W9-BEV-310

ENTERPRISE SERVICE ORIENTED ARCHITECTURES

Enterprise Service Oriented Architectures

Concepts, Challenges, Recommendations

by

JAMES MCGOVERN

OLIVER SIMS

ASHISH JAIN

MARK LITTLE

A C.I.P. Catalogue record for this book is available from the Library of Congress.

ISBN-10 1-4020-3704-X (HB)
ISBN-13 978-1-4020-3704-7 (HB)
ISBN-10 1-4020-3705-8 (e-book)
ISBN-13 978-1-4020-3705-4 (e-book)

Published by Springer,
P.O. Box 17, 3300 AA Dordrecht, The Netherlands.

www.springer.com

Printed on acid-free paper

Printed in the Netherlands.

The condition of an enlightened mind is a surrendered heart.
Alan Redpath

Author Team

To those who are savage in the pursuit of excellence ...

James

To my wife Sherry and sons James and Sylvester who provide and replenish the energy necessary for me to complete the exciting work as well as the mundane. To Mom and Dad, thanks for the encouragement and persistence.

Oliver

To my wife, Heather, for just about everything, and to my children Christopher, Richard, and David, of whom I am inordinately proud, and who have kept me firmly rooted in reality.

Ashish

To my wife Nishma and children Eshan and Ronit for their love, patience and support. To my parents, for their encouragement throughout the years.

Mark

I'd like to send my love to all my family, particularly my wife Paula and our children Daniel and Adam, who have acted as an anchor for me through the years, keeping me sane throughout the storms.

TABLE OF CONTENTS

ENDORSEMENTS

You can't live a perfect day without doing something
for someone who will never be able to repay you.
John Wooden

"*Enterprise SOA is well written and insightful. This book covers enormous ground and readers will find it the best, single source on SOA. Highly recommended!*"

Ron Widitz
Enterprise Architect
Discover Financial

"*This book was truly a guide for all levels of individuals developing business applications in today's global, open market. It clearly summarizes key concepts for executive management, provides the framework of architectural guidelines and standards, as well as provided detailed coding examples for entry level developers. This book should be a must read for all interested in leading their organization's business model into the future.*"

Damon Rothstein
Enterprise Network Architect
Piper Jaffray and Companies

"*Concise, readable and useful as a tool in the running of a business. You truly pull concepts together with real world examples.*"

W.M. Douglas Crawford
VP NASDAQ Technology & Operations
Advest

"*Enterprise SOA provides architects and developers with an excellent source of much needed information on understanding how to utilize enterprise technologies such as*

SOA, orchestration, components, and registries to solve problems that currently face the enterprise. Understanding these technologies will help architects develop systems that can solve current problems as well as lay down an architecture that will adapt to on going changes in the business environment."

Suneet Shah
CTO and Chief Architect
Diamelle

"*Enterprise Service-Oriented Architectures provides a unique and worthwhile lifecycle-perspective to realizing a SOA. A number of concepts such as components, registries, web-service security, management, business processes, etc. are addressed in the context of different stages during the realization of a SOA, including : translating SOA requirements to design, design to implementation, and implementation to deployment.*"

Sekhar Sarukkai
Technical Evangelist
Oblix

"*This book is an outstanding and insightful work on the perspectives and potential of service-oriented architecture. A must read for every Enterprise Architect who needs to know how to succeed in the face of architectural challenges presented as part of his/her daily chores.*"

Nitin Narayan
CEO
Mavenz, India

"*This book is the product of some of the leading thinkers in Information Technology today. The concepts included in this book are being debated and analyzed by most of the Information Officers in the world right now. This book provides a history of how we got to SOAs, what they mean today, and where they will lead tomorrow. The implications of SOAs, Web Services, Federation, BPEL, and Grid computing, will revolutionize the IT industry. We are living in truly interesting times. Those of us in the IT community have our work cut out for us to lead our companies and customers into the next generation of computing. Thank you for this great book to help spearhead the charge!*"

Joe Gibson
Senior Practice Director, Integration
East Area Technology Services
Oracle

ABOUT THE SERIES

Before you can inspire with emotion, you must be swamped with it yourself. Before you can move their tears, your own must flow. To convince them, you must yourself believe.
Winston Churchill

The new enterprise requires a new type of leadership based on the logical continuation of historical effort, while not doing what has been done just because it has been done that way in the past. Agility and leadership when combined is a cohesive presentation of common sense mined from the few truly successful projects as opposed to the aggregation of every (predominately failed) effort declared complete not only successful projects but projects that really add value to a business imperative. We are living in a new era where one seeks uncommon approaches while maintaining common virtues.

The art of leadership is about knowing and influencing people so that they can come to share common values resulting in more efficiency in achieving the strategic vision for the enterprise. Leadership must also embrace diversity which will lead to a much more lively dialectic.

The Enterprise Series has earned its place as a valuable resource to those who want to ramp up quickly and stay ahead of the curve. The authors of books within this series are not writers hired to cover the "hot" topic of the minute. Instead they are thought leaders and expert practitioners who bring insight to the community at large based on real-world experience. More importantly, they are not theorists but actually practice what they preach.

This series is founded on the conviction that enterprises should differentiate themselves, their architecture and their people based on the way they think as much as on the products or services they sell. Thought leadership is all about time-honored expertise and comprehensive capabilities. Its inflection point however is new thinking and original perspectives.

We hope you find this series and this book to be a practical guide and trusted advisor leading you successfully on your journey.

James McGovern
Rajanish Dass
Anthony Finkelstein
John Gøtze

Series Editors

James McGovern

James is an industry thought leader and the co-author of several recent books on service-oriented architectures, enterprise architectures and technology leadership. He is employed as an Enterprise Architect for The Hartford Financial Services Group, Inc. He holds industry certifications from Microsoft, Cisco and Sun. James is a popular speaker at elite technology conferences around the globe. He is member of the Java Community Process and the Worldwide Institute of Software Architects.

Rajanish Dass

Rajanish is a Fellow at IIM Calcutta and his primary research and teaching interests are in the area of Information Systems Management and its applications to various arenas of doing business. Particular interests lie in the area of real-time Data Mining and Business Intelligence techniques, developing algorithms and heuristics for performance enhancement, applications of Business Intelligence techniques for various areas of business like supply chain management, network intrusion detection, privacy and security enhancement, anti-spamming techniques, retailing, finance and business policy making, Competitive Intelligence, etc.

A rank holder throughout his career; he has experiences in working for high-ended projects at the IBM Research Laboratory India and at the Tata Consultancy Services. He has published a number of research papers in forums of international repute and of national significance. He is currently doing research in collaboration with world renowned research labs of MIT, Oracle Centre of Excellence, Messagelabs, etc.

Anthony Finkelstein

Anthony is Professor of Software Systems Engineering at University College London. He is a founder of London Software Systems a new joint research institute established jointly by UCL and Imperial College. He has contributed to research on software specification methods, software development processes, tool and environment support for software development. Recent work has included significant contributions to work on tools for managing model integrity in software development, specification from multiple viewpoints and requirements engineering. His current interest's area is the managing of distributed information in software development. He is the Head of the Department of Computer Science and founder of Systemwire a technology spinout company.

John Gøtze

John is chief consultant and enterprise architect in the Danish Ministry of Science, Technology and Innovation, where he since 2001 has been heavily involved in establishing and managing the Danish government's enterprise architecture program, as an important part of the national e-government policy. Recent work has included policy documents as well as academic publications on cross-governmental interoperability, architecture frameworks, service-oriented architecture and open standards. He is also a non-tenured associate professor at Copenhagen Business School and the IT University of Copenhagen, where he teaches masters classes and supervises theses. He holds a PhD and MSc from the Technical University of Denmark.

FOREWORD

We live in an interesting (in the sense of the "*May your life be interesting*" Chinese proverb) moment of the IT industry. Finally, many of the disciplines required to manage IT in a structured and agile way are converging together. We now have the theoretical concepts and practical experience to align IT to the business, manage IT as a business, define enterprise architectures, and align IT initiatives and individual projects (not only as far as development is concerned, but also with regards to outsourcing, deployment, integration, governance, and the other IT concerns). Nearly any imaginable technology IT challenges can currently be solved (or has been solved) by some company in the industry. Companies willing to invest the time and money and having the experience (or the luck ...) to do it can truly take advantage of IT to achieve their business objectives. And we have many failures and successes to learn from, and to build upon.

A key architectural and technology element of this convergence is an architectural style that became known in the year 2000 as "Service-Oriented Architecture". Since 2003, this has started to morph toward an architectural style with the potential of impacting the vast majority of IT: "an Enterprise Service-Oriented Architecture" (ESOA). In its widest meaning, this term indicates the architectural style enabling an interoperability layer reducing the costs of integration, creating a technical and functional decoupling between applications, and supporting an enterprise-wide rationalization of IT applications. When ESOA is fully adopted, enterprises can align IT to their business processes and create a transitioning path toward a normalized IT portfolio. As such, an ESOA has the potential to profoundly impact both business and IT.

It is indeed the first time in our industry that the IT disciplines, technologies, approaches are coming together to this extent. And still, IT is today more complex than ever: addressing IT this way is still beyond the capability of most organizations, both due to the costs and to the complexity of the task. The industry still needs to mature to bring costs and complexity down. For this to happen, among other things we need to see books addressing the required architectural elements. This is one of those books.

In 1996, Oliver Sims and I were working together on a large product development (over 500 hundred developers building an ERP product with thousands of tables). Oliver introduced a concept he called "semantic messages". A semantic message was a message that contained not only the data that needed to be sent, but also tags describing the data being sent. For a couple of years, we explored together the many challenges of addressing interoperability through "semantic messages" to address development, interoperability, and deployment "in-the-large". We built a simple language for describing these semantic messages. This was the first time I had met the concept of what I later called a "strongly-tagged language". We also built the infrastructure, patterns, architectures, modeling tools and code-generation tools, repositories, and processes to define these semantic messages in an architecturally consistent way. As often happens in our industry, in time I discovered that many other teams had been working with similar approaches in their companies.

These approaches were not standards, but rather very proprietary approaches. So when XML came out, many people were happy to finally see a "tagged language" that was being standardized <u>and</u> adopted industry-wide: something for which we had unsuccessfully lobbied in various standard bodies for years. Now finally the industry had a standard as a basis for what we believed was the best way to address many interoperability issues.

Of course, XML is just a very basic language, alone it cannot do much: to achieve its potential, it needed a whole set of additional standards, technologies, infrastructures, frameworks and tools to cover the whole spectrum of what is needed for interoperability. Today, this is reflected in the many Web Services standards, and in the many products being sold to support Web Services. But, once these basic technical layers are addressed, any serious project needs to address, among other things, the architectural issues. The point is not (and has never been) the technology: the point is how to use these technologies in the various architectural choices we have to make to address the requirements.

The industry has come a long way. Many Web Services technology providers have come and gone. The industry is stabilizing and consolidating. The Open Source movement has brought costs down. Second-generation architectural approaches provide maturity models for component blueprints and models enabling faster and more reliable software manaufacturing. Now we have much experience with Web Services infrastructures, and, not only in specific companies but industry-wide, we know what works and what doesn't. For the business, this promises the elimination of costly, redundant, and proprietary approaches, and the ability to integrate applications quickly and easily. IT is rapidly commoditizing, and ESOA helps drive value higher and higher up the IT chain.

And finally, we start to see books not treating the problem as a simple "standard" or technology problem, not focusing only on the basic Web Services bricks, but positioning Web Services within the larger architectural perspective. The book you hold in your hands is a fine example of this.

This book has the advantage of having been written by industry practitioners covering many perspectives in IT: the authors together have the right mix of technology product perspective, consultant perspective, and large IT shop perspective. The book covers many of the most important topics: components, registries, security, management, transactions, and events. As such, it addresses an important need: bridging the gap between technology and architecture.

Enterprise Service-Oriented Architectures are one of the most significant evolutions in the IT industry in the past few years. They share the spotlight with other significant evolutions and trends. These include the wide-spread adoption of enterprise architectures, the creation of an enterprise architecture discipline that looks well beyond "software architecture" to address the many business, functional, structural and technical aspects of IT today, the maturity of governance and compliance process frameworks, and the application of agile concepts to all aspects of IT (including deployment of packaged software and outsourcing). But software architecture remains the critical prerequisite for success in IT and in ESOA in particular: this book addresses this prerequisite.

Thanks, guys, for putting together a fine and timely book.

Peter Herzum
President, Herzum Software

PREFACE

Don't tell people how to do things, tell them what to do
and let them surprise you with their results ...
George S. Patton

Service-oriented architectures (SOA) fundamentally changes the way enterprise software is developed and deployed. SOA enterprise applications evolve. The change will morph existing software, as we currently know it away from using monolithic approaches. Instead, SOA will enable virtualized on-demand execution models that break the current economic and technological bottleneck caused by traditional approaches.

Software as a service has become pervasive as a model for forward looking enterprises to streamline operations, lower cost of ownership and provides competitive differentiation in the marketplace. SOA is not a silver bullet that will address all of the deficiencies within an enterprise related to integration, reusability or the elimination of redundant systems. SOA can assist in these problem domains in an incremental manner while providing guidance on business architecture as well.

Service orientation has become a viable opportunity for enterprises to increase the internal rate of return on a project-by-project basis, react to rapidly changing market conditions and conduct transactions with business partners at will. Loosely coupled, standards-based architectures are one approach to distributed computing that will allow software resources available on the network to be leveraged. Applications that separate business processes, presentation rules, business rules and data access into separate loosely coupled layers will not only assist in the construction of better software but also make it more adaptable to future change.

Service-oriented architectures will allow for combining existing functions with new development efforts, allowing the creation of composite applications. Leveraging high-quality low-cost applications that can be procured from third party suppliers to

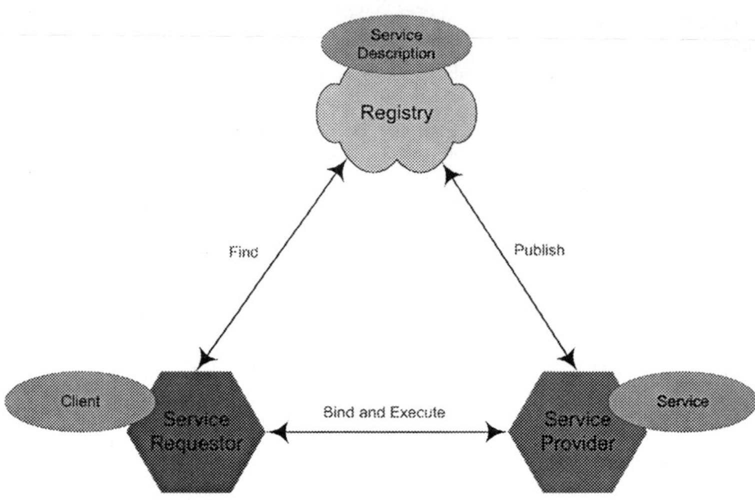

***Figure 1.* Service-Oriented Architecture**

replace lower quality components lowers the risks in software development projects. By reusing existing functions that are of high quality, it leads to faster deliverables and increases the potential for overall higher quality.

Loose coupling helps preserve the future by allowing parts of the business and the technology that provides support to change at their own pace without the risks linked to costly migrations using monolithic approaches. SOA allows business users to focus on business problems at hand without worrying about the technical constraints within existing IT applications as they can choose to replace components incrementally. For the individuals who develop solutions, SOA helps in the following manner:

- Business analysts focus on higher order responsibilities in the development lifecycle while increasing their own knowledge of the business domain.

- Separating functionality into component-based services that can be tackled by multiple teams enables parallel development.

- Quality assurance and unit testing become more efficient; while errors using SOA have the potential to be discovered much later in the lifecycle, the overall quantity will be reduced to support better service level agreements (SLA) and development specifications.

- Component-based approaches when used within a service-oriented architecture can aid in becoming reusable assets for systems and software that are constructed using proper software development techniques.

- Functional decomposition of services and their underlying components with respect to the business process helps preserve the flexibility, future maintainability and eases integration efforts.
- Security rules defined for consumers and providers based on role, function, context and method of interface that helps solve many security considerations within the enterprise.

Implementing a service-oriented architecture will not happen overnight nor requires enterprises to throw existing technology investments. The challenge will be in deciding which services are core to your business and investing in them and leveraging services provided by others as appropriate. In all technology revolutions the prior generation usually remains a vital part of the infrastructure but not the only part. Software built to support services significantly reduces the need for enterprise software; not eliminate it. Service-oriented architecture is an economically responsive model to the needs of IT and enables the corporation to focus more on the business process and the applications rather than the deployment of more enterprise software.

Service-oriented architectures also provide an opportunity for an organization to mature their enterprise architecture perspective. Enterprise architecture provides the necessary framework for categorizing everything for the purpose of supporting future business planning. Both business and IT executives should be able to look at the enterprise architecture and understand the tradeoffs in using various systems, processes, technologies and so on. SOA can be the next level of specification and provide guidance on the best ways to realize many of the goals of enterprise architecture.

ABOUT THIS BOOK

The great revolution in our generation is that of human beings, who by changing the inner attitudes of their minds, can change the outer aspects of their lives.
Marilyn Ferguson

The goal of this book is to share insight gathered by industry thought leaders in a practical easy to read manner. This book contains many leading edge examples that illustrate how agile approaches to enterprise architecture can be applied to existing business and technology issues. It will help one focus on how to think concretely about enterprise architecture while providing solutions to today's problems.

Within the covers of this book, you will learn about the following topics:

- Fundamentals of a Service-Oriented Architecture,
- Component-Based Services,
- Orchestration,
- Registries,
- Management,
- Transactions,
- Event-Driven Architecture, and
- Understanding Distributed Computing.

Audience

This book is for every Java and .NET developer and architects of Fortune 1000 enterprises and the consultancies that service them who have the drive to spend extra hours feverishly seeking bits of wisdom on their craft and who want to gain the latest insights and strategies for leveraging emerging enterprise SOA disciplines for value creation, increased business agility and strategic competitive advantage.

This book does assume that one has significant IT experience under their belt and have worked on projects that were both large and small; on time as well as those which are over budget using different project management, software development and infrastructure paradigms. This book is not for those who desire all the information they require in a single book as this is an impossible goal to achieve; rather this is best suited for those who want to gain insight from thought leaders and are willing to be savage in the leap from good to great.

Finally, this book is aimed at the people who must create applications in the real world day-in, day-out. Many of the best practices books treat each tip as the sole focus of a chapter with no discussion of integrating it into a real application. Real applications are tenuous at best, requiring lots of moving parts in order to function together. Concepts and recommendations within this book are presented in context of a living enterprise with all the places that the real world intersects with the academia of the problem space at hand.

The hardest part of starting an enterprise service-oriented architecture initiative is knowing where to begin. We hope that our insights will be a useful starting point for a set of well-managed endeavors for many an architect.

What This Book Is Not!

First, this is not a book for beginners. If you are looking for introductory material on service-oriented architectures, we recommend searching for articles on the Internet using search engines such as Google. Second, while this book may sporadically use SOAP, WSDL and UDDI snippets to describe SOA concepts, this book is not about web services. If you require a book on web services, we recommend *Java Web Services Architecture* published in 2003 by Morgan Kaufmann.

Many of the examples contained within this book use XML. If you do not have a thorough understanding, we recommend the following books:

- Learning XML, Second Edition – O'Reilly.

- Effective XML: 50 Specific Ways to Improve your XML – O'Reilly.

The authors recommend that the readers have a thorough understanding of general software development, design patterns, enterprise integration and network infrastructure as a foundation to truly understanding the material contained within. Some good books are:

- *Enterprise Integration Patterns* – Addison Wesley.
- *Pattern-Oriented Software Architecture*, Volume 1 – Wiley.
- *Network Security Architectures* – Cisco Press.
- *Introduction to Networking* – McGraw-Hill.
- *Software Architecture in Practice* – Addison Wesley.

Finally, if you have not programmed using a modern language such as Java and/or .NET, we recommend the following books as a good starting point:

- *Java 2 Enterprise Edition Bible* – John Wiley & Sons.
- *Bitter Java* – Manning Publications.
- *Java 2: A Beginner's Guide* – McGraw Hill.
- *Beginning VB.NET (Programmer to Programmer)* – Wrox.

How to Use This Book

The authors have taken deliberate action to avoid filling this book with lots of code and specification information. This book strives to provide vivid insight into the dynamics of SOA and a strategic approach to successfully integrate technology into business decisions and the day-to-day actions of the workforce, business partners and the consumer to reduce waste of resource and enhance the deliverables of the enterprise.

The goal of this book is to strive to be both practical and philosophical. Sections of the book may discuss general principles with examples that illustrate them: examples drawn not from trivial demonstration programs (i.e. pet stores, shopping carts, etc.) but rather actual architectures used in production systems in industry applications such as financial services, supply chains, manufacturing, defense and telecommunications.

Motivation for Writing This Book

There is an abundance of books on Web Services on the market many of which are bestsellers. The vast majority of texts simply explain vendor product offerings, APIs and very brief tutorials without providing the reader with sufficient understanding of the problems that exist within enterprises. The authors felt it is not sufficient to merely learn the technology and APIs but to understand the principles behind them so that they can be appropriately incorporated into existing systems and applications.

Many books also explain the happy path to software development. Knowing what works is good (design pattern), but knowing what doesn?t work is better (anti-pattern). Where appropriate, this book will outline potential pitfalls. The authors of this book have been doing service-oriented software development before it became a hot topic in industry magazines and journals. The authors themselves are relentless in the pursuit of finding better ways to develop software, which relies on thinking about problems of the past differently. Success is bred by not simply understanding technology but also by understanding agile methods for realizing the business goal.

The author team's primary motivation in writing this book is to share our working experience to bridge the gap between the knowledge of industry gurus and newcomers to service-oriented architectures. Many powerful techniques lay hidden in magazine articles, conference proceedings, vendor marketing materials and academic papers for years before becoming recognized by the masses.

NOTE: For those who are not familiar with Agile Methods, we recommend you read the Agile Manifesto at http://www.agilemanifesto.org.

Disclaimer

The advice, diagrams and recommendations contained within this book may be used as your heart desires, with the sole discretion that you may not claim that you were the author. The publisher, authors or their respective employers do not provide any form of warranty or guarantee its usefulness for any particular purpose.

This book is 100% error free! Not! If you believed us even for a second, I have a suspension bridge in my backyard that I would like to sell you. The author team and editors have worked hard to bring you an easy to understand, accurate guide on Enterprise Service-Oriented Architectures. If you find any mistakes in this book, we would appreciate your contacting us via email at serviceorientedbook@yahoogroups.com.

This book may use from time to time examples of a fictitious organization. Any example companies, organizations, products, domain names, email addresses, people, places, events depicted herein are fictitious. No association with any real company, organization, product, domain name, email address, person, places or events is intended or should be inferred.

About the Authors

James McGovern

James is the co-author of several bestselling books, including *A Practical Guide to Enterprise Architecture*. He is employed as an Enterprise Architect for The Hartford, a Fortune 100 financial services firm. James is a popular speaker at elite technology conferences around the globe. He is a member of the Java Community Process and the Worldwide Institute of Software Architects.

Oliver Sims

Oliver is a recognized leader in the architecture, design, and implementation of service-oriented and component-based enterprise systems. Currently an independent consultant, Oliver has held a number of senior technical positions in software product and service companies. He was a founding member of the OMG Architecture Board, has been active in several OMG Task Forces, and has contributed to the development of MDA. Co-author of *Business Component Factory* and *Building Business Objects*, and author of *Business Objects*.

Oliver has many published articles to his credit. Oliver's experience in IT and software spans three decades, and he has accumulated wide practical experience in a number of roles and with many kinds of system. He was one of the first to prove the synergy between components and distributed objects, and was chief architect for a groundbreaking component container middleware product in the mid 1990s. Most recently Oliver has helped IT organizations in their transition to effective component-based high-productivity development of service-oriented systems.

Ashish Jain

Ashish is an enterprise architect with over 11 years of industry experience with expertise in the architecture, development and mentoring of the mid-tier and server-side components. He currently works as a Principal Architect with Ping Identity Corporation, a leading provider of solutions for identity federation. Prior to joining Ping Identity, he worked with BEA Systems where his role was to assist BEA customers in designing and implementing their e-business strategies using solutions based on J2EE. He holds several industry certifications from SUN and BEA and is also a board member for the Denver BEA User Group. He is also the co-author of *The J2EE 1.4 Bible* (ISBN: 0-7645-3966-3, http://www.amazon.com/exec/obidos/tg/detail/-/0764539663).

Mark Little

Mark is Chief Architect for Arjuna Technologies Ltd., a spin-off company from Hewlett-Packard, specializing in the development of reliable middleware. At HP Mark was a Distinguished Engineer and architect working on their transation and Web Service products. He is one of the primary authors of the OMG Activity Service specification and is on the expert group for the same work in J2EE (JSR 95). He is also the specification lead for JSR 156: Java API for XML Transactions. He is on the OMG's OTS Revision Task Force and the OASIS Business Transactions Protocol, OASIS WS-CAF and OASIS WS-TX Technical Committees, to name a few.

Before joining HP he was for over 10 years a member of the Arjuna team within the University of Newcastle upon Tyne (where he continues to have a Visiting Fellowship). His research within the Arjuna team included replication and transactions support, which include the construction of an OTS/JTS compliant transaction processing system. Mark has published extensively in the *Web Services Journal*, *Java Developers Journal* and other journals and magazines. He is also the co-author of several books including *Java Transactions Processing: Design and Implementation* and *The J2EE 1.4 Bible.*

ACKNOWLEDGEMENTS

When the character of a man is not clear to you, look at his friends.
Japanese Proverb

A book like this is never just the work of those whose names appear on the cover. Like the academy awards, "there are so many people we would like to thank …" We are immensely grateful for all those who have encouraged us, provided practical advice, debated the finer points on controversial topics and whose insights have honed our own.

The authors have benefited immensely in their own professions by reading papers from other industry thought leaders including but not limited to (in no particular order):

Jeff Schneider
Martin Fowler
Anne Thomas Manes
Doug Barry
Doug Kaye
Peter Herzum

The author team would also like to thank other writers we have worked with in the past and desire to work with in the future (in no particular order):

Per Bothner
Kurt Cagle
Yakov Fain
Jason Gordon
James Linn
Lynn Denoia
Leeanne Phillips
Sunil Mathew
Vaidyanathan Nagarajan
Sameer Tyagi
Alan Williamson
Vikas Sharan
Elias Jo
Scott W. Ambler
Dave Hollander
Nitin Narayan
Rahul Tyagi
Kito Mann

Finally, the author team would like to thank our editor, Robbert van Berckelaer, for allowing our ideas to be published in a manner the community sorely needs and most importantly our copy editor, Jolanda Karada, for painstakingly copyediting and ensuring this book is error-free.

James McGovern

Best wishes to the reluctant warriors within the Armed Forces who spread freedom throughout the planet. Prayers to the families in Palestine, Israel and other parts of the Middle East who seek peace and those who have lost their lifes in pursuit of it. To all of my coworkers at The Hartford who have been merciless in the support of speed, agility and balance in our daily lives. To Democrats, who make thievery and cowardice sound so romantic. To Republicans, who make Democrats look principled.

Regardless of land, religion or language, there is just but one God. I must thank our creator whom has bestowed upon me many favors. I am grateful for being blessed with a great family, doing the things I love and working for such a great employer. To say that I am not worthy of such blessings is obvious to anyone who knows me, which makes me all the more grateful.

Oliver Sims

Such insights as I may have developed over the years have been mainly due to the many valued colleagues with whom I have had the honor of working. In particular, I would like to thank Martin Anderson, Alan Boother, Roger Brown, Peter Eeles, David Frankel, Mike Guttman, Peter Herzum, Haim Kilov, Wojtek Kozaczynski, Maurice Perks, Dave Roberts, Mike Rosen, Trevor Sharpe, Sandy Tyndale-Biscoe, Rick Williams, and Bryan Wood.

Ashish Jain

I would like to thank all my colleagues at Ping Identity for helping me learn everyday. In particular, I would like to thank Darren Platt and Brian Whitney for taking the time to share their real world experiences with me. I would also like to thank my ex-colleagues at BEA, John Funk and Bob Webster, for reviewing the content and their invaluable comments.

Mark Little

I would like to thank all of my colleagues at Arjuna Technologies, who have helped to make it a great working environment over the years. In particular Stuart Wheater, Barry Hodgson, Dave Ingham, Steve Caughey and the members of the transactions team, past and present. Many thanks go to Professor Santosh Shrivastava of the University of Newcastle upon Tyne, who started my career off in this direction and has been a constant friend over the many years. Thanks to my ex-Bluestone and Hewlett-Packard friends and colleagues, including Bob Bickel, ex-general manager of Hewlett-Packard Middleware, Al Smith, Greg Pavlik and Jon Maron, who showed me that the best things in life are free.

ABOUT THE REVIEWERS

Synergism is the simultaneous actions of separate entities which together have greater total effect than the sum of their individual effects.
Buchholz and Roth

The author team owes a debt of gratitude to all of the reviewers who provided guidance, feedback, constructive criticism, praise and encouragement throughout the manuscript writing process. Our reviewers came with diverse backgrounds: from people who believe in traditional processes to those who have embraced agile methods; from those whose native tongue is English, to those who speak joyous languages such as Arabic, Chinese, French, Hindi, Spanish, Urdu and others; from those who are lowly developers and project managers to those who are senior executives, this book would not be what it is without you.

The author team deeply appreciates all of the feedback received during the manuscript writing process from the following individuals (company affiliations are included where permitted):

Argentina

Daniel J. Biondi, Regional CT, EDS Latin America Solution Centres, Buenos Aires

Australia

Shaji Sethu, Solutions Architect, Volante, North Ryde, NSW

Belgium

Fanuel Dewever, Consultant, Human Capital Management, IBM Business Consulting Services

Robin Mulkers, Head Application Architect, Christelijke Mutualiteit

Canada

Henry Chiu, Architect/Trainer/Mentor, ObjectSoft Solutions, Ontario

Finland

Anders Aspnas, Solution Architect, Fujitsu Services OY

Germany

Stefan Tilkov, Managing Director, innoQ Deutschland GmbH, Ratingen

India

Naveen Gabrani, Software Project Manager, Computer Sciences Corporation
Rohit, S. Gulati, CISA, CSQA, Iflex Solutions, Bangalore
Shivprasad Koirala, AG Technologies, Nepal

Israel & Palestine

Issac Goldstand, Owner, Mirimar Networks, Jerusalem

Pakistan

Ammad Amjad, Systems Architect, Lahore Stock Exchange

Scotland

Jon C. Ferguson, PhD, Director and Architect, Omega Software, Ltd., Aberdeenshire

Singapore

Victor Putra Lesmana, IBM

Ukraine

Ruslan Shevchenko, Director, Grad-Soft Ltd., Kiev

United Kingdom

Max Kington, Technical Architect, Cantor Fitzgerald, London

United States

Wayne Allen, Product Development Manager, Corillian, Portland, Oregon
Matt Anderson, Senior Enterprise Architect, Great American Insurance Company, Ohio
Adolfo Lagomasino, Architect, Lucent Technologies, Landover, Maryland
Barbara McGowin, Principal, McGowin Enterprises, Goose Creek, South Carolina
Robert W. Meriam, Chief Infosec Officer, Catholic Health Services of Long Island, Melville, New York
David L. Nicol, Founder and CTO, TipJar LLC, Kansas City, Missouri
Donna M. Schaeffer, Associate Professor, University of San Francisco, California
Ravi Sharma, Senior Enterprise Architect, Systems Development Factory, General Motors, Detroit, Michigan

1 UNDERSTANDING SERVICE-ORIENTED ARCHITECTURE

Man's mind, once stretched by a new idea, never regains its original dimensions.
Oliver Wendell Holmes

The idea of software modules providing services to other software modules is a long-established approach to software design. A "service" has three fundamental attributes: the service's description in the form of an interface definition, a mechanism for accessing or "consuming" the service by invoking its interface, and an implementation or a "provision" of the service – that is, the code behind the interface. Today, this approach is being revitalized by a new and standard technology – Web Services.

In the past, Enterprise Systems have been dogged with a plethora of different kinds of interface, each tied to a specific technology or commercial product. Project teams have had to master a whole array of different ways of invoking interfaces – of binding or tying their software to other software – often at high levels of technical complexity. And it is the process of binding software modules or subsystems together that often presents the greatest development problems. It has been said that plumbing never leaks in the middle of a pipe: it always leaks at the joints; and so it is with software. Although there have been a number of approaches to this problem, there has been a lack of effective standards that apply not only between enterprises but all the way down to between modules or subsystems co-located on the same machine. Companies have developed their own in-house standards, sometimes centered on an enterprise bus approach. However, whenever a new piece of software was acquired, it had to be "wrapped" with the in-house interface.

Produced by the World Wide Web Consortium (W3C), Web Services are a set of standards not only for defining interfaces but also for accessing those interfaces. Together they provide a way to tie systems – and modules – together. They are increasingly being adopted by software vendors, whether the software is middleware such as BPM (Business Process Management) products or application packages. This provides obvious advantages for enterprise IT organizations. However, many still see web services as being for inter-enterprise use only. This is probably due to the word "web" in the title. But nothing could be further from the truth. Unless the standards groups that control the evolution of web services prevent it (a hugely self-defeating proposition!), the same standard can be used within the enterprise and across a wide technical scope. Sometimes it does make sense to not develop web services. In situations where you have full control of both service and client there are often considerable savings to be made (both in development effort and communications latency/bandwidth) by avoiding web services and adopting a more streamlined integration approach. Some of the web services middleware now available even provide local optimization for access between software modules in the same address space, making this less relevant from a performance perspective for in-house consumed services.

But although it is the arrival of web services that has put the "service-orientation" into Enterprise Service-Oriented Architecture (ESOA), there is much more to service orientation than just a technology standard for interfaces. Service orientation in the enterprise context is not just a neat technology that is also an international standard. Service orientation is a pervasive mindset – a way of thinking about things – that can help transform IT responsiveness and agility. Thus the business defines services it wants to provide to customers and partners. IT defines services for and to the business. IT develops or buys application modules that provide services to other application modules, and applications to other applications. But the thinking can be usefully extended further, even to organizational units within IT, so that they provide services to each other. That is why ESOA is so much more than just web services. Service orientation concentrates architects' minds on provision of value, whether from one module to another, or from one discipline to another, or from one part of IT to another. Web service standards and technology, although perhaps the catalyst for ESOA, are by themselves merely the icing on the cake. And who wants icing without the cake when they can have both?

In this book we aim to show how to make a head start on baking a fully-iced cake. We focus on the main areas where service orientation makes a difference, and also on the major architectural concerns that are affected by service orientation. We start with an introduction to web services in the context of enterprise architecture. The following chapters address component-based services, service orchestration, service registries, security, service management, transactions, and event-driven architecture. We hope that readers will find how enterprise architecture can be re-vitalized not only by the introduction of web services technology but also by the way a service-oriented approach can make a desirable difference to enterprise architecture.

Introduction

This chapter presents the major aspects of a service-oriented architecture for the enterprise. To be effective, such an architecture must address more than the technical design of services: it must also provide a design for IT agility in the face of increasing time-to-market and responsiveness pressures.

Enterprise Service-Oriented Architecture is centered on three major concepts:

- Services offered over the web and within the enterprise using XML-based standards both for the specification of invokeable services and for the message flows involved in requesting and delivering those services. This is often referred to as just "service-oriented architecture" (SOA).
- Implementation of services using component-based software engineering (CBSE) architecture (see Chapter 3), which not only addresses structuring new applications, but also embraces such aspects as legacy wrapping, workflow, and Business-to-Business (B2B) specifications.
- An architectural, procedural, and organizational mindset that is service-oriented, and which can merge the web services technology and CBSE potential into a synergistic whole that can be hugely productive.

The first of these concepts is becoming well known. Some services will be provided by suppliers outside the enterprise. However, most enterprises know that competitive advantage depends on their core systems and processes. They also think it foolhardy to cede control of these, and more importantly the valuable in-house business domain knowledge, to a third party. Hence the core services will continue to be provided in-house, either though in-house development, outsourcing, or through packages.

It is sometimes thought that SOA means building applications by composing third-party services. However, someone somewhere has to build the code that provides the services. A key question often overlooked is, how are the implementations of business-oriented services best designed, structured, and built? The second concept provides the answer to this question, and is addressed separately in Chapter 3.

Underlying these more technical considerations is the pressing need for a major improvement in flexibility and timeliness of systems. The third concept – that of a service-oriented mindset – has developed as an important part of the response to this need.

The chapter is structured into four parts as follows:

Section 1 (Introducing Service-Oriented Architectures) shows how a single architecture based on mature CBSE can address a wide range of capabilities including Business-to-Business (B2B), Business-to-Customer (B2C), Business-to-Government (B2G), workflow, Business Process Management (BPM), and legacy wrapping, and at the same time can provide the scalable enterprise services needed. In addition, we show how a Service-Oriented Architecture can establish better separation between major enterprise components, and enable inherently more adaptable back end applications. CBSE itself is addressed separately in Chapter 3.

Section 2 (Service-Based Collaboration) examines how the basic service orientation concepts can enable effective intra- and inter-enterprise collaboration. The key to collaboration is federation – a concept that enables loosely-coupled but effective integration – through "higher-level" services. Federation as the basis for collaboration and integration can enable much more rapid business evolution and responsiveness than other approaches, such as providing a new packaged or purpose-built application for each new service requirement, or re-engineering two existing services into a single combined service implementation that also provides the new higher-level service required.

Building an Enterprise Service-Oriented Architecture (ESOA) is not easy. It is true that some impressive immediate gains can be made, but the challenge is to ensure that those early gains become the foundation of a truly productive and responsive service-oriented system. Without such a foundation, the danger is that after a few years all that has been created are yet more rigid and inflexible stovepipes – service-oriented legacy! The ESOA that positions you not only for the present but also for the future rests on a firm architectural basis that delivers:

- Separation of technology platforms from the business services offered, and from the business logic that implements those services.
- Flexibility and responsiveness so that the services offered both within and outside the enterprise can respond fast to the evolution of the business.

Section 3 (The Platform) deals with technology platforms that supports business services, and, more importantly, its separation from those services. Such separation is crucial in enabling business services to evolve at the speed of the business, rather than being constrained by technology change.

Section 4 (Transition) briefly discusses a process that can address the key aspects of a transition to service-orientation. Moving to an agile ESOA environment is not a simple task. A major inhibitor is the effort and management focus needed to plan and take the first steps towards the cohesive holistic environment required. This work may well include some organizational aspects.

Of course, to be effective, and to truly enable business agility, there must be clear traceability between business requirements and system implementation. Otherwise the services provided may well not be those the business requires and needs. What is needed is to connect business requirements directly with the kind of ESOA discussed here, The next chapter discusses an approach for providing a near-seamless progression from business requirements to service implementation.

1. Introducing Service-Oriented Architectures

First we provide an introduction to Web Services and the place they can play in enterprise systems. The aim is to provide an overall understanding of the technology rather than a tutorial on its detailed application. A high-level model of our enterprise system context is also presented to aid the discussion. Second, we examine the extent to which web services can be used within an enterprise system, and conclude that they can. This means that a single worldwide standard for services can be used not only between enterprises, but also within them, even within a single address space! All parts of an enterprise system can be provided with the same standard technology, fronting legacy systems, message buses, new systems, business processes, and workflow. Thus the current Tower of Babel surrounding interface definition and invocation can be conquered, and a new level of simplification becomes achievable.

1.1. Web Services

Web services have been standardized through the World Wide Web Consortium

(W3C). The specifications mainly use XML as their "alphabet".[1] The reason for their success over the past few years is that the specifications are:

- platform-independent,
- effectively, a single platform-independent type system,
- international standards,
- relatively simple,
- freely available, and
- supportive of loose coupling.

These standards provide a highly effective "lingua franca" for inter-system communication. The two standards of concern[2] for this chapter are at the heart of web services, and are:

- WSDL (Web Services Description Language), and
- SOAP (Simple Object Access Protocol).

A third standard, also used in web services, is the Universal Description, Discovery and Integration registry (UDDI).[3] This provides for service publishing and discovery.

Before describing these three standards, let us first describe our context through a high-level and much-simplified model of an enterprise system that provides external web services to other organizations.

1.1.1. Enterprise IT and Web Services

Web services are often thought of as an inter-enterprise concern. Later, we will show how this is a very constraining view. For the time being, however, in order to illustrate what, technically, web services look like, we retain this context. The main parts of an enterprise IT system that provides and implements web services are illustrated in Figure 1, and are as follows:

[1] As a standard for carrying not only data but also the names of that data, XML provides for a degree of resilience in the face of "interface creep"; however, most standards do not make use of this capability, insisting on a rigidity that is often, in our opinion, somewhat over-specified.

[2] Another W3C standard – "XML Schemas" – is important for the design of XML structures. However, further description of this standard is beyond the scope of this chapter.

[3] Although primarily designed for use with web services, the UDDI standard is not from W3C – it is from the Organization for the Advancement of Structured Information Standards (OASIS – see www.oasis-open.org).

- The **Core Enterprise System** is the set of custom applications and bought-in packages that form the heart of the IT system and that run on distributed servers and/or mainframes. Security and scalability are of major importance here. The Core Enterprise System is protected by firewalls and other security mechanisms. The code that implements the core business logic behind web services, and also manages core data assets, is here.

- The **Web Services Integration Broker** is the set of middleware responsible for handling B2B and B2G interactions with external systems.[4] This includes storage of the collaboration specifications and their execution, and also invocation of services provided by the Core Enterprise System.

- **Web/Application Servers** handle user and B2C requests from browsers, both within the enterprise and outside. User sessions, often long-running, are also managed here. The sessions make requests for services to the Core Enterprise System. For scalability reasons, these requests are typically "one-shot" requests, such as "update order" or "get stock details".

- A Process **Engine** manages automated business processes and workflows, and is also responsible for storage of specifications and their execution. There may be more than one process engine. For workflow, such engines typically provide a user interface so that users can see and manipulate their work list, and so that the work items can be managed. A process engine that addresses EAI will often provide numerous adapters for a range of packaged applications, while a Business Process Management engine may well provide complex peer-to-peer protocols for collaborations with third parties' systems.

- **User Systems** are typically PCs on user's desks, and are included here for completeness. Some user systems access the core enterprise system directly using a client/server style of interaction.

The typical interactions between these parts of the IT environment are shown by the dotted arrows.

Now let us look in more detail at the technology of web services – WSDL, SOAP, and UDDI.

---

[4] For an excellent white paper on the internals of this, see Cummins (2002). Broker function is almost always provided within commercial Web Services products.

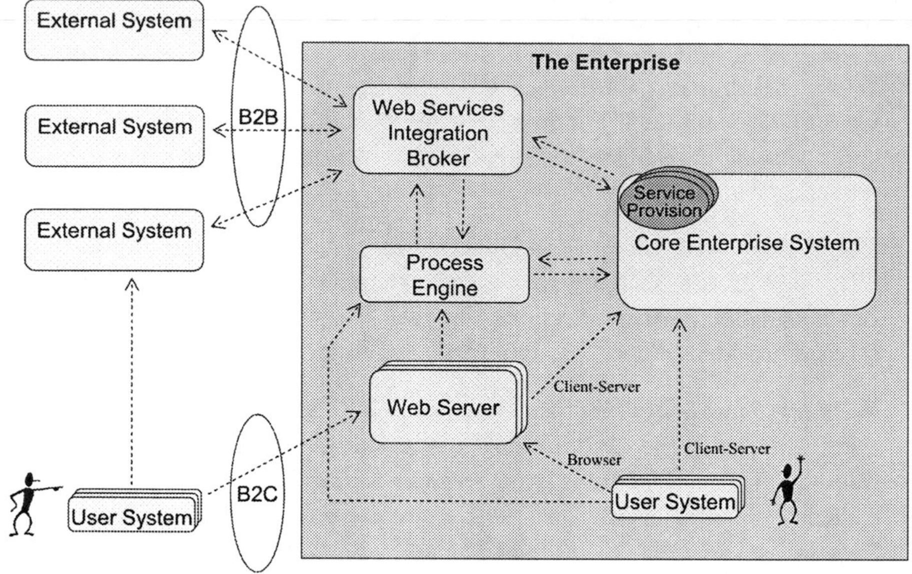

Figure 1. **An IT View of the Enterprise and Its Partners**[5]

1.1.2. WSDL and SOAP

WSDL or Web Services Description Language is a way of defining an interface to a service. It is the external view – seen by the developer – of the service. The vast majority of the time, developers will use a graphical IDE to interpret WSDL to display it in a user-friendly manner. SOAP (Simple Object Access protocol) defines the protocol – on the wire – for making requests and receiving responses. The creators of WSDL decided to use the then-existing SOAP standard as the protocol for accessing web services defined by WSDL. Together they form the basis of web services – the definition of services and the subsequent invocation of them.

This section illustrates how web services work through a highly simplified example. Consider a B2B service that allows products to be ordered. The service specifies that a request containing customer number and product number should be sent, upon which the product will be ordered, and the purchase order number will be returned. Error conditions are not considered in our example.

[5] The figure mentions "B2B" and "B2C". B2G and Business-to-Employee (B2E) have been omitted for clarity, but should be assumed to be beside B2B and B2C respectively. B2E in particular is starting to exploit mobile, wireless, and telecommuting trends for external access by employees, especially since user systems are becoming more than browsers with rich client and smart device technologies.

If the interface were written using CORBA IDL,[6] the order placement function might look like this:

```
interface Ordering {
  void placeOrder(in string CustNum, in string ProdNum, out
short PONum);
  ...
};
```

However, in the web service world, the interaction is described using WSDL (often pronounced "wizdle" by practitioners), and the WSDL file is stored by the enterprise's Web Services Integration Broker.[7] A simplified version of the WSDL corresponding to the preceding interface definition is as follows:[8]

WSDL fragment for an "Ordering" Service

```
<definitions name="OrderingService"

  <!-- Message definitions including parameters -->

  <message name="placeOrderRequest>
    <part name="custNum" type="string"/>
    <part name="prodNum" type="string"/>
  </message>

  <message name="placeOrderResponse">
    <part name="PONum" type="int"/>
  </message>

  <!-- PortTypes referring to message definitions -->

  <portType name="OrderingPort">
    <operation name="placeOrder">
      <input message="placeOrderRequest"/>
```

6 CORBA is the OMG's Common Object Request Broker Architecture. IDL stands for Interface Definition Language.

7 This repository is indexed using another web standard, UDDI (Universal Description, Discovery and Integration), whereby the service defined in the WSDL file can be found when potential users of the service do not know its web location. In our example, we assume the location is known, and so UDDI is not used.

8 WSDL examples in this chapter are based on WSDL version 1. At the time of writing, version 2 is in preparation. Version 2 introduces new terminology and a different approach to packaging the various elements of a service definition. However, the overall discussion here will not be materially affected by the new version.

```
      <output message="placeOrderResponse"/>
    </operation>
    ...
  </portType>

  <!-- Bindings for each operation in the PortTypes section. -->

  <binding type="OrderingPort" name="OrderingBinding">
    <soap:binding style="rpc" transport="http"/>
    <operation name="placeOrder">
    </operation>
            ...
  </binding>

  <!-- Services: Specifies the port address for each binding -->

  <service name="SalesOrderService">
    <port binding="OrderingBinding">
      <soap:address location="http://.../ordering.asp"/>
    </port>
  </service>

</definitions>
```

The purpose here is not to provide a full explanation of WSDL, but merely to illustrate the kind of thing it is. Note, however, that the "placeOrder" service is handled by two separate messages – one incoming from the external system to the system providing the service ("placeOrderRequest", and one outgoing from the service provider to the requesting external system ("placeOrderResponse").

The WSDL file constitutes a definition of the service provided at run-time. This includes the service's location (the URI to invoke the service), and the input and output messages (if any) that will flow in a service execution as SOAP messages. In this way, WSDL abstracts access to the underlying application data and processes – there is no specification whatsoever of the service implementation itself. The link with the service implementation is specified, in the service-providing system, quite separately from the WSDL service definition. Thus there is an absolute separation between the interface (the "service definition") and its implementation.This is a crucial aspect of Web Services: not only are interface and implementation logically separated, but they are also physically separated. It is precisely this that enables WSDL interfaces to be provided for a very wide variety of service implementations, from Java on an app server to COBOL on a mainframe – all accessible from a huge variety of clients. And it is largely this that make WSDL such an effective universal standard.

The (simplified) SOAP messages that flow across the wire during a service execution could look something like this:

SOAP messages on the wire

```
<!-- Sent by client to request the service: -->

<Envelope>
  <Body>
    <placeOrderRequest>
      <custNum>AB123</custNum>
      <ProdNum>XY-238/5<ProdNum>
    </placeOrderRequest>
  </Body>
</Envelope>

<!-- Received back from server (response): -->

<Envelope>
  <Body>
    <placeOrderResponse>
      <PONum>845273</PONum>
    </placeOrderResponse>
  </Body>
</Envelope>
```

A system that requests a service typically does so through some application that sends the appropriate SOAP message. Creation of the application code that does the mapping of (say) Java objects to SOAP messages, and the actual invocation, is handled by tools. This code is often called a "proxy" – the code that represents in the client the actual service implementation in the service-providing system.

Just as tools generate proxy code at the requesting end or "consumer end-point", so the code that invokes the implementation of the service at the service provider endpoint can also be generated. This code receives SOAP messages and maps them (in various ways according to the particular web services integration broker middleware) to the native language (e.g., Java) code that implements the service. Responses follow the reverse path.

But how are services found? In a world of ubiquitous services, there has to be a standard way for finding services that can be used. The UDDI standard (Universal Description, Discovery and Integration) provides the basis for this.

1.1.3. UDDI

UDDI (Universal Description, Discovery and Integration) is a standard for registering and searching web services within directories – yellow pages as it were – containing web services. UDDI is comprehensively addressed in the Registries Chapter, and only a brief overview is provided here. UDDI's main function is to provide for the discovery of services. First, a service provider uses UDDI to store the who, what, where, and how of a service – that is, the publisher, service description, location of the service, and the interfaces to access the service. Using these elements (as well as registry-specific service categorizations) potential consumers of web services can search for services. Then a potential consumer can use UDDI to locate an appropriate service. This can be done by a human using a browser, or programmatically. Generally, design-time discovery of services is a manual process performed through a browser. A consumer of a service will iron out with the publisher details such as the suitability of the service (does it meet enterprise requirements for availability, disaster recovery), and register to use the service if authentication is required. Finally, the consumer can connect to and use (interact with) the service. SOAP is used for messaging (with other messaging standards also being allowed for).

An additional strength of UDDI is run-time binding. Web service clients should be designed to cache the endpoint of the web service they access. Should a communications failure occur, the client should query UDDI and retrieve the endpoint for the service. It may well turn out that the reason for the failure is that the URL of the service has changed, and hence the service access can be re-tried. In this way, web service providers can move their web services (for example to perform routine hardware maintenance, failover within a cluster architecture, or disaster recovery) while minimizing impact on consumers.

The UDDI standard defines interfaces to a directory that are themselves web services described by a WSDL. Web page interfaces to UDDI execute those UDDI web services based upon human input through the browser, and display the results of those web services.[9]

Although there is some provision made within the UDDI standard for some limited semantics to describe a service, within the context of an enterprise UDDI is probably likely to be used by humans to browse for services. In other words, it may turn out to be more useful as a repository of services available than as an automated discovery facility.

[9] Examining UDDI's API documentation, schema and WSDL can serve as an introduction to more complex web services and their use. For example, see http://www.oasis-open.org/committees/uddi-spec/doc/tcspecs.htm#uddiv2. See also http://uddi.org/.

Having introduced the technical elements of web services, we now examine how a developer would use them. Again, the intent is to provide an overview rather than a tutorial.

Creating and Accessing a Web Service

Within the enterprise's IT organization, a developer first defines a service using a WSDL tool, and stores the resulting WSDL file in a repository managed by the Web Services Integration Broker. This is shown as step A in Figure 2 (the developer is shown at a "user system": a developer is a user too – of a system providing the development environment). Part of this task is identifying the module within the core enterprise system that will actually deliver the service.

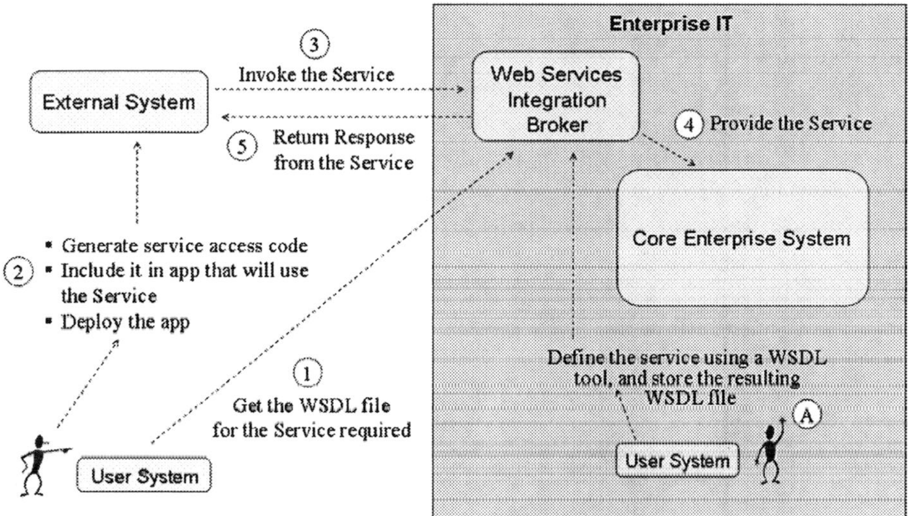

Figure 2. **Creating a Web Service**

To access the service, a developer in the external enterprise:

1. Uses a tool to retrieve the WSDL file.

2. The tool then generates a proxy for the service in the programming language of choice. The proxy is a programming language class that provides a friendly interface, in the programming language of choice, for the developer to invoke the service. Generated code inside the proxy handles SOAP formatting based on the WSDL specification and communication with the system providing the service. The proxy (and the application containing it) is installed on the external organization's system.

3. When the application runs, it calls the proxy, which does everything necessary to map the native language request made to it to SOAP requests that go across the wire to access the service.

4. When a request is received by the enterprise's Web Services Integration Broker, it is mapped to a specific service provider (the implementation of the service – the thing that provides it) in the core IT system. This could be a legacy application, an EJB, or some other application. Once serviced, a response is sent to the Integration Broker (not shown in the diagram).

5. A SOAP response is sent back to the requesting system.

With proxies and adapters in mind, our picture of enterprise IT is now as shown in Figure 3. The adapter effectively provides the route between the incoming SOAP message and the service provider. The WS Broker and the service provider together make up "the service". But Enterprise SOA (ESOA) is not only about the design of the service interfaces and the use of web standards such as SOAP and WSDL. It is not only about the internal structure of the Web Service Integration Broker (not discussed in this chapter). ESOA is also about the design and structure of the internals of the service, and the extent to which service orientation using web services technology can be usefully applied elsewhere within the enterprise IT system.

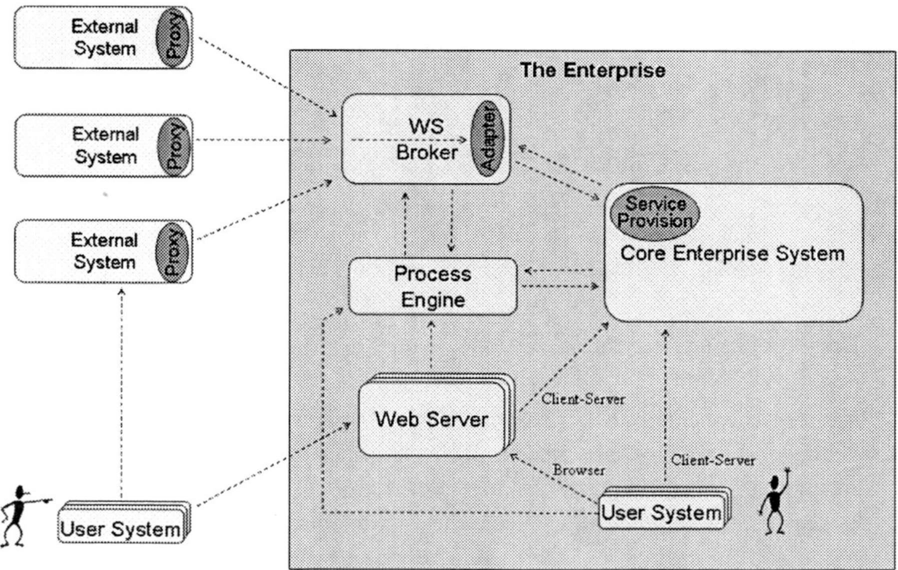

Figure 3. **Web Service Proxies and Adapters**

1.1.4. The Beginnings of Enterprise Service Orientation

Consider the service interface provided by the Web Services Broker Adapter in Figure 3. Now consider the service provision module in the same figure. This module also has an interface of some sort – otherwise it could not be called. Other parts of the enterprise IT picture also have their own interfaces – workflow, B2B as a service to internal parts, EAI systems that integrate legacy and/or packaged systems, BPM systems, etc. There are in fact many different interfaces that developers must deal with. Can we do anything about this tower of Babel?

Well, consider the advantages of web services listed previously. There is no reason why these should not apply *inside* enterprise IT as well as outside. The result would be a single kind of interface, using the same technology, for all internal systems that provide a service. Many existing systems would need to be wrapped of course. And performance would have to be considered. However, the potential advantage of a single interface type, that maps to many programming languages, is a huge simplifier for enterprise systems. It is like a common hub. Indeed, considering the number of other technologies that go with web services – such as message queuing – a single interfaced type is almost a must – a highly compelling simplifier. And simplification means effort reduction, which means cost reduction and/or faster response to business needs.

Figure 4 shows web service interfaces (the gray [green in e-book version] "lollipops") not only on the B2B collaborations (our WSDL/SOAP example was an extremely simple example of a B2B service), but also on the core system modules that provide or implement services. In addition, web service interfaces are also wrapped around the process engine so that process instances (including workflow and BPM instances) can be kicked off using a web service interface.

Note that this also reduces the variety of invocation mechanisms. In Figure 3, the order placement service provided by the core enterprise system is invoked using quite possibly four different mechanisms, for example:

- CORBA from the Web Service Integration Broker;
- MQ from a BPM or workflow instance;
- JMS from the web server;
- COM from a PC using client/server.

Each of these has its own programming model, and this is often visible in the applications making the requests. Wrapping all of these mechanisms with web

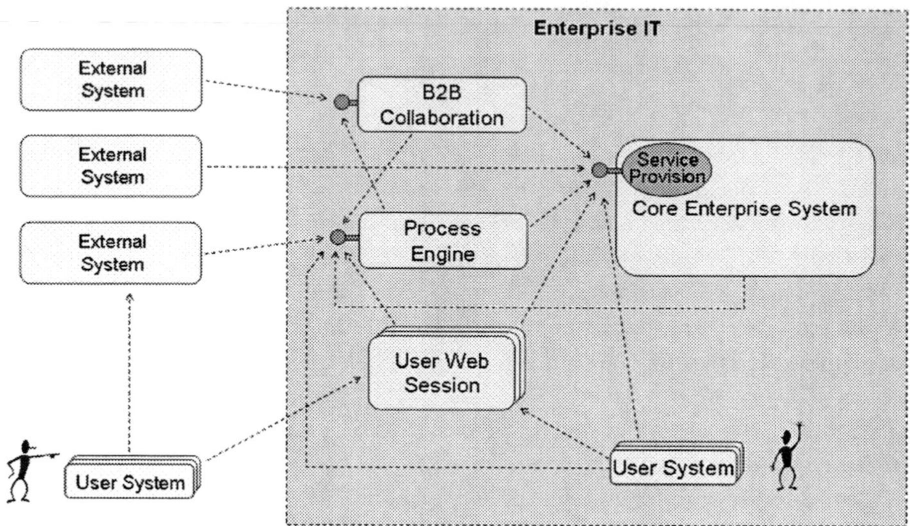

Figure 4. **Internal Web Service Interfaces**

services not only provides simplicity for the application developers, it also separates the communications and messaging infrastructures from applications. This simplifies evolution of the service without impacting other applications.

One significant benefit is that the debate around synchronous and asynchronous messaging models can now be divorced from the communications middleware, and brought back to where it rightly belongs – in the business developer's scope. For occasionally, it is required that a service should be invoked asynchronously *with respect to the invoking code*. It has been said that the only way to do this is with an asynchronous communications mechanism, such as a MOM (Message-Oriented Middleware). It has been further stated that CORBA (for example) is inherently a synchronous mechanism. However, proxy design can cater for either kind of communication. Further, a proxy can be designed to provide either or both a synchronous and asynchronous interface for the developer using the proxy. Hence the developer may invoke a service either synchronously or asynchronously with respect to his code, without being concerned about the precise communications mechanism.

So far we have treated the core IT systems as if they merely implemented services. But what about their own internal structure? For this, we turn to component-based development. Not the hyped "components" of third-party off-the-shelf plug-n-play modules, but the much more realistic and valuable modules of mature CBSE (Component-Based Software Engineering), which have been service-oriented from their beginning (some time before the term came into general use). CBSE in the context of the Service-Oriented Enterprise System is discussed in the next chapter. For the time being, we assume that web services have CBSE-based implementations which access the appropriate corporate resource. This assumption also addresses granularity and dependency management issues for modules that implement a service.

1.2. Enterprise Service-Oriented Architecture

Now we bring the two main threads – web services and CBSE – together. The result is an enterprise SOA that applies to both web services made available externally and also to core business component services built or specified for internal use. Figure 5 illustrates this. The business components within the Core Enterprise System area have "web service" interfaces – that is, they are specified using WSDL and invoked using SOAP. It may appear that performance will be unacceptable when components are co-located. Co-location can also have the potential of lack of support of distributed transactions, security context propagation/trust and other important concerns. Good middleware will optimize access, so that components in the same address space will be automatically invoked directly rather than via SOAP messages.[10] (If the middleware chosen does not provide such optimization, then of course performance considerations may well dictate a dropping-back to possibly multiple different interface technologies. In addition, groupings of tightly-coupled applications can be wrapped.)

Figure 5 also shows "wrapper components" that wrap legacy and/or packaged applications for either process or data access. The wrapper components look like components from the outside, but their internal implementation consists of whatever is needed to access the legacy or packaged application, plus the relevant part of that application itself.

The result is a single way of providing and invoking service interfaces, whether externally or internally.[11] In addition, all the advantages of CBSE accrue. Indeed, Enterprise SOA has some unique advantages:

---

[10] It is an ancient dictate of middleware, going back at least to the mid-1970s that remote/local access should be transparent to the application developer, with local access being optimized. The introduction of "local" interfaces in J2EE seems to have ignored this rule, and in some eyes was a giant leap backwards in the annals of effective middleware. However, server middleware is available today that does observe the rule.

[11] Some might say that services of different granularity require that they be implemented using different invocation or "binding" technologies. This was a reasonable position prior to the advent of Web Services technology. However – and so long as middleware suppliers provide for local optimization of service invocations – it is difficult to see how this position remains generally viable into the future. Certainly in certain proprietary implementations of service and component concepts in the 1990s, the advantages were reasonably well-proven for a wide range of situations.

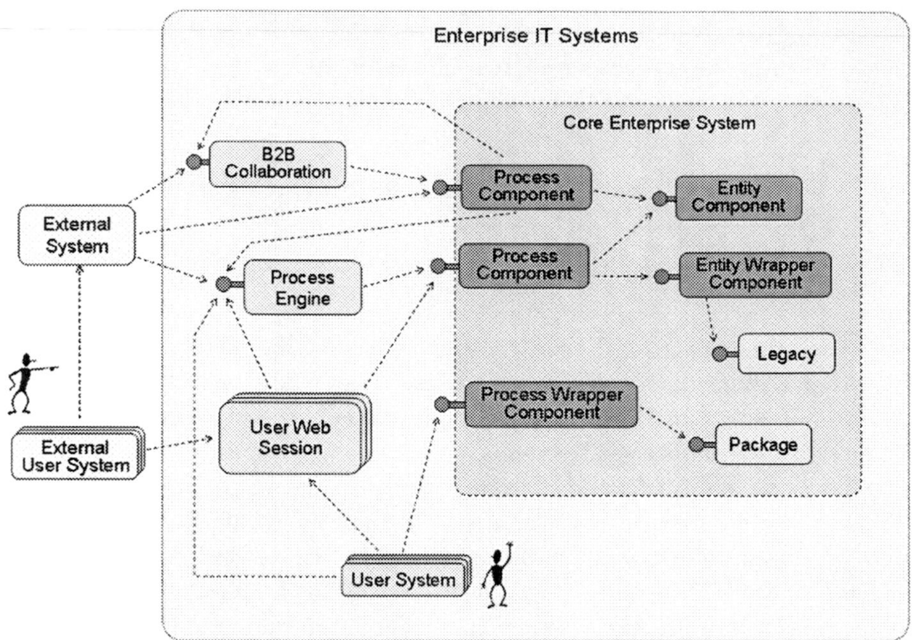

Figure 5. **Enterprise Service-Oriented Architecture**

- Provides, through the use of web service interfaces, a single interface and service access design, which is independent of the underlying platforms;
- Provides a single type system for interactions across and outside the enterprise;
- Provides a clear architecture for the internal implementation of services;
- Is tailor-made for use of model-driven development, such as the OMG's Model-Driven Architecture (MDA – see (OMG1)) strategy or Microsoft's Domain-Specific Language (DSL) developments (Greenfield and Short 2004).
- Separates much more clearly the business logic in code, business rules, work-flow, or B2B collaboration specifications from the underlying middleware which includes integration subsystems, communication subsystems, component containers, etc.;
- Simplifies the whole enterprise development environment.

In conclusion, Enterprise SOA is a concept whose time has come, and which will form the foundation for future enterprise systems. Perhaps CBSE and Web Services are indeed a marriage made in heaven.

2. Service-Based Collaboration through Federation

The ability to have services collaborate to provide new services is an important part of Enterprise Service-Oriented Architecture (ESOA). Without this, the various services are islands – silos – tomorrow's legacy. In order to achieve service-based collaboration, our ESOA must address how services are "federated" such that they deliver the collaborations required. A collaboration can then be said to be achieved through a "federation" of services.

2.1. A Federation Is ...

Federal/federating/federation – pertaining to "a system of government in which several States form a unity but remain independent in internal affairs; ... an association of largely independent units." (COD 1982)

But what, in our context, are the units being associated? Answer: services. We are talking about federations of services. Federation is therefore about creating an environment where common services are made available for use in conjunction with others.[12]

Let us start with a typical situation faced by many enterprises today. Figure 6 shows three legacy systems (X, Y, and Z) that have been given a service interface (the gray [blue in e-book version] "lollipops") through wrappers, which could use EAI technology. The term "service interface" refers to a programmatic interface whose description conforms to the WSDL standard, as described previously in Section 1 of this chapter. The wrapper is implemented using the approaches described in the same section.

Now assume the enterprise wishes to deploy a service that is a combination of the existing services. It can do so by defining a business process (using one of the many tools on the market) that firstly provides a service interface, and secondly is largely implemented through invocation of the existing services provided by the legacy systems. Process A in Figure 6 gives an example of this approach. And what we have here is a federation: Services provided by applications X and Y are "federated" by Process A to provide a new service.

[12] If services are federated, this must imply that service providers are also federated. Federation of providers can be implicit or explicit, and there is a range of governance issues that may apply such federations. However, in this chapter we do not address these issues.

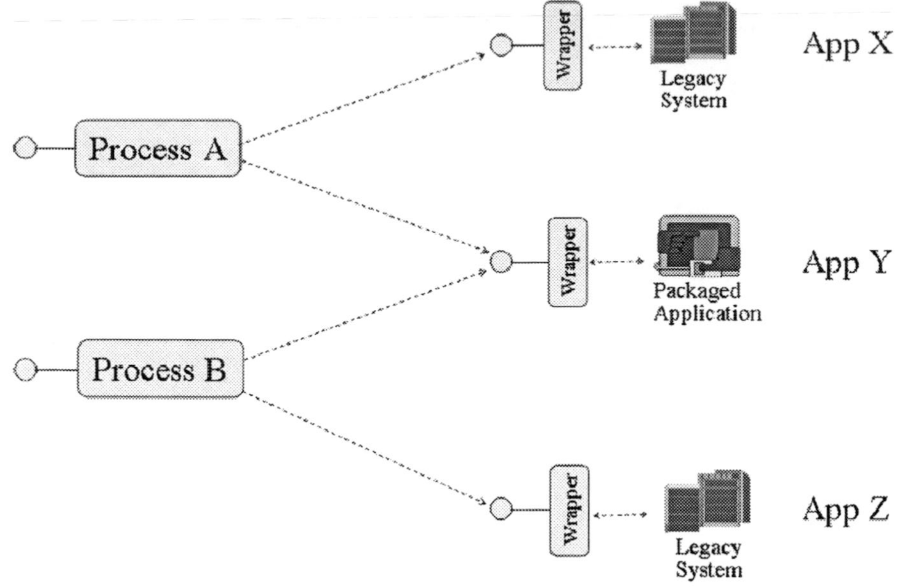

Figure 6. **Service Federation**

There are three things in this picture worthy of note:

1. Apps X and Y are not modified in any way.
2. Current services are unaffected.
3. The service provided by App Y is re-used by a second federated service (Process B).

There are also three things wrong with the picture:

1. The legacy and packaged applications are often monolithic: although they may contain many useful smaller-grained services, they are often not usable because the application designers did not provide ways of invoking them from outside the application.
2. Because of the monolithic nature of the applications, the service wrappings are limited in their scope for service evolution.
3. The function made accessible by the applications may or may not map to the function the business needs, and hence further federation opportunities are limited.

What is happening in Figure 6 is that, while there may be impressive advantages in providing services outside the enterprise, in a short time it will become apparent that the drawbacks of legacy systems – lack of flexibility, high maintenance costs, etc. – will leak through to service provision. In effect, the enterprise will be exporting the drawbacks of monolithic systems to their customers. When the business evolves, while the service interface can be rapidly changed due to current technologies, the provision of those services – the applications – cannot. A good service, valued by customers, can become a poor service over a relatively short time by being unable to evolve at the same (or faster) rate of a competitors' service. We are in danger of exporting the symptoms of our current legacy integration problem outside the enterprise – slow response to change, high cost of maintenance, possible poor performance, etc.

What we have in Figure 6 is a set of new legacy services! For example, a sales order placed through Process A in Figure 6 is unlikely to be processed in a single ACID transaction. This means that it may well not be committed. Handling situations where compensating transaction must be launched in order to undo a unit of work are well-understood. Propagating errors back to requestors is also well understood. Providing for both in a federation over networks and across disparate systems is another level of complexity. However, even were this to be achieved, conveying the correct semantics of an error across a federation is a major challenge. Even within a single system, we often cannot provide understandable error messages to the human being who needs to know what has happened! In our example, somewhere there will be a human being who is interested in the fate of the sales order – even if it is only as a monitor of exceptions in a fully-automated supply chain. How will that person know whether or not the order was actually placed?

So service federation is not just about gluing together what is there already; it is about seeing federated services as the basis for future systems architecture, from medium-grained to very large-grained services. When we said that federation is about creating an environment where common services are made available for use in conjunction with others, we omitted the context, which is that of flexible, evolvable, low-maintenance service provision, so that the business's time-to-market and responsiveness goals are met.

What is a "Service"?

We have referred to "services", "service interfaces", and "service implementation". Figure 7 shows a simplified UML[13] *model of these concepts (cardinalities have been omitted, since they are quite complex, and the model is, we believe, sufficient for current purposes without them). The topmost class is the concept of a service instance. This consists of a service interface, through which the service is programmatically invoked or requested at run-time, and a service implementation, which is the code that implements and provides the service. The lower three classes are the development-time definitions and specifications that, when put into production in the run-time, offer and provide a given service.*[14]

Federation means that a service implementation may be nothing more than an invocation of another "lower-level" service, although federation will normally involve at least a minimal amount of business logic and/or data mapping. Such a service is often referred to as a "choreography", since it causes the underlying services to "dance", as it were, to the tune of the federating service. However, in addition to choreography, and unless the federation is entirely within the IT facilities of a single enterprise, there will also be important additional issues such as security, data model semantics, and trust.

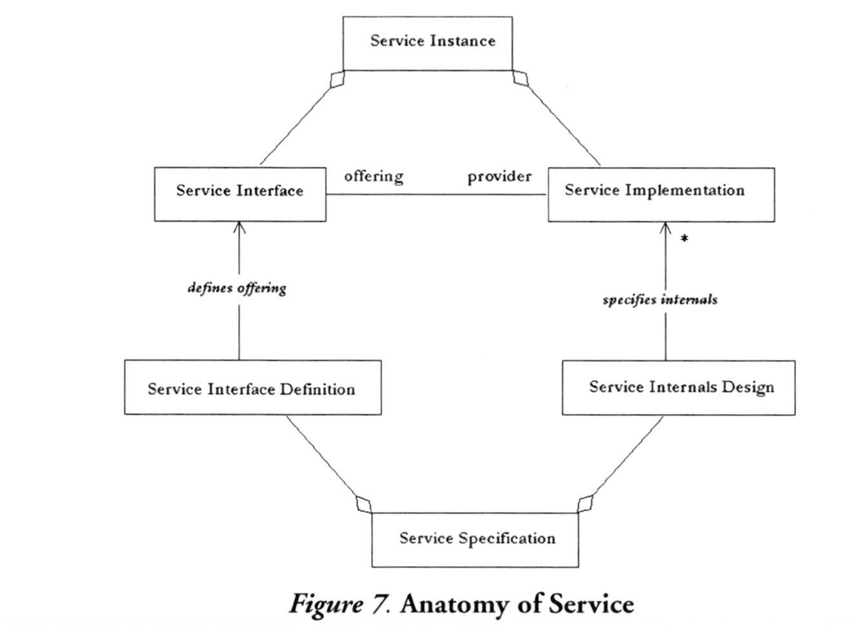

Figure 7. **Anatomy of Service**

[13] Unified Modeling Language – see OMG2 (2003) for the formal UML version 1 specification. UML version 2 is nearing finalization at the time of writing (see OMG3 2004).

[14] In those cases where services are dynamically bound based on run-time discovery, then the interface definition is a run-time artifact for the service consumer as well as a development-time artifact for the service provider.

2.2. Federation and Mature CBSE

For many organizations, the legacy problem is possibly the most significant barrier to evolving modern application architectures. However, while it is occasionally intractable, many EAI products enable a programmatic interface to be provided. The key question is what should these interfaces be? This is addressed in the next chapter, where we show how business "elements" can be identified and mapped one-to-one to service interfaces, such that the interfaces provided by application-level code reflect the important business areas of interest. In other words, the interfaces that wrap legacy should be modelled on this basis, so that they map directly to business needs.

In addition, Section 1 argued that new or re-factored applications should be modularized according to mature CBSE principles. Such modules, implemented as components, and aligned with business elements, can very easily be provided with service interfaces. While a mature component approach offered this capability, relatively few organizations have succeeded in achieving it. This has primarily been because:

- The initial focus for CBSE was on off-the-shelf markets in components. This focus has not proved fruitful, as the lack of such markets today shows. Another strand of CBSE focused on components as a better way of modularizing, and this focus has been far more fruitful (see Chapter 3) if less widely-known.[15]

- Focus on component technology per se. Effective component design and build does not need component container middleware, although such middleware makes the job considerably easier. But component container middleware alone does not produce well-designed systems that meet the goals of CBSE.

- Lack of focus on architecture, especially dependency management. Mature CBSE requires several things to be combined into an effective design and build environment, all informed by a clearly defined architecture which shows how application systems built in conformance with that architecture will meet the business's needs for responsiveness and time-to-market. Lack of such architecture, together with lack of processes that support a direct and clear link with business requirements, has resulted in approaches to service-orientation that have delivered new monoliths – with rather pleasant service-oriented interfaces that are slow and difficult to evolve over time.

[15] The academic world seems to have focussed on CBSE as providing a market of off-the-shelf components. One professor recently said to me that CBSE is dead, and service-orientation is the new thing, and applications will be built simply by invoking appropriate services, regardless of where these are or who implemented them. He seemed to have forgotten that a service must be implemented by something somewhere, else it is like a chain letter!

- Component middleware not only leaves technology "glue" to be built by most if not all organizations making significant use of them, but they it also tends to have built-in design biases (such as EJB's rigid session/entity dichotomy) that can sometimes make effective design more difficult.
- Lastly, but probably most importantly, an inability (for varying reasons) to make the organizational changes necessary. We will re-visit this question in Section 4 of this chapter.

Making mature CBSE viable has probably mostly been driven by what now can be seen as a systemic service orientation. This not only applies to architecture, but also to organization. This involves organizing the development environment in a way that rigorously separates implementation and provision of the development and run-time infrastructure from that of service definition and implementation. The infrastructure organization provides services to the service development group. Thus effective CBSE is to some extent dependent on a "service" approach being taken to the IT organization itself (as recommended by the "product line" approach (Clements and Northrop 2002), and also by the "component factory" approach (Herzum and Sims 2000).

On the architectural level, mature CBSE requires that components should be as autonomous as possible. However, they are designed from the start to cooperate with other components to deliver a solution. This drives stringent dependency-management approaches in the architecture. One of the more important dependency management schemes is based on the mediator pattern (Gamma et al. 1995). The business element approach described in Chapter 3 helps with this through the realization that business elements are naturally organized in this way. That is, there is a spectrum within which collaboration of autonomous components happens; the spectrum stretches from entities with very few business rules attached to them other than basic validation through to high-level processes.

2.3. The Federation Spectrum

Figure 8 illustrates this spectrum applied to a simplified "core business" component-based system that provides Invoice Management services. An Invoice Manager component contains the main invoice-related processes and/or procedures such as create invoice, print invoice, update invoice, etc. Important entities such as Invoice and Customer contain the business rules and validation associated with the entities themselves, irrespective of which process invokes them. Such an entity may make use of bottom-level "utility" components, such as an address database manager, or "Address Book" component. Utility components tend to be commodity in nature; that is, if the enterprise could buy them off-the-shelf from a third party, it would.

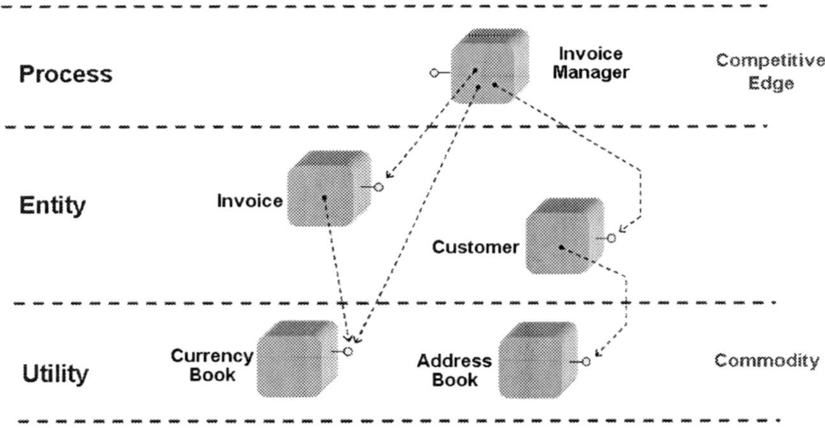

Figure 8. **Federation in the Core Business System**

Processes, however, tend to provide competitive edge, and hence are likely to be built in-house, or be based on a package that allows extensive customization.

A component higher in the spectrum can invoke any of those beneath it. This is in effect a use of the mediator pattern in the large. The dependencies create an open directed acyclic graph.

Now consider a second system, providing Order Management services, as shown in Figure 9. Here we see re-use of the Customer and Currency Book components. Since Customer is dependent on Address Book, this also appears.

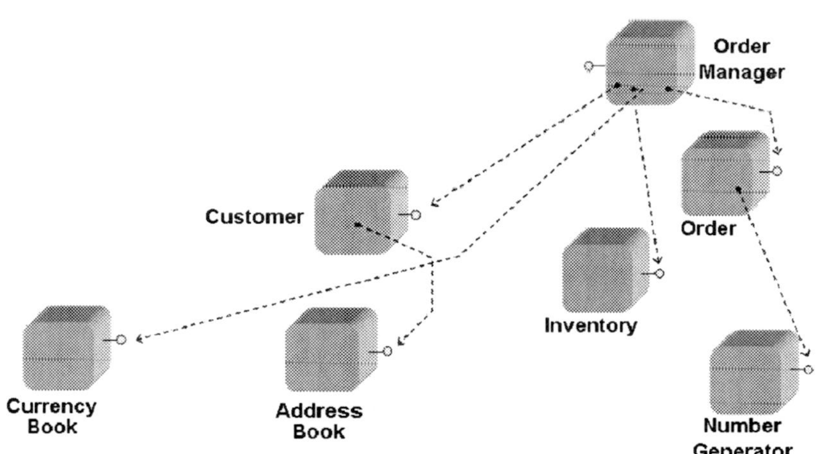

Figure 9. **Simplified Order Management System**

These two systems could well be deployed, as shown in Figure 10. Hence these components must be designed such that they provide services to any appropriate requestor – or consumer. A key part of this approach is firstly that the components map to business elements as defined (or better discovered) in the requirements phase of development, and secondly that each component is highly service-oriented such that they can collaborate with others in providing business solutions. Thus in the evolution of mature CBSE, there has been a shift from reuse of components as pluggable modules of software technology to business-oriented reuse and business collaboration of business services – the components themselves being the service implementations.[16]

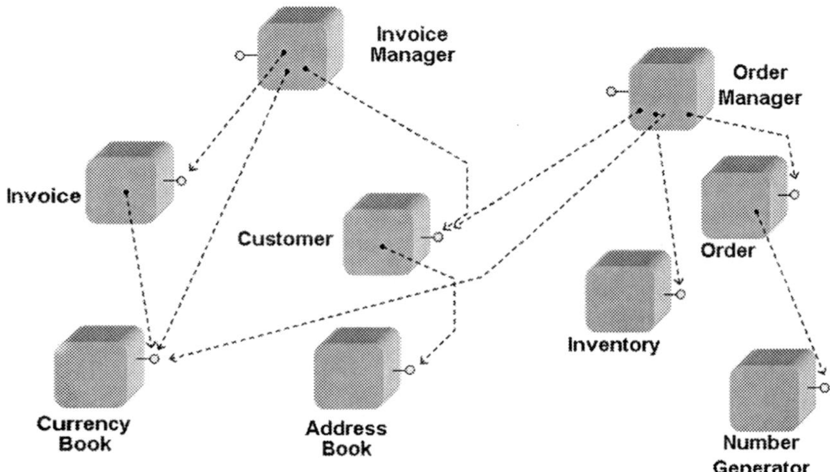

Figure 10. **Federation with Common Components**

Finally, notice that the Invoice Manager and the Order Manager components provide service interfaces. In this way, the collaborations that they "choreograph" are in themselves large-grained components, which provide service interfaces to higher-level components. But what are these higher-level components? They are the business service implementations that that make use of "lower-level" processes. For example, a customer order fulfilment service could span order placements and invoice creation as well as other things such as delivery scheduling. The execution of a given instance could take several weeks to complete.

One way of implementing this might be to modify existing services such as Invoice Manager, so that the new process is embedded within them. However, this would be a gross breach of encapsulation, and would be exceptionally poor design. Much better

[16] Students of the history of this evolution can find an early application of components as business-oriented pluggable modules in Sims (1994).

is to develop a "higher-level" service implementation that invokes the lower-level ones.

Figure 11 illustrates a "Fulfill Order" service (probably implemented using BPM-type tools) that makes use of the services provided by the lower-level Invoice Manager and Order Manager services. These in turn make use of the even lower-level entity services provided by Customer, Order, Invoice, etc. In effect, each service implementation is a combination of a process or set of business rules plus specific usage of lower-level services. The term often used is that higher-level components "choreograph" those at a lower level. This is the essence of federation.

Thus we can see a loose hierarchy of processes. At the bottom, the processes become procedures and algorithms, and indeed at the limit morph into data access components, whose main function is to hide or separate the specific details of data access. For example, the "processes" within a Customer or Order entity service implementation are typically the sets of algorithms and business rules to do with validating the internal contents of a Customer or Order (for example, "order header must have more than one order line", and "each order line must refer to a valid product").

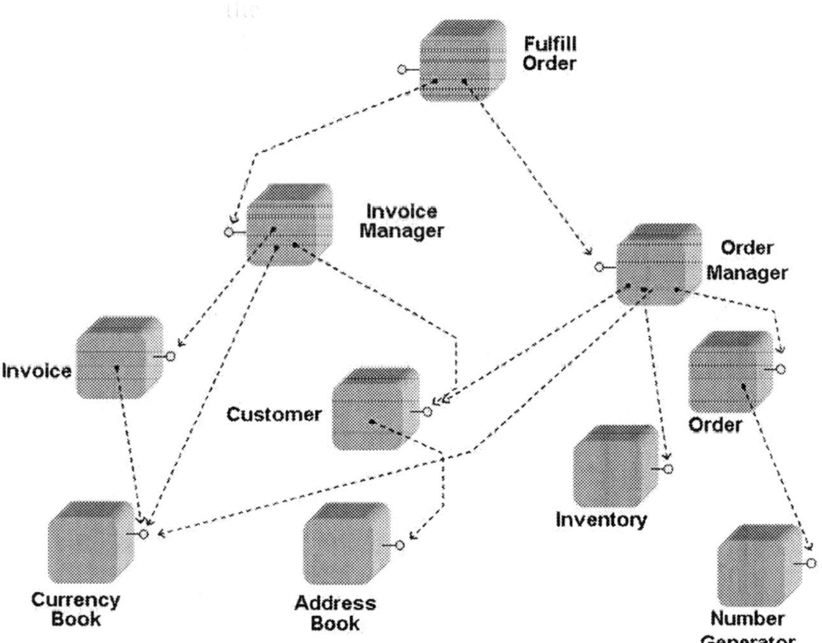

Figure 11. **Federation Using a BPM Component**

2.4. The Spectrum as a Service Taxonomy

The spectrum then is partly data through process, but more importantly it is a spectrum of business scope. Hence the main difference between different levels in the spectrum is the business scope addressed by the service. This implies that the greater the scope, the larger the granularity of the resulting federation. Service granularity means the amount of process (and consequential state change) you get from a single invocation of a service.

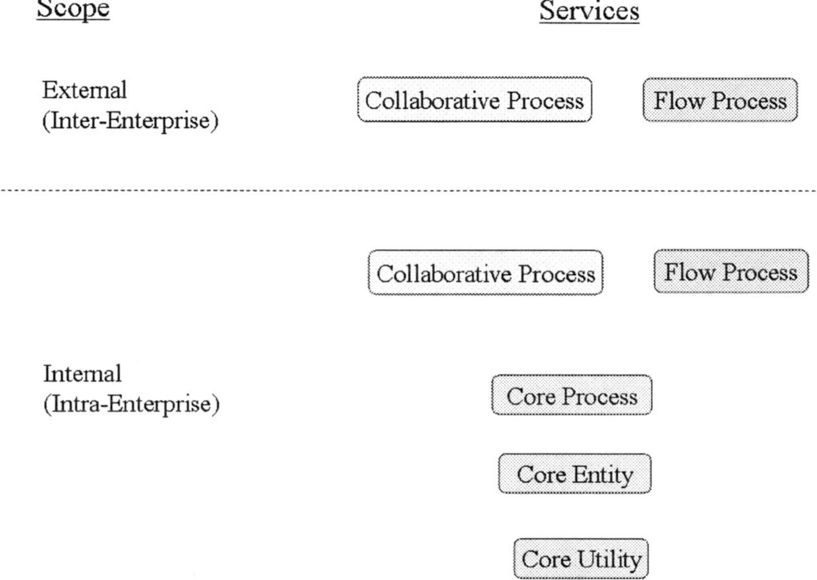

Figure 12. **A Service Taxonomy**

Figure 12 suggests a service ontology based on these concepts. While not a rigid classification, it has proved useful in separating concerns, and in ascribing implementation technologies. Thus higher-level services are implemented by peer-to-peer collaborations, or "flow" processes such as business process flows or workflow. These levels are typically implemented by business process management systems or workflow systems. Tools[17] in these areas tend to provide for high-level definition of processes

[17] Higher-level "processes" can be categorized into B2B collaborations, flow-type business processes, and workflow. However, this categorization is partly driven by the past evolution of tools. Tools in this area tend to implement various developing standards such as BPML (Business Process Modeling Language) and BPEL4WS (Business Process Execution Language for Web Services). These standards are currently in considerable flux, and it is not yet evident which will win out in the longer term. The tools and middleware that enables business processes to be specified, and provides for their execution,

(the service implementation), such that the service implementation is interpretive. Lower-level service implementations tend to be much more algorithmic in nature, and (with today's technology at least) tend to be implemented in programming languages such as Java, through formal IT development processes, and running on middleware providing for high transactions rates and scalability (such as component container and transaction processing middleware).

This figure shows a "spectrum of services", both internal to the enterprise or organization, and also external services. Lower-level services are federated by higher-level services.

Figure 12 may seem to suggest that a given process should be placeable at one of the five levels shown. However, useful sub-levels can be defined. For example, working in a number of industries, we have seen that the bottom three levels in Figure 12 can be expressed as eight or so useful levels (Herzum and Sims 2002). Furthermore, these levels tend to be the same within an industry area. For example, Supply Chain Management systems have core processes that can be sub-divided into two layers: core business processes (such as Inventory Management) and "support" processes such as credit checking. Core entities can be sub-divided into contracts (e.g. sales order), trading parters (e.g. customer), basic concepts (e.g. price, or inventory), and materials (e.g. item or product). Finally, core utilities may be classed as "books" (e.g. addresses) or "support" items (e.g. notes).

Higher-level and broader-scope services can also have multiple layers, and work is on-going as to whether there are useful industry-wide categorizations.

Finally, the spectrum could be called a "spectrum of instability", since the higher the level, in general, the more frequently the processes change. We prefer the term "spectrum of flexibility", to reflect where high flexibility and ability to rapidly evolve are vital aspects of architecture technology selection. The lower levels, down to the essential entities of the business, are relatively more stable, although specific sets of business rules can sometimes change frequently. This argues for maintenance of those sets of business rules such that new versions can be "plugged into" a component. Further discussion of how this can be done is beyond the scope of this chapter.

Thus in a given situation, flow and collaboration services will appear at a number of levels. What is important here is:

---

are often called Business Process Management Systems (BPMSs). Workflow systems are addressed by the WorkFlow Coalition (WFC), and have broadly the same overall characteristics as BPMSs. At the detail level, they are quite different, and currently products on the market tend to be either BPMSs or Workflow Systems. It is not yet clear whether in future they will coalesce into a single kind of product, although we see no a priori reasons why they should not eventually be able to come together.

- Each is service-oriented, business function is provided through federations of services.
- Services are designed and implemented according to mature CBSE principle for responsiveness and agility in the face of business evolution.
- The SOA framework for federation is equally applicable for service use internal and external to the organization.

These characteristics provide for organizational adaptability.[18]

In summary, enterprise SOA (ESOA) is the basis for enabling federation through good modularization (components), clear identification of business elements that are service-oriented and whose implementation will be components, architecture that embraces the flexibility spectrum, and, at the technical level, definition of WSDL as the means to define and invoke services. The latter factor is often overlooked, but is of considerable importance. As mentioned in Section 1, WSDL scales very well. It is applicable to all levels of the service spectrum. And it is a widely-accepted standard, supported by a large and growing number of products and tools. For the first time we have a standard for all service interfaces, that can apply from the lowest-level service to a majority of required standards.

Note that WSDL is not the sole web service definition language out there, http://hinchcliffe.org/archive/2005/05/10/215.aspx

2.5. Federation Example

The various levels of service can be federated in many different ways. Figure 13 illustrates one example, where three enterprises (B, C, and D) collaborate in a virtual enterprise (A in the figure). We can see at least four federations (the figure does not show all the service interactions or federations):

- Enterprise A provides a business process flow service (*Provision Customer*), whose implementation is a federation that includes, at one of its parts, invocation of a B2B collaboration process service (*Contract Negotiation*) among B, C and D.
- D's part of *Contract Negotiation* involves (when the contract has been agreed) a federation of existing business flow services, one of which is *Fulfill Order*. This in turn ...

[18] A good exposition of how service orientation can affect organization is to be found in the first several chapters of Harmon et al. (2001).

- ... federates several core process services, one of them being *Order Manager*, which in turn ...
- ... federates several core entity services.

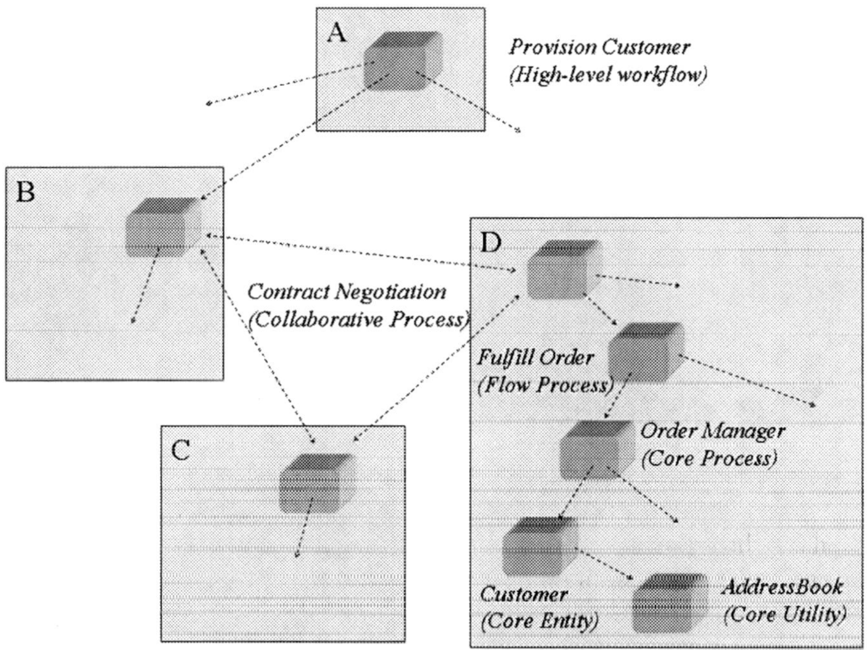

Figure 13. **Enterprise Collaboration**

Thinking service orientation at the enterprise level leads inexorably to thinking in terms of systemic service orientation, both within the enterprise and outside. In this section, we have discussed federation of services, where the federations themselves become higher-level services in their own right – but which are implemented by well-modularized and accessible components, each of which provides its own services and also will probably federate other components of lower granularity. This is the essence of ESOA. Granularity is to do with business scope, not in the sense of the scope of enterprise that needs to know about it, but in terms of managerial ownership. The important consideration is that separations between levels of service federations are not a technology matter but are formed by business drivers and concerns.

The goal for ESOA is nothing less than a worldwide mesh of collaborating services, allowing each enterprise to focus on its core competence. A key part of this is the concept of applying the same model internally, so that within an enterprise each subsidiary, division, region, location, and even each department has its core competence published as a service.

But we cannot just build each service implementation as a new stovepipe. We need to bring different services together as and when required, without touching the implementation of those services. The process of doing this is called "federation".

This section has shown, based on concepts developed in earlier sections, how services that are federations, and how federations of services, can be achieved. But achieving service federations alone is not sufficient. We also need to change and evolve them – and introduce new services – without being tied by the underlying technology. Thus we must consider how to separate the business-level services and service implementations from their underlying technology base. We need to provide a platform that appears to business developers as substantially more stable and unified than before, while retaining our ability to evolve the many underlying technologies at their natural pace. Thus we need to consider the platform that supports an ESOA.

3. The Platform

ESOA is quintessentially about satisfying enterprise business requirements in a responsive and efficient way. A major inhibitor to this is that the business changes and evolves at a quite different rate than the rate of change in underlying software and hardware technology. Why is this an inhibitor? Because most current approaches to application software development fail to separate business logic needed to implement services from the "platform" – that is, the set of DBMSs, application servers, GUI infrastructures, BPM engines, messaging systems, communications stacks, system services such as logging, configuration, naming, etc., that underlie the business services, and upon which they run.

Look at any business-level application code today, and the chances are you will find all sorts of technology code buried inextricably with the business logic, from GUI-driving code to thread and transaction management code. This means that changes to business function can drag in technology concerns, and changes to technology impact business logic. And this is not some minor techie problem. It means is that every time the business needs something to change, or needs some new function, the business logic developers are immediately immersed in software technology, and vice-versa. Figure 14 illustrates the effect: not only do both business and technology changes result in modifications to the IT systems, but also each change is one of both business and technology, thus doubling the effect of each change! By the way, this applies to new function too, not just changes. And what if we need to move to a new platform, or we are developing services for two or more platforms? It is imperative that we shield our service implementations as much as possible from the impact of underlying software technology, whether from changes to that technology, or from the need to run services on several different platforms.

It has been said that model-driven development approaches – as in the OMG's Model-Driven Architecture (OMG) – will remove this problem. However, if a model generates not only business logic but also the technology glue, then we have certainly simplified one part of the problem, but have introduced another – the problem of maintaining an increasing amount of glue-generating code! The argument for clear separation of these two major aspects – business and technology, in both models and code – remains.

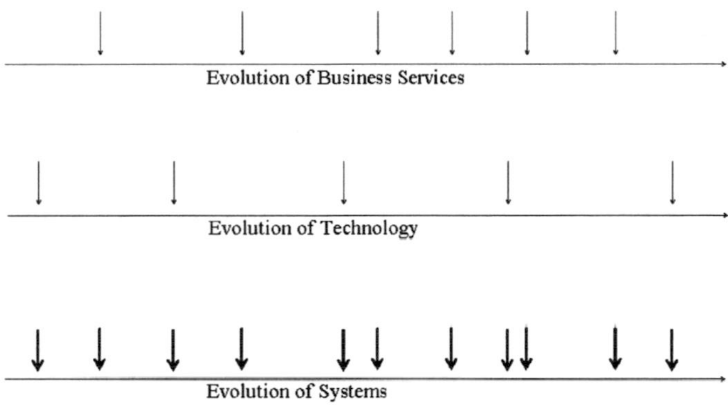

Figure 14. **Development Churn**

In this section, we take a top-down view of the technology "platform" and describe an approach that protects, as much as possible, the business services and their implementations from the evolution and change that must occur as platforms mature or change.

3.1. The ESOA "Blueprint"

How do we get a handle on separating software technology function from software business services? Well, the "A" in ESOA stands for "architecture". This is not there just to pad out a snappy acronym. It means that service-orientation at the enterprise level must be clearly designed, and that design must be visible. In other words it must have an architecture. But "architecture" can mean many things. Here, we use it in the sense of a "blueprint" that applies to a range of different applications, all built according to the same structural principles. When a number of different applications can all share the same structure, and where the relationships between the parts of the structure are very similar, then we have what might be called an "architectural style" (Hubert 2002). Much the same concept is also called a "product line" (Clements and Northrop 2002), or part of an "approach" (Herzum and Sims 2000). An architectural style can be expressed through what is sometimes called a "blueprint" (also called a "metamodel"). Such a blueprint becomes the expression of the "architecture" in ESOA. It is a detailed design for:

- The structure of the modules to be defined and built by business developers (including their dependencies and statefulness), how they relate to each other, where the services are offered, and to whom (internal, external, etc.).
- The transparencies enjoyed by business developers – that is, the extent to which software technology is hidden from them.
- A specification of how extra-functional challenges such as scalability, buildability, performance, etc. will be addressed.

One part of such a blueprint is the model of what a "component" is (see Chapter 2). A further example of what the blueprint addresses is the "distribution" part of a distributed system – that is, the logical distribution tiers. These are areas of responsibility – or "aspects" – of business logic *as seen by the business developer*. They are separate from, but mappable to, the physical distributed system. For reasons beyond the scope of this chapter, we prefer a four-tier model to the often-used three-tier model. Briefly, the tiers are:

- User – the specification of the user interaction with some device (including screen layouts).
- Workspace – the business logic involved with managing a user's session. This tier provides services to the user tier.
- Enterprise – the business logic involved in providing enterprise-level services to authorized requestors, and also the business logic inherent in "business objects" – the business-level resources that business processes depend upon. This tier provides services to the workspace tier, and also to other areas such as B2B collaborations
- Resource – the business logic required to access resources such as data (or printing). This tier provides resource services to the enterprise tier.

Figure 15 illustrates these four logical tiers, and shows how they can be mapped to a variety of physical systems.

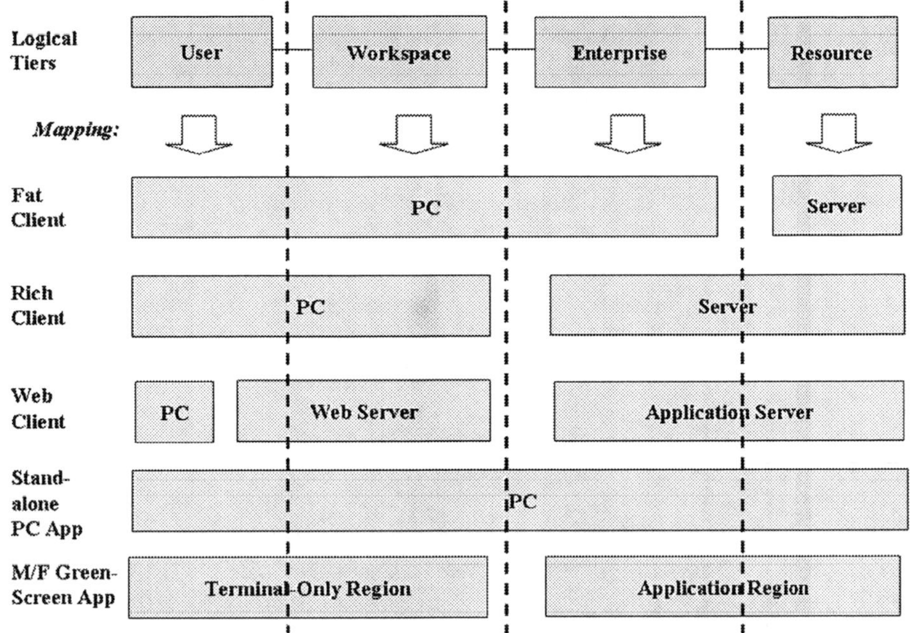

***Figure 15.* The Four-Tier Distribution Model**

Figure 15 is fairly high-level, and illustrates the "distribution" concept that is part of the set of core concepts within an ESOA.[19] However, the objective for the ESOA blueprint is to define things, based on these core concepts, at a sufficient level of detail that the same business-level code can be mapped to several different physical system structures, and to differing software technology platforms. This requires two things:

- A concept of development that rigorously separates business logic from the technology infrastructure, and also explicitly addresses mapping of platform-independent designs to the necessary platform-specific artifacts. This is exactly the province of the OMG's new strategy, "Model-Driven Architecture" or MDA (OMG1 2003).

- A concept and implementation of "platform" that enables the separation to be as complete as possible. Of course, it can never be completely separate: if it were,

[19] Note that this approach separates the orthogonal concerns of distribution of logical areas of responsibility (workspace, enterprise, etc.) from those of separation of logical business responsibilities (process, entity, etc.). It is not uncommon to find these two concerns conflated, resulting in business processes being placed in a PC or in web server session logic, leaving only entities or "business objects" in the shared server. This makes provision of business services difficult, since they either have to be duplicated on the server, or an important part of the system must be re-engineered to separate them properly.

then business logic could not run! But we can push the boundary of the platform upwards so that separation becomes as clean and as complete as possible.[20]

The key to separation is to define a "virtual platform" for business developers that is deterministically mappable to a number of real platforms. Figure 16 illustrates this. Note the additional blueprints (designs) for the virtual platform and for the real platforms. For example, components built according to the business service blueprint could be mapped or transformed to J2EE or a CORBA Component Model (CCM) implementation or .NET, all of which support the component concept. It can also be mapped to some transaction processors such as IBM's CICS. The mapping or transformation (or partial transformation) would produce business service components that are of the specific form supported by the target platform.

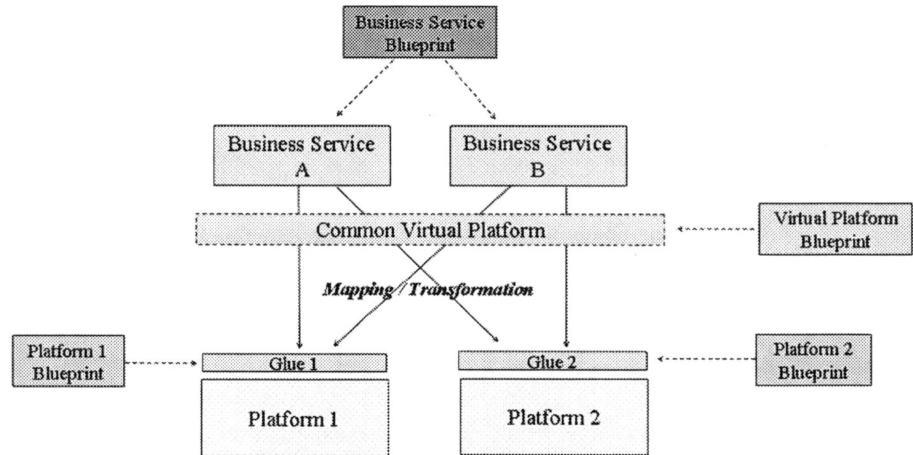

Figure 16. **The "Virtual Platform"**

Now this all seems like a huge task. But it is not. Most IT departments have skilled people who produce bits of code, or add-ons to development tools, that hide complexity and make things easier for application developers. A run-time example of "glue" is a logging service (it is surprising how many real platforms do not provide this, or provide one whose function needs to be expanded in some way). A development-time example of glue is a script that takes an analysis-level model and transforms it into the beginnings of a design-level model. In each case, what is really being done is to define a virtual platform and to provide for the glue to map that higher-level platform to the real COTS (commercial off-the-shelf) platforms.

[20] MDA defines "platform" as follows: "A platform in general is a set of subsystems/technologies that provide a coherent set of functionality through interfaces and specified usage patterns that any subsystem that depends on the platform can use without concern for the details of how the functionality provided by the platform is implemented." (OMG1 2003, pp. 2–3).

However, the blueprints generally only exist in the minds for the glue providers, and are often lost when the project ends. Figure 16 suggests that this process, so common in so many projects across the industry, should be formalized and applied explicitly within the enterprise so that they are not lost and re-invented project by project. Section 4 presents a process whereby this problem can be fixed.

3.2. Current Status for ESOA Platforms

A mature ESOA platform actually comprises two important "platforms": the run-time platform, and the "development platform" used by business developers to build service components that will run on the run-time platform. However, despite the wide range of commercial off-the-shelf (COTS) products that are available today, implementing an ESOA is difficult. There are three reasons for this:

1. COTS products are point solutions, not ESOA solutions;
2. COTS products are general-purpose; and
3. IT development is (typically) project-based.

3.2.1. Point Solutions

IT development organizations today are faced with a huge choice of middleware and development tools. Somewhere on the market, you can find everything needed to implement an ESOA. The main constituent parts of EOSA run-time platform include such things as an application server (component container middleware), Web Service support, DBMS, and a user interface infrastructure. The function required includes:

- Web Service definition and publishing;
- Optimization mechanisms so that web services can be used where required within a single address space;
- XML handling;
- Transaction processing and Concurrency support;
- Event management through a notification service;
- Workflow and B2B support;
- User Interface infrastructure;

- DBMS;
- Caching mechanisms.

And for each of these, there are a number of sub-functions needed – for example, effective transaction processing needs thread and connection pooling, and event management needs queuing.

The development platform includes such things as web service definition tools, compilers, repositories, GUI design tools, and modeling tools. Again, sub-functions are needed, such as the ability to interchange artifacts among the various tools.

The overall problem is that, although everything required is available, it is not available in a single integrated product. This results in high levels of complication across the whole development environment. From the CIO/Chief Architect's view, all you can buy from vendors today are big construction kits, where you often have to make up your own assembly and operation instructions. There are lots of specs and instructions for the individual parts, and much advice on sub-assemblies – assuming you understand all the parts. The main areas of complexity are:

- Technical complications throughout the development environment. Addressing these requires high levels of scarce skill for many development projects. The result is low effective skill levels applied to many developments, with the inevitable poor quality and re-work.
- Rapid change in and evolution of software technologies. This results in high levels of technology churn, and a disinclination to install new or upgraded products. When technology is changed, this has a severe knock-on effect on the business function portfolio. This is exacerbated by business evolution and change (naturally) being out of sync with technology change.
- Lack of focus on an ESOA architectural style.

Thus we have a situation where a great deal of work is needed to turn the collection of products into an effective ESOA platform.

3.2.2. General-Purpose COTS Products

The reason there are holes in the COTS products available today is that producers have not appreciated the concept of architectural styles. Hence they have had to produce very general-purpose platforms, suitable for many architectural styles. However, it is the concept of architectural style that enables a platform to be very high level. Implementing services in a distributed enterprise system can done with a particular architectural style, and hence the platform for that style could be much higher-level than that provided by the general-purpose COTS products. There are some indications that this may – just may – be changing. But do not hold your breath for the next two years.

3.2.3. Project-Based Development

The third impediment to effective ESOA implementation is a strong "project orientation" within the development organization. Of course, this does not mean that projects per se are an impediment. However, where each development project has significant authority to choose (some of) its own technology code or products, and also to build its own glue, then it can be extremely difficult to achieve a sensible separation between software technology and business function. This is because in such an environment:

- There is little funding for efforts outside the project, and so:
- There is limited re-use of common artifacts, whether software technology or application modules, across projects; rather, there is often a great deal of re-invention.[21]

Such organization means that expertise and artifacts are not shared across projects, and so valuable learning and knowledge is dissipated at the end of each project. This adds to the cost of each project, but such costs are not visible because the cost basis is project-oriented, not service-oriented. Figure 17 illustrates this.

Now one of the striking things about IT organizations is that they are often relatively impervious to the business pressure for dramatic time-to-market improvements. This is because IT organizations are fighting on two major fronts:

1. Time-to-market pressures from business stakeholders, and
2. Dealing with rapid and wide-ranging technology "churn".

And this when much current application development and design thinking is optimized for yesterday's environment, characterized by OO and fat client design plus rapid development processes such as RAD and XP. To this has been added distributed system thinking characterized by thin or "rich" clients and app server technologies. Finally, the underlying software technology is often researched and

[21] By "re-use" I do not mean harvesting something, then adapting it, then testing it, then teaching people about the adaptation, etc. I mean taking some asset and using it *unchanged* in a project. Experience shows that re-use of this kind is a perfectly viable proposition – but probably not in a tradition project-based organization.

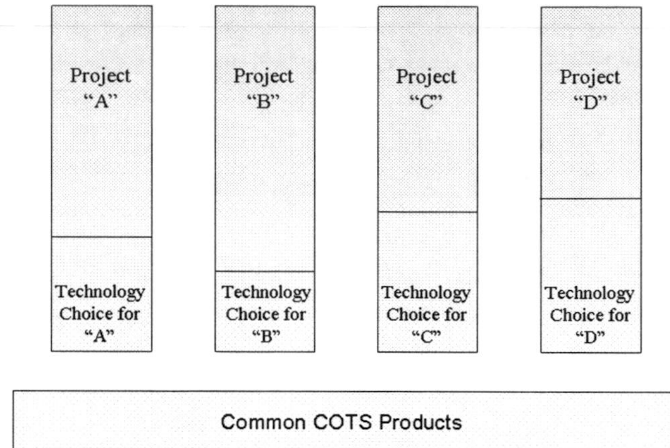

Figure 17. **Project Orientation**

adopted on a per-project basis, with little other than operating systems and major middleware products being used as a common infrastructure across projects.

Changing to more productive development environments while facing such pressures is difficult, and implies organizational as well as design paradigm changes. The major inhibitor is the lack of an end-to-end cohesive product that directly aims at lifting productivity – an "enterprise productivity platform" (EPP). While few organizations are able to meet the challenge of building an EPP as a marketable product, many can move in the right direction using existing products combined with a tight focus on harvesting their skills, and the assets that those skills have produced, to provide an in-house equivalent. The objective is to share assets across projects, and have a single way of filling the holes in the existing product providing the run-time platform and the development environment. Without such a move within IT, business stakeholders are likely to continue to be disappointed.

3.3. Filling the Holes

We talked about the prevalence of "glue" code, and the need to take an enterprise view of the effort in producing it. To summarize this, Figure 18 shows the requirement at the top, what is available in the middle (showing the holes), and the way that glue fills the gaps at the bottom. From the business service developer's point of view, where much ingenuity and time must be applied to providing the business logic (processes, procedures, algorithms, data handling, etc.), the less software technology the better. However, much glue function is built from the bottom up, with important aspects left to the business developer "in case they're needed". With a clear blueprint, the things that are needed can be pre-defined, and a great deal of software technology can be hidden much more effectively.

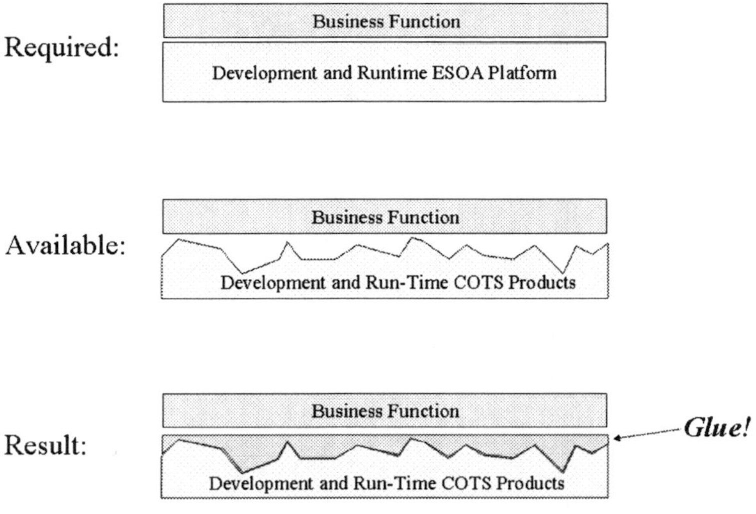

Figure 18. **The Importance of "Glue"**

In other words, there is an urgent need to view the glue as creating a virtual platform for service developers. Space prevents detailed discussion, but two examples can illustrate the kinds of concerns involved. Both look at providing simplicity and transparency to business service developers in ways that are specific to the ESOA architectural style, but independent of underlying platform technology. The two examples involve invoking services at the client end, and building a GUI front-end.

3.3.1. Invoking a Business Service

First, we look at an example of the kind of glue code often provided for business developers on an ad hoc basis by friendly colleagues working in the same project. The example is one where a business developer needs to invoke a "Place_Order" service (say from a PC or from a web server). The information he or she has is the order data (in a variable `order_data`), and a key – the string "Place_Order" – to the URL that identifies the WSDL that is the effective interface to the service implementation. The code the developer might write to place the order is as follows, where the code is actually simple pseudocode, and lines beginning "//" are comments:

```
// Get the URL of the web service
url = wsdl_location_service.find("Place_Order");
// Bind to web service whose WSDL is at the specified URL
```

```
web_service = wsdl_system.bind(url);
// Create a proxy to use to access the web service;
order_proxy = proxy_service.makeproxy(web_service)
// Now invoke Create Order:
 error = order_proxy.create(order_data);
```

Notice the three functions used by the developer: wsdl_location_service, wsdl_system, and proxy_service. At least one, probably two, and perhaps all of these are "helper" functions written locally to assist the business developer, and not provided by the web service COTS product being used. The friendly colleagues have, on an ad-hoc basis, picked out the parts that they believed could do with some help, and have provided it in a way that reduces software technology complexity to some extent.

Now let us take a top-down view, and ask, if I am a business developer, what might I prefer to code here. A good answer is:

```
// Find the "Place_Order" service:
bus_service = system_service.find("Place_Order");
// Invoke the service:
error = bus_service.create(order_data);
```

Experience suggests that this simplification is not only eminently do-able, but also better than the following even briefer and still viable approach:

```
// Invoke the Place_Order service:
Error = bus_service.invoke("Place_Order","create",order_data);
```

Support for either of the above two approaches is more complex to write, even if it is much more helpful to the business developer. However, this is the kind of thing that is defined in the blueprint, written once, and provided as a standard aspect of the virtual platform for all business developers. It clearly separates business logic from software technology since this form can be mapped within the virtual platform to a number of different technologies – not only different web service COTS products, but also, other non-web technologies such as CORBA. It can also provide for performance enhancements.

3.3.2. User Interface

The user interface is an area often assigned to junior programmers to implement. This is a mistake. The user interface is where the system actually delivers benefit to the enterprise. The less usable it is, the less benefit. In addition, UI code is particularly difficult to write well, requiring much low-level technical detail that is technology-specific. For example, an HTML-defined UI is quite different from one using Swing. However, it is possible to construct a UI framework – part of the virtual platform – that not only simplifies things a great deal, but can also shield the business developer from technology differences. Such an infrastructure includes such capabilities as:

- Navigation schemes;
- Widget standards;
- Internationalization concerns;
- Performance framework (so that the users do not experience the "sticky mouse" syndrome, nor do they wait for server access when performing trivial operations such as tabbing off a field).

Today, XML is starting to be applied to the UI. In the mid-90s, I helped build a component container middleware product which used a pre-cursor to XML as the only way to define GUIs. A layout tool produced XML-like definitions, which were interpreted dynamically. This worked well on 16MHz processors running Windows 3.1, and on slightly more powerful PCs running Windows95. Performance was not a problem. Neither was UI building (Eeles and Sims 1998). Today, this approach is being developed using XML: XUL (XML User interface definition Language) (XUL) is an interesting approach to simplification, as is Microsoft's forthcoming XAML (Extensible Application Markup Language – pronounced "Zamel", to rhyme with "camel" (Petzold 2004)). Here is an example of a simple XUL panel definition

```
<xul>
<window title="Nexaweb Example" >
<button text="Button 1"/>
<button text="Button 2"/>
</window>
</xul>
```

Given an appropriate run-time container, this can dynamically produce a window containing two push-buttons. We can expand this to make the push-buttons do something:

```
<xul>
<window title="Simple Example Window" >
<button text="Button 1" oncommand="/myapp/button1click.jsp"/>
<button text="Button 2" oncommand="/myapp/button2click.jsp"/>
</window>
</xul>
```

There is already work being done to produce a layout tool, so that you do not have to write raw XML. However, much of the work visible on the web is still a point solution. Our experience in this area has taught us that a holistic system-wide approach is required to integrate this effectively into an overall system where data shown on user interfaces is obtained from a large shared database. For example, consider a user getting a partial list of entities (e.g. Customers) from the enterprise database, and double-clicking on one item in the list to open a window showing that customer's details. The function involved in this can be generalized to cover any entity, so that all the developer has to do for a given entity type is to specify the display format of the list, and of the panel where details will be shown.

3.4. Summing Up the Platform

COTS platform products tend to be point solutions, and are not integrated with other products. It is a significant job to integrate them, and to provide some support for business service developers. Where that support is not provided, then the integration task is placed on the business developers, and this overhead is sometimes repeated in each development project. When support is provided, it is often ad hoc, and useful glue is often not captured for re-use elsewhere.

Mature ESOA suggests doing this work once, capturing it, and re-applying it across service provisioning projects. This involves consciously providing and maintaining an ESOA virtual platform. While this is unlikely to increase overall costs over a period, and should reduce them - perhaps significantly, the cost profile within a development organization will certainly change.

This does not mean a big bang approach. Proven techniques exist to evolve towards an EPP for ESOA. The major inhibitor is the effort and management focus needed to plan and take the first steps towards the cohesive holistic environment required. This means that in-house efforts to create an EPP cannot provide "instant gratification" – indeed, it may be six months from the start before benefit is seen.[22] The solution to this is a focused transition program to move from IT's current state to the ESOA virtual platform and EPP.

The next section addresses just such a process for transitioning to an ESOA virtual platform, and the organizational implications of such a move.

[22] The book *Business Component Factory* (Herzum and Sims 2000) was based on an early proprietary Productivity Platform that was highly successful in the late 1990s.

4. Transitioning to ESOA

The previous sections have discussed the nature of web services, scaling up to federations or collaborations of services, and separation of business from platform concerns. While all of these are necessary for truly effective ESOA implementation, by themselves none are sufficient. Applied together, they are mutually supportive and highly synergistic. However, making them so is not just a matter of throwing them all into the ring and hoping that something good will emerge. Rather it needs a focused process to weld them together, and an organization that supports their application rather than hinders it. Indeed, experience suggests that the greatest inhibitor to effective ESOA implementation is lack of an appropriate organizational structure.

A "big bang" approach is almost certain to fail. This leaves evolution – and so we need an evolution process aimed at enabling the IT organization to make the journey – or transition – to the desired goal. This section first discusses the goal of ESOA, and also ways of articulating the "vision" at the start of a transition towards the goal. Second, we briefly discuss how moving to ESOA involves organizational changes, so that the core concepts are supported by the organizational structure rather than inhibited by them. A process for achieving the transition can usefully follow the general approach described by Guttman and Matthews (1998/1999); further description of such a process is outside of the scope of this book.

4.1. The Goal

We assume that the overall business goals, and the supporting objectives set by the business for IT, have already been clearly stated, and have resulted in a determination to move to a service-oriented environment. The goal then is agile provisioning of enterprise services, and avoidance of "legacy service" creation. "Agile" means responsiveness and flexibility; that is, not only can new or changed business function be deployed rapidly in terms of minimal impacts on existing services; it also means that the development organization can produce those new or changed services quickly.

Two key factors are instrumental in achieving this goal:

1. A set of core concepts that show the technical feasibility of the goal. These should be articulated in sufficient detail as to enable people to say, "Yes, this can work, there's no magic." The previous sections of this chapter have introduced the essential core concepts.

2. A process for achieving the goal – that is, for applying these core concepts in the development organization.

Taking this as a model, the first thing to do is to articulate the "vision" of the desired end state. This includes:

- The core architectural concepts, which together define the technical vision.
- Separation of concerns along "product line" principles (Clements and Northrop 2002), to produce an "ESOA Productivity Platform" (EPP).

There are several ways to articulate the vision, including a PowerPoint presentation with accompanying text, and a scenario of what things will be like for developers and project managers (an example is provided later in this section). In addition a "target programmer's model" is also highly useful. This is typically defined early in the transition process, and comprises target component code and target development procedures. The target code is the code involved in a sample service implementation, written with an eye to eliminating as much software technology as possible. The code is annotated to identify how things work, and what facilities will be required of the EPP to enable this code to run. The target developer procedures should be written with an eye to eliminating as much work as possible from the development process itself. This will typically assume integrated tools and an effective repository, thereby identifying further function required in the EPP.

4.2. Separation of Concerns

Focusing on the development organization, there are four major areas of concern:

1. Service Design and Implementation;
2. The EPP;
3. The ESOA blueprint; and
4. Development Goals.

When these areas are well designed, teams can work at their own pace, based on their resource/need balance, without overt interference. This is a critical success factor. Figure 19 shows how these areas relate to each other.

The Service Provisioning area is responsible for the agile design, development, and delivery of service-oriented application systems to the enterprise, including not only new systems, but also such things as (the business logic involved in) EAI, and in business process definition and testing.

Service Provisioning is the customer of the EPP area, which provides it with the required high-productivity build and test environment. To meet his goals of agility

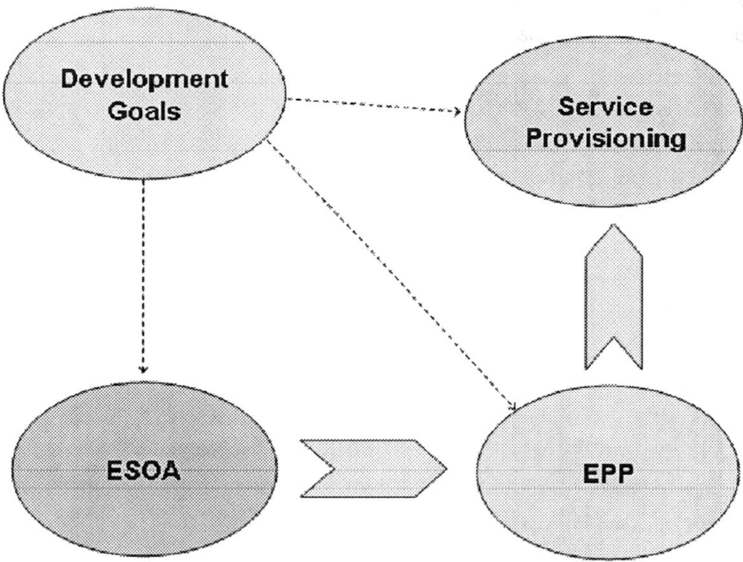

Figure 19. **Organizational Separation of Concerns**

and responsiveness, the manager of this area is motivated to demand the most productive level of EPP as is possible. It is no bad thing if the Service Provisioning area is empowered to obtain EPP artifacts from other sources than the EPP. This keeps the EPP area on its toes, as it must satisfy the requirements of the Service Provisioning area, which will be motivated by the demands of the enterprise for responsiveness, time-to-market, etc. – in other words, agility.

In turn, the EPP area is the customer of the ESOA area, which is responsible for the core concepts and for architectural blueprints. They produce architectural deliverables tailored to the needs of the EPP area. In other words, they provide an architectural service. The manager of the EPP area is motivated to demand the most productive mechanism for the delivery of architecture. For example, a 2000-page architecture manual is much less use than a set of well-designed and tested UML profiles. It is no bad thing for people working within this area to be regularly seconded to the EPP and Service Provisioning areas.

Finally, the Development Goals area, often a sub-group reporting to the CIO, is the management function that:

- Maintains the other three areas focused on the goals of the development organization (which in turn must support the goals defined for IT by the enterprise); and

- Ensures that the appropriate provider/producer dynamics are maintained between the other three areas.

It might be argued that other elements such as Process, Software Engineering, Project Office, and Facilities (networks, operating systems, email, etc.) are also of key importance; and so they are. However, experience suggests very strongly that organizing such that the four areas discussed have clear and overt presence is a vital and necessary aspect of achieving agile service-orientation goals. In addition, experience also suggests that the other essential elements can be accommodated quite happily alongside or within the four major areas shown here.

We deliberately use the term "area" for these four elements. This is because precise organizational structures can vary significantly. But however the actual organization might be arranged, it is vital that these four areas are made very evident as autonomous units, and that they are managed as such, with the usual management prerogative of authority over resource allocation.

5. Summary

We started this chapter discussing web services, which can provide an international technology standard for enterprise IT. Accessible not only from outside the enterprise, this technology is also widely usable internally – even within the same address space on a single machine. So now all interfacing problems are solved? Well, no. Web services provide the potential for a single software interfacing standard throughout enterprise IT. But the realization of that potential must be consciously designed – or architected.

This chapter has outlined the major aspects of such an enterprise architecture based on service orientation. Starting with the nature of the web services technology, we have indicated how it can be applied systemically across the enterprise, how services can be federated, and how business logic can be separated from underlying platform technology. And we have briefly discussed how a project or program to evolve to an ESOA can be planned. In the next chapter, we look at the implementation of services, and also discuss an approach to lessening the divide between business requirements and the IT systems that deliver solutions to meet them.

2 COMPONENT-BASED SERVICES

Success is neither magical nor mysterious. Success is the natural consequence of consistently applying the basic fundamentals
Jim Rohn

Recently, someone (who should have known better) said of service-oriented architecture, "SOA means that we don't have to build applications any more – all we have to do is invoke other people's services." Thus a service implementation is merely a collection of service invocations, and the services invoked are implemented by other service invocations, and so on ad infinitum. Like a successful pyramid or chain letter scheme. Would that it were so easy!

The concept of a service can be usefully seen as comprising three parts:

- Service definition – defined by a service provider, and seen by a service consumer.
- Service implementation – code that, when executed, performs the business logic required to provide the service. (The term "code" is intended to cover not only application code but also specifications or definitions that are interpreted by an "engine" – as occurs with Enterprise Application Integration (EAI), or Workflow, or Business Process Management (BPM) products.)
- Service execution – an instance of a service being provided and consumed at run-time.

The idea that SOA can work without a service implementation is absurd. Clearly there has to be an implementation somewhere.

Chapter 1 dealt primarily with the service definition and execution. This chapter addresses the implementation of a service. The implementation may well consist of a choreography of other services, and they themselves may be implemented by yet further services. Thus there can be a chain of subsidiary services involved in the implementation of some "top level" service.[1] Wherever in this chain there is some business logic, then someone somewhere must define and implement that logic. This applies not only to process definitions that are interpreted by a BPM (Business Process Management)[2] or an EAI (Enterprise Application Integration) infrastructure, but also to code written by application developers. In the latter case, as well as defining the business logic, someone must also decide how to structure the software that implements the service.

In the past, poor design structure has resulted in monolithic and opaque code that has been costly to evolve, and where traceability of business requirements is lost. In implementing services, it is essential to avoid creating tomorrow's legacy. This chapter proposes that services are best implemented through component-based software engineering (CBSE).[3] CBSE is much more than merely using component container middleware. It is a design discipline whose core focus is modularization based on the natural "modularization" of the problem domain. It is also a design discipline that not only includes the best of previous software structuring practice, but also allows for crucial architectural concerns such as granularity, distribution, flexibility, and rigorous dependency management to be addressed in a coherent way. A design discipline such as this is an essential pre-requisite for development agility, applying as much to out-sourced work as to in-house. Finally, we shall see how a unified component concept cannot only address code structure, but can also encompass BPM and EAI definitions.

The chapter is structured as follows:

- First, the nature of mature CBSE is described.

[1] In this chapter, we ignore the possibility, which could at least theoretically eventuate in an open and trusted worldwide chain of dynamically-discovered and invoked services, of a loop!

[2] In this chapter, and unless specified otherwise in the text, we use the term BPM to apply to both business process definitions and to workflow definitions. The difference between the two is often held to be that workflow includes steps that are performed by humans, whereas business processes do not. This differentiation is useful when considering infrastructures provided by BPM and EAI vendors versus those provided by Workflow vendors. From an architectural point of view, on the other hand, there are many similarities between the two.

[3] CBSE is sometimes referred to by the term "Component-Based Development" or CBD, although "CBD" has also been applied to other arguably less formal approaches.

- Second, we define what is meant by the word "component", building upon the UML version 2.0 definition (OMG3 2004), which is very different from that of previous UML versions.
- Third, we consider the major architectural concerns inherent in mature CBSE, and suggest by brief examples how these concerns can be addressed in a way that exploits and expands CBSE.
- Finally, to be effective, and to truly enable business agility, there must be clear traceability between business requirements and system implementation. Otherwise the services provided may well not be those that the business requires and needs. Section 4 discusses an approach that can deliver a seamless progression from a business requirements definition to service implementation with little information loss.

1. Component-Based Software Engineering (CBSE)

There has been much market hype about components being things bought from third-party suppliers, so that application development becomes merely the assembly of third-party components. However, given the almost complete lack of interfacing and composition standards, together with the lack of definition about what a component was – and what it was not – such hype was never very likely to bear fruit, and indeed in the enterprise application area it has not (although there are some useful technology-level components, mostly in the GUI area).

Components were also seen by many as being a technology thing (COM, EJB, CORBA Component Model), where key technical characteristics have been tight coupling (generally static) of low-level programmatic interfaces and synchronous RPC-style messaging. This contrasts with the dynamic binding (loose coupling) provided by such technologies as SOAP and WSDL, with their ability to invoke services across different technology platforms, and support for several interaction styles from RPC to asynchronous loosely coupled collaborations. (However, as we shall see in section 2.3 Network-Style Interfaces, thinking of components as merely tightly-coupled technology artifacts and hence inappropriate for SOA is to dramatically miss the point!)

In short, CBSE has come to be seen as yesterday's hype, with little to show for it other than some useful technology. However, if ever there was a case of the baby being thrown out with the bathwater, this is it!

1.1. Understanding CBSE

Over the past ten years or so, CBSE has taken two quite different paths: first the "market in components" approach that has failed to bear much fruit (see Section 2.2 Federation and Mature CBSE of the previous chapter), and second a mature software design discipline. The second approach (for example, see Herzum and Sims 2000; and Hubert 2002) is a quite different animal from the unlamented "market in components" hype of the 1990s. This approach, having been continuously developed since the late 1980s, might be called "mature CBSE".

Mature CBSE is primarily a way of thinking about application design (and then applying that thinking of course). How you think about design is probably the most important design choice of all. For example, forty years ago many application designers thought of an application as a kind of written report, an algorithm that started at the beginning (of the coding pad), went on until it reached the end, and then stopped. When this structure did not match the problem domain that the application was trying to implement, the result was reams of spaghetti code.

The history of software can be viewed as a search for better ways to think about application design structures. First there was the idea of splitting applications into separate "jobs", each implemented by a separate batch program. In the 70s came insight into the program internals, so that each program was split into modules, based on its function. Inside each module, code was organized according the four main structured programming concepts.[4] This structure was well suited for the batch systems of the time, but did not suit the event-driven systems that started to become prevalent in the 80s.

Object orientation, introduced in the 80s, promised much. The concept was right – modules of code each of which implemented a clear "thing", and which were event-driven. The idea was to represent in software the "things of the problem domain", for example things such as "customer", "order", "trade", etc. But at this point, something went grievously wrong. OO was implemented through programming languages. But a programming language addresses the inside of a module – how you code the internals. The result was that the "objects of the problem domain" disappeared inside an amorphous module which itself did not represent anything recognizable

[4] The four main structured programming concepts were: Sequence (of code statements), If-Then-Else, DoWhile, and Case.

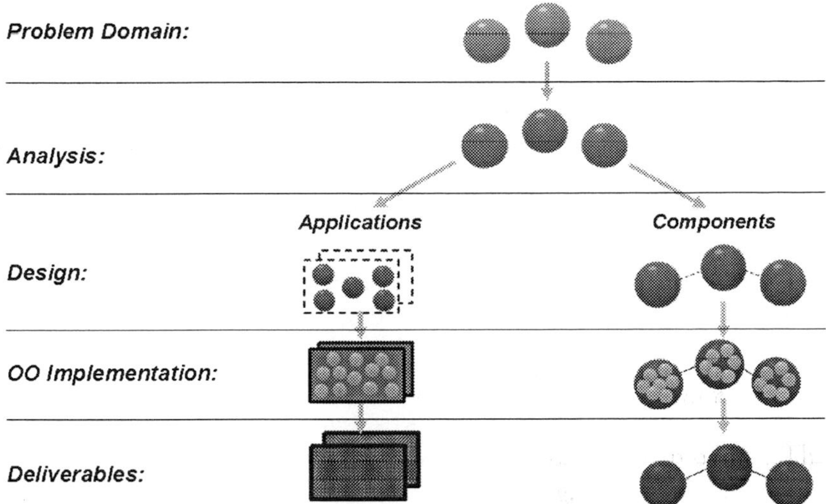

Figure 1. **Applications vs. Components**

by domain experts.[5] Some modules were a whole application. We were back to the single-module application of the 50s and 60s! This is illustrated in Figure 1, where the important[6] concepts in the problem domain are seen at the first stages of the development lifecycle (labeled "Analysis" here), after which, if going down the traditional "application" track, they start to become successively buried in the opaque deliverable which is an "application" in one or more anonymous modules. Mature CBSE, on the other hand, refines the domain concepts and delivers them as software modules that are invokeable through their interfaces, and which can plug autonomously into the platform.

Now there is nothing wrong with the concepts behind OO. What went wrong was that these concepts were not implemented by sensible middleware – it was all left to the application programmer. What a difference it would have made if the major software objects had each been a separate module containing more minor objects, each major module relating to an important and real thing in the problem domain,

[5] Ivar Jacobsen once said that in the problem domain he could see objects; during analysis and design the objects were all there; but once the programmers got hold of them they disappeared, and never returned, being buried invisibly in applications. (Private communication to the author in 1993).

[6] Few development processes address the issue of granularity in the business domain. Hence there is often a problem with using vague terms such as "important" and "major". Examples of "major" things are "customer", "contract", and "sales order taking process"; examples of "minor" things are "product number", "balance-on-hand", and "address". Minor things are contained in major things. Section 4 of this chapter shows an approach to formalizing this.

and independently pluggable into a system. But such pluggability needs something to plug into – a software socket provided by the middleware platform.

But which platform? Here we are not talking about the technology platform (J2EE, .NET, CICS, etc.) but rather the "virtual platform" described in Section 3.1 of the previous chapter. There is no point in building a component if a large part of that component consists of bits and pieces of technology code. All that does is to increase the "surface area" of the component – increases the complexity of the "plug" that is a necessary part of each component, and which plugs into the "socket" provided by the virtual platform. A major reason why component technology platforms do not deliver the goods as far as truly pluggable components are concerned is that they leave far too many aspects to be handled by the developer of the component. For example, such things as transactions, concurrency, activation, and access to platform services such as logging, error management, publish/subscribe, and so forth.

But, one might argue, all such code can be generated, especially with the growing availability of tools implementing the various flavors of model-driven development (for example, implementations of OMG's MDA, Microsoft's Domain-Specific Language (DSL) initiative, IBM's EMF, to say nothing of the many modeling tools available today that provide for code generation). However, there are problems with code generation. First, technology code generated for one component (for example code providing for transactional behavior) may conflict with code generated for another, which means that these two components often cannot co-exist within a given system. So much for pluggability and interoperability! We need platforms that provide high levels of technology services, plus a standard policy configuration approach, where each component is, on deployment, configured for a defined policy. Second, the more code generated, the more must be re-tested and re-deployed when something in that code changes. If all components contain significant fragments of platform-related (non-business) code, then changes to the platform can result in massive re-generation, re-testing, and re-deployment.

All these points lead to a clear conclusion – that raising the level of the platform to as high a level of abstraction as possible is much more than a nice-to-have: it is a necessity. Part of that high level of abstraction will be interfaces to platform services that allow for flexibility as those interfaces evolve – which they will. The key is to slow down the rate of impact on the business-level components. These too are evolving as the business changes. An effective virtual platform will help a great deal with this. Instead of both technology and business changes impacting business-level components, in the main only business changes will impact them. Technology changes will affect mainly the virtual platform.

Components, then, are objects writ large, with appropriate middleware to support them. Components realize much of the original vision of object orientation. Components are language-neutral and can be written using either OO or procedural languages.[7] Components are also coupling-agnostic; that is, they may be tightly or loosely coupled.

But wait a minute – consider a system such as supply chain management. A count of the software repository would show thousands – more probably tens of thousands – of OO classes. Does that mean tens of thousands of components? Well, no. As indicated previously, a component is normally a collection of classes. An important CBSE concern is defining which classes belong to which component (remember that a component is not only a deployable module, it is also seen as a "big" class in its own right). So, for example, a Sales Order component could consist of an Order Header class, an Order Line class, a collection class (an instance of which would hold the Order Line instances), and several smaller classes such as Currency, Order Value Calculator, etc. CBSE is also concerned with identifying and scoping the components in a system. So our supply chain management system could end up with perhaps 300–500 components, each consisting of a number of classes.

Let us now define what a component is in more detail.

2. A Component Definition

What is a "component"? There have been many descriptions and definitions of "component". A useful summary of various aspects, including component vs. class, and component as a type or as an instance, can be found in Atkinson et al. (2002). Over the past several years, there has been a developing consensus as to what a component is, culminating in the OMG's UML2 definition (OMG3 2004). This is quite different from that given in UML1, and Section 2.1 reviews the new definition.

However, the OMG's definition deliberately applies to many different kinds of component, including low-level technology components such as GUI components. For ESOA, it is useful to refine the OMG's definition, and a definition of an

[7] Although not available today, probably due to the justified lack of interest in procedural languages, in the mid-90s there was middleware available that supported mixing components each written in a different language all in the same address space.

"enterprise component" is presented in Section 2.2. One of the key differences between a UML2 component and an enterprise component is the nature of the latter's interface. Section 2.3 discusses the "network-style" interface provided (and required) by enterprise components.

2.1. The UML2 Component

The OMG has recently standardized version 2.0 of the Unified Modeling Language (UML). An important aspect of UML2 is its much-expanded component concept. Whereas UML version 1 saw a component as essentially a build-time and deployment-time module, UML2 has hugely enlarged the concept, and has extended it across the development lifecycle, so providing standard support for what many architects involved in mature CBSE have been modeling for some time now using their own UML profiles. A UML2 component is a three-part construct consisting of:

- A type;
- One or more interfaces (both required and provided); and
- A realization.

The standard (OMG3 2004) states, "The component concept addresses the area of component-based development and component-based system structuring, where a component is modeled throughout the development lifecycle and successively refined into deployment and run-time. ... A component defines its behavior in terms of provided and required interfaces. As such, a component serves as a type, whose conformance is defined by these provided and required interfaces (encompassing both their static as well as dynamic semantics)." Figure 2, a slight simplification of the diagram in OMG3 (2004) illustrates the three-part nature of a UML component.

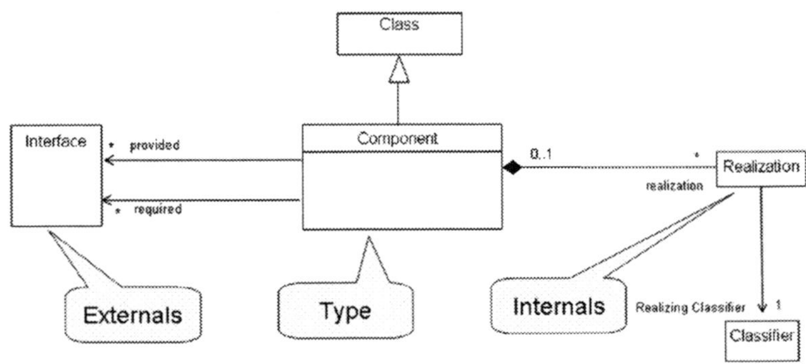

Figure 2. **The UML 2.0 Component**

A component, then, is a kind of class. However, this is not the class you would use in normal modeling. It is a special kind of class, defined by UML2, and whose properties include:[8]

- Ability to have an internal structure and ports (a port is a distinct interaction point both externally with the environment, and also internally to internal parts).
- May be designated as having its own thread of control, or of executing within the context of something else.
- May specify which signals (such as events) can be handled
- Behavior that can be fully or partly described by the collaboration of owned or referenced classifiers. (A "classifier" is essentially an abstract supertype within UML that is a type, that defines a "classification of instances" (a set of instances that have features in common), that can include features of various sorts, and that can be sub-typed.)

Based on this supertype, UML 2.0 defines a component as follows:

> *A component represents a modular part of a system that encapsulates its contents and whose manifestation is replaceable within its environment. A component defines its behavior in terms of provided and required interfaces. As such, a component serves as a type, whose conformance is defined by these provided and required interfaces (encompassing both their static as well as dynamic semantics). One component may therefore be substituted by another only if the two are type conformant. Larger pieces of a system's functionality may be assembled by re-using components as parts in an encompassing component or assembly of components, and wiring together their required and provided interfaces.*
>
> *A component is modeled throughout the development lifecycle and successively refined into deployment and run-time. A component may be manifest by one or more artifacts, and in turn, that artifact may be deployed to its execution environment. A deployment specification may define values that parameterize the component's execution.*

Note that the realization of a component can include other components. This allows for various granularity strategies to be applied. In addition, it is expected that a component that does not include other components will be realized by a number of classifiers, and a good example of a classifier is a class. An example of realization specifications are shown in Figure 3, which is a modification of an example in OMG3 (2004) and illustrates a "wiring diagram" of components. This is a new kind of diagram introduced in UML2.

[8] For full details, see Section 8 "Components" of OMG1 (2003).

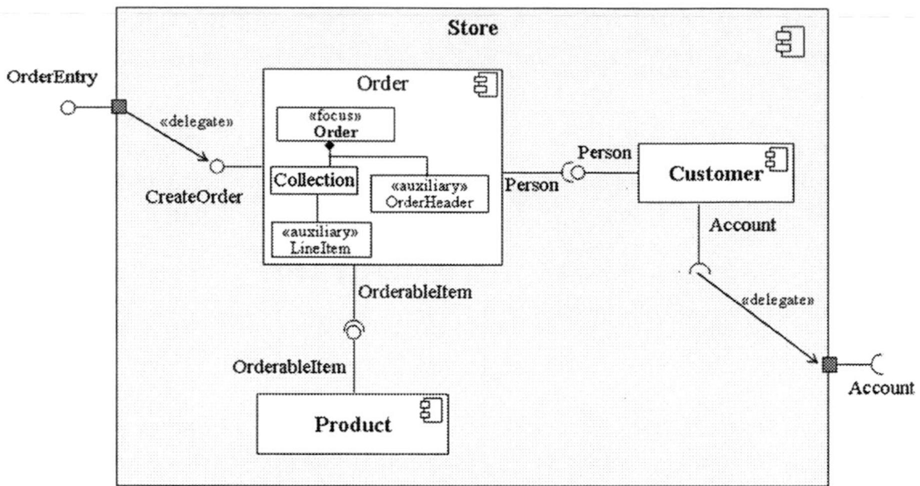

***Figure 3.* Component Wiring and Component Internals (UML2)**

Four components are shown here: Store, Order, Product, and Customer. Store provides an OrderEntry service, and its realization comprises three other components, Order, Product, and Customer. Store provides an interface called OrderEntry, and requires an interface of type Account. Store delegates implementation of its OrderEntry interface to the Order component via its CreateOrder interface. The Order component requires OrderableItem and Person interfaces. Product provides an OrderableItem interface, and Customer provides a Person interface. In addition, Customer requires Account, which is delegated to Store's required interface.

Note that Product and Customer should be designed so as to provide services to other components. This is what "autonomous" means, and is really a design statement. That is, Product and Customer (and Order and Store for that matter) should be managed during their design and construction on the basis that they are autonomous, that their services may be used by a number of different components, and that they are in the business of providing services to those as yet un-named components.

Experience suggests that (at least when working with the kind of "virtual platform" discussed in Section 3 of Chapter 1) the effort to design a service-oriented component autonomously is no greater than designing one that turns out to be constrained to work only with one calling component.

But do we really want to design, say, a Customer component, that might be a "core entity" (see Section 2.4 of Chapter 1), so that its services are available on the web to all and sundry? Of course not! We design such a component so that its services are used by other components executing within a domain that is behind firewalls etc. This means that the services provided by each component should have a defined scope of visibility within the enterprise as well as outside.

Figure 3 also shows another realization – that of Order. Four classes are shown is realizing Order: Order, OrderHeader, LineItem, and Collection. Order has the UML-provided stereotype "focus", showing that the Order class provides the Order component with its essential type. Other classes are auxiliary (this stereotype is also provided by UML) and show that they play the role of the supporting cast as it were within the component, assisting the Order class to fulfill its role as the focus within the component.

In this way, the dichotomy of type is resolved. In a business information model, one may well expect to see the classes Order, OrderLine, possibly OrderHeader, and also many others such as Customer, Address, etc. Domain experts will assert that there is a concept Order that has within it the concepts of Order Header and Line Item. But there is also the concept Order that both provides business logic and also choreographs the other classes involved. So we have Order as a group that ignores any internal arrangement and choreography of classes, and we also have Order as the choreographer and holder of some of the business logic. This is the dichotomy. UML provides for (and so resolves design difficulties associated with) this dichotomy. The component model element (a type) is used to represent the concept Order, and the component realization is used to show the choreographing Order class and also the other classes involved – without which Order would not be an Order!

Finally note that there is nothing visible in the diagram to show whether Store physically composes the other three components. Typically, components are not physically composed; rather Store refers to them.

Now let us return to SOA. The key aspects of the UML2 component that are really useful for service-oriented architecture are that it:

- Is a type;
- Can be visible and tangible throughout the development lifecycle and also in the run-time;
- Can be built and deployed autonomously (an example of autonomous deployment is updating a system with a new version of the component); and
- Is intended to be combined and composed with other components with which it collaborates to deliver solutions.

The UML2 component goes far in providing what is needed for service implementation. Based on the UML2 component, we can define an "Enterprise" component – the kind used in building enterprise-strength service-oriented systems.

2.2. The Enterprise Component

An Enterprise Component is an extension of the UML2 component that exhibits all of the following characteristics:

- Represents and encapsulates a single business concept (process or entity) that provides one or more business services through its interfaces;
- Is of medium to large granularity;
- Has one or more well-defined "network-style" service-related interfaces;[9]
- Is intended to be managed at run-time by a middleware container which provides the run-time technology "socket" into which the component "plugs". In other words, it enjoys the separation from technology concerns via the kind of "virtual platform" described in Section 3 of Chapter 1;[10]
- Addresses the scalability and distribution challenges of enterprise distributed systems;
- Can publish events and can subscribe to them (assuming the availability of a notification service);
- Can be managed at design time by a modeling tool that can be said to provide a "development-time socket" – that is, it knows about components, and can import a component model (or design) into a larger "system" model that comprises collaborating components;
- Supports both synchronous and asynchronous messaging, synchronicity being with respect to the flow of control within the component, and not to the underlying communications stack. In this way, message synchronicity is completely separated from underlying messaging middleware. Although middleware

[9] An enterprise component will also have an "administrative" interface which can provide for aspects such as systems management and monitoring. These are not considered further here.

[10] With such a "virtual platform", the design of an Enterprise Component may ignore a whole host of technology factors such as transactions, event management, configuration, activation/passivation, systems management, and provision of any required technology-oriented interfaces. Late in the development cycle, the code required for implementation of technology bindings, and also of policies, can be generated or merged (perhaps using aspect-oriented weaving techniques) into the component.

supporting this and other transparencies has existed in the past,[11] providing this transparency today requires "glue" to be added to the available middleware. This capability can be implemented in proxies that are typically generated. The underlying invocation will be a Web Service invocation as described in Section 3.3 of the preceding chapter.

A component also has an internal implementation or "realization". This realization appears both at design time and at build-time. The detailed realization of a component can vary widely in nature. However, it is useful to distinguish between two main forms:

1. A "programmed" realization – that is, the internals are coded using a programming language such as Java or C# (or even a procedural language such as COBOL in some circumstances!), or by an interpreted language such as Python. The number of classes in a component implementation typically varies from around five to as many as one hundred and twenty or so. An example of a programmed component is a server-side component implemented with EJB technology and written in Java. A programmed component is generally intended to be run on component middleware such J2EE or .NET, and its creation requires IT technical and management skills.

2. A "declarative" realization – that is, the internals take the form of a declarative script, such as a BPM process definition (usually defined using a GUI-oriented tool, with the script itself being stored by the tool as an XML document). The "code" that executes the script is an interpreter provided by middleware (such as BPM middleware). Examples include workflow and B2B definitions. Production of a declarative component does not always require IT technical and management skills.

It is important to understand that an Enterprise Component is primarily a design and application code construct, and is mapped to underlying middleware technology as far towards the end of the development lifecycle as possible. In addition, it assumes a reasonably high level of virtual platform. Thus it is ideal as the design vehicle for systems built according to the emerging concept of model-driven development such as OMG's MDA.

2.3. Network-Style Interfaces

A "network-style interface" is an interface that can be invoked from other address spaces in the same system, or from geographically remote systems, or even from within the same address space. Invocation from within the same address space

[11] See Sims (1994).

requires middleware that provides optimization of the invocation. There are two important initial constraints on an interface that makes it a "network-style" interface:

- References passed as operation parameters must be references to other components.[12]

- Instances of classes are always passed by value, never by reference. That is, a reference to something that is not a component, but which must be passed as a parameter (for example, an Order Header class), is always passed by value.

These two constraints make it much easier to avoid the "object spaghetti" that resulted in some early distributed object implementations where designers assumed that all objects could be distributed, and ended up with dense webs of dependencies – in the form of object invocations – that flowed across networks. Systems built this way were quickly found to be unworkable due to seriously appalling performance: iterating an OOPL collection instance across a network is not a good idea! And, of course, maintenance of such systems, with multiple cross-network low-level dependencies was in many situations quite impossible. The lesson is that some important techniques in classical object-oriented design and implementation, although good for code that runs entirely in a single address space, do not scale.

A network-style interface is also loosely-coupled in the following ways:

- Data carried on a request to an enterprise component should carry associated metadata (data labels or tags). Experience over the past twenty years or so has shown that use of metadata in messages can be exploited in some very valuable and innovative ways. These include better management of "interface creep", and a number of ways of providing generic code that dynamically adjusts its behavior based on the metadata provided to it. Prior to XML, this was done using proprietary mechanisms. Today, service orientation assumes that the messaging mechanism will be web services using XML as the data format. This means that advantageous exploitation already identified, but not widely-known because of the lack of standardization of the data formats, now becomes available to service-oriented architectures (although they do not seem to have yet been picked up by the Web Services community).

  Note that this is a design not an implementation statement. Loose coupling can be implemented using web services, and for example J2EE component

[12] Strictly speaking, this statement implies that there is a concept of "reference scope", where any given kind of reference has a specific scope. For example, a URL (for a web service for example) can have worldwide scope; a CORBA IOR has scope within a given network of interconnected CORBA systems (which may be extended by, for example, the COM-CORBA inter-working standard); a C++ object reference has validity at most within a given address space in a single computer.

container providers are beginning to provide for this. However, there will be times when tighter coupling is needed. In this case, a network-style interface can be implemented using a more tightly-coupled interface technology. The opposite is generally not true.

- Middleware implementations of network-style interfaces will normally provide some means of optimizing invocations if the target component is co-located – that is, in the same address space as the invoking code. If this is not available, then either appropriate glue code must be provided (quite a tricky task), or compromises must be made.

  One such compromise is to assume the existence of network-style interfaces until build time, when tightly-coupled interfaces are substituted. With MDA, such a decision could be parameter-driven, with the necessary code being generated.

- Can be invoked regardless of the underlying communications infrastructure. That is, the component designer/programmer does not need to know over what communications channel the component will be invoked. Thus a component is insensitive as to whether an invocation is carried by a language call from within the same address space, by RMI, JMS, CORBA, HTTP/SOAP, etc.

- Can be invoked across asynchronous or synchronous communications stacks.

- Is insensitive as to whether an incoming message was originally sent synchronously or asynchronously with respect to the invoking code. Providing this level of transparency with current COTS middleware will require additional glue code, but the advantages in simplicity for the application developer are great. Some of the glue code may well be resident in the component, but such code can be generated.

- Can operate as a "port". That is, can accept data without there being an operation name. This provides for Enterprise Components that model business processes to be implemented as BPM specifications.

It may seem that these kinds of capabilities will result in an unwelcome overhead for a component. However, aside from optimizations and function provided in middleware, an enterprise component is large enough in terms of number of classes in its implementation to be able to handle some overhead. Remember that a component (specifically a programmed component) is a kind of small program. Indeed, when compared with a class, an enterprise component is best thought of as an adult in the software world – responsible for its own fate (thus, for example, when deactivated by middleware for garbage collection reasons – as opposed to shutdown – an enterprise component should be able to decline deactivation. This would be specified through policy rather than coding.

This mind-set, when well supported by the virtual platform, can provide for further technology transparencies, and so make life simpler for the application developer. As a useful piece of serendipity, the nature of the Web Services model provides support for this concept. For example, there is no concept in Web Services, as there is in some component middleware, of a client having to "create" the component with which it wishes to communicate.

Finally, circumstances often exist which prevent full implementation of enterprise components according the description given above. Experience suggests that getting as close as possible, and being clear about where the boundaries are, still gives significant benefit. For example, in a web-based distributed application, application artifacts that run on a web server and a browser are such things as Javascript, ASP pages, servlets, and HTML GUI panels. While the separations of concern, and the design mindset of CBSE and the enterprise component concept are still very useful and can be applied to some extent, it is not appropriate for example to try to provide a servlet with all the attributes of the network-style interface. Hence common sense compromises based on the virtual platform – which will depend on the COTS middleware capabilities – are always appropriate.

3. Component Granularity

This section discusses the often thorny issue of component granularity. There are a number of approaches to handling component granularity, and we choose to describe the approach taken by Herzum and Sims (2000). The advantages of this scheme are:

- Defines three clearly different kinds of enterprise component that range from a component consisting of a small number of classes up to an entire application;
- Provides for a component design scheme that is platform independent, and that can be mapped to a number of different platforms;
- Integrates scalability and dependency management aspects;
- Extends across the distributed system from GUI to database;
- Addresses re-use directly, and clearly defines what is intended to be potentially re-usable and what is not;

- Provides for a direct linkage from a requirements model (see Section 4 of this chapter);
- Defines a granularity level that is of immediate assistance as a viable unit of project management;
- Can be applied partly or wholly depending on circumstances.

The granularity scheme presented here assumes the presence of a virtual platform as described in the previous chapter. This means that components will largely implement only business-related concerns, and for present purposes we assume that this is wholly the case. In reality there will be some non-business software technology that must exist within components and that will be visible to application developers; however, such technology as there is does not invalidate the assumption.

Since one of the levels of granularity includes distribution, we begin by describing a distribution architecture that provides four logical distribution tiers, and that can map to a number of physical tiers. Section 3.2 then presents the four different granularities, and finally Section 3.3 discusses the main aspects of dependency management.

3.1. Distribution Domains and Tiers

The previous chapter (in Section 3.1) introduced a four-tier model, where each tier is a logical area of concern, as follows: user tier, workspace tier, enterprise tier, and resource tier. This section briefly presents a conceptual background – the big picture – which defines distribution tiers and domains, and then describes each.

3.1.1. Looking at the Big Picture

The four-tier model actually consists of two linked two-tier models, each based on the concept of an "inner" or "core" tier, and an "outer" or "external" tier. This is shown in Figure 4, where a system is seen as comprising a number of logical distribution tiers. A distribution tier is a logical area of responsibility in the distribution dimension of a system.

At this point, we should re-iterate a crucial point: the distribution tiers being discussed here relate to application code only, assuming a high-level virtual platform. That is, they are tiers as seen by the application developer. While a similar tier analysis can be made for middleware, and is then of use to middleware developers, this aspect is not considered further here.

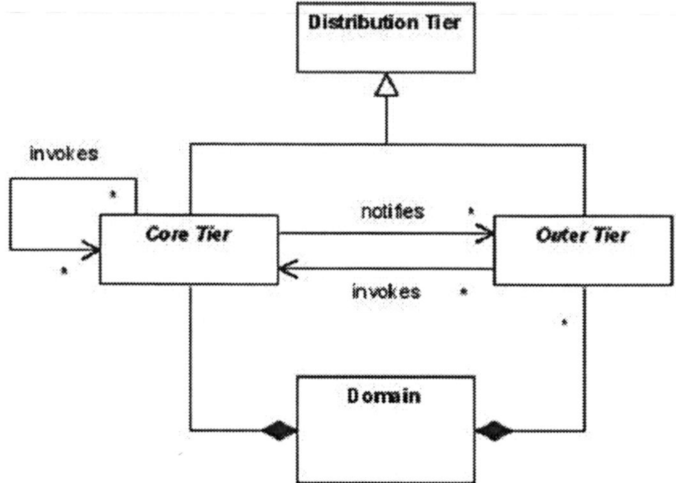

Figure 4. **Logical Tiers and Domains**

Since a distribution tier is a logical construct, it can be mapped to one or more physical tiers (for example an application server, a web server, a browser, a PC). It can also share a physical tier with other logical tiers. A distribution tier can have many components placed within it. Finally, inasmuch as a distribution tier is the result of an architectural separation of concerns, the concept can also apply (very beneficially) to non-distributed applications.

An application code can be seen as having two different kinds of logical responsibility:

- Core Tier: a logical distribution tier that realizes business function rather than the handling of external devices such as GUIs or DBMSs. It is the result of the architectural separation of concerns between managing externals and implementing business logic. It can be seen as the "business core" of a system. A core tier may be accessed by several outer tiers, and occasionally by none. In other words, the core tier provides services to zero or more outer tiers.

- Outer Tier: a logical distribution tier whose responsibility within the system is to manage, define, or access a resource such as a user interface, a data base, a B2B link, and so forth. It handles "external" protocols and data formats, and maps them to/from the internal canonical form(s) defined for the core tier. An outer tier may have trivial business logic embedded in it (for example, maintaining a total of amounts entered on a GUI).

Logical Distribution Tiers can be combined to form a "Domain". For example, the Application and Data tiers of the traditional three-tier model might be seen as making up a "server domain". A Domain is a significant logical part of a system that has a specific responsibility within the system, and that is the focus of interest across many viewpoints. It is also a technical management domain; it is an area of the enterprise IT system that is technically managed as a unit. Examples are the business-related application software artifacts on a user's workstation, and the set of address spaces and systems within which an ACID[13] transaction is supported. Chapter 7 discusses transactions in some depth.

Figure 4 shows the relationships between tier and domain concepts. The term "invokes" in the figure means some form of programmatic invocation, such as a Web Service invocation, a CORBA or RMI call, a message sent via a message queuing middleware, or sometimes an intra-process transfer of control. A Domain consists of one Core Tier and usually one or more Outer Tiers, although sometimes a Domain has no Outside Tiers.

It can be shown that the three-tier model is in fact a core and two outer tiers, all within a single domain. But the essence of enterprise distributed systems is that there are two kinds of domain in the end-to-end distribution area, and a third domain that addresses BPM. Let us first look at the two end-to-end domains, and the tiers within each.

3.1.2. Distribution Domains and Tiers

The two end-to-end distribution domains are the "user-workspace domain" and the "enterprise resource domain", as shown at the bottom of Figure 5.

The **User Workspace Domain** (UWD) is responsible for support within the wider system for a single person using a user interface, and consists of a User Tier and a Workspace Tier. The User Workspace Domain accesses one or more Enterprise Resource Domains in order to access data (read or write), or other system resources that are also shared by more than one person.[14]

The **Enterprise Resource Domain** (ERD) is responsible for provision of services to multiple concurrent authorized requestors, and also for the integrity and protection of those resources. A given Enterprise Resource Domain is defined by the scope of an ACID transaction running in that Domain, (possibly over several physical systems). Hence a given system may include more than one Enterprise Resource Domain. If so,

---

[13] ACID is a transaction processing acronym that stands for Atomicity, Consistency, Isolation, and Durability – the required attributes of a recoverable transaction.

[14] For example, in a rich client situation, the UWD normally resides on the PC. In a browser plus web server situation, the UWD normally maps to the "browser plus the one or more sessions on the web server that are dedicated to a single user".

then responsibility for coordinating transactions lies outside the Enterprise Resource Domains.

The nature of requests for services made to an ERD from another Domain can be an important scalability factor in distributed systems. Where a single service request is handled within a single ACID transaction, scalability is significantly enhanced. If a transaction is held open over several requests, then the system scalability reduces. The architecture should enforce this "single shot" ERD access pattern. The ERD provides one or more services. When one is requested, it runs in a single transaction.[15]

This rule maps well to a common business rule. That is, the business requires some change of state to be either completed or not done at all, and is not interested in any intermediate state, and wants the change to be made as fast as practicable.

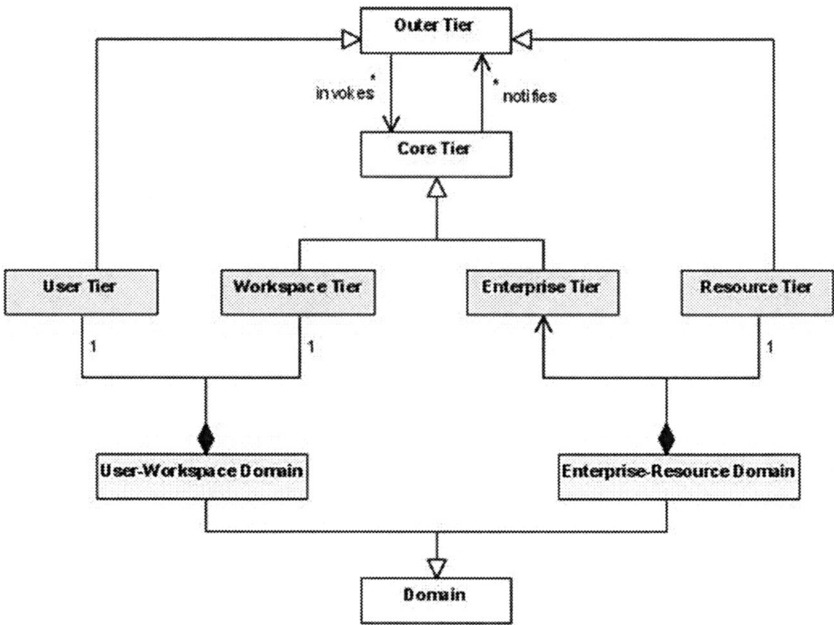

Figure 5. **The Four-Tier Model**

Within each of these domains are two tiers, making the four-tier model shown in Figure 5. The tiers are:

1. The **User Tier** is an outer tier that provides user interaction logic through a set of user interface components such as windows, panels, menus, and prompts (or

[15] This rule implies that even queries (read-only) will needlessly run in a transaction. For some systems, this will incur an unacceptable overhead. In this case, the architecture should be changed to show read-only requests running non-transactionally.

their voice equivalent). It depends on the Workspace Tier for its source and sink of data, and for its management in terms of user sessions.

2. The **Workspace Tier** is a core tier that provides a user's model, and contains user session logic and user-side representations of processes and information. This tier consists of a set of components that communicate with components in the enterprise tier.

It is possible that non-re-usable components are in this tier too, components that are really to specific to one application can be potentially re-used elsewhere.

3. The **Enterprise Tier** is a core tier that provides enterprise-level business function services, and is also responsible for protecting the integrity of enterprise resources at the business logic level. Services can be either process-oriented (which typically provide the service interface required by, for example, web services), or entity-oriented (which typically provide entity services for the process services and are typically not exposed outside this tier). The Enterprise Tier depends on the Resource Tier for access to data and other resources (such as high-volume printing).

4. The **Resource Tier** is an outer tier that provides components for access and/or updating data and other resources. The Resource Tier provides persistent storage services to the Enterprise Tier, and accesses mechanisms for storing data in some manner, such as a standard relational DBMS, or an object-oriented database. It may also provide access mechanisms to legacy system data.

Finally, the User Workspace Domain sometimes has its own persistence tier (not shown in Figure 5). This can occur when it is important to persist the state of a user session when the user logs off (for example, to go home at the end of a day when a unit of work is only partly complete). Thus the User Workspace Domain can sometimes have three tiers – user, workspace, and user-resource; or, in other words, presentation, application, and data.

3.1.3. The BPM Domain

One additional domain completes the picture. This is the BPM domain, which is usefully seen as orthogonal to the User Workspace and Enterprise-Resource domains. This is because a single workflow definition, for example, may invoke both workspace and enterprise tier components. The BPM domain often has only one tier – a core tier. It may be argued that an outside tier is necessary, in that adapters (to legacy systems or to COTS application packages) are needed. However, we assume that such adapters are effectively part of the infrastructure, and that application developers need not be concerned with them. This is not always the case; business-oriented developers may need to define data transformations to do with integrating data from different adapters. In that case, an outer tier – which might be called the "data transformation specification" tier, can be defined. Again, workflow requires some form of work list visible on a user's screen. However, these are typically provided by the workflow product, and as such are not the concern of the application developer. The BPM domain is discussed in detail in Chapter 5.

Having discussed distribution aspects, we now move on to consider a useful scheme of component granularity, one level of which will use distribution concepts.

3.2. Granularity Scheme

A service-oriented architecture must define clear levels of granularity for service implementations. Since services are assumed to be provided by components, then this means that component granularity must be defined. Without this, it becomes difficult to define how components are composed, and how the various scalability aspects are taken into account. Several different granularity schemes have been proposed; here we briefly present the scheme described in Herzum and Sims (2000) (and used with some variation in Combine (2003)) which defines three levels of granularity within the user-workspace and enterprise-resource domains:

1. Distributed Component (DC);
2. Business Component (BC); and
3. Application Component (AC).[16]

The relationships between these three are as shown in Figure 6. The most coarse-grained is the application component, which consists of a number of business components, which in turn are composed of distributed components.

[16] This level of granularity is called a "System-Level Component" in Herzum and Sims (2000). Here we use the term given to this concept by Combine (2003).

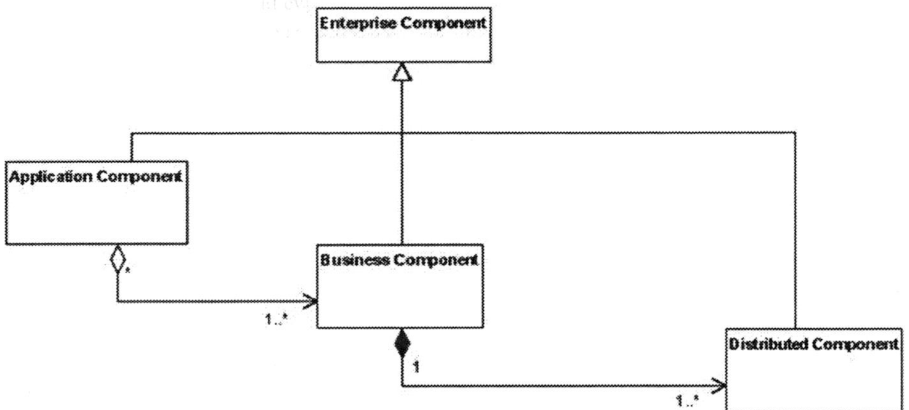

Figure 6. **Three Levels of Component Granularity**

3.2.1. The Distributed Component (DC)[17]

A Distributed Component or DC is an enterprise component (as defined previously) that is typically implemented by platform component models such as EJB, CORBA component, COM component,[18] various BPM definitions, and even a set of CICS transaction programs. The DC is the smallest level of granularity, and is responsible for the implementation of services. EDOC (OMG2 2004) uses the same term,[19] but Combine (2003) refers to it as a "Service Component". In general, most component architectures provide for this level of granularity.

In spite of its name, a DC exists in a single distribution tier. Put another way, a given distribution tier consists of a number of DCs. Figure 7 illustrates how this works, where round-cornered boxes are DCs of various kinds. Enterprise component architectures often define different kinds of DC; the kinds in the figure derive from Herzum and Sims (2000), where "EDC" for example means "Enterprise-tier DC",

[17] When first mooted as a concept at a higher level of abstraction than code, the DC was named "distributable component", reflecting its network-style interfaces, together with the idea that it could be moved to a different machine and (pace performance) would still work correctly. However, it turned out that "distributable component" was much more difficult to use in conversation than "distributed component", which in turn is usually shortened to "DC".

[18] CORBA Component middleware is now becoming available; for example, see http://openccm.objectweb.org/.

[19] It was the intention when EDOC was being defined to include a full specification of a "distributed component". However, for various non-technical reasons, the specification was not completed at the time EDOC was standardized.

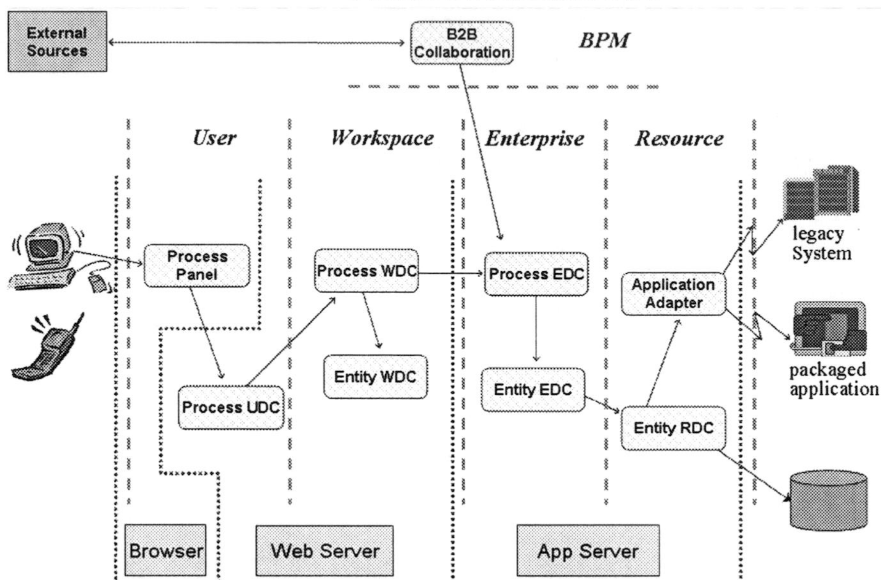

Figure 7. **Different Kinds of Distributed Component**

this being further divided into process and entity DCs. Other authors give them different names – for example, Harmon et al. (2001) call this a "Process Controller".

The user tier in Figure 7 illustrates how the artifacts of a DC – and hence a logical distribution tier – can at run-time be distributed over more than one physical tier. The "process panel" which is a GUI panel relating to a process that is deployed in a browser (probably dynamically generated from the definition on the web server). For example, this might be an order processing "workbench", which would embed other panels relating to entities (entity panels not shown in the figure). The Process UDC, which Harmon et al. (2001) call a "view controller", is located on the web server. Hence at run-time, the user tier artifacts appear on two physical tiers.

In summary, a DC can have a number of quite different implementations. A user-tier DC could consist of a C# module and a panel definition (emerging XML-based technologies for GUI panel definition, such as Microsoft's XAML (Rector 2003), are of interest here). An enterprise tier DC could be implemented as an EJB, and a BPM domain DC could be implemented as a workflow specification or B2B collaboration script.

The several different ways that a DC can be implemented illustrates a really important aspect of the DC concept: it is a design concept that maps well to a wide variety of different technologies. Each DC provides services, some local, others of very wide scope. In addition, the DC concept is sufficiently closely specified[20] to provide for rich design models at the MDA Platform-Independent Model (PIM) level, with the concepts preferably presented through a UML profile in an appropriate modeling tool. Finally, a DC is large enough to be able to carry some overhead to help provide transparencies for the application developer. For example, mapping from/to XML can be handled at run-time by generated code within the DC, so that the application developer deals only with normal classes in the programming language being used.

3.2.2. The Business Component (BC)

Consider a system that has no concept of, say, "customer" (a rather artificial supposition, but useful for exposition). Now ask the question, what artifacts would be required to add "Customer" to this system? We might immediately say a Customer DC. But of course, there is much more than that:

- Customer GUI panels for users to list, inspect, and perhaps update Customer records;
- A Customer DB schema; and
- Pass-by-value objects that contain Customer data.

The list could go on. The important point is that the implementation of the Customer concept could well require artifacts in each of the four distribution tiers. A "business component" or BC is an enterprise component that implements all and only a given business concept (process or entity) in a system. As such, it also provides for the business concept's distribution throughout the system, across the four distribution tiers described previously. It also maps well to business concepts in a requirements and/or business model, and the beneficial implications of this are discussed in Section 4 of this chapter.

Distribution Aspect

A BC consists of at least one DC, and it must have at least one workspace tier or one enterprise tier DC. Of course, it may have both, and it sometimes has more than one DC in a given tier. Each DC fulfills the responsibilities of its tier within the BC.

An example of a BC consisting of only an enterprise tier DC is a calculation engine that it implemented as a DC. For example, in ERP systems, a price calculator, often very complex, may be produced as a BC whose realization is a single enterprise-tier DC.

---

20 For further information, see Sims (2002).

A BC is not required to have to have all four tiers. However, its tiers are always adjacent tiers in the four-tier model. That is, while one BC may have all four tiers (user, workspace, enterprise, resource), or perhaps only two – for example, enterprise and resource only, it will never consist of tiers that are not adjacent. For example, a BC consisting of only user and resource tiers would be invalid.

The interfaces of a BC are provided by (delegated to) one of the DCs in the enterprise tier, and optionally one of the DCs in the workspace tier.

Business Function Aspect

A BC can represent both process and entity business concepts. Thus an application consists of a number of business components that collaborate to deliver application functionality across the distribution tiers. In turn, a DC within a BC is either a process or an entity DC based on what the BC is. It is often useful to divide entity components into two layers: entity and "utility". A utility BC is one that provides widely-used business services to both entity and process BCs. Examples include Address Book, Number Generator, and Currency.

A key consideration in component design is to minimize dependencies so that components can be composed and re-composed (re-used) as freely as possible. A component architecture should feature specific interaction patterns that minimize dependencies, such as the mediator pattern. The BC internals and also its external relationships with other BCs are the obvious place to apply dependency management patterns.

Service Orientation

A BC provides business-related services through its interfaces not only at the required "server" (enterprise tier) level, but also, where advanced user interaction designs are being applied, at the workspace tier level as well. Enterprise services are provided by process BCs to BPM components and also to external requestors. Entity services are provided to process BCs and also to BPM components.

BC Benefits

The BC concept does a number of important things, and in particular provides five valuable benefits:

1. Link with Requirements: It provides a direct link with the business requirements model – which knows nothing about distribution tiers (see Section 4 of this chapter).

2. Project Management Unit: As a cohesive collection of DCs, the BC is an ideal unit of project management, and valuable and meaningful metrics can be easily derived. This makes for much more accurate prediction than is often the case.

And when application development is mainly done through outsourcing, the BC, or an assembly of BCs, is an ideal "module" to outsource. Otherwise, outsourcing, while cost-effective, may reduce its usefulness by building yet more "silos" that are not interoperable, nor very maintainable through lack of effective modularization – to say nothing of re-use.

3. Lifecycle Continuity: As it moves through its lifecycle, a business component is realized by different artifacts at different stages. At analysis time, the artifacts comprising the business component will be UML models, and documents (specifications). Design time will add detail to these artifacts, so that code can be produced. The code will consist of some DCs, plus other artifacts such as GUI panels and DB schema definitions. A component architecture will define what completeness means at the end of each stage, defines the stages, and shows how traceability is provided. Thus a BC encapsulates all development artifacts within it. Its life starts with the business concept and is refined throughout its development. Indeed, with appropriate support, the BC can actually "run" as soon as it is conceived (through a standard "administrative" interface). This approach has been called "component metamorphosis" (Hubert 2002) and is extremely attractive, especially when combined with a capability for immediate prototyping in order to gain quick and early feedback from subject matter experts (see Pawson and Matthews 2002).

4. Domain knowledge: The BC also acts as a focus for domain knowledge within an application development group. And since the BC extends across the distribution tiers, there is not only shared domain expertise across tiers, but also within a small team (say, two to six people) there is some cross-familiarization in the various technology concerns found across tiers – from user interface through transactions to data base concerns. All of this can be hugely useful in terms of skill growth. However, it does assume a good virtual platform and a separate organization that provides the platform.

5. Unit of Ownership: Re-usable software artifacts are valuable enterprise assets, and must therefore be "owned" by a manager within the IT organization. However, to avoid one manager looking after ten thousand individual assets – which is not humanly possible, asset ownership must be structured, such that ownership of a large asset implies ownership of embedded assets.

The BC is an ideal unit of asset management, since it "owns" all of the assets that go into the DCs that make up the BC, and among these there will normally be a number that are re-usable. Without a larger "owning" construct, such re-usable assets are often difficult to categorize, and can quickly become lost. Examples of smaller assets that are usefully "owned" by a BC are proxy classes required to access the DCs in the business component, and also "business data types" (pass-by-value classes that are used as parameters in operation signatures) that are defined for the provided interfaces. For further detail, see Sims (2001).

The value of the BC as a unit of asset ownership is enhanced by the development lifecycle aspect, where a BC's lifecycle must also be managed, from the start of its development, then into operational use, through subsequent evolution, to its retirement perhaps many years later.

A full treatment of the richness of the business component concept is beyond the scope of this chapter, but is presented well in Herzum and Sims (2000). Other authors also suggest a similar concept. Richard Hubert, for example, talks of a component having both client and server personalities, and says, "These personalities exist to cleanly encapsulate and denote the two design partitions inevitably required of any component if it to be distributed." (Hubert 2002, p. 87)

3.2.3. The Application Component (AC)

Business components collaborate to provide a business solution. The assembly of BCs that together provide such a solution effectively make an "application". When this assembly is deliberately produced to be a component in its own right, with one or more service-oriented interfaces, then the assembly is called an "Application Component".

We can define an application component as an assembly of collaborating BCs that provides a defined set of business services. This concept is similar to EDOC's "Application Component" (OMG2 2004). A legacy system wrapped with a service-oriented interface looks like an AC to its clients.

Figure 8 shows an example of an AC. It consists of five BCs, each having up to four tiers, and together providing a simplified Invoice Management service. Business function layers (process-entity-utility) are shown vertically, and within each BC, the distribution tiers are shown as a stack of slices. User tiers are gray (blue in e-book version), and resource tiers are light grey (yellow in e-book version). Interfaces for the workspace and enterprise tiers are shown. Some of the business components have less than four tiers, and this is quite normal.

This AC might be called the Invoice Management component.[21] As with most ACs, its interface is defined as being the interface of the topmost process BC (Invoice

[21] In any architecture, naming conventions are important. This architecture chooses to call process components "X Managers", application components "X Management", and entity components just "X". Hence Invoice Management, Invoice Manager, and Invoice. This does not necessarily mean that somewhere there is a Customer Manager. If managing a Customer requires no other component, then

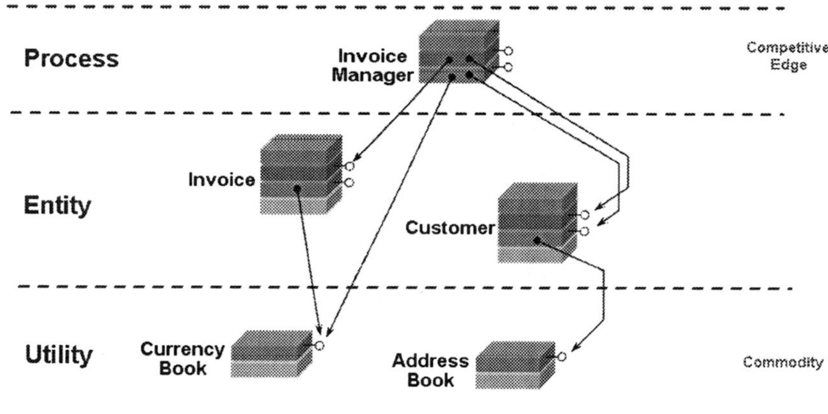

Figure 8. **Application Component Composed of Business Components**

Manager in the example); that is, a union of the Invoice Manager's workspace tier and enterprise tier interfaces. The enterprise service interface – that is, the interface that would be published in a UDDI repository – is almost always the enterprise tier interface only. (See Chapter 6 for a more detailed discussion of UDDI.)

In order to show how the tiers within each business component interact, we can flatten the figure out, the result being shown in Figure 9. Each BC is shown as a gray (blue in e-book version) rectangle. Within each BC are DCs implementing its various tiers. The DCs are named by their tier, so that, for example, the DC implementing the enterprise tier of the Customer BC is known as the "Customer Enterprise-Tier Distributed Component" – or just "Customer EDC" for short. Other naming conventions are possible, of course, but this one, although a little acronym-heavy at first glance, has proven simple for developers to use once the concepts have been introduced.

Black solid arrows show intra- and inter-BC invocations. The assumed component architecture allows intra-BC invocations between workspace and enterprise tiers; some architectures disallow this, routing all invocations through the top-level process BC.

---

the Customer business component can manage itself. Actually, this is unlikely for "customer" in most businesses, since normally at least a credit check is required as part of the "add new customer" business process. See Herzum and Sims (2000) for a discussion of naming conventions, and also for a discussion of styles of entity components.

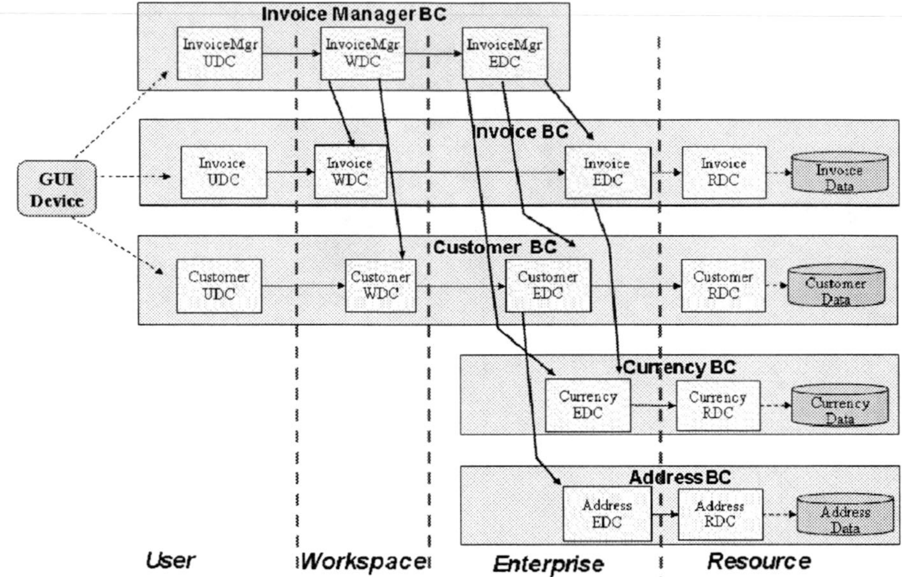

Figure 9. **Invoice Management Application Component**

Figure 9 does not repeat the process/entity/utility layering, although it is more or less implicit in the positions of the BC.

Finally, with regard to Figure 9, it is worth saying something about the DCs in the user tier. In the figure, they each appear to presents a different panel to the user. This is certainly not the intent. The various panels are normally presented as panes and/or pop-up windows within a window that presents a "tool" appearance.

Several views of the essential component model are needed. The diagrams above show component-centric views. A common additional view is that of the data base schemas. Another is the set of user workspace domain components, and yet another is a view of the set of enterprise resource domain elements. Such views are normally provided through development tools.

Finally, note that the user and workspace tiers in an AC constitute its user-workspace domain. It is not unusual for an AC to provide for a number of different user experiences such as browser, PC, PDA, and phone. In this case there will be a separate user-workspace domain for each experience, although it is quite possible that many of the same workspace tier DCs will be used in each domain.

3.3. Dependency Management

A focus in a component architecture on dependency management is essential. Without this, component interactions can become highly complicated, so slowing business evolution as changes take much longer to make and test. Two important dependency management patterns used in BCs and ACs are:

1. Inter-tier interactions; and
2. Business function layers.

3.3.1. Inter-Tier Interactions

Some of the constraints on inter-tier communication have been noted previously. Figure 10 illustrates a set of constraints that have been found useful. Essentially each tier (or more precisely, the DCs in each tier) provides services to the tier on the left. The BPM tier provides services to both workspace and enterprise tiers, and vice-versa. That is, BPM components (process or workflow specifications) can be kicked off by DCs in either the workspace or the enterprise tier.

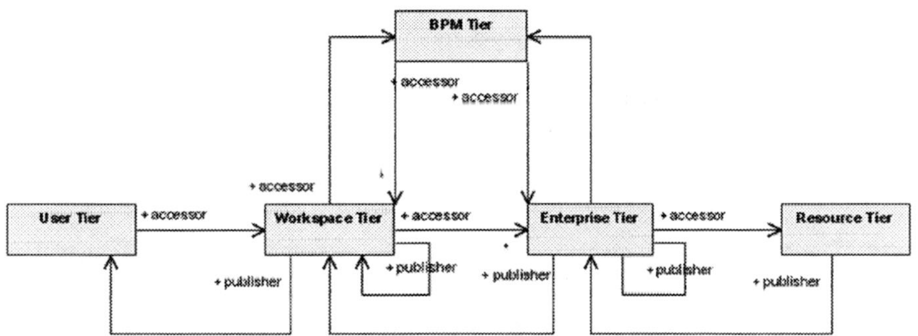

Figure 10. **Inter-Tier Interactions**

Note that Figure 10 could be part of a UML profile. Loosely speaking, a UML profile is a kind of template, or conceptual model. However, a UML profile not only defines the concepts to be used; it can also be applied by a modeling tool so that an application developer's model is constrained to use the concepts expressed in the profile.[22] For example, the developer can be constrained to design components and component interactions that conform to the profile. Tools can then check the

[22] One example of such a tool is "Objecteering" from Softeam (www.softeam.com). The latest version of this tool provides not only normal UML modeling, but also a profile building tool.

correctness of the model as far as proper use of the profiled concepts is concerned. This is an excellent way of delivering architecture to the application developer. When a profile defines scalability patterns and constraints, then the result is that run-time implementations whose structure is generated from the design models are likely to be inherently scalable, and also conform in all respects to the modularization and re-use standards defined by the profile. This approach is an important aspect of the OMG's MDA (Model-Driven Architecture) strategy (OMG1 2003).

3.3.2. Business Function Layers

It is useful to separate the orthogonal concerns of distribution tiers and application layers. A distributed system has a number of logical tiers which are essentially IT-related responsibilities. A business has a number of logical business-related responsibilities that we call "layers". These responsibilities are, briefly, process and entity.

Some architectures conflate these two quite different concerns. Thus we see architectures that suggest a user tier, a workspace or "session" tier, a "business service" tier (process), and a "business object tier" (entity).

However, there is more or less universal agreement now that process components should be separated from entity components, and that the pattern governing their collaboration should be the mediator pattern (Gamma et al. 1995). This is a very useful dependency management pattern, and is an example of a pattern developed in the context of object-oriented design that does indeed scale. This pattern is well established, being formalized in EJB (session and entity EJBs) and similarly (although richer) in the CORBA Component Model.

However, business function layering is richer than merely a separation into two parts. Business function is more a spectrum, from process to entity. Of course, this spectrum applies not only to business components (and hence to DCs) but also to the BPM domain, where the separations are sometimes considered to be continuous, and sometimes discrete. However, here we focus on the three component granularities described previously, based on the architecture described in Herzum and Sims (2000). This firstly separates the layers into three categories of process, entity, and utility. It appears that, by industry sector, these can usefully be further subdivided.

Within an application component, the process-utility layers play an important part in the architectural separation of concerns, and contribute significantly to reducing complexity through dependency management through application of the mediator pattern. This is done by having process BCs mediate (or choreograph) entity BCs. Utility components, however, provide services both to entity and to process components.

Figure 8 illustrates this pattern, with the process BC at the top invoking entity components in lower layers. A formal model of the constraints inherent in this approach would show a directed acyclic graph of invocation dependencies. Essentially this says that Process Components use Entity Components and/or Utility Components. Entity Components can use Utility Components, and finally Process Components can invoke other Process Components when the process layer is further sub-divided. BPM components operate at a higher layer than the process BC, which is how application components are federated.

An Entity component is responsible for managing a specific set of data, and can be thought of as "owning" that data. It provides entity services to other (typically process) components, and protects the integrity of the data as far as enforcement of business rules directly to do with that data is concerned (for example, validation).

A significant advantage of entities owning their data is the reduction of dependencies between data access mechanisms and schema on one hand, and business logic on the other. Often a traditional application that needs to access, say, customer data, will do so directly using SQL. This creates a web of dependencies between the database and multiple applications. The entity component approach helps to address DB schema dependency management. In the enterprise tier, entity DCs effectively provide a service-oriented component structure to otherwise monolithic process-oriented services.

A utility BC is a kind of entity that is of widespread use across many business functions. An example could be an "address list" containing addresses for customers, suppliers, business partners, and employees. Another example might be a "currency book" that handles currency conversions, currency arithmetic, and provides exchange rate information.[23]

4. From Requirements to Design

An important aspect of ESOA is that the services provided, and the components that implement them, should map as directly as possible to the needs of the business. Then, when the business evolves, it is very quickly clear what parts of the IT system are affected and which new or changed services and components should be provided. However, current methodologies often do not provide this (although some

[23] An example of this is the FbcCurrency Module in the OMG Currency Specification (OMG document formal/00-06-29).

go part-way towards it), nor do they help with structuring already-defined services. The resulting impedance mismatch can cause loss of information and traceability.

Without a solution to this problem, it is hard to see how any software initiative, by itself, can hope to make business more agile, responsive, or IT become more productive so that it can meet time-to-market, flexibility, and service-orientation goals. Failure in this area means that much of what IT delivers is likely either to not do what the business needs IT to do, or to result in "service silos". Either way, the result is loss of agility.

So we need to be able to specify business needs with minimal information loss while crossing the bridge between business rules and structures to IT algorithms and modules. Many current requirements analysis methods provide mapping of the business rules to IT algorithms. However, those IT algorithms usually end up buried in code modules that bear little resemblance to business structures. Real and effective traceability becomes very difficult; the bridge weakens, sometimes to the point of collapse. But such traceability is particularly important for ESOA, where proper identification of the components that provide the services is the key to agile IT.

The approach described in this section, called the "Business Element Approach",[24] provides for changes to business processes or rules being quickly and unambiguously be traced to one or more specific components. In addition, new business structures and algorithms are analyzed such that the structures defined in the requirements activity become the start of the IT design model.

We start by suggesting a particular approach to requirements. Then we show how the resulting business-oriented model can be directly implemented by the kinds of software component discussed previously.

4.1. Requirements

The objective of the requirements activity[25] is to define precisely what services the planned system should provide, how they are carried out, and what business features it should exhibit. The requirements activity ends when all relevant business questions have been answered. Therefore, it is not some high-level scoping activity (although

[24] This term is due to Taylor (1995), and his approach is further described in Hubert (2002). Extension of this work was done within the COMBINE project (Combine 2003), and also after that project completed.

[25] We use the generic term "requirements" as the name of the activity that defines precisely what the business wants and needs of IT. This activity goes by many names in the industry, including "business modeling", "requirements", "requirements analysis", "scoping and definition", etc.

that is part of it); rather it is a significant part of the system development effort, and goes into substantial business detail. However, it does not include IT system design.

The main elements of the process are as follows:

- Define scope, vision, and goals;
- Define the business requirements in terms of business processes and resources used or created by those processes ("resources" are sometimes known as business objects, or entities);
- Define the "business elements" that the IT system will implement; and
- Define user interaction requirements.

It should not be assumed that this list implies a sequence. More importantly, following description of business elements should certainly not be interpreted as implying a waterfall-style process. Such is certainly not the case.

4.1.1. Business Elements

A business element is a process, a resource, or an organizational unit. These three are inter-dependent: organizations perform specified processes; a process requires both an organization to perform it and resources as input or things produced; resources are assets of an organization, and are used or produced by processes. For current purposes we focus only on process and resource BEs.

Informally, we can say that a Business Element (BE) is an identifiable "chunk" of the business that is seen as important by business people.[26] A BE can be process-oriented or resource-oriented. Examples are "Sales Order Service", "Invoice Management", "Customer", "Booking", and "Sales Order".

But how are these BEs identified? With experience, many BEs rather jump out at one, and indeed some candidate BEs can often be suggested at the start of requirements based on experience in other organizations in the same industry. However, there is a set of heuristics that enable candidates to be identified based on process and resource models.

4.1.2. Processes and Resources

The Business Element approach requires that we define clearly:

---

[26] A precise definition of what "important" means in this context is beyond the scope of this book. However, Tyndale-Biscoe et al. (2002) provides a useful exposition.

- Business processes, each of which has one or more steps, and where each step is, where appropriate, further refined as a process in its own right. A process provides a service (possibly an internal service), and the steps define how the service is provided. A bottom-level process is often a set of steps that constitute what might be called a "procedure" or algorithm.[27]

- Resources[28] used by or produced by steps, and which provide limited-scope services to processes.

Processes may be captured in text within use case models, or more formally by UML classes or action states. We can identify a number of different kinds of process, differentiated by business-related factors. Of relevance here is an "immediate" process. An immediate process is one that is required to complete as soon as possible, and whose intermediate states are of no concern to the business in that they are not required to be remembered after the process has completed. An immediate process is performed autonomously, with no intervention from a human. It typically defines a service that would be provided by the core enterprise system (see Section 1 of the previous chapter). Other kinds of processes would map to BPM specifications.

Resources are captured in a "business object model" or an "entity model". Examples are "Customer", "Balance", "Address", and "Order Line". Given models of immediate processes, and resources, we can define the set of "business elements" that are within the scope of a given project.

4.2. Business Element Analysis

Three different kinds of business element can be derived from resource and process models:

1. Resource Business Element (RBE) – the important resources in the business. An RBE is a candidate for implementation in the eventual IT system as a Business Component.

2. Service Business Element (SBE) – a set of related services provided by the business and implemented by a business process. An SBE is a candidate for implementation in the eventual IT system as a process-style programmed Distributed Component.

---

27 There may be a number of kinds of resources, such as entities, performers, and actors. Here we are concerned only with those resources that are entities.

28 Some business modelers prefer not to analyze down to this level while in a business requirements activity. Others prefer to do so, arguing that business modeling only stops when, within the scope selected, there are now more questions about the business.

3. Delivery Business Element (DBE) – a defined grouping of service and resource business elements that provides a coherent set of services related to an organizational unit. A DBE is a candidate for implementation in the eventual IT system as a Distributed Component (implemented using such technologies as EJB, CORBA, .NET, etc.).

Note that, although the word "element" implies a single thing, a business element is in fact a group of things.

4.2.1. Resource Business Element (RBE)

A Resource Business Element (RBE) encapsulates a group of resources. The group is focused around a particular resource that is "real and independent" in the business domain. Other resources are "auxiliary", inasmuch as they support the primary resource in some way (for example, a Customer resource may be supported by a Customer Balance resource).

Real: A real resource is one that is both used and understood by subject matter experts (SMEs). It is not abstract. For example, in a manufacturing business, "customer", "address", and "invoice line item" would probably be real, while "legal entity", "location", and "collection member" might not. That is, an SME would assert that while a "customer" is a common everyday concrete thing, a "legal entity" is not (although there might be agreement that, hypothetically, it would be a good super-type of "customer").[29]

Independent: An independent resource is one that can be talked about by SMEs without first saying to what it belongs. That is, its scope is implied and understood, and is probably that of the business or of an important organizational unit within the business. For example, in a manufacturing business, a "customer" probably does not have to be qualified, so it is independent. "Address" or "Balance", on the other hand, would have to be qualified to be meaningful, for example, "customer address" or "supplier address". Of course, this is context-dependent; for example, addresses are often kept separate from the resources they relate to, especially in distribution-oriented organizations.

Looking at the business resource model in this way, certain resources can be identified as real and independent, and are called "focus" resources, while the others are called "auxiliary" resources. These terms follow UML semantics (see [UML]).

---

[29] For a full discussion of this topic, see under "Trading Partners" in Herzum and Sims (2000, p. 463).

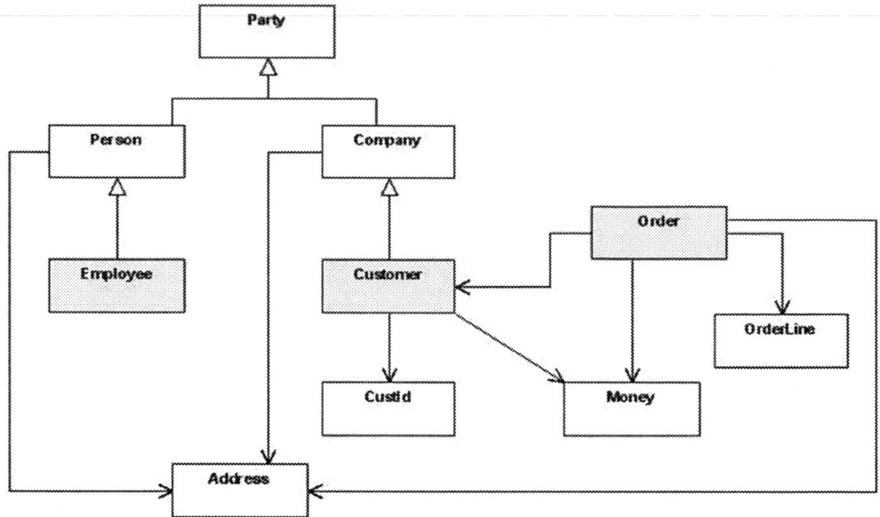

Figure 11. **Sample Resource Model Showing Focus Resources (Fragment)**

Identification

The following heuristic can be used to identify resource business elements (RBEs):

1. Consider each resource in the business resource model, and ask whether it is "real" and "independent". If it is, then it is the focus resource for a RBE. Other resources are "auxiliary" resources.[30]

2. Navigate the relationships (including upward generalizations) from the focus resource, to and through auxiliary resources, stopping when another focus resource is reached. Note the auxiliary resources encountered. Those auxiliary resources, plus the focus resource, form the first-cut definition of a group called the "focus group". Note that this is not an entirely automatic process; some judgment on where to stop is sometimes needed.

3. When all RBEs have been identified, create an RBE relationships class diagram. This is essential for comprehension of relationships between RBEs.

Example

The RBE example starts from a business resource model (or business object model). Figure 11 shows a highly simplified sample resource (or business) model. Let us assume that Employee, Customer, and Order are identified as the focus resources. Following the identification heuristic to group auxiliary resources results in the three focus groups illustrated in Figure 12.

---

30 The terms "focus" and "auxiliary" are UML stereotypes, and have the same semantics here.

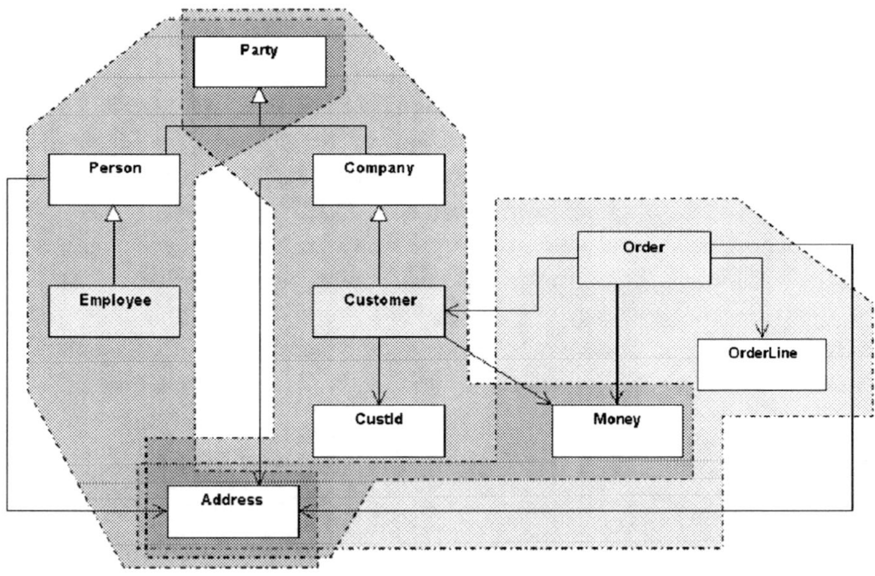

Figure 12. **Focus Groups**

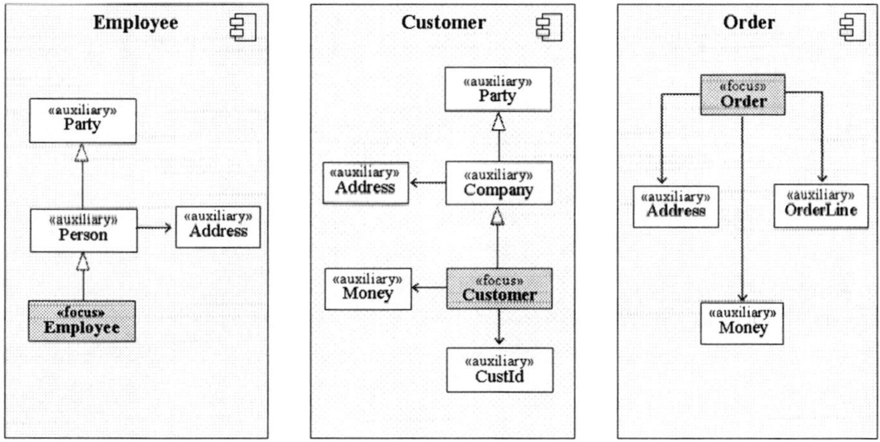

Figure 13. **Resource Business Elements**

When these are disentangled, three distinct resource business elements emerge, as shown in Figure 13. The result is a significant simplification of the original resource model, and no information is lost. Indeed, some has been gained, since the resource model can now be shown in its RBE view, which presents only the "important" resources. One of the interesting simplifications is that the various relationships have also been "grouped", leaving only one inter-RBE relationship. Finally, note that some auxiliary resources appear in more than one RBE. This is not surprising. However, a given focus resource appears in only one RBE.

Before leaving subject of RBEs, it can be seen that each RBE is represented in Figure 13 as a UML2 component. This illustrates well one of the intents of UML2 components – that they should apply throughout the development lifecycle – including the business model, or "Computation-Independent Model" (CIM) in the OMG's MDA parlance. In this case, we can use the component's concept of "type" and also it is concept of realization. Some business modelers may think this use of the UML2 component concept is wrong – that a business model should not show the least indication of something that may be misinterpreted as eventual implementation. In that case, a suitable model element for an RBE could be a UML package.

4.2.2. The Service Business Element (SBE)

A service business element is a collection of "immediate" steps as discussed previously in Section 4.1. The reason for grouping the steps (and their sub-steps) is that a given organizational unit is often responsible for the set of processes (steps) surrounding a Resource BE. These steps are often closely related in terms of the kinds of things they do, and together provide a coherent service. In effect, we apply the tested modularization principles of high cohesion and low coupling to these "chunks" of the business.

Identification Heuristic

To identify Service Business Elements (SBEs):

1. Identify the highest-level immediate steps in the business process model. These are services provided by the core business systems. The name of each step is probably of the form "verb-noun". Many of the nouns will probably be the names of RBEs, for example Supplier, Shipment, Contract, Schedule, Invoice, or Product.

2. Group the steps by RBE. It is likely that each group will include the CRUD[31] lifecycle of the RBE.

   Many groups will involve more than one resource BE. For example, a Sales Order group could include steps that not only direct the lifecycle of a Sales Order in some way, but also update Inventory and Customer Balance. However, the focus of the group is often a specific resource (such as Sales Order).

   Some groups may involve only one RBE. In this case, it is possible that the step forms part of the responsibilities of the RBE rather than the SBE.

[31] CRUD: Create, Read, Update, Delete.

3. Iterate on the next level of immediate steps in the business process model. If no further SBEs are found, then the immediate steps at this level of iteration are candidates for the business logic within the SBE, or possibly even within an RBE (such as "validate data provided"). If there are no lower-level immediate steps found, then stop.

Each SBE will normally map to an organizational unit, and is a candidate for implementation as a process component. The various verbs in the names of the immediate steps are candidate operations in the interfaces of that component. Subsidiary immediate steps associated with each higher-level immediate step typically constitute the process that provides the service indicated by the higher-level immediate step.

This identification heuristic groups immediate steps such that the groups – service business elements – make sense in business terms, and not only provide the basis for a service-oriented enterprise system, but also exhibit best practice modularization along high cohesion and low coupling principles.

SBE Identification Example

Suppose the following services (top-level immediate steps) were defined in the process model:

- Amend Customer Record;
- Handle Order (place a new Order);
- Remove Employee;
- Record New Customer;
- Amend Existing Order;
- Cancel Order;
- Hire New Employee.

Many of these steps will have subsidiary immediate steps. For example, the "Amend Customer Record" and "Handle Order" steps could well have the following subsidiary steps:

Service	Subsidiary Immediate Steps
Amend Customer Record	Validate customer details provided
–	Review credit limit by running a Credit Check
–	Record Customer details
–	Check for relationships with other Customers, update where necessary
–	Send the standard "your details changed" letter
Handle Order	Validate data submitted
–	Check Customer is valid
–	Calculate value of Order
–	Check for credit
–	Allocate inventory
–	Create Back-Orders where necessary
–	Create the Order
–	Send an Order Acknowledgment

Based on the example above of seven services (top-level immediate steps), the identification and grouping heuristic could produce the following (incomplete) SBEs:

SBE	Service	Subsidiary Immediate Steps
Customer Service	Amend Customer Record	Validate customer details provided
–		Review credit limit ...
–		Record Customer details
–		Check for relationships ...
–		Send the standard letter
–	Record New Customer	...
Order Service	Handle Order (place a new Order)	Validate data submitted
–		Check Customer is valid
–		Calculate value of Order
–		Check for credit
–		Allocate inventory
–		Create Back-Orders where necessary
–		Create the Order
–		Send an Order Acknowledgment
–	Amend Existing Order	...
–	Cancel Order	...
Employee Service	Hire New Employee	...
	Remove Employee	...

As can be seen, each top-level immediate step provides a service (e.g. "Amend Customer record"). Each service in turn will usually consist of a set of subsidiary immediate steps.

4.2.3. Delivery Business Element (DBE)

Specific subsets of Service and Resource BEs are used by an organizational unit in the business to deliver some required capability. For example, an Order Service SBE plus several RBEs such as Customer, Product, and Sales Order are used to deliver order management capabilities to a Sale Order Processing department in the business. Such specific groups can be seen as providing defined services to other parts of the organization, as well as to customers and suppliers. The grouping itself usefully forms a third kind of business element, which we call a Delivery BE, since it is this group that delivers functionality for the business. Consider: an RBE can do nothing by itself (no process), and likewise, an SBE by itself is pretty useless (no resources!). The Delivery BE is the set of assets that delivers value.

A Delivery Business Element (DBE) is a grouping of Service and Resource Business Elements that together deliver a business solution to a business problem, and which provides services to requestors.

A given DBE often corresponds to a major responsibility of a department or larger organizational unit in the business. For example, the services and resources involved in a "Sales Order Management" DBE would reflect the major responsibilities of the Sales Processing Department in a business.

A simplified example of a DBE is shown in Figure 14.

Identification

Delivery Business Elements can be identified by finding the top-level SBEs. A "top-level" SBE is one that is not a dependant of any other SBE. For each top-level SBE, identify the set of BEs that this SBE needs to function correctly. That is, identify the dependent BEs of the top-level SBE. The resulting set, plus the top-level SBE, comprises the Delivery Business Element.

Hint: In small-to-medium projects, there may only be top level SBEs. In very small projects, there may indeed be only one, and hence the DBE will correspond to an "application".

A BE diagram can be constructed as BEs are identified. Applying the mediator pattern for usages by one BE of other BEs typically results in a directed acyclic graph (as illustrated in Figure 14). The DBE will normally be a subset of this diagram.

Example

Figure 14 illustrates the dependencies between two SBEs (Order Service and Pricing) and three Resource Business Elements. This set of business elements together comprises the "Order Management" delivery business element. Note that the UML2 component is used in the diagram to represent business elements. Only the "type" part of the component is used – interfaces and implementation detail are normally added later during the IT design phase. This illustrates well a realization of the UML2 objectives for the component concept– that it should apply throughout the development lifecycle – including the requirements phase.

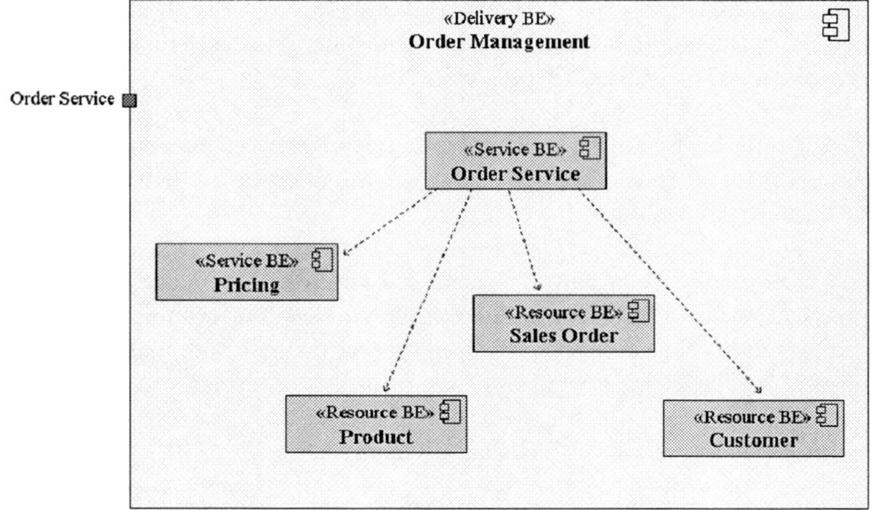

Figure 14. **Delivery Business Element**

4.3. Mapping to Components

A BE captures an important business concept. CBSE defines a set of structuring concepts that are ideal for implementation of BEs in an IT system. This is because little or no transformation is required between the BEs and the technical design model. That is, each BE is mapped one-to-one to a candidate component in the design model. This means that traceability between components in the IT system and the business is direct and visible to business people. Each business element maps isomorphically to a specific kind of component, as follows:

- **Service BE to Process Business Component**: Each immediate step provided by a service BE is mapped to an operation on a process business component in the IT design. Thus immediate steps become services provided by the system (for example, "Modify Customer record").

- **Resource BE to Entity Business Component**: Again, the mapping is direct: each resource BE can be (largely automatically) transformed into the beginnings of an entity business component, complete with focus and auxiliary classes. As with the process component, the transformation has no information loss.

- **Delivery BE to Application Component**: Earlier in this chapter we showed how process and entity components collaborate, and a simplified example of a sales order management application component was given. This collaboration maps extremely well to a Delivery Business Element, and the transformation is exceptionally simple. Dependencies between BEs map to operation invocations between components.

In MDA terms, the business elements comprise part of a CIM (Computation-Independent Model), and can be (largely automatically) transformed into the beginnings of a component PIM (Platform-Independent Model). Because no structural changes are made, the transformation is simple, and has no information loss.

The component model is then refined, behavior added, etc., to move through the development lifecycle to an operational IT system.

In other words, we have a clear and unambiguous bridge between the business and the IT system, with one-to-one mapping.

This, then, is the essence of the "bridge" between business requirements and the IT system. Extra-functional requirements (such as scalability and security) are typically handled either through the architectural features of the component model (e.g. the legitimate interactions between tiers) or as part of the virtual platform.

In this way, traceability between components in the IT system and the business is direct and visible to business people; and reverse traceability is similarly isomorphic and visible. Just as SBEs "choreograph" the use of RBEs and sometimes other SBEs, so process components choreograph the usage of other components. Each component provides clear services; for example entity components provide "entity services" to process components, which in turn provide published enterprise services both to business users and to requestors outside the business. Because each component is designed and built autonomously, capturing autonomous business elements, then just as business elements in the business can be re-used, so can the components. There is as much re-use of components as there is of business elements. Further technical re-use is also possible within the IT domain. For example, auxiliary classes within components can often be re-used in other components.

5. Summary

In summary, process business elements can be said to be the "modules" of the business. Mature CBSE gives us a technology whereby business elements can be captured on a one-to-one basis. This means that the IT system that supports the business is structured along the same lines as the business.

Now suppose we provide systemic event management in the IT system, so that each component can publish business events as they happen. It then becomes possible to think of installing probes into the message stream which can not only measure the flow rate between given components, but also can interrogate the message content itself (remember that the message context is XML).

Ability to probe messages for their semantic content? This starts to sound like a kind of "business nervous system"! And indeed, some enterprises today are beginning to think along these terms. Why? Because the concept of a "business control room" for real-time management of organizational units is one that has been around since the 1970s (e.g., Beer 1979). Then, it was not only the technology that was lacking, it was also the set of software structuring concepts. Today, enterprise service-oriented architecture can provide both the technology and the software structuring concepts.

Hence ESOA may well provide the basis for a situation where the business models, or "CIMs" in MDA-speak, may be become a live model of the business, in the same way that a railroad control center provides a live model of a railway system. And the design models or MDA "PIMs" (platform-independent models) could become the main focus and tool for synchronized business and IT agility and evolution. The "naked objects" initiative (Pawson and Matthews 2002) provides the basis for technology whereby even partly-built components can be automatically visualized on a GUI. But here we stop: further extrapolation and exploration is beyond the scope of this chapter.

3 ORCHESTRATION

None of us is as smart as all of us.
Anonymous

Even before the advent of Web services, an increasingly large number of distributed applications were constructed by composing them out of existing applications. Enterprise Application Integration (EAI) techniques grew up from the realization that no one infrastructural technology (e.g., CORBA or DCOM) will ever be adopted by all of the software industry. Furthermore, although sourcing a solution to a problem (large or small) from a single vendor is possible in the short term, in the long term it is often the case that a corporate intranet will be running systems from a variety of vendors, not all of which will be able to interoperate. Large multi-national corporations often evolve through acquisitions of smaller companies who may have different infrastructural investments. We have often heard the statement that "It's easier to interoperate with a different company than to talk to different divisions within the same company." Therefore it should come as no surprise to learn that large-scale applications are rarely built from scratch; rather they are constructed by composing them out of existing applications.

Providing solutions that enable disparate (heterogeneous) technologies and applications to communicate is extremely important. Without them, a company's infrastructure would either not be able to grow (leading to islands of isolation) or would be at the mercy of a single vendor. For several years EAI solutions have made it possible to compose an application out of component applications in a uniform manner, irrespective of the languages in which the component applications have been written and the operating systems of the host platforms. Unfortunately, most EAI platforms offer solutions that are not interoperable with one another. Web services offer a potential solution to this important drawback.

The resulting applications can be very complex in structure, containing many temporal and dataflow dependencies between their constituent applications. An additional complication is that the execution of such an application may take a long time to complete and may contain long periods of inactivity (minutes, hours, days, weeks, etc.), often due to the constituent applications requiring user interactions. In a distributed environment, it is inevitable that long running applications will require support for fault-tolerance and dynamic reconfiguration: machines may fail, services may be moved or withdrawn and application requirements may change. In such an environment it is essential that the structure of applications can be modified to reflect these changes. In general, *composite applications* are increasing in importance as companies combine off-the-shelf and homegrown Web services into new applications. Various mechanisms are being proposed and delivered to market daily to help improve this process. New "fourth generation" language development tools are emerging that are specifically designed to stitch together Web services from any source, regardless of the underlying implementation.

A large number of vendors are starting to sell business process management, workflow and orchestration tools for use in combining Web services into automatic business process execution flows. In addition, a growing number of businesses find themselves creating new applications by combining their own Web services with Web services available from the Internet supplied by the likes of Amazon.com and Google.com. These types of composite applications represent a variety of requirements, from needing a simple way to share persistent data to the ability to manage recovery scenarios that include various types of transactional software. Composite applications therefore represent a significant challenge for Web services standards since they are intended to handle complex, potentially long-running interactions among multiple Web services as well as simple and short-lived interactions.

Workflow systems have been around for many years, pre-dating Web Services and SOA. The core concepts behind the notion of workflow are not tied to any specific implementation environment. Therefore, in the following sections we will examine workflows from an architectural perspective before describing the Web Services Business Execution Language (WS-BPEL) (WSBPEL), which is the current contender for the title of workflow standard for SOA.

1. Workflow and Business Process Management

A *business relationship* is any distributed state maintained by two or more parties, which is subject to some contractual constraints previously agreed by those parties. A business transaction can therefore be considered as a consistent change in the state of a business relationship between parties. Each party participating in a business transaction holds its own application state corresponding to the business relationship with other parties involved in that transaction. During the course of a business transaction, this state may change.

Traditional methods for integration of these business transactions typically involve embedded logic inside of functionality-oriented IT applications. The development, testing and deployment effort required to change these applications make integration and process changes very costly and complex. To address these issues, proprietary EAI and Business Process Management (BPM) products emerged to abstract integration and process automation. These software products (*workflow systems*) liberated the integration and process tasks from the underlying functional IT applications so they could be more effectively changed, managed and optimized.

Workflows are rule-based management software that direct, coordinate and monitor execution of tasks arranged to form *workflow applications* representing business processes. *Tasks* (*activities*) are application specific units of work that may involve multiple services or components. A *Workflow schema* (*workflow script*) is used to explicitly represent the dependency between the tasks and in many ways may look like a traditional programming language, with branch statements, conditional executions, etc. The structure of many workflow management systems is based on the Workflow Reference Model developed by the Workflow Management Coalition (WfMC). Figure 1 depicts the Reference Model.

This model provides for the manipulation and execution of workflow instances (interfaces 2, 3 and 5) as well as for the definition and management of workflow schemas (interfaces 1 and 5). According to the base workflow model, a workflow application is modeled as a collection of tasks. A task is the unit of activity within a workflow application; typically you can equate a task with an interaction on a service or services; for example, booking a flight on an airline.

The structure of the workflow application is expressed by the interdependencies between its constituent tasks. A dependency could be just a *notification* (*temporal*) dependency (shown by a dotted line in Figure 2, indicating that t2 can start only

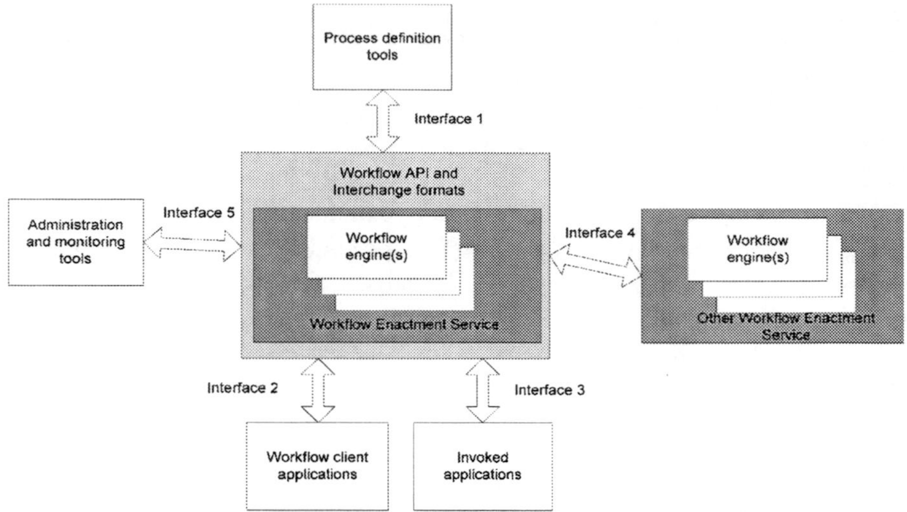

Figure 1. **WfMC Workflow Reference Model**

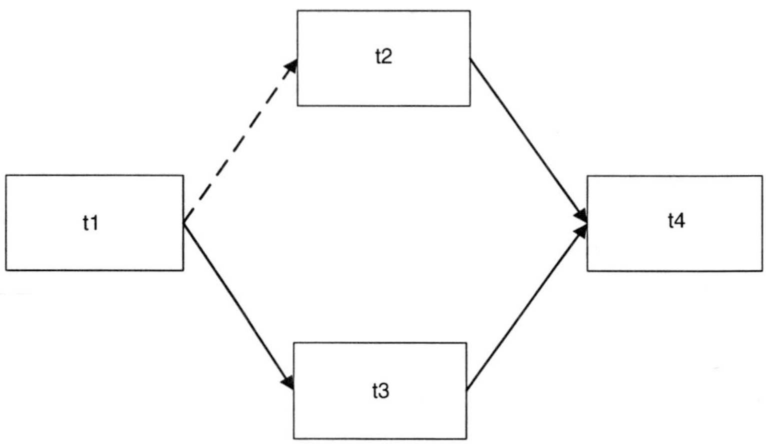

Figure 2. **Inter-Dependency Tasks**

after t1 has terminated) or a *dataflow* dependency (shown by a solid line, indicating that, say t3, needs to be notified of the availability of input data from t1).

A task is typically modeled as a having a set of *inputs* and a set of *outputs*. The execution of a task is triggered by the availability of an input(s) message. A task can terminate producing one of a set of output messages. The outputs will, if required, be propagated to other tasks as sources of input. In addition, a task can be composed from other tasks to form a compound task.

A workflow system allows the specification of task dependencies and their interrelationships and then controls the execution of that workflow specification. Typically this specification will be maintained in a persistent manner such that failures of the workflow system or individual tasks will be recoverable to ensure that the required specification is executed to completion.

For example, let us consider a workflow application that involves processing a customer's order for a book from an online shop. It may be modeled as a compound task *processOrderApplication* which contains four constituent simple task instances: *paymentAuthorization*, *checkStock*, *dispatch* and *paymentCapture*. The relationship between the tasks is shown in Figure 3.

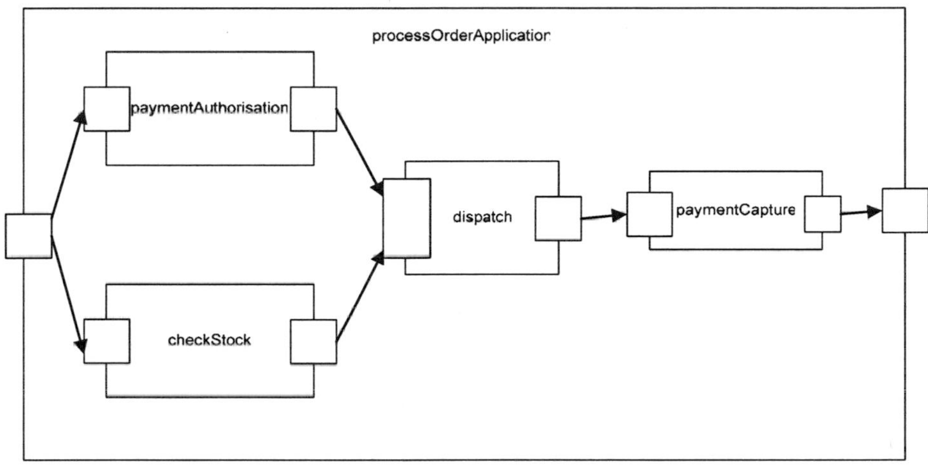

Figure 3. **Process Order Application Example**

To process an order, *paymentAuthorization* and *checkStock* tasks are executed concurrently. If both complete successfully then *dispatch* task is started and if that task is successful then the *paymentCapture* task is started. Obviously you may want to structure tasks slightly differently in some situations, e.g., run *paymentCapture* before *dispatch*, or run them concurrently. However, for our illustrative purposes this structuring is sufficient.

Note that although to define these business constraints (interactions) requires precise knowledge of the interaction protocols involved, the publicly visible exchange pattern of each of the parties involved, it does not require internal implementation specific details of the various parties. For example, if we return to the process order example, it is not necessary to understand how the `checkStock` or `dispatch` tasks are actually implemented: as a user of their services all that is required is that they conform to some pre-agreed contract.

This is an important point and one which is exemplified by the overall Web services model. Web services are specifically about fostering systems interoperability. What makes Web services so interesting is the fact that the architecture is deliberately not prescriptive about what happens behind service endpoints – Web services are ultimately only concerned with the transfer of structured data between parties, plus any meta-level information to safeguard such transfers (e.g., by encrypting or digitally signing messages). As we have already seen, this gives flexibility of implementation, allowing systems to adapt to changes in requirements, technology etc. without directly affecting users. Furthermore, most businesses will not want to expose their back-end implementation decisions and strategies to users for a variety of reasons.

Some workflow implementations allow the internal structure of a compound task to be modified (sometimes dynamically, as the workflow executes) without affecting the tasks which supply it with inputs or use it for inputs. In this case it would be possible to change the payment and stock management policies, for example, causing payment capture even if the item is not presently in stock, or the addition of a task which could check the stock levels of the suppliers of the company and arrange direct dispatch from them.

1.1. Intra-Enterprise Workflows

As you can imagine, workflow systems are extremely useful in controlling the execution of processes that form an application, both within a single domain, e.g., a corporate intranet as well as between domains, e.g., business-to-business interactions. At present it is true to say that the majority of workflow systems are typically being used to glue together services and components within a single domain, but that is likely to change. Many examples of this exist today, including the purchase order scenario we have already considered. For example, some large software organizations model their issue-tracking systems on what is often referred to as the *trouble ticket* scenario: a bug or problem is identified; it must be recorded; the record must be checked for accuracy; from a single instance of a problem, the underlying cause is identified; a resolution is identified, which must be communicated back to the original party with the problem.

Trying to model either the purchase order or trouble ticket scenarios manually is obviously possible, since these kinds of applications existed before there was anything identifiable as a workflow system. However, it requires a lot of skill and effort on behalf of the application programmer, especially when issues such as reliability, fault tolerance and adaptability are concerned. For example, at some point during its execution a long running application is likely to encounter changes to the environment within which it is executing. These environmental changes could include machine failures, services being moved or withdrawn, or even the application's functional requirements being changed. Trying to implement this for a bespoke application is hard enough without sacrificing flexibility. Luckily, some of the more advanced workflow systems provide mechanisms that will allow workflow applications to change their internal structures to ensure forward progress can be made.

1.2. Interoperability Concerns

Whilst workflow systems and standards have been around for many years, there has remained a significant problem with these systems: interoperability. Despite the fact that a standard for non-Web services workflow systems exists (the WfMC standard), it is written in such a way that many different, un-interoperable implementations are possible, which can still claim to be compliant with the standard. The problems this can cause are obvious and difficult to resolve without help from the individual vendors, whose initial responses are likely to be to try to persuade you to move to a homogeneous system. For example, we know of at least one major aircraft manufacturing company that in the late 1990s had seven different workflow systems that were compliant with the WfMC standard and yet could not talk to one another! With the advent of Web services, the hope is that this will change.

In the following sections we will look at the efforts going on in the world of Web Services to provide a standard for workflow definition and interactions that is intended to lower the entry barrier for implementers as well as users.

2. *The Business Process Execution Language (BPEL)*

Standard interaction protocols such as XML and SOAP are all well and good, but the full power of Web services as an integration platform can only be realized when there is a standard process integration model. In July 2002, BEA, IBM, and Microsoft released a trio of specifications designed to support business transactions over Web services. These specifications, BPEL4WS (BSPEL), WS-Transaction (WSAA, WSBA) and WS-Coordination (WSC), together form the basis for reliably choreographing Web services-based applications, providing business process management, transactional integrity and generic coordination facilities respectively. We will look at WS-Transaction and WS-Coordination in Chapter 7, so do not worry if this chapter is rather brief on those specifications.

The value of BPEL4WS is that the orchestration and refinement of the individual processes that go to make up a business application is critical to an enterprise's viability in the marketplace. Those businesses whose processes are agile and flexible will be able to adapt rapidly to and exploit new market conditions. In the rest of this paper we will talk about BPEL4WS (Business Process Execution Language for Web services). It is important to know that in May 2003, IBM, Microsoft, BEA and partners submitted a version 1.1 of BPEL4WS to OASIS under the WS-BPEL (Web Services Business Process Execution Language) Technical Committee, and it is this version we will concentrate on. However, it is worth remembering that as we have already seen, a standard does not necessarily imply interoperability.

Note that it is beyond the scope of this chapter to be able to present a tutorial of BPEL (which is still evolving through the standards process anyway). There are several good books and tutorials accompanying BPEL software that can dedicate much more space to this subject than we can in this chapter. However, it is our intention to give a sound architectural grounding in the concepts and techniques involved in understanding and using the language. As such we will cover the fundamental aspects of the BPEL language from a requirements perspective, but will have to omit some of the syntax elements and capabilities.

BPEL is an example of a workflow scripting language for specifying business process behavior based on Web services. The language can be used to formally define the behavior of business processes and their interactions. Processes in BPEL export and import functionality exclusively using Web services and the language is *entirely* XML-based. As we will see, because of the cross-industry support, BPEL looks like providing the standard integration model and language for BPM. It has the potential to commoditize the capabilities provided by the old workflow and proprietary EAI and BPM solutions. This is extremely important because it should allow integration tasks to leverage existing (legacy) investments in EAI and provide an integration path between different vendor implementations.

Unfortunately, although one of the original goals of the initial WS-BPEL specification was to foster interoperability between different implementations and to provide for fault-tolerant tasks through the use of transactions, during its progression through the OASIS standardization process these aspects have been removed. It is likely that true interoperability between heterogeneous BPEL implementations based on the final OASIS BPEL 1.0 specification will be difficult to achieve.

2.1. Relationship to XPath

The default language for expressions in BPEL is XPath 1.0 [XPATH], although the specification allows other query languages to be used. This means that basic computations constrained by XPath can be performed as part of an activity. BPEL supports the following distinct kinds of expressions:

- Boolean valued expressions where the evaluation results in a true or false result. Such expressions are used to manage process control flow.
- Deadline valued expressions where the evaluation results in a string which is compatible with the format of either XML Schema `date` or `dateTime` types. Such expressions are used in timed wait and pick activities with a fixed deadline, as we will see later.
- Duration valued expressions where the evaluation results in a string which is compatible with the format XML Schema `duration`. These expressions are used in timed `wait` situations with a relative deadline.
- General expressions where any of the XPath types (string, number, or Boolean) can be the result. Such expressions are used for assignment and may use different operators (e.g., <=, +, *, etc.) depending on the result type.

In addition, BPEL also defines a number of other extensions in the BPEL namespace http://schema.xmlsoap.org/ws/2003/03/business-process/. The "`bpws:`" is associated with this namespace and when it is used in the rest of this chapter you should remember this.

2.2. Variables

During the course of a business process it is likely that application data will have to be updated or inspected. BPEL provides the `variable` construct for this purpose. A BPEL `variable` is a typed data structure which stores messages associated with a workflow instance. As with any workflow, the state of the application is a function of the messages that have been exchanged and variables are used to maintain this state. Variables provide the means for holding messages that state of the business process. The messages held may be those that have been received from partners or are to be sent to partners. In addition, they can also hold data that are needed for holding state related to the process but are not exchanged with partners. Variables begin in an un-initialized state and are populated over time by the arrival of messages, or computations being executed which populate them.

For example, let us assume that the checkStock process returns a message containing the number of the required items still in the warehouse. Code 1 shows how a BPEL variable may be created based on this message type.

```
<wsdl:types>
      <xsd:schema>
            <xsd:simpleType name="stockCountType">
                  <xsd:restriction base="xsd:int"/>
            </xsd:simpleType>
      </xsd:schema>
</wsdl:types>

<variables>
      <variable name="itemsAvailable"
      type="props:stockCountType"/>
</variables>
```

Code 1. An example of a BPEL variable

As we mentioned earlier, BPEL defines some XPath extension functions. One of those functions is shown in Code 2 and is used to get a variable's value:

```
bpws:getVariableProperty('variableName', 'propertyName')
```

Code 2. The XPath function to return a property value from a message

The first parameter is the name of a source variable (message type) and the second is a qualified name (`QName`) of a property to select from within that variable. If the property does not appear in the message, then it is implementation dependant as to what is returned. Otherwise, a node set containing the single node representing the property is returned.

For example, let us return to the *checkStock* process that returns a message indicating the amount of stock left. Our workflow process may prioritize clients and only fulfill a purchase request for a specific low-priority client if it does not drop the stock below a specific level, in case a high-priority client request comes in before the stock can be replenished. Code 3 illustrates how this could be modeled: the source variable `stockResult` is the message returned by executing the checkStock process and part of this message has an element `level` that contains the current amount of the request items remaining in stock.

```
<case condition="bpws:getVariableProperty(stockResult,level)
> 100">
      <flow>
            <!-- there is enough stock to allow a low-priority
            order -->
      </flow>
</case>
```

Code 3. An example of using getVariableProperty

We have looked at some of the basics of BPEL, such as variables and the ability to define expressions. In the next section we will build on these to show how relationships between business processes can be defined and interactions between those processes controlled.

2.3. Defining Business Relationships

Because BPEL is a flow definition language it has to provide a means of capturing enterprise interdependencies with various roles known as *partner link*, *partner link types* and *business partners*. The partner link type is used to characterize the conversational relationship between two services, by defining the type of role each service plays in a specific interaction. For example, the `purchaseOrderProducer` and `purchaseOrderConsumer` roles could be represented as shown in Code 4:

```
<partnerLinkType name="OrderProducerConsumerLink"
xmlns="http://schemas.xmlsoap.org/ws/2003/05/partner-link/">
      <role name="Consumer">
            <portType name="consume:ConsumerPortType"/>
      </role>
      <role name="Producer">
            <portType name="produce:ProducerPortType"/>
      </role>
</partnerLinkType>
```

Code 4. The purchase order Producer and Consumer PartnerLinkType

As you can see, each role specifies exactly one `portType`. Importantly, the partner link type can either be defined independently of the services' WSDL, or may appear within the WSDL document. Although it is more usual to find a partner link type with two roles, as above, there are situations where a single role may be appropriate and this is allowed for within the BPEL syntax. For example, a service that wishes to be able to interact with any other service without knowing the type of the service a priori (a general logging service may fall into this category if it is implemented to take log information from any service in a corporate network).

The partner links are used to model the actual service with which a business process interacts. It is important to understand the distinction between partner links and partner link types: more than one partner link can be characterized by the same `partnerLinkType`. If we go back to the process order application, it is possible that the `checkStock` task may use more than one supplier, but the same `partnerLinkType`. The syntax for a partnerLink is shown in Code 5:

```
<partnerLinks>
      <partnerLink name="ncname" partnerLinkType="qname"
                   myRole="ncname"? partnerRole="ncname"?>+
      </partnerLink>
</partnerLinks>
```

Code 5. The partnerLink syntax

As can be seen, each `partnerLink` must be named and this name is used for all interactions via that link. `myRole` is used to indicate the role of the business process, whereas `partnerRole` shows the role of the partner.

The business partner role is used to represent relationships with a specific partner. Such business partnerships often require more than one conversational relationship. For example, as shown in Code 6, the `AuthorizationCapture` partner is required to provide the roles of both payment authorization and payment capture. The definition of these capabilities appears in the `partner` element:

```
<partner name="AuthorizationCapture"
    xmlns="http://schemas.xmlsoap.org/ws/2003/05/partner-link/">
  <partnerLink name="PaymentAuthorization"/>
  <partnerLink name="PaymentCapture"/>
</partner>
```

Code 6. An example of a business partner role

Partner definitions are optional and need not cover the entire partner links defined in the process. From the process perspective a partner definition introduces a constraint on the functionality that a business partner is required to provide. It is important that partner definitions do not overlap, i.e., a partner link cannot appear in more than one partner definition.

2.4. Message Correlation

Once we have captured the relationships between our enterprise and its partners, we can begin to exchange messages based on these relationships. However, WSDL is essentially a stateless model based on two possible patterns:

- Synchronous (remote procedure call) interactions, where the underlying communication system ties together requests and their responses, or
- Asynchronous interactions, where request messages and any possible responses have to be tied together at the application level. Usually this happens in an ad hoc manner; for example by encoding a unique sequence number in the outgoing request that the sender of the response echoes back. (Actually that is pretty much what happens in the synchronous case too, but the communication system takes care of it for you.)

During a business activity, a given process will often interact with many different partners in order to conduct work. Those interactions may be based on either synchronous or asynchronous transport mechanisms. However, the typical interaction pattern is based on asynchronous (one way) messages because this has the benefit of allowing loose coupling of application entities: the sender of a given message that requires a response need not be the same as the ultimate receiver of that response. This allows for great flexibility in choosing service deployments, particularly in environments that may be error prone or require dynamic changes to roles and responsibilities.

As we mentioned above, in this case some kind of message correlation is required in order to ensure that messages are delivered to the right BPEL instance: it is obviously important that messages belonging to one business relationship do not get mixed with another. Fortunately BPEL does not mandate a specific interaction pattern, but it does provide language-level support for asynchronous interactions through *correlation sets*. For example, let us return to the process order scenario and look at the possible message interactions between the various processes in a BPEL implementation, as shown via the UML interaction diagram in Figure 4. Here we have added an *Order Process Orchestrator*, which is meant to represent the overall controlling aspect of the BPEL flow. As you can see, in this example we have modelled all interactions as asynchronous one-way operations, although we could just as easily produced a diagram that relied on synchronous interactions.

However, because we are using one-way operations, it is necessary to tie up responses with requests. For example, if you look at the interaction between the Order Process Orchestrator and the Payment Authorization Process you can see the `paymentAuthorization` request and the `paymentAuthorized` response.

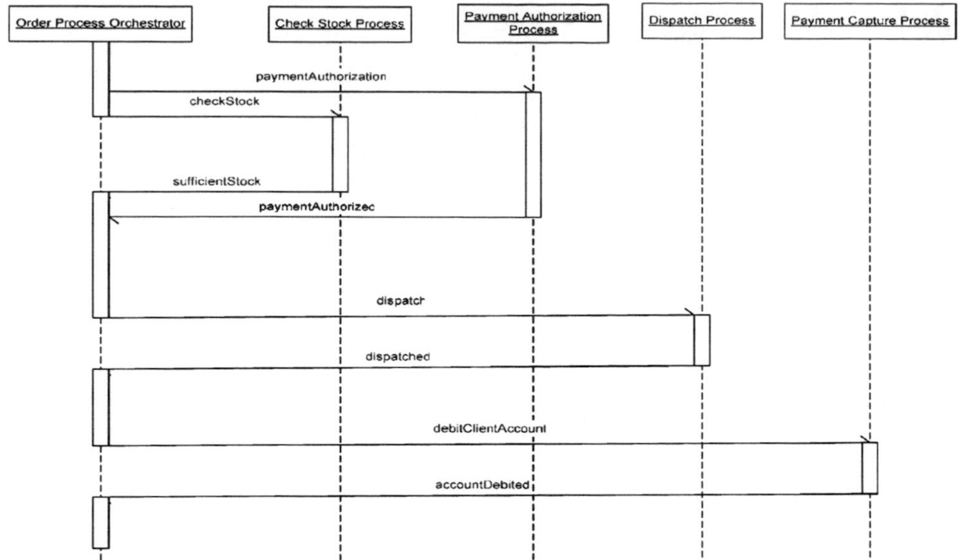

Figure 4. **Message Interactions for the Process Order Example**

The order process workflow will probably be dealing with many client order requests concurrently, so the Orchestrator will be sending and receiving many `paymentAuthorization` and `paymentAuthorized messages`. It is obviously important that it can match up these responses with their requests. That is where correlation sets come in.

A correlation set is a declarative mechanism for defining related groups of operations within a service instance. It is a mechanism for defining a named group of properties that serve as a way to uniquely identify an application-level conversation within a specific business protocol (e.g., the `paymentAuthorization` and `paymentAuthorized` interaction we saw earlier). Application messages are associated with correlation sets and the BPEL implementation is responsible for ensuring that requests and responses are matched using this unique data.

In order to declare a correlation set for a message it is necessary to define which subset of the message properties declared for a message type can uniquely identify a message instance. Let us look at the order process example in more detail and see how correlation sets may be defined for it. We will begin by defining three message properties: `customerID`, `orderNumber` and `dispatchNumber`. All of these properties, illustrated in Code 7, are defined as part of the `processOrderCorrelation.wsdl`:

```
<definitions name="properties"
targetNamespace="http://example.com/orderProcessCorrelation.wsdl"
xmlns:poc="http://example.com/processOrderCorrelation.wsdl"
xmlns:bpws="http://schemas.xmlsoap.org/ws/2003/03/business-
process/"
xmlns="http://schemas.xmlsoap.org/wsdl/">
      <!-- define correlation properties -->
      <bpws:property name="customerID" type="xsd:string"/>
      <bpws:property name="orderNumber" type="xsd:int"/>
      <bpws:property name="dispatchNumber" type="xsd:id"/>
</definitions>
```

Code 7. An example of message properties

Then we can define the process order messages, shown in Code 8. For the sake of simplicity we will ignore error conditions and associated messages:

```
<definitions name="correlatedMessages"
targetNamespace="http://example.com/processOrderMessages.wsdl"
xmlns:pom="http://example.com/processOrderMessages.wsdl"
xmlns:poc="http://example.com/processOrderCorrelation.wsdl"
xmlns:bpws="http://schemas.xmlsoap.org/ws/2003/03/business-
process/"
xmlns="http://schemas.xmlsoap.org/wsdl/">
<!-- define types for Process Order and dispatch information -->
     <types>
           <xsd:schema>
           <xsd:complexType name="ProcessOrder">
                 <xsd:element name="CID" type="xsd:string"/>
                 <xsd:element name="order" type="xsd:int"/>
                 ...
           </xsd:complexType>
           <xsd:complexType name="ProcessOrderResponse">
                 <xsd:element name="CID" type="xsd:string"/>
                 <xsd:element name="order" type="xsd:int"/>
                 ...
           </xsd:complexType>
           <xsd:complexType name="Dispatch">
                 <xsd:element name="VID" type="xsd:string"/>
                 <xsd:element name="dispNum" type="xsd:int"/>
           </xsd:complexType>
           </xsd:schema>
     </types>
```

```
    <message name="POMessage">
          <part name="PO" type="pom:ProcessOrder"/>
    </message>
    <message name="POResponse">
          <part name="PO" type="pom:ProcessOrder"/>
    </message>
    <message name="DispatchMessage">
          <part name="IVC" type="pom:Dispatch"/>
    </message>
    <bpws:propertyAlias propertyName="poc:customerID"
    messageType="pom:POMessage" part="PO"
    query="/PO/CID"/>
    <bpws:propertyAlias propertyName="poc:orderNumber"
    messageType="pom:POMessage" part="PO"
    query="/PO/Order"/>
    <bpws:propertyAlias propertyName="poc:dispatchNumber"
    messageType="pom:DispMessage" part="IVC"
    query="/IVC/InvNum"/>
    ...
</definitions>
```

Code 8. The process order messages

Finally, the portType used is defined, in a separate WSDL document, as shown in Code 9. This example shows both the synchronous (request-response) and asynchronous (one-way) operations.

```
<definitions name="orderingPortType"
targetNamespace="http://example.com/ordering.wsdl"
xmlns:pom="http://example.com/processOrderMessages.wsdl"
xmlns="http://schemas.xmlsoap.org/wsdl/">
      <portType name="OrderingPortType">
            <operation name="SynchronousOrder">
                  <input message="pom:POMessage"/>
                  <output message="pom:POResponse"/>
            </operation>
            <operation name="AsynchronousOrder">
                  <input message="pom:POMessage"/>
            </operation>
      </portType>
      <portType name="OrderSubmitterPT">
            <operation name="AsynchronousOrderResponse">
                  <input message="pom:POResponse"/>
```

```
            </operation>
        </portType>
</definitions>
```

Code 9. Process order portType

Both the properties and their mapping to purchase order and invoice messages will be used in the correlation set examples shown in Code 10:

```
<correlationSets
xmlns:poc="http://example.com/processOrderCorrelation.wsdl">
<!-- Order numbers are particular to a customer, this set is
carried in application data -->
      <correlationSet name="ProcessOrder"
properties="poc:customerID poc:orderNumber"/>

<!-- Dispatch numbers are particular to a completed order, this
set is carried in application data -->
      <correlationSet name="Dispatch"
      properties="poc:invoiceNumber"/>
</correlationSets>
```

Code 10. The process order correlation sets

If we take the case of the ProcessOrder operation, then we can see how it is supposed to work. Figure 5 shows the interaction messages between the client and the process order service in a UML interaction diagram. For simplicity we have omitted the interactions between the Orchestrator and the internal processes we saw in Figure 4. In this case the `customerID` and `orderNumber` will be associated with the request message. The combination of the values of these properties must be unique in the scope of this workflow. Any response message will also have these values associated with it such that the response can be delivered to the right process instance. As we have already mentioned, it is up to the BPEL implementation to ensure that these messages are correctly delivered, so all you need to do is make sure that a correlation set is appropriately defined and related to your message invocations.

Now that we have seen how to create business relationships and manage the interactions between them through correlation sets, we need to discuss how an actual workflow (or business process interaction flow) can be defined within BPEL. We will do that in the next section, where we will discuss in some detail the different types of interaction patterns that BPEL supports.

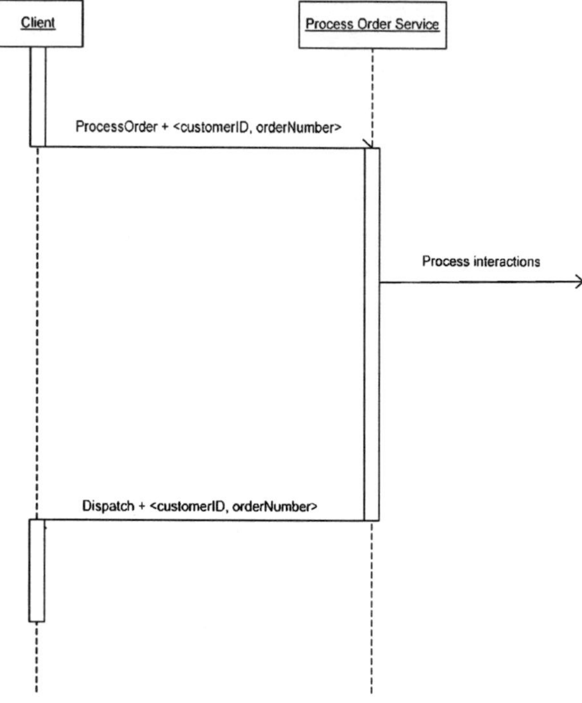

***Figure 5.* Client Interactions with the Order Process System**

2.5. Activities

As we saw when first talking about workflow systems, they are typically used when controlling the flow of an application within a corporate intranet. However, there is nothing intrinsically restrictive about workflow models that prevent them from being used across an enterprise boundary. In fact this is precisely the area where BPEL is aimed: describing inter-enterprise business interactions, where the individual business processes from each enterprise are represented as Web services.

BPEL models all stages of a workflow as *activities*. Activities are composed into *scopes* to form algorithmic workflows. Each scope has a primary activity that defines its normal behavior; the primary activity can be arbitrarily complex and be composed of many sub-activities (nested activities). In this case, the scope is shared by all nested activities.

In order to execute a process, we must have some means of describing its behavior. The BPEL language provides a number of fundamental activities which form the basic building blocks of the workflow and provide support to manipulate data, iterate, call external functions etc., and how to compose these primitives into meaningful workflows. The language also provides for the structuring of activities to manage control flow dependencies in a workflow. They are responsible for serializing and parallelizing activities, choosing from alternative paths in a workflow, etc.

BPEL classifies these activities as either *basic* or *structured* types. Basic activities deal with state management, communication and exception handling, while structured activities deal with process control-flow issues. In the following sections we will briefly examine the different activity types. If you are familiar with most high-level programming languages (e.g., C++, Java, C# etc.), then most of the principles behind these primitives should be fairly intuitive.

2.5.1. <assign>

This construct can be used to update the values of variables with new data (e.g., messages). It can contain any number of elementary assignments and it is important to understand that the type of the source from which the data comes *must* be the same as the type of the destination to which it is being assigned.

A typical example of assignment is where the contents of one message are copied into another. This is illustrated in Code 11, where the address details of a customer placing a purchase order are copied to some dispatch data prior to shipping the order.

```
<assign>
     <copy>
        <from variable="processOrder" part="customerAddress"/>
        <to variable="dispatchData" part="customerAddress"/>
     </copy>
</assign>
```

Code 11. An assign example

The syntax for `<assign>` is actually quite powerful. The syntax for from is captured in Code 12:

```
<from variable="ncname" part="ncname"?/>
<from partnerLink="ncname"
endpointReference="myRole|partnerRole"/>
<from variable="ncname" property="qname"/>
<from expression="general-expr"/>
<from> ... literal value ... </from>
```

Code 12. The assign-from syntax

The to field must be one of the following, shown in Code 13:

```
<to variable="ncname" part="ncname"?/>
<to partnerLink="ncname"/>
<to variable="ncname" property="qname"/>
```

Code 13. The assign-to syntax

As we saw in the example, the first from and to variants simply provide the name of the variable. If the type of the variable is a WSDL message, then the optional part attribute can be used to provide the name of a part within that variable (so that only a subset of the message can be selected).

The second variation of from and to allows for dynamic manipulation of the endpoint references associated with partner links. The value of the partnerLink attributed is the name of a partnerLink declared in the process. You can see that in the case of from, the role of the link must be specified: this is because a process may need to communicate an endpoint reference corresponding to either its own role or that of the partner's role.

The third form of from and to allows the manipulation of message properties. They provide a way to clearly define how distinguished data elements in messages can be used. The fourth form of from allows processed to perform basic computations on properties and variables, while the fifth allows a literal value to be given as the source value.

Let us look at how some of the other features of <assign> could be used. Assume we have three variables customerName, dispatchToName, and dispatchToAddress, representing the name of the customer who places a purchase order, the name of the person to whom the order should be dispatched and the address to use when dispatching the order, respectively, as shown in Code 14:

```
<variable name="customerName" messageType="foo:person"/>
<variable name="dispatchToName" messageType="foo:person"/>
<variable name="dispatchToAddress" element="foo:address"/>
```

Code 14 Variable setups

The BPEL sample below illustrates copying one variable to another as well as copying a part of a variable to a compatible element type:

```
<assign>
      <copy>
            <from variable="customerName"/>
```

```
            <to variable="dispatchToName"/>
      </copy>
      <copy>
            <from variable="customerName" part="address"/>
            <to variable="dispatchToAddress"/>
      </copy>
</assign>
```

Code 15. An extended assign example

2.5.2. <receive>

Web service operations are exposed to the outside world by a `receive` activity. This construct allows the business process to do a blocking wait for a matching message to arrive. The `receive` activity is the workflow entity which a WSDL operation maps onto, and so it specifies the `partner` it expects to invoke the corresponding operation, and `portType` and `operation` that it expects the partner to invoke.

Code 16 shows the `<receive>` activity that the purchase order system might expose as its `ProcessOrder` operation. The workflow uses a variable called `PO` to hold incoming messages from customers. When a `POMessage` is received from a customer the `<receive>` activity is activated and a new instance of the workflow is created to run.

```
<variables>
      <variable name="PO" messageType="POMessage">
</variables>
<receive partnerLink="ordering" portType="purchaseOrderPortType"
operation="ProcessOrder" variable="PO">
</receive>
```

Code 16. A receive example

`<receive>` is a blocking activity, which means that any workflow process that depends upon the receipt of an appropriate message cannot execute until that event occurs. The creation of process instances in BPEL is always implicit. Activities that receive messages (`<receive>` and the `<pick>` activity we will see later) can be annotated to indicate that the triggering of that activity should cause a new instance of the business process to be created. This is done by setting the `createInstance` attribute on the activity to "yes". To be instantiated, each business process must contain at least one such start (initial) activity; obviously such an activity cannot have a preceding activity in the flow.

In some cases it may be possible for a flow to be started by the arrival of one of a number of different messages and it may not be possible to determine a priori which message will arrive first (it is non-deterministic). To cater for this situation, BPEL allows multiple initial activities to be declared. It is up to the BPEL implementation to determine which of the concurrent arriving messages will actually trigger the instantiation of the workflow, though this will typically be the first message to arrive. Subsequent messages will be routed to the newly created workflow.

2.5.3. <invoke>

This construct allows the business process to invoke a one-way or request-response operation on a portType offered by a partner. In order to execute a request-response operation, two variables are required for input (request) and output (response) messages.

```
<invoke partnerLink="PlacePurchaseOrder"
      portType="PurchaseOrderSystemPortType"
      operation="ProcessOrder"
      inputVariable="CustomerDetails"
      outputVariable="InvoiceDetails"/>
```

Code 17. An invoke example

In Code 17, the invoke activity calls the ProcessOrder operation (from the PurchaseOrderSystemPortType which is exposed by the PlacePurchaseOrder partner) when a message from the CustomerDetails variable is received. The result of executing the operation is the placement of a message in the InvoiceDetails variable. Obviously sending a message may result in an error (the recipient has crashed, for example), so a request-response operation may also have to deal with fault messages, but we will look at those later.

An asynchronous one-way operation is slightly simpler, since there is no outputVariable. This would fit the scenario where interactions between partners may occur over a long period of time, for example, as illustrated in Figure 5. The response to a given one-way operation would then be another one-way operation. If you consider the example above, we could imagine separating the message request for the purchase from the message response that is the invoice into two one-way interactions.

2.5.4. <reply>

This construct allows the business process to send a synchronous message in reply to a message that was received through a <receive>. The combination of a <receive> and a <reply> forms a request/response operation on the WSDL portType for the process.

```
<reply partnerLink="purchasing" portType="purchaseOrderPortType"
      operation="sendPurchaseOrder" variable="Invoice"/>
```

Code 18 A reply example

In Code 18 you can see the purchaseOrder system's response to the initial purchase request. The purchasing partner is sent a message from the Invoice variable (which contains messages with invoice details), as a result of invoking the sendPurchaseOrder operation.

2.5.5. <throw>

This activity generates a fault from inside the business process. Every fault is required to have a globally unique name, and the <throw> must provide the name for the fault; it can optionally provide additional data (via variables) that may give more information about the fault. A *fault handler* can then use the data to inspect and handle the fault and perhaps use the information to populate any fault messages that may need to be sent to other services; we will examine fault handlers in the next section.

```
<throw faultName="CustomerNotSubscribed"
            faultVariable="CustomerOrderFailureVariable"/>
```

Code 19. A throw example

For example, in Code 19, we have slightly modified the orderProcess flow that we have seen already. In this case, only customers who have previously subscribed with the system are allowed to place orders. Therefore, in the case where a customer who has not subscribed attempts to place an order, the <throw> activity will populate the CustomerOrderFailureVariable with sufficient data so that the workflow process that deals with the initial placement of orders can create an appropriate failure message and sent it to the prospective customer.

2.5.6. <catch>

Handling faults is also follows a similar pattern to common programming languages like C++, Java, and C#. A <catch> declaration is used to handle specific faults occurring within a scope, and a catchAll declaration within the activity's scope faultHandlers declarations will handle any faults not handled by a more specific <catch> at the same scope.

For example, in Code 20 we have defined two specific faults that clients of our order process system may encounter when attempting to place an order and which we can handle explicitly: the CustomerNotSubscribed fault we mentioned earlier and a fault that indicates that the system may be unavailable (e.g., crashed), OrderProcessSystemNotResponding. However, other faults may arise that cannot be handled by these two fault handlers and in which case we rely on the catchall activity.

```
<bpws:faultHandlers>
  <bpws:catch faultName="CustomerNotSubscribed">
    <!-- Handle the fault -->
  </bpws:catch>
  <bpws:catch faultName="OrderProcessSystemNotResponding">
    <!-- Handle the fault -->
  </bpws:catch>
  <bpws:catchAll>
    <!-- Unexpected fault, shutdown -->
...
  </bpws:catchAll>
</bpws:faultHandlers>
```

Code 20 An example of using the catch activity

2.5.7. <terminate>

When this activity is carried out, the process instance is immediately terminated without the ongoing work being undone and compensated. The BPEL implementation must terminate all running activities in the process as soon as possible without any attempt at fault handling.

If we look at Code 21, we can now use <terminate> in the catchall block to exit the process if any unexpected error occurs. Obviously, this may not be the best course of action for all processes, but this is just an example.

```
<bpws:faultHandlers>
  <bpws:catch faultName="CustomerNotSubscribed">
    <!-- Handle the fault -->
  </bpws:catch>
  <bpws:catch faultName="OrderProcessSystemNotResponding">
    <!-- Handle the fault -->
  </bpws:catch>
  <bpws:catchAll>
    <!-- Unexpected fault, shutdown -->
<terminate/>
  </bpws:catchAll>
</bpws:faultHandlers>
```

Code 21 Using terminate in the catchall handler

2.5.8. <sequence>

This construct allows you to define a collection of activities to be performed sequentially in lexical order (the order in which they occur in the syntax). In the example below, the sub-activities are executed serially.

```
<sequence>
<invoke partnerLink="paymentAuthorization" .../>
<invoke partnerLink="dispatch" .../>
<invoke partnerLink="paymentCapture" .../>
</sequence>
```

Code 22 An example of the sequence activity

2.5.9. <flow>

This construct allows you to specify one or more activities to be performed concurrently. A `<flow>` completes when all of its constituent activities have completed. If you look back at the process order scenario depicted in Figure 3, it is possible to see that when an order is first made, the Authorization stage (whether the client can place orders) and the checking of whether the order can be fulfilled, occur in parallel. How this may be accomplished in BPEL is shown in Code 23, where the two `<invoke>` activities (`PaymentAuthorization` and `CheckStock`) are enabled to start concurrently as soon as the `<flow>` is started. The `<flow>` completes when both of the activities respond (we will assume they are invoked in a synchronous request/response manner). The Dispatch is invoked only after the `<flow>` completes (we will assume that there are no preceding errors).

```
<sequence>
      <flow>
            <invoke partnerLink="PaymentAuthorization" .../>
            <invoke partnerLink="CheckStock" .../>
      </flow>
<invoke partnerLink="Dispatch" .../>
</sequence>
```

Code 23 The process order example in BPEL

In the example above, the two concurrent activities have no dependencies between them. This is not always going to be the case and synchronization dependencies will exist between activities in a `<flow>`, i.e., some activities may have to be executed in a specific order. As such, BPEL provides a link construct that can be used to express these dependencies. A `link` is named and all links in a `<flow>` must be defined separately. Two activities can be linked together using `source` and `target` elements. Every link must have precisely one activity in the `<flow>` as its `source` and precisely one `<flow>` activity as its target. The source may also specify a transition condition through the `transitionCondition` attribute of the source element. All links that do not have an explicit `transitionCondition` attribute have a default attribute associated with them with a value of true.

BPEL provides another XPath extension to assist in using `links`, which is shown in Code 24:

```
bpws:getLinkStatus ('linkName')
```

Code 24 The XPath function for checking the status of a link

This function returns a Boolean value which indicates the status of the link in the parameter. The status of a link is determined by evaluating its `transitionCondition` attribute. This evaluation occurs on the actual values of the variables referenced in the expression, so if they are also modifiable via a concurrent path, the result may be non-deterministic. If the evaluated result is true then the status is positive, otherwise it is negative.

`getLinkStatus` can only be used in a `<join>` condition. The parameter must refer to the name of an incoming link for the activity associated with the `<join>`.

In the example shown in Code 25, we have taken the example of sourcing a book from an online book shop, pricing shipping and handling and insurance costs, and then charging the entire cost to a bank account. Locating the book, shipping and handling and insurance costs can all occur in parallel and the example BPEL code shows this because each service interaction is a separate `<sequence>` or `<invoke>`.

However, the final operation, debiting the bank account, cannot occur until all three previous activities have completed. This is ensured because it is related to the other activities through the `link` synchronizations defined at the top of the `<flow>`.

```
<bpws:flow>
  <bpws:links>
    <bpws:link name="BookCost"/>
    <bpws:link name="ShippingCost"/>
    <bpws:link name="InsuranceCost"/>
  </bpws:links>
<bpws:flow>
   <!-- Buy the book -->
   <bpws:sequence>
     <bpws:invoke name="OnlineBookShopInvocation"
       partner="BookShop">
       ...
     </bpws:invoke>
     <bpws:receive name="BookShopResponse" ...>
       <bpws:source link="BookCost" .../>
     </bpws:receive>
   </bpws:sequence>

   <!-- Buy shipping and handling -->
   <bpws:sequence>
     <bpws:invoke name="ShippingInvocation"
       partner="ShippingAndHandlingService">
       ...
     </bpws:invoke>
     <bpws:receive name="ShippingResponse" ...>
       <bpws:source link="ShippingCost" .../>
     </bpws:receive>
   </bpws:sequence>

   <!-- Buy insurance -->
   <bpws:invoke name="InsuranceInvocation"
     partner="InsuranceBroker">
     <bpws:source link="InsuranceCost"/>
     ...
   </bpws:invoke>

  <!-- Online bank account -->
  <bpws:invoke name="BankAccountInvocation"
    partner="Bank" ...>
```

```
      <bpws:target link="BookCost"/>
      <bpws:target link="ShippingCost"/>
      <bpws:target link="InsuranceCost"/>
      ...
    </bpws:invoke>
  </bpws:flow>
```

Code 25. An example of flow and link

2.5.10. <scope>

This construct allows you to define a nested activity with its own associated variables, fault handlers and compensation handler. It is a way of allowing activities to share common error handling and compensation routines. A `<scope>` consists of the primary activity that defines the behaviour of the `<scope>`, a set of optional fault handlers and a single optional compensation handler. Each `<scope>` can be named, which is important when you may have to refer to one `<scope>` from within another.

```
<bpws:scope>
  <bpws:faultHandlers>
    <bpws:catch faultName="OutOfStockFault" .../>
    <bpws:catch faultName="UnknownStockFault" .../>
    <bpws:catch faultName="UnauthorizedClientFault" .../>
    <bpws:catchAll>
      <bpws:compensate/>
    </bpws:catchAll>
  </bpws:faultHandlers>
  <!-- place order -->
</bpws:scope>
```

Code 26. An example of the scope activity

Code 26 illustrates how an order may be placed against the `processOrderApplication`. At the bottom of the `<scope>` is the normal behaviour of the activity, i.e., the placement of an order by a client. However, the `<scope>` declares a number of fault handlers with `catch` activities; the aim of these handlers it to provide a means to cope with the different types of failures that may occur during the order placement process. For example, the quantity of the item that is required by the client may not be available in the warehouse and as such an error message (`OutOfStockFault`) will be returned and caught; the process then had the opportunity to try something else, e.g., request less stock, or wait until the warehouse has been restocked.

The `catchall` handler has been declared slightly differently in this example: if we assume that the other fault handlers allow the application to continue to make forward progress (albeit at a reduced capacity), what happens if an error occurs that simply cannot be handled in this way or is unexpected? The answer is that in these situations the entire `<scope>` may have to be compensated. In the example, the compensate activity runs the `compensationHandler` for all of the inner scopes, which will perform any work necessary to bring the application to the state it had before the scope was executed. If nested scopes were named, it would be possible to limit the compensation to a specific scope.

```
<scope>
      <compensationHandler>
            <invoke partnerLink="Buyer"
    portType="SP:OrderPlacement"
            operation="CancelOrder"
            inputVariable="getResponse"
            outputVariable="getConfirmation">
            </invoke>
      </compensationHandler>
</scope>
```

Code 27. A compensationHandler example

Compensation is an important requirement for long running business processes and had existed in workflow systems from the start. Automatic compensation of failures is possible in only the simplest of situations for business transactions, which rely on traditional ACID transaction systems to scope their work. In these cases, backward compensation is provided for by the underlying transaction system, which does not have (nor does it need to have) any semantic knowledge of the application or what it is compensating. However, in the case of long running business transactions, ACID transactions are unsuitable and automatic compensation is not possible: in order to compensate for complex business-to-business interactions does require semantic knowledge of the application. As such, compensation handlers have to be written by the application programmer, since this where the semantic knowledge resides.

Where fault handlers provide alternative forward execution paths through a `scope`, compensation handlers, when invoked, undo the work performed by a `scope`. Since a `compensationHandler` for a specific `scope` reverses that scope's work, the handler can potentially be as complex and intricate as the scope's normal original activity.

A compensationHandler can also be set to compensate an entire business process after its normal completion (instead of individual scopes).

2.5.11. <wait>

This construct allows a process to unconditionally wait for a given (fixed amount) time period or until a certain time has passed. A typical use for this feature is shown in Code 28, where the *checkStock* process waits for a specific time before it checks.

```
<bpws:while condition="true">
  <!-- XML Schema string form 24 hours -->
  <bpws:wait until="'2004-11-12T18:00+01:00'"/>
  <!-- Inventory process -->
</bpws:while>
```

Code 28. An example of the wait activity

2.5.12. <pick>

This activity type allows you to block and wait for a suitable message to arrive or for a timeout to expire. When one of these triggering events occurs, the associated activity is performed. A <pick> activity declares events that it will trigger on and corresponding activities to execute once those events occur. Events can take the form of either the receipt of a message or a time-based event including both duration (time relative from now) and deadline (fixed future time).

It is possible for a <pick> activity to be the first activity executed by a workflow by being the first recipient of a message in that workflow, in which case it acts like a receive activity and is annotated with a createInstance="yes" attribute.

Irrespective of whether or not a <pick> activity is used to instantiate a workflow instance, every such activity contains at least one onMessage event. For those <pick> activities which do not instantiate workflows, the onMessage events constrain the scope in which the activity becomes active.

An example <pick> activity is shown in Code 29, where the activity waits on a response message from the checkStock system via its onMessage declaration. In this example, the checkStock system should respond within 1 day and 10 hours or an error is assumed to have occurred and a timeout is triggered through the onAlarm; we will assume some fault handling mechanism is executed here.

```
<bpws:pick createInstance="no">
  <bpws:onMessage partner="CheckStock"
    portType="CheckStockPortType"
    operation="checkResponse" variable="WarehouseResponses">
    <bpws:correlations>
       <bpws:correlation set="BookingsCorrelationSet"/>
    </bpws:correlations>
    <!-- Continue with booking -->
  </bpws:onMessage>
  <bpws:onAlarm for="'P1DT10H'">
    <!-- Stock warehouse did not respond! Problem! -->
  </bpws:onAlarm>
</bpws:pick>
```

Code 29. An example of a pick activity

2.5.13. <switch>

This construct allows you to select exactly one branch of activity from a set of possible choices. It is similar in name and design to switch statements you will find in popular languages such as C++ and Java. As you can see in Code 30 (which illustrates the `checkStock` process using the `getVariableProperty` XPath extension we discussed earlier), the `case` activity consists of an ordered list of one or more conditional branches (defined by `case` elements), followed by an optional `otherwise` branch (the same as the `default` case branch in most programming languages).

```
<bpws:switch>
  <bpws:case condition="bpws:getVariableProperty(stockLevel,
                                             level) < 10" >
    <!-- place a high priority request for more stock -->
  </bpws:case>
  <bpws:case condition="bpws:getVariableProperty(stockLevel,
                                             level) <=  100" >
    <!-- place a low priority request for more stock -->
  </bpws:case>
  <bpws:otherwise>
    <!-- stock level is ok -->
  </bpws:otherwise>
</bpws:switch>
```

Code 30. An example of the switch activity

2.5.14. <while>

This construct allows you to indicate that an activity is to be repeated until a certain success criteria has been met. For example, as shown in Code 31, part of the `checkStock` process checks the level of stock in the warehouse and while it remains below a threshold level it places a request for more stock and waits until the request has been fulfilled.

```
...
<variable name="stockLevel" type="xsd:integer"/>
...
<while condition= "bpws:getVariableData(stockLevel) <= 10">
<scope>
      <!-- place order for more stock -->
</scope>
</while>
```

Code 31. A while activity example

2.5.15. <empty>

This construct (shown in Code 32) allows for the insertion of a null-operation instruction into a business process, which may be useful for synchronization of concurrent activities.

```
<empty standard-attributes>
      standard-elements
</empty>
```

Code 32. Syntax of the empty activity

So far we have discussed how to define business relationships and manage their interactions. However, we have not talked about *transactions*: the ability to scope units of work such that either all of that work happens or none of it does, despite failures of any of the processes involved in the work. As we saw earlier, when BPEL4WS was originally released, it came with two other specifications; the WS-Coordination and WS-Transaction specifications. Although we will talk much more about transactions in a later chapter, it is worth discussing how they relate to BPEL in the following section.

2.6. Transactions

At this stage you may be wondering about the relationship between BPEL and Web Services transactions. For example, in some cases it may seem appropriate to map a `<scope>` with its `compensationHandlers` to an atomic transaction: the `<scope>` is the body of the transaction, while the compensation is the normal behavior of a transaction that is forced to roll back (abort). However, you will have noticed that none of the BPEL elements mention transactions and neither does the OASIS specification. The reasons for a lack of transactions in BPEL are both technical and political. As we will see in Chapter 7, the traditional transaction model is not always appropriate in a long running business process example. As such, other transaction models (such as those based on forward compensation techniques) may be more appropriate. Chapter 7 will show that these extended transaction models (and specifications based around them) exist in the area of Web Services. Unfortunately, none of them have yet become the standard for Web Services transactions.

The original BPEL4WS specification did refer to the IBM, Microsoft and BEA Web Services Transactions specification. However, since BPEL has entered OASIS, it has gained a wider audience who are not as ready to jump on the proprietary IBM, Microsoft and BEA bandwagon of specifications in other areas. One proposed solution in the BPEL standards process was to abstract away from the specifics of a give transaction specification: define *what* is required without defining *how* it is implemented. The other solution was to remove transactions entirely. Due to time constraints, at this moment the BPEL committee has settled on the latter solution.

What this means is that BPEL implementations do not have to provide any transaction support in order to be compliant with the specification. However, in our experience, when deploying workflow systems inter- and intra-enterprise, some form of transaction support (whether it be traditional ACID transactions or forward compensation-based transactions) is required. Therefore, it is likely that the more advanced and enterprise ready BPEL implementations will provide transaction support over and above what the OASIS specification requires. Obviously this may affect the portability of any workflows implemented.

To help place all of what we have just discussed into context and make it much more concrete, in the rest of this chapter we will look at a worked example. We will slowly build up this example, using various aspects of BPEL that we have mentioned, to illustrate how it can be applied to fairly complex business relationships.

3. A Worked Example of Web Services Orchestration

To illustrate the utility of BPEL we will now take our processOrder scenario and show how it could be implemented using the BPEL 1.1 language. To do this we obviously need a BPEL implementation. For an area that is relatively new to Web Services, there are already a large number of implementations. In the J2EE space, for example, there are:

- Collaxa BPEL Server (http://www.collaxa.com), now owned by Oracle,
- IBM BPWS4J (http://www.alphaworks.ibm.com/tech/bpws4j) for IBM WebSphere Application Server,
- OpenStorm Service Orchestrator (http://www.openstorm.com), and
- Vergil VCAB Server (http://www.vergiltech.com/products_VCAB.php),

while in the .NET space:

- Microsoft BizTalk 2004 (http://www.microsoft.com/biztalk/), and
- OpenStorm Service Orchestrator (http://www.openstorm.com).

It is worth noting that many vendors are splitting their offerings into the *graphical design-time tool*, which should produce vendor-neutral BPEL flows, and the *run-time execution engine*, which is used to drive these flows. Although you could write BPEL scripts in any editor (after all, it is only XML schema), BPEL is extremely powerful and complex, with the result that your application structures may also become complex. Using a graphical tool to layout the flows is much better as they allow you to see immediately this structure and assist in reasoning about it, especially in the case of failures.

For this chapter we have chosen to use the offerings from Collaxa, who were an independent company until 2004 when they were acquired by Oracle, who is now offering the product embedded in their Web Services toolkit. However, it is still possible to use the software stand-alone or with other application servers.

The Collaxa BPEL implementation is split into two components: the design-time graphical tool (Collaxa BPEL Designer 1.0.3), and the run-time BPEL engine (Collaxa BPEL Server v2.0 rc6).

Note that it is not going to be possible to demonstrate all of the functionality available from the BPEL language in the scenario we have been using. Neither will it be possible to show the full power and flexibility of the tools we will use. However, we hope to give you a flavor of what is possible with BPEL and encourage you to explore this area more. As we have already said, tying together Web Services into process flows offers a powerful opportunity to leverage existing infrastructural investments without being tied into one specific vendor.

The example scenario we are going to look at in more depth is the order process example we have seen throughout this chapter and is illustrated in Figure 3. Unfortunately, to show how to implement this entire scenario in BPEL, covering all aspects including failure cases, will take more space than we have available. Therefore, we will concentrate on one specific aspect of the scenario, the payment authorization segment, and give an overview of how the rest could be tackled.

4. Design-Time Demonstration

In this section we will look at what it means to design a BPEL application using the tools available. We will examine the design tool and process execution engine and explain the fundamental steps in implementing this scenario.

4.1. Task Definitions

If you look at the process order scenario again, you will see that there is the *processOrderApplication*, which will be a single Web Service, and four sub-tasks:

1. *paymentAuthorization*: this task determines whether or not the client of *processOrderApplication* is allowed to place orders. What criteria this uses will depend upon the implementation, but for now we will assume it is based on the name of the client.

2. *checkStock*: this task determines whether or not there is sufficient stock available to fulfill the client's order. Again, what criteria it uses will be implementation-dependent, and we have already discussed some alternatives in this chapter and how they might be implemented in BPEL.

3. *dispatch*: this task is responsible for fulfilling and sending the clients order. This could involve another BPEL process flow, for example between the *processOrderApplication* vendor and the delivery company.

4. *paymentCapture*: this task bills the client. Again it could involve another flow, for example with an online bank facility.

As we have already mentioned, to show how all of this scenario could be implemented in BPEL will consume too much space. So, we will concentrate on the *paymentAuthorization* task and how it is related to the overall *processOrderApplication* service.

Note that in the following examples we are going to use basic Web Service implementations that do very little in the way of real business process. This is because we are going to focus on BPEL and how the scripting language can be used to glue together Web Services. As we mentioned at the start of this chapter, the advantage of the Service-Oriented Architecture approach to application development is that the underlying implementations of specific services can change without affecting the application. Therefore, replacing the basic Web Services with real-world equivalents is straightforward, but beyond the scope of this chapter because of space limitations.

4.2. The ProcessOrderApplication Flow

We begin by defining the *processOrderApplication* Web Service (and by definition, the global coordinating BPEL flow). In the Collaxa Designer, this is straightforward: you simply create a new project and the design tool will populate it with templates for the services' WSDL and the flow.

If you look at Figure 6, you can see how this appears in the graphical designer, with the input (`<receive>`) and response (`<reply>`) activities labeled. Part of the XML corresponding to the *ProcessOrderApplication* definition of the basic types and service WSDL is shown in Code 33 (we have removed some of the elements for brevity).

```
<types>
    <element name="ProcessOrderApplicationRequest">
        <complexType>
            <sequence>
                <element name="clientName" type="string"/>
                <element name="item" type="string"/>
                <element name="delivery-address"
                type="string"/>
            </sequence>
        </complexType>
    </element>
    <element name="ProcessOrderApplicationResponse">
        <complexType>
            <sequence>
                <element name="result" type="string"/>
```

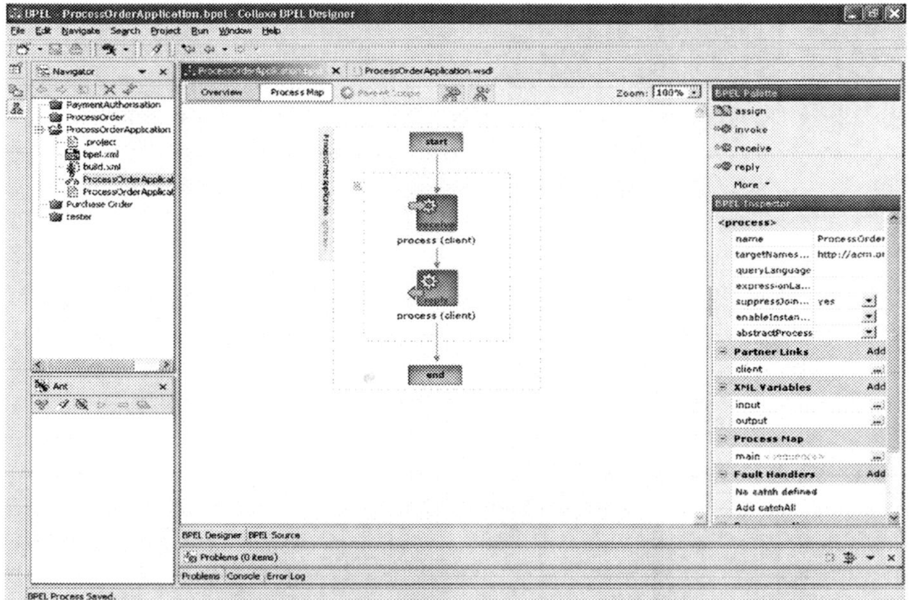

Figure 6. **Initial ProcessOrderApplication BPEL Flow**

```
            </sequence>
        </complexType>
    </element>
 </types>
<message name="ProcessOrderApplicationRequestMessage">
    <part name="payload"
    element="tns:ProcessOrderApplicationRequest"/>
 </message>
 <message name="ProcessOrderApplicationResponseMessage">
    <part name="payload"
    element="tns:ProcessOrderApplicationResponse"/>
 </message>
 <portType name="ProcessOrderApplication">
    <operation name="process">
        <input message=
        "tns:ProcessOrderApplicationRequestMessage"/>
        <output message=
        "tns:ProcessOrderApplicationResponseMessage"/>
    </operation>
```

Code 33. The BPEL process definition for ProcessOrderApplication

As you can see from the `portType`, the Web Service that clients interact with has an input and an output (for simplicity we will model this as a synchronous invocation). The invocation from the client (`input`) is expected to carry the client's name, the name of the item being requested and the delivery address for the order (assuming that it is allowed and can be fulfilled). The response to the client (`output`) will eventually be a string indicating whether or not the order has been allowed. We will add error handling later.

4.3. The PaymentAuthorization Sub-Task

At the moment our flow does not do much, so let us move on to the *paymentAuthorization* sub-task. As with the previous service, we will define a `PaymentAuthorization` Web Service and associated BPEL flow from scratch. Obviously if you already have a Web Service defined and implemented, then you would be able to import that definition to this flow instead. By default, the Collaxa designer will give us the same basic message definitions and WSDL templates. So we obviously need to change these to more accurately reflect what this sub-task will do. For simplicity, we will assume that the authorization criterion is that each client must be pre-registered with the order process system before they can place an order. Upon registering, each client is given a unique login name that must be used when making orders; we will assume that the names all begin with "1234".

So the definition of input and output message types for our `PaymentAuthorization` service can be defined as shown in Code 34:

```
<element name="PaymentAuthorizationRequest">
    <complexType>
        <sequence>
            <element name="clientName" type="string"/>
        </sequence>
    </complexType>
</element>
<element name="PaymentAuthorizationResponse">
    <complexType>
        <sequence>
            <element name="result" type="boolean"/>
        </sequence>
    </complexType>
</element>
```

Code 34. The input and output message type definitions for PaymentAuthorization

This will take as input the client's name and then return a Boolean indicating whether or not the client is authorized to place the order. How the actual Web Service performs this validation is an implementation choice and could involve diving down into a specific programming language such as Java or C#. However, the Collaxa design tool gives us the flexibility of staying entirely within the BPEL domain and we will use that because it further illustrates the power of BPEL and some of the activities we previously mentioned.

So, the first thing we want to do is define an `<assign>` activity that will look at the input message for our `PaymentAuthorization` service and based on the contents, determine what the output message will be. We can do this by dragging and dropping an `<assign>` activity to after the `<receive>` activity, but before the `<reply>` activity, as shown in Figure 7.

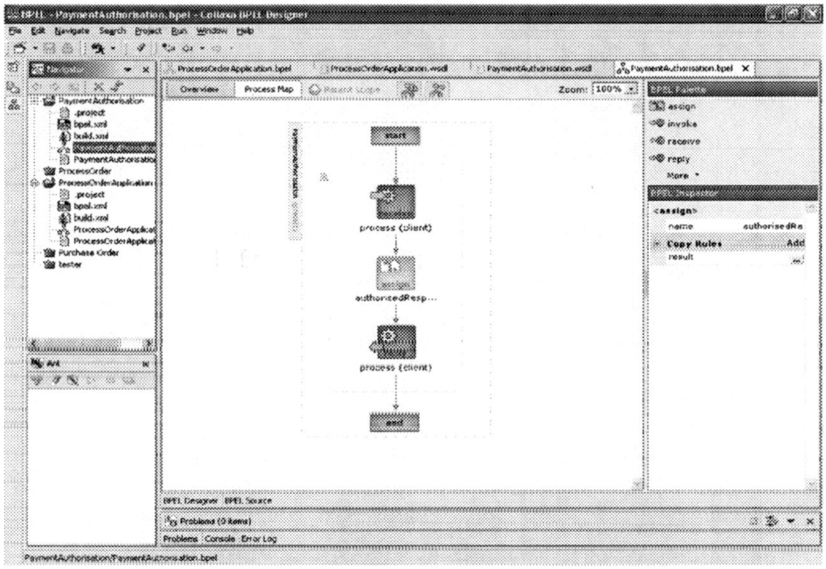

***Figure 7.* PaymentAuthorization and the <assign> Activity**

At this stage we have a blank `<assign>` activity, so we need to make it do something useful. Working within the design tool, we can associate a copy-rule with our activity, as shown in Figure 8.

Here, the from-field is defined as coming from an XPath expression, which uses the input message (the client's name) and checks whether or not it starts with "1234". The entire expression is shown in Code 35:

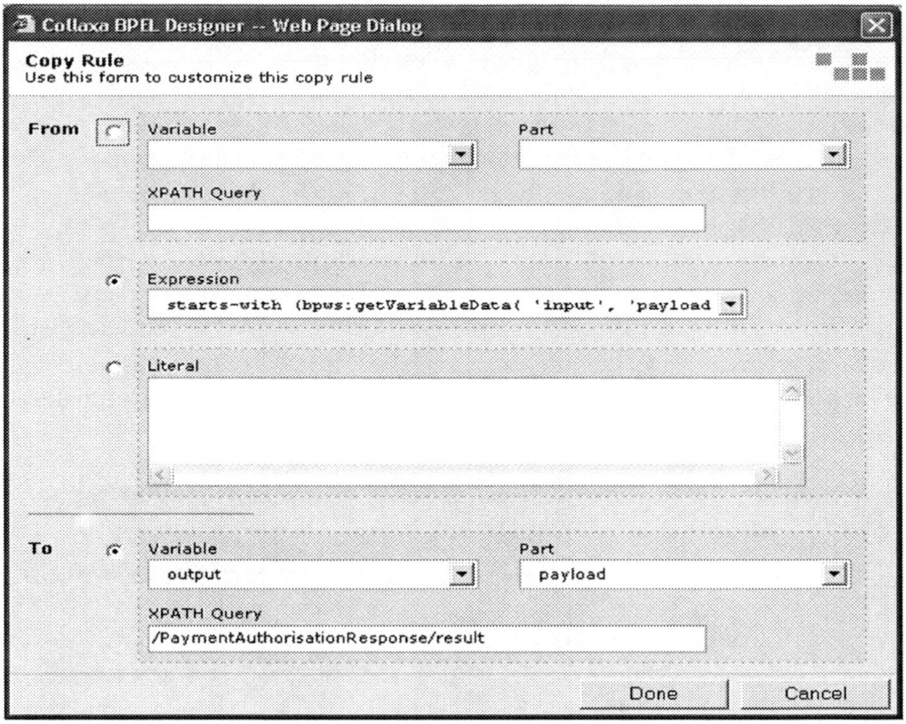

Figure 8. **The PaymentAuthorization Copy Rule**

```
starts-with (bpws:getVariableData( 'input',
'payload','/PaymentAuthorizationRequest/clientName' ), '1234')
```

Code 35. A sample XPath expression

You should recognize the `getVariableData` XPath extension that we mentioned earlier: it was created specifically by the BPEL authors for this kind of use. It works by scanning the payload portion of the input message for the element `clientName` within the `PaymentAuthorizationRequest`.

4.3.1. Testing the Sub-Task within the Design Tool

Using the design tool and the execution engine we can test this flow and associated service. This is shown in Figure 9, where our client requesting an order will be called "`badname`", which obviously should not pass the validation criterion. As you can see, the Collaxa run-time engine provides us with a form that allows us to construct a suitable input message for the flow. It also allows us to send that message to the flow and await a response. This is an important and very useful feature because it allows

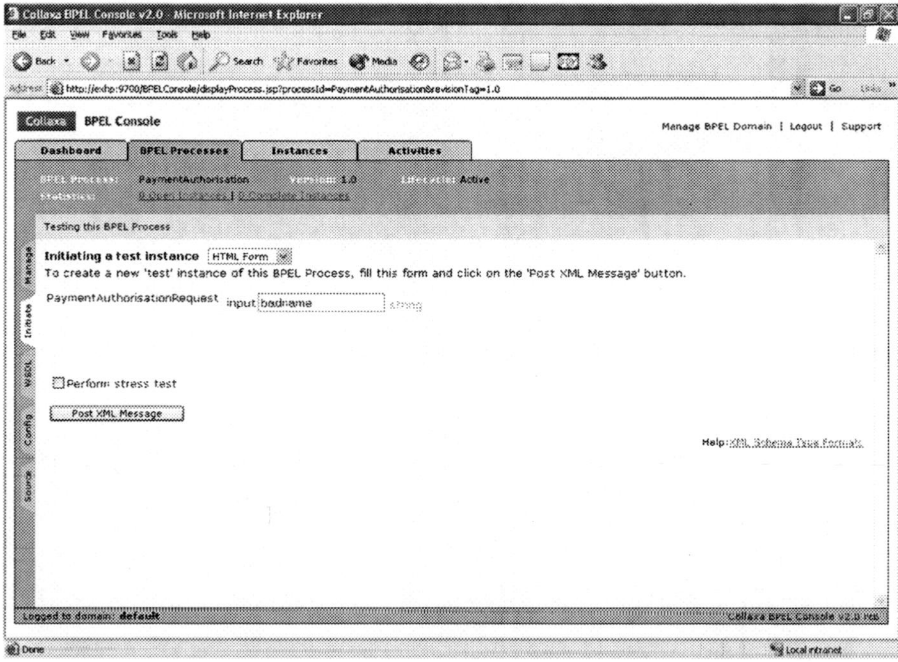

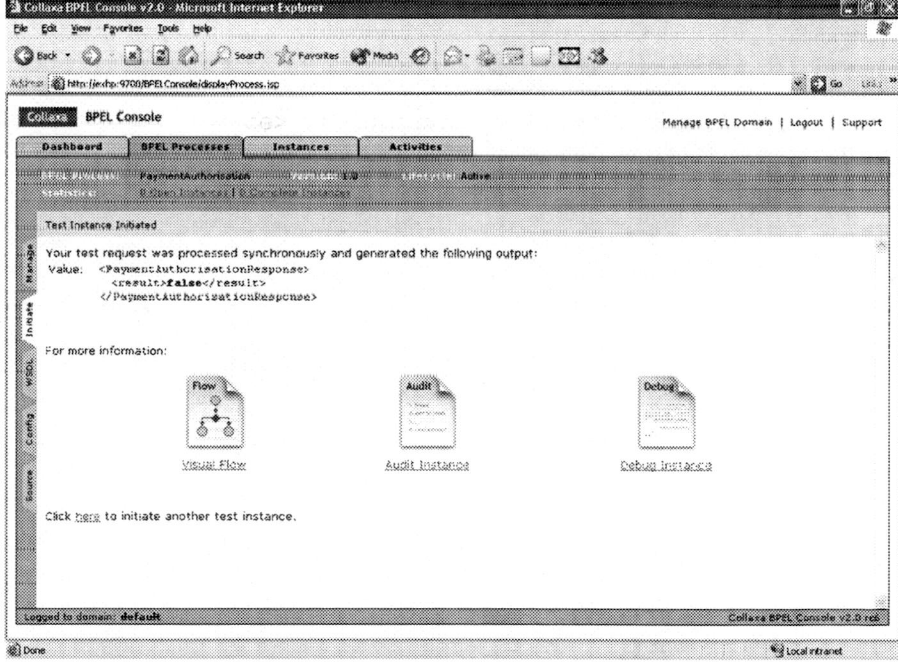

Figure 9. **An Unauthorized Client**

us to stay entirely in the BPEL world in order to test our flow. Even if we eventually replace the sample Web Service with one that does authorization in a more realistic manner, the fact that we can test and validate the required message interaction with a "dummy" service means that we can isolate any future problems to the service implementation or a lack in our requirement specification.

If you are interested in seeing what the equivalent BPEL source is that the design tool has auto-generated for us, then this is shown in Code 36.

```
<!-- PaymentAuthorization BPEL Process -->
<process name="PaymentAuthorization"
targetNamespace="http://acm.org/samples"
suppressJoinFailure="yes"
xmlns:tns="http://acm.org/samples"
xmlns="http://schemas.xmlsoap.org/ws/2003/03/business-process/"
xmlns:bpelx="http://schemas.collaxa.com/bpel/extension">
      <!--
~~~~~~~~~~~~~~~~~~~~~~~~~~~~~~~~~~~~~~~~~~~~~~~~~~~~~~~~~~~~
      PARTNERLINKS:List of services participating in this BPEL
      process
~~~~~~~~~~~~~~~~~~~~~~~~~~~~~~~~~~~~~~~~~~~~~~~~~~~~~~~~~~~ -->
      <partnerLinks>
            <!-- The 'client' role represents the requester of
    this service. -->
            <partnerLink name="client"
partnerLinkType="tns:PaymentAuthorization"
myRole="PaymentAuthorizationProvider"/>
</partnerLinks>
<!--
~~~~~~~~~~~~~~~~~~~~~~~~~~~~~~~~~~~~~~~~~~~~~~~~~~~~~~~~~~~~
      VARIABLES: List of messages and XML documents used in this
      process
~~~~~~~~~~~~~~~~~~~~~~~~~~~~~~~~~~~~~~~~~~~~~~~~~~~~~~~~~~~ -->
      <variables>
            <!-- Reference to the message passed as input during
initiation -->
            <variable name="input"
messageType="tns:PaymentAuthorizationRequestMessage"/>
            <!-- Reference to the message that will be returned
to the requester -->
<variable name="output"
messageType="tns:PaymentAuthorizationResponseMessage"/>
      </variables>
```

```
      <!--
~~~~~~~~~~~~~~~~~~~~~~~~~~~~~~~~~~~~~~~~~~~~~~~~~~~~~~~~~~~~~~~~~~~~
      ORCHESTRATION LOGIC: Set of activities coordinating the
      flow of messages across the services integrated within
      this business process
~~~~~~~~~~~~~~~~~~~~~~~~~~~~~~~~~~~~~~~~~~~~~~~~~~~~~~~~~~~~~~~~~~~~ -->
      <sequence name="main">
            <!-- Receive input from requester.
             Note: This maps to operation defined in
PaymentAuthorization.wsdl -->
            <receive name="receiveInput" partnerLink="client"
portType="tns:PaymentAuthorization" operation="process"
variable="input" createInstance="yes"/>
            <!-- Generate reply to synchronous request -->
            <assign name="authorisedResponse">
                    <copy>
                          <from expression="starts-with
(bpws:getVariableData( 'input', 'payload',
'/PaymentAuthorizationRequest' ), '1234')">
                          </from>
  <to variable="output" part="payload"
query="/PaymentAuthorizationResponse/result"/>
                    </copy>
              </assign>
      <reply name="replyOutput" partnerLink="client"
portType="tns:PaymentAuthorization" operation="process"
variable="output"/>
       </sequence>
</process>
```

Code 36. BPEL language for the PaymentAuthorization service

If we then rerun the example with a valid name ("1234goodclient" in this case), the results are as expected, and shown in Figure 10.

Hopefully, at this stage you can see how relatively straightforward it would be to replace the default `PaymentAuthorization` Web Service with one that was based on something more meaningful.

Finally, we will publish our `PaymentAuthorization` service so that it can be integrated within the overall business scenario. How the service is made available to the rest of the world is a deployment choice that will typically be based on a number of factors, including trust relationships between partners. For example, the WSDL

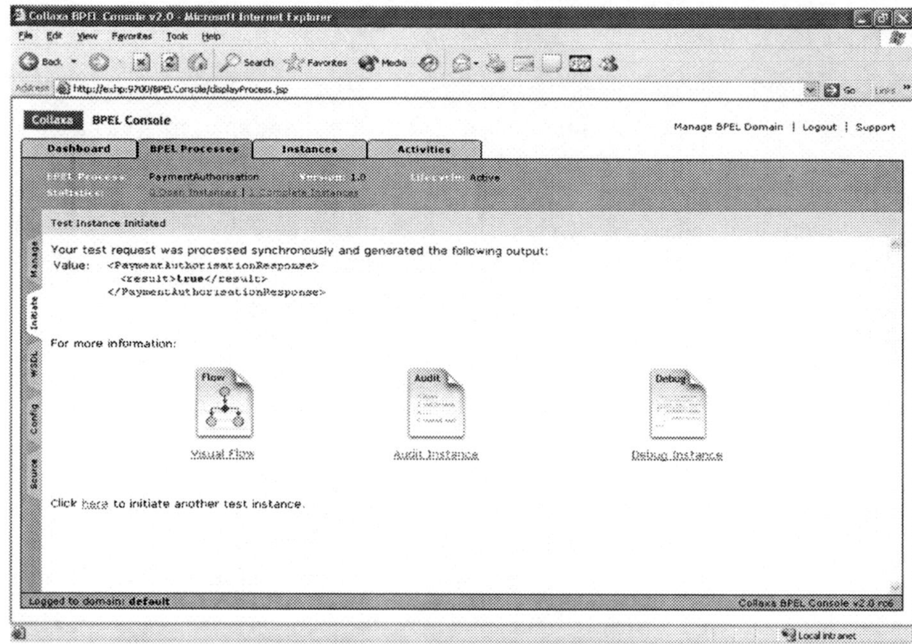

***Figure 10.* An Authorized Client**

could be exported as a plain text file that is available by virtue of a shared disk. Another alternative would be to use a UDDI registry. There may be other options that are specific to the BPEL implementation that you use. The Collaxa design tool allows, for example, allows a deployment into a jar or zip file. In this example, however, we will use the simplest approach and export our service to the BPEL run-time engine.

4.4. Gluing Them Together

If we now return to the global BPEL flow, we can start to glue together the *processOrderApplication* into a form similar to the one in Figure 3. If you remember, so far we have a flow shown in Figure 6 for the `ProcessOrderApplication` flow. Now we can add in the `PaymentAuthorization` service we have just defined. For the sake of this example, in what follows we will ignore the *checkStock* sub-task because we have not defined it yet.

First we will begin by adding an authorization `<scope>` activity, because we want to be able to catch any failures that may occur and we also need to be able to create variables for our flow to use. As with most things in the design-tool, we can drag-and-drop the desired activity.

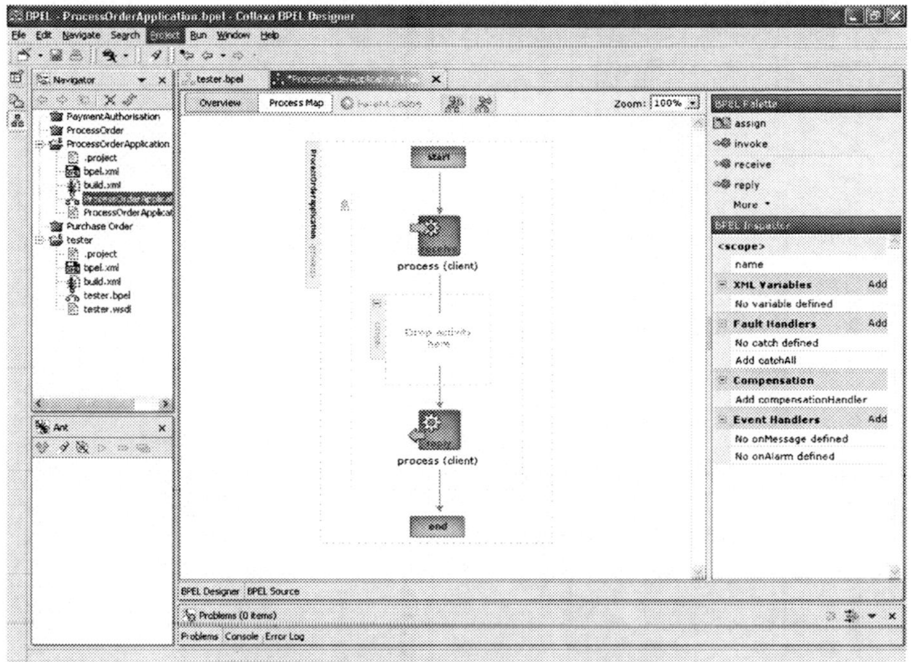

Figure 11. **The Blank Scope Activity**

As one can see from Figure 11, initially the <scope> has no fault handlers and does nothing. However, we can quickly rectify this by putting an <invoke> activity within the scope. Remember, what we are modeling is the `ProcessOrderApplication` process requesting of the `PaymentAuthorization` task to validate the client's credentials.

In order to do this with the <invoke> activity, we must define the partner link relationship. In the design tool that we are using, once the <invoke> activity has been installed within the <scope>, a special partner link creation template is made available for that activity, which is shown in Figure 12. In this template, we first define the name of the partner link (`PaymentAuthorizationPartner`) and then give the location of the WSDL for that partner. As you can see, this tool allows us to specify the WSDL location either explicitly (which we do here), or we could browse a UDDI registry.

Once the WSDL has been defined, the tool goes and fetches it so that it can offer us the `partnerLinkType` and `partnerRole` definitions. The resultant BPEL `partnerLink` definition is shown in Code 37. Once again, this is all automatically generated by the tool.

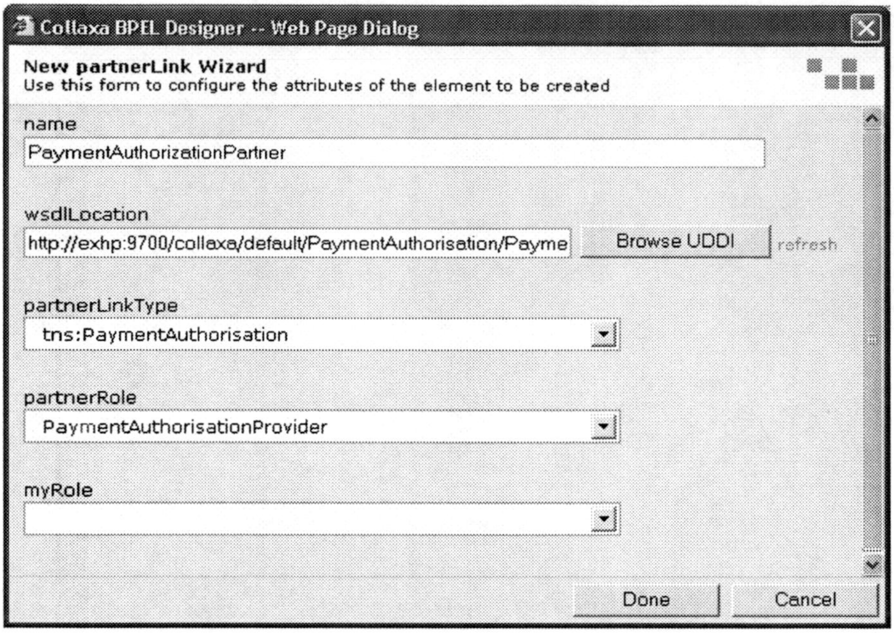

Figure 12. **Establishing a PartnerLink**

```
<sequence name="main">
     <!-- Receive input from requester.
 Note: This maps to operation defined in
 ProcessOrderApplication.wsdl -->
     <receive name="receiveInput" partnerLink="client"
portType="tns:ProcessOrderApplication" operation="process"
variable="input" createInstance="yes"/>
     <!-- Generate reply to synchronous request -->
     <scope>
           <invoke partnerLink="PaymentAuthorizationPartner"
portType="tns:PaymentAuthorization"/>
</scope>
<reply name="replyOutput" partnerLink="client"
portType="tns:ProcessOrderApplication" operation="process"
variable="output"/>
</sequence>
```

Code 37. Sample partnerLink definition

Next we have to be able to take some of the message that was input to the `ProcessOrderApplication` (the client name) and pass them through to the

PaymentAuthorization sub-task. Likewise, we want to take the result of the PaymentAuthorization sub-task and be able to use it within the rest of our application. As you may have guessed by now, we do this through the use of <assign> activities. However, we need to create some global variables to store intermediate data. We do this by establishing that the operation we want ProcessOrderApplication to invoke is process, which has both input and output messages; the design tool knows from the XML definition, what then types of these messages are as well.

We will need a global variable for storing the outgoing client data in (called clientCredentials), and one for storing the PaymentAuthorization response (called clientValidation). Using the tool we establish these as the input and output variables for the <invoke> activity. Now we need to use <assign> to set up these two variables. For brevity we will only show how this is accomplished for clientCredentials. The <assign> template is shown in Figure 13, with the relevant XPath expression for extracting the clientName element from the ProcessOrderApplication input message.

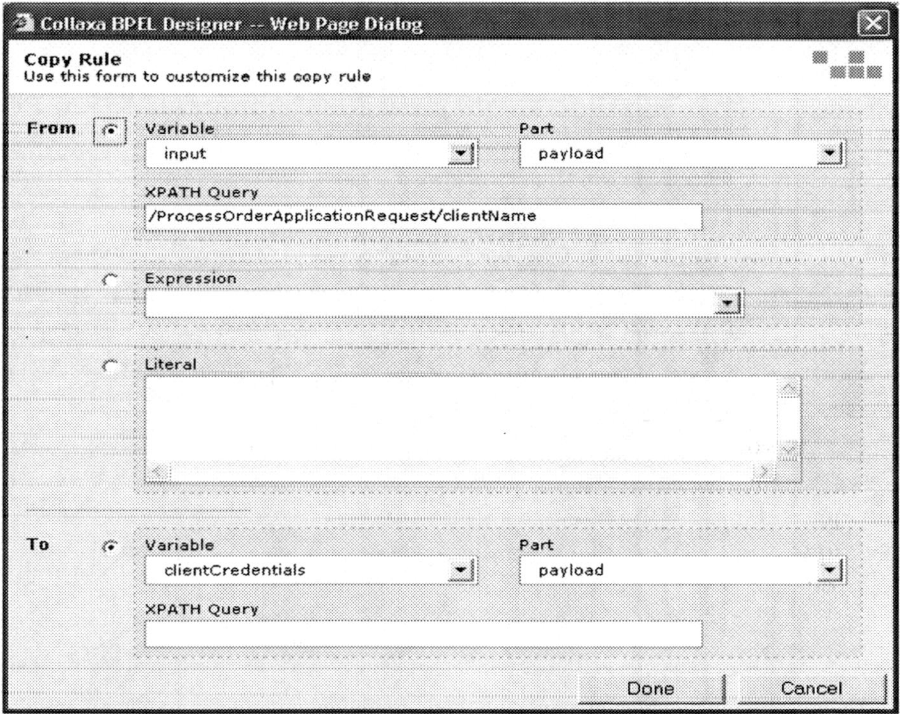

Figure 13. **Initializing the ClientCredentials Variable**

The resulting flow is shown in Code 38, and illustrated graphically in Figure 14.

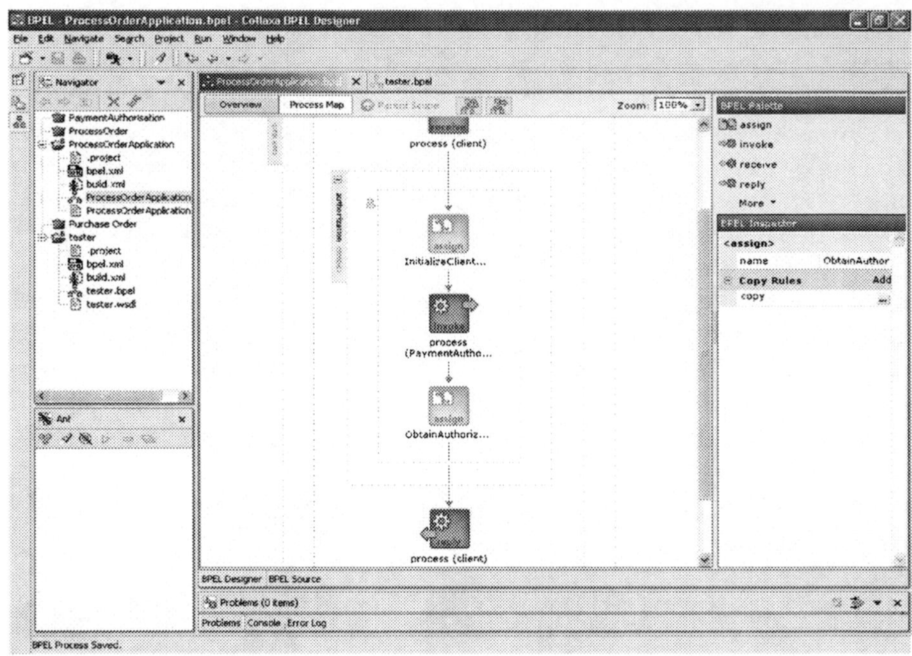

Figure 14. **The PaymentAuthorization Scope Activity**

```
<sequence name="main">
            <!-- Receive input from requester.
             Note: This maps to operation defined in
ProcessOrderApplication.wsdl -->
            <receive name="receiveInput" partnerLink="client"
portType="tns:ProcessOrderApplication" operation="process"
variable="input" createInstance="yes"/>
            <!-- Generate reply to synchronous request -->
            <scope name="authorization">
                <sequence>
                    <assign name="InitializeClientCredentials">
                          <copy>
              <from variable="input"
part="payload" query="/ProcessOrderApplication/clientName">
             </from>
    <to variable="clientCredentials"
part="payload"/>
  </copy>
    </assign>
<invoke
```

```
partnerLink="PaymentAuthorizationPartner"
portType="tns:PaymentAuthorisation" name="paymentAuthorization"
inputVariable="clientCredentials"
outputVariable="clientValidation" operation="process"/>
    <assign name="ObtainAuthorizationResponse">
  <copy>
      <from variable="clientValidation"
part="payload">
      </from>
    <to variable="output"
part="payload"/>
  </copy>
    </assign>
</sequence>
    </scope>
    <reply name="replyOutput" partnerLink="client"
portType="tns:ProcessOrderApplication" operation="process"
variable="output"/>
      </sequence>
```

Code 38. The BPEL source for the PaymentAuthorization scope activity

4.5. Fault Handling

So far we have ignored any faults that may occur during the flow of our application. Unfortunately faults of one kind or another are common place. For example, they may occur because of a machine or process failure, or simply because of invalid input data. As we have already seen, BPEL provides a fairly comprehensive suite of facilities to both model faults (e.g., the `<throw>` activity) and deal with them (e.g., fault handlers).If we consider the `PaymentAuthorization` section of our `ProcessOrderApplication`, then there are several types of fault that we may want to model and deal with. For example, if the format of the `clientName element` is invalid, then we would want to report that back to the client; this could be through a normal response message, or (probably more useful) through an error response, i.e., a fault message.

Likewise, the client identified by `clientName` may actually be in debt to the order system, and in which case the next time that client attempts to place an order an entirely separate process flow may be required, e.g., a `DebtCollectionService`. There are obviously other failure scenarios that we could model here, but the aim is not to include them all but to give a flavor of *how* such fault types can be catered for within BPEL. In order to model these two types of fault we need to return to the PaymentAuthorization service and allow it to throw these two fault types: ClientNameFormatFault and UnpaidBillFault respectively. Then we go back to the authorization <scope> activity we declared earlier in the ProcessOrderApplication flow. If we remember from Figure 11, the design tool shows that the activity has scope for fault handlers as well as a compensation handler and event handlers (e.g., onMessage). It is relatively straightforward to add two fault handlers to this scope, one for each of the faults that the PaymentAuthorization service can now throw. Figure 15 shows the handler for the UnpaidBillFault.

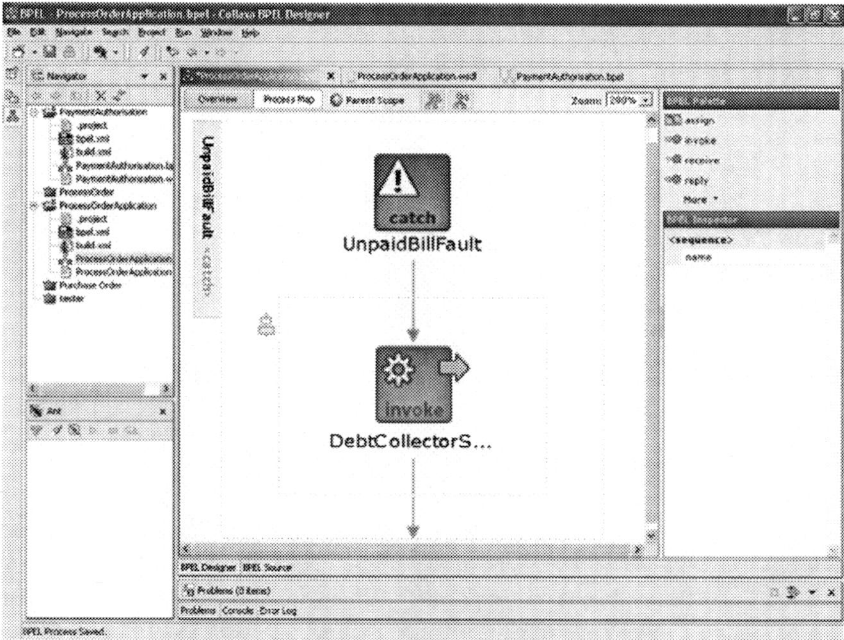

***Figure 15.* Handling the UnpaidBillFault**

4.6. The Entire Flow

With a little more effort it is possible to define the entire *processOrder* application in BPEL. This is shown in Figure 16 and looks a lot like what we saw in Figure 3.

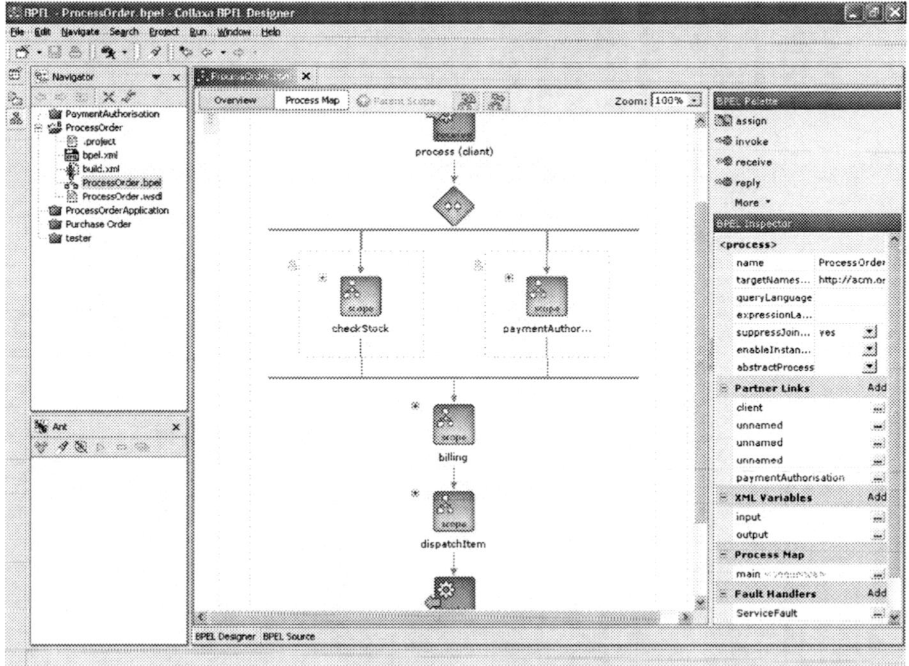

Figure 16. **All of the Order Process Application in BPEL**

5. Run-Time Demonstration

Now that we have designed our `ProcessOrderApplication`, we can execute it and examine what actually happens from one step to another. As we did when designing it, we will only concentrate on the `PaymentAuthorization` sub-task for simplicity.

5.1. Tracking the Flow

If one recalls, the `ProcessOrderApplication` is invoked with three pieces of information:

1. The client name.
2. The type of item required.
3. The client's shipping address.

It then invokes the `PaymentAuthorization` sub-task, passing it the client name, to determine if the client is allowed to place an order. We previously saw how the

`ProcessOrderApplication` and `PaymentAuthorization` processes have been glued together, so now let us see how they execute. Once again the Collaxa run-time engine facilitates this by providing us with a suitable form, as shown in Figure 17. Here we have three fields, one for each of the data variables that a client must supply.

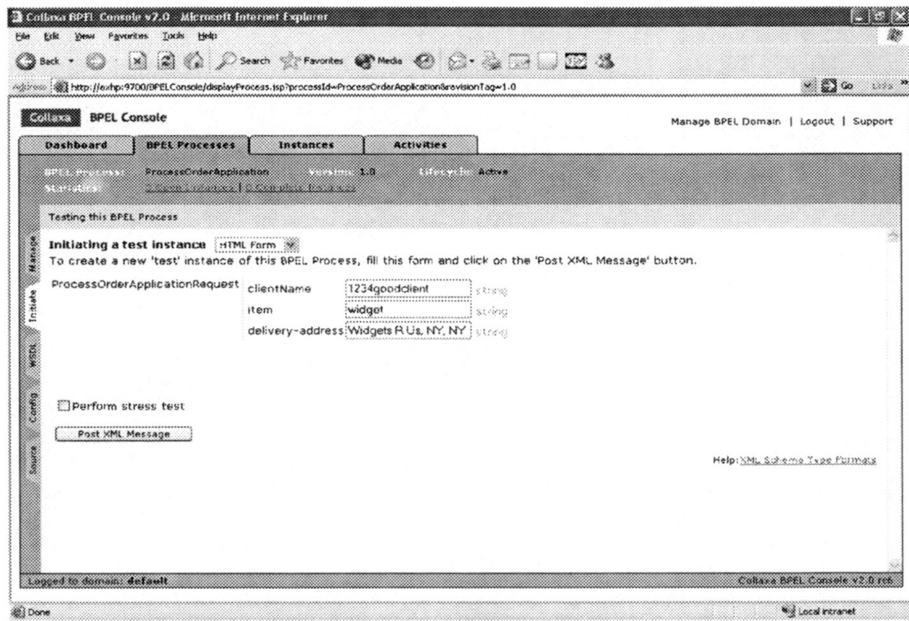

Figure 17. **Placing an Order**

Through its *Flow* option, the Collaxa Server interface allows us to see all of the message exchanges that occur in this flow. The result of submitting this form is a message being posted to the `ProcessOrderApplication`. The format of that message is shown in Code 39.

```
<input>
      <part name="payload">
            <ProcessOrderApplicationRequest
      xmlns="http://acm.org/samples">
                  <clientName>1234goodclient</clientName>
                  <item>widget</item>
                  <delivery-address>Widgets R Us, NY, NY
          </delivery-address>
            </ProcessOrderApplicationRequest>
      </part>
</input>
```

Code 39. The client message to the ProcessOrderApplication flow

Upon receiving the client's message, the `InitializeClientCredentials` `<assign>` activity we saw earlier scans the message for the `clientName` field, as shown in Code 40, in order to update the `clientCredentials` global variable.

```
<clientCredentials>
      <part name="payload">
            <PaymentAuthorisationRequest
            xmlns="http://acm.org/samples">1234goodclient
    </PaymentAuthorisationRequest>
      </part>
</clientCredentials>
```

Code 40. Updating the clientCredentials variable

Once the `clientCredentials` variable has been successfully initialized, the `PaymentAuthorization` flow can be invoked. The message that the `ProcessOrderApplication` sends to this sub-task is shown in Code 41, along with the response that eventually comes back.

```
<messages>
      <clientCredentials>
            <part name="payload">
                  <PaymentAuthorisationRequest
  mlns="http://acm.org/samples">1234goodclient
  </PaymentAuthorisationRequest>
            </part>
      </clientCredentials>
      <clientValidation>
            <part name="payload">
                        <PaymentAuthorisationResponse
  xmlns="http://acm.org/samples">
       <result>true</result>
</PaymentAuthorisationResponse>
    </part>
      </clientValidation>
</messages>
```

Code 41. The PaymentAuthorization request and response

Likewise, the response is placed in the `clientValidation` variable and eventually used in the rest of the `ProcessOrderApplication` flow.

5.2. The Audit Trail

Through the interface to the Collaxa Server run-time, it is possible to obtain an audit trail of this segment of the `ProcessOrderApplication`. This gives similar information to the Flow we saw previously, but in a slightly different format, as shown in Figure 18.

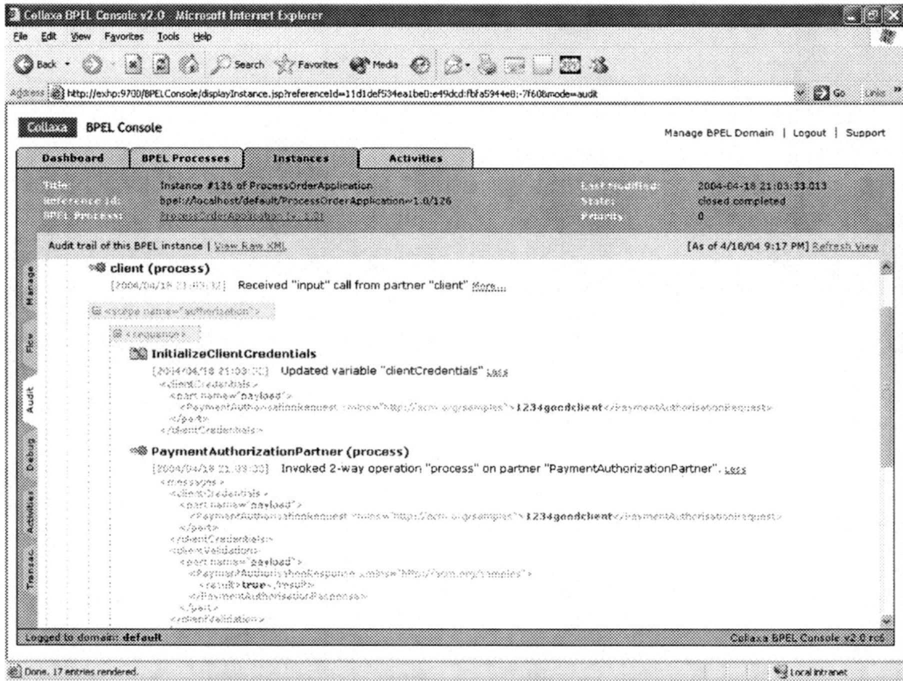

Figure 18. **An Example of the Audit Option**

6. Summary

In this chapter we have looked at the principles behind workflow systems and why they have been used successfully for a variety of enterprise integration strategies. However, as we saw, the lack of a rigorous standard for workflow that concentrated on interoperability of implementations often resulted in vendor lock-in. Fortunately, Web services are specifically about fostering systems interoperability and the SOA is deliberately not prescriptive about what happens behind service endpoints: Web services are ultimately only concerned with the transfer of structured data between parties, plus any meta-level information to safeguard such transfers.

As a result, combining Web Services and workflow offers the best of both worlds: an interoperable integration strategy that allows you to leverage existing investments. We then discussed the Business Process Execution Language (BPEL) now in OASIS, but originally from BEA, IBM and Microsoft, which is a workflow scripting language for specifying business process behavior, based on Web services and is rapidly becoming the standard for Web Services workflow. The language (entirely XML-based) can be used to formally define the behavior of business processes and their interactions.

More importantly, BPEL has the potential to commoditize the capabilities provided by the old workflow and proprietary EAI and BPM solutions. This is extremely important because it should allow integration tasks to leverage existing (legacy) investments in EAI and provide an integration path between different vendor implementations.

After discussing the principles behind BPEL we further illustrated the advantages that it offers by using a worked example (an order process scenario). As we saw, with the aid of a suitable graphical tool, designing fairly complex process flows using BPEL is relatively straightforward. With only a few mouse-clicks and a basic understanding of the BPEL language, we were able to define the *paymentAuthorisation* task of our original *processOrder* application. What BPEL (and by implication Web Services), its supporters and implementers have done is to take the once elitist area of workflow systems and bring them to the masses. It is no longer a requirement that specialist EAI vendors have to be the first and only port of call for corporations large and small who wish to automate their internal or external business processes.

4 WORKING WITH REGISTRY AND UDDI

Look at a day when you are supremely satisfied at the end. It's not a day when you lounge around doing nothing, it's when you've had everything to do and you've done it!
Margaret Thatcher

The demeanor of conducting business has changed over the past decade. However, there are certain entities, the real players in a transaction that have remained the same – *buyers*, *sellers* and *marketplaces*. Whether you buy a book over the Internet, shop at the nearest mall or take advantage of the spa service at your local club, the above entities hold true. The buyers and sellers meet at a market place where the seller showcases its products and services. The buyer browses through it, evaluates it and may decide to perform the transaction. In the context of SOA, a registry resembles a market place. It provides applications and businesses a central point to store information about their services. It is expected to provide the same level of information and the same breadth of services to its clients as that of a conventional market place. However, the vision of a registry solution does not end here. The dream of the enterprise architects is to have a solution that facilitates the automated discovery and execution of e-commerce transactions and enabling a liquid and frictionless environment for business transactions. Therefore, a registry is more than an "e-business directory". It is an inherent component of the SOA infrastructure that should be mature to propose pragmatic standards yet flexible enough to manage the growing complexity and dynamism in business relationships and interoperability.

There are more than one industry initiatives to handle the issue of registry. In this chapter, we will take a look at Universal Description, Discovery and Integration (UDDI). Before we examine UDDI, it is imperative to understand the role and basic elements of a registry solution in business transactions.

1. Introducing the Registry

A Service-Oriented Architecture is based on the interactions between three primary functionaries: service provider, service registry and service requestor. The service provider creates the service and publishes the service description in a registry. The service requestor finds the service description in the registry and uses the information to bind and execute the service. The following diagram illustrates this concept.

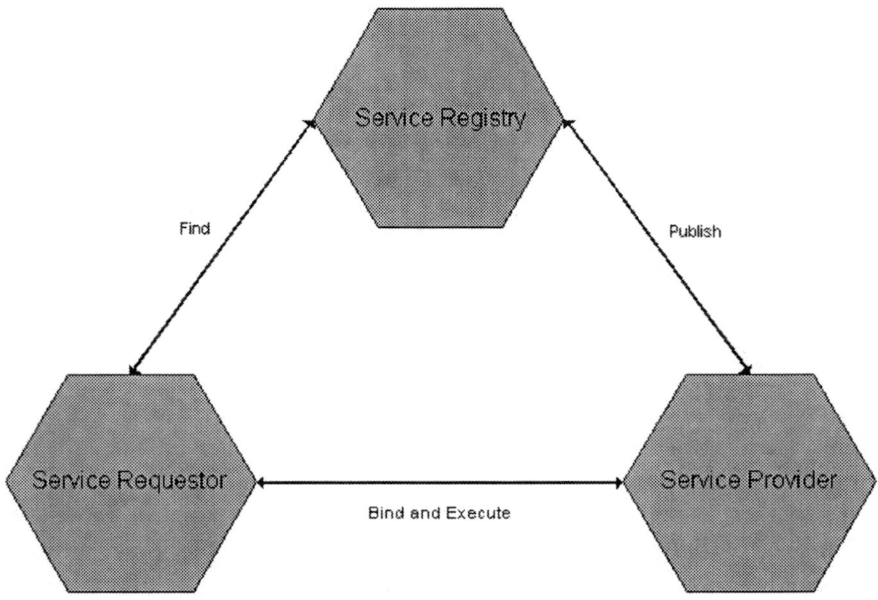

Figure 1. **Publish, Find and Execute**

1.1. Why Do I Need It?

On a small scale, it is not very difficult to discover, manage and interface with business partners. One option is to call each partner on the phone, and then try to find the right person to talk with. It?s cumbersome but still possible to maintain a list of partner companies that adhere to your requirements and their service access points and interfaces. However, this model breaks down, as the number of companies that you need to interact with grows, along with the number and types of interfaces they export. To manage the list of growing partners and their changing interfaces becomes an exponential task. It not only makes your system frail but it also restricts your business ability to discover and collaborate with new partners. A registry solution based on agreed upon standards provides a common way to publish and discover services. It offers a central place where you query whether a partner has a service that is compatible with in-house technologies or to find a list of companies that supports shipping services on the other side of the globe.

1.2. How Do I Use It?

The repository of services has several different uses, based on the perspective of who is using it. From a business analyst's perspective, it is similar to an Internet search engine for business processes. Similar to a web user that uses a search engine like Google to find websites of interest, a business analyst can browse one ore more registries to find new businesses. A series of marketplaces and business search portals are coming up to assist business analysts with the right tools in their quest to discover new partners.

The other set of users are the software developers who use the registry's programming APIs to publish services and query the registry to discover services matching various criteria. Figures 2 describes the relationship between registries and its users.

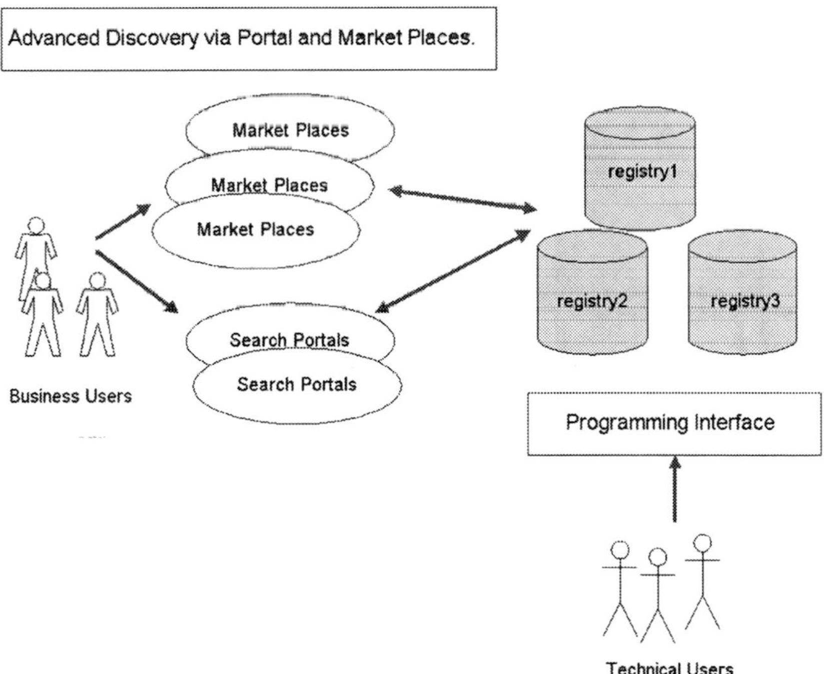

Figure 2. **Registry Usage**

1.3. Registry vs Repository

It is important to note that registry is an enabler of services and that it is not a part of the service. It allows for the registration of services, discovery of metadata and classification of entities into predefined categories. Unlike a repository, it does not have the ability to store business process definitions or WSDL or any other documents that are required for trading agreements. A registry stores information about the items and not the items themselves. A repository, on the other hand, is used to physically store the items. Thus a repository serves as data storage and makes use of a registry service as an interface to outside parties.

A registry service can be thought of as an advanced address book, where every entry contains information in a pre-defined format and the entries are organized for easy access. Whenever a consumer or client is looking for a service, it can browse or search the address book by specifying its criterion. Any distributed programming framework needs a module to serve this need. J2EE has the notion of JNDI, where the client Java programs can look up for distributed objects like EJBs. CORBA provides a similar COS Naming Service that allows the clients to look up CORBA objects by name. Web Service Inspection Language (WS-Inspection) and WS-ServiceGroup from the WS-Resource Framework specifications also attempt to address the issue of service discovery. Electronic business XML (ebXML) that makes use of XML and provides a standard, non-proprietary way of handing Electronic Data Interchange (EDI) between business partners also has a discovery solution. However, due to the simplicity, flexibility and a strong focus on the business and service listings, Universal Description, Discover and Integration (UDDI), the topic of this chapter has gained the maximum traction in the ESOA context.

2. *Universal Description, Discovery and Integration (UDDI)*

A good registry solution should provide a platform-independent way of describing services, discovering businesses, and integrating business services using the Internet. It should facilitate consumption of these services by providing the clients the ability to query and retrieve details about the business, the services offered and details about the services, such as how and where to invoke them. The Universal Description, Discovery and Integration projects provides an open, standardized and flexible way to achieve the above.

Microsoft, IBM and Ariba first proposed the UDDI specifications in the year 2000. By the time version 3.0 of the specifications was released in the year 2002, the UDDI consortium consisted of more than 200 members. Keeping with the spirit of open standards, the consortium handed over the future UDDI development efforts to the open-standards organization OASIS. The specifications have gone under significant evolution since its first inception. While the initial UDDI specification focused on Web service description and discovery on an Internet scale, subsequent UDDI refinements helped it become a more effective and pragmatic solution. The introduction of the subscription API and the means to facilitate the gradual migration of a service from an internal development setting to the enterprise level registry and finally to the web is evidence that the specifications have matured enough to handle real world issues.

In simplistic terms, a registry solution can be compared to a phone book. It provides the ability for service providers to register their services and for service consumers to easily locate the business entities and the services they provide. Conceptually, a business can register three types of information into a UDDI registry.

1. White pages
   Basic contact information and identifies about a company, including business name, address, contact information and unique identifiers such has DUNS or tax ids. This information allows consumers to locate your serivce based upon your business identification. This is similar to looking up either the phone number or address of a business when you know the business's name.

2. Yellow pages
   Yellow pages describe a service using classification information. For instance, the phone directory can provide information to find an Italian restaurant in the San Francisco area. It allows consumers to discover a service based upon its categorization (taxonomy). We will discuss more about taxonomies later in this chapter.

3. Green pages
   Green pages allow to describe the service that the business offers. They contain technical information about the behavior, support functions and access point for the service.

2.1. Technical Overview

Figure 3 illustrates how UDDI fits into an overall stack of services. Rather than trying to reinvent the technologies, it builds on a network transport layer and a SOAP-based XML messaging layer and uses WSDL for the definitions of services.

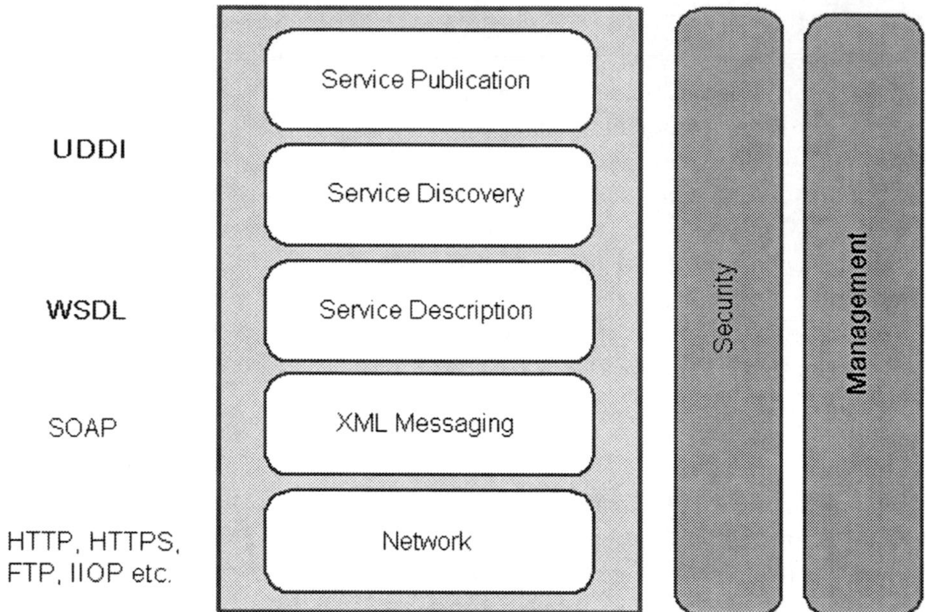

Figure 3. **Stack of Elements Required for an Established Service**

UDDI presents a number of APIs such as inquiry API, publisher API and subscriber API for the consumers to access the registry. The specifications also present an information model composed of instances of persistent data structures called entities. The core entities are `businessEntity`, `businessService`, `bindingTemplate` and `tModel`. Each of the entities are expressed in XML and are persistently stored by UDDI nodes. A set of services that implements at least one UDDI API set is termed as a *UDDI node*. One or more UDDI nodes may form a *UDDI registry*, with the restriction that a node may belong to one, and only one, registry. The nodes of a registry collectively manage a well-defined set of UDDI data. Typically, this is supported by the use of UDDI replication between the nodes in the registry, which reside on different systems. The nodes are hosted by operators who are responsible for durable recording and backup of all data, providing security and maintaining the integrity of data.

Within a registry, each instance of the core data structures is uniquely identified by a UDDI key. By choosing appropriate policies, multiple registries may form a group, known as an "affiliation", whose purpose is to permit controlled copying of core data structures among them. In the next few sections, we will examine each of above concepts in more detail.

2.2. Informational Structural Model

UDDI registry consists of four core data structure types, the `businessEntity`, the `businessService`, the `bindingTemplate` and the `tModel`. Additionally, `publisherAssertion` data structure is used to define relationships between the entities and `operationalInfo` can be used to maintain the tracking information. The data structures and their relationships are displayed in Figure 4.

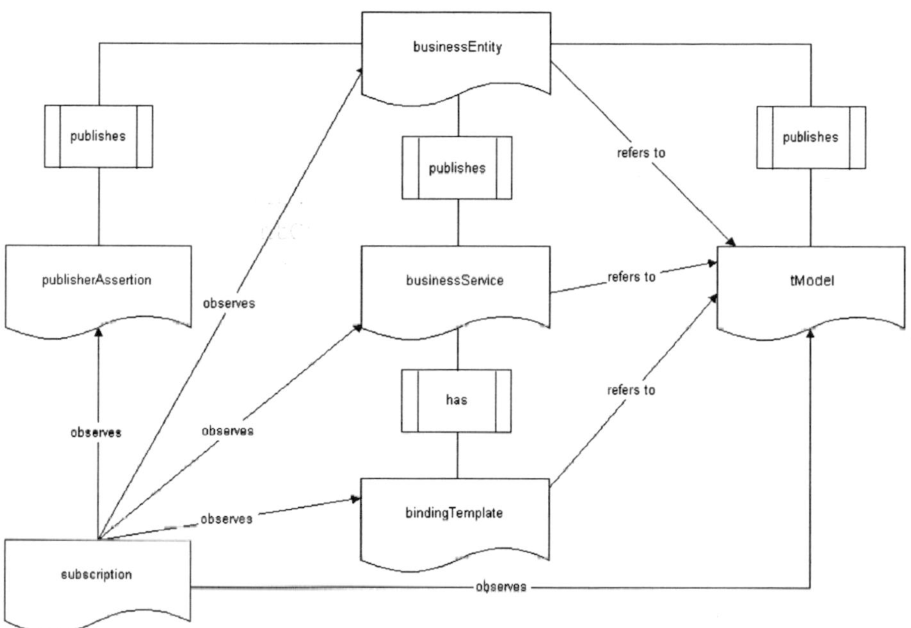

Figure 4. **Structural Model**

To summarize the relationship described in the above diagram, the `businessEntity` element represents a business and contains references to one or more `businessService` elements. `businessService` and `bindingTemplate` elements defines the technical and business descriptions of the service and contains a reference to one or more `tModels`. The `tModel` element is used to define the technical specification for the service. Additionally, `publisherAssertion` element can be used to define a relationship between two or more `businessEntity` elements. Let us examine each of these elements in more detail.

2.2.1. Business Information: The BusinessEntity Element

Partners should be able to discover your business with a small set of facts about your business such as your name, category or some other key identifier. The `<businessEntity>` structure serves as a top-level information manager. Each `<businessEntity>` entity contains descriptive information about a business or organization. This information includes contact information, categorization, identifiers, descriptions, and relationships to other businesses. From an XML standpoint, the `<businessEntity>` is the top-level data structure that holds descriptive information about the business or organization it describes. Figure 5 lists the elements that are contained in the structure. Each `<businessEntity>` is identified by its `businessKey`. If a `businessKey` is not specified at publication time, the registry automatically generates one. `categoryBag` and `identifierBag` are used for classification of entities and are discussed later in the section. The `Signature` element specifies the digital signature of the publisher and can be used to verify the integrity of the data. Each contained `<businessService>` describes a logical service offered by the business or organization.

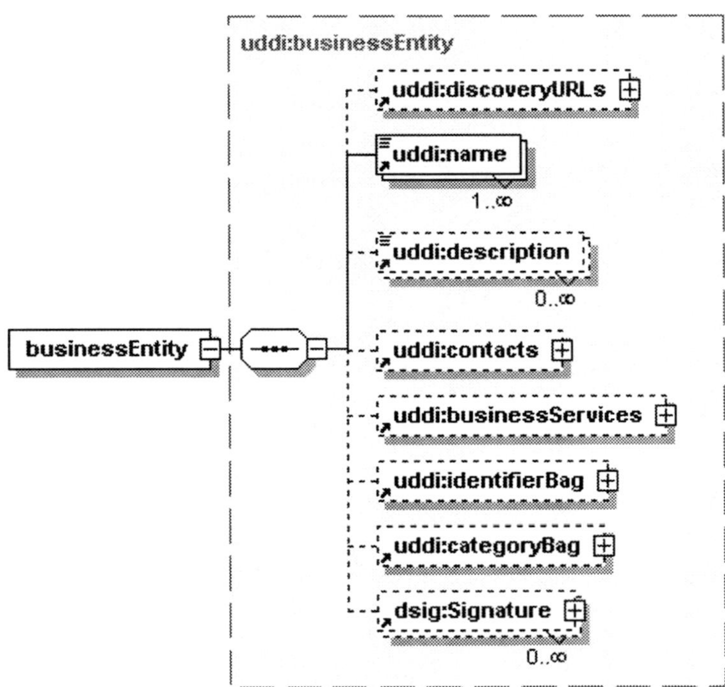

Figure 5. **BusinessEntity**

2.2.2. Service Information: The BusinessService element

A <businessEntity> contains one or more <businessService> structures. A <businessService> structure represents a logical service and contains descriptive information in business. A <businessService> document is re-usable, i.e. a <businessService> element can be used by several <businessEntity> elements. For instance, a large enterprise may decide to publish multiple <businessEntity> structures, one each of its several subdivisions. But it has a shipping service that it would like to be published within each of the entities. It can do so by using service projection where the <businessService> will be included by reference as opposed to containment.

Technical information about the <businessService> is found in the contained <bindingTemplate> entities. Figure 6 lists the various elements of <businessService> structure.

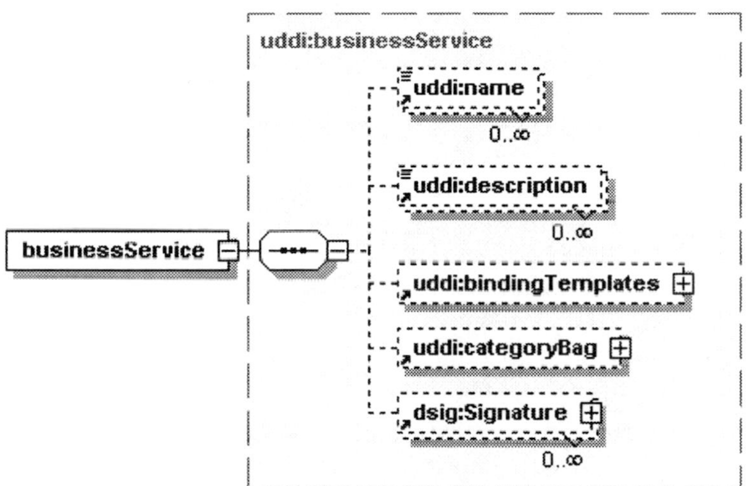

Figure 6. **BusinessService**

2.2.3. Specification Information: The BindingTemplate Element

A <bindingTemplate> contains pointers to technical descriptions and the access point URL, but does not contain the details of the service's specifications. It describes the type of service being offered using references to <tModels>, application-specific parameters, and settings. The key to a <bindingTemplate> is that it allows a service to expose what bindings it supports. A service may choose to support multiple binding protocols, including HTTP, HTTPS, SMTP and so forth. Figure 7 describes the <bindingTemplate> structure.

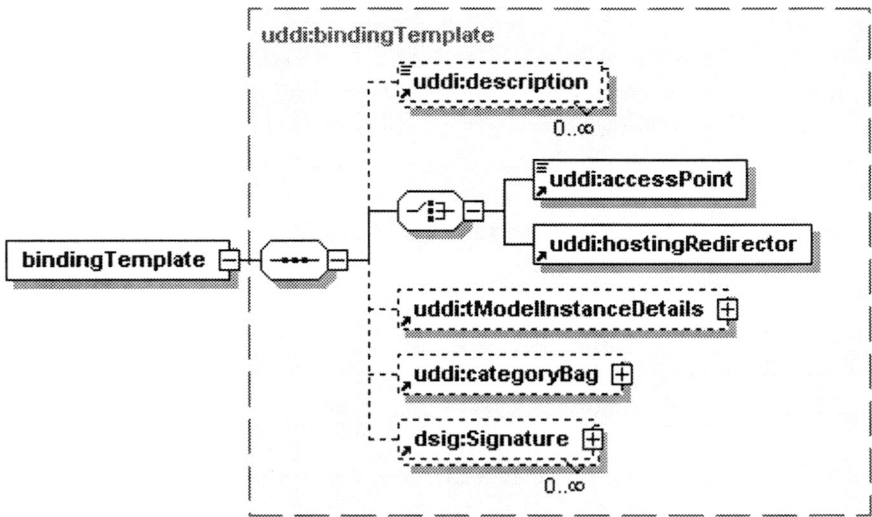

Figure 7. **BindingTemplate**

2.2.4. Technical Fingerprint: The TModel Element

Software that communicates with other software invariably adheres to some pre-agreed specifications. In order to invoke a purchase order service with a business partner, you need more than a URL. You need to know the format of the purchase order, the required protocols, security handshake and the expected result type. This is achieved by publishing information about the specification in a <tModel> (Technical Model). A <tModel> acts as an abstract description of a particular specification or behavior to which the web service adheres. It is a type of digital "fingerprint" for determining the specifics of how to interact with a particular service. It is important to note that the actual specification or set of documents that describes the concept of a <tModel> is not a part of the registry and is remotely referenced using the overviewDoc structure. Once a <tModel> is published, other parties can express the availability of Web services that are compliant with a specification the <tModel> represents. They can do so by simply including a reference to the <tModel> – i.e., its tModelKey – in their technical service descriptions <bindingTemplate> data. Companies can use the information pointed to by a <tModel> to determine whether a service is compatible with their business requirements. For example, let us consider the situation where the company DummyMortgages has a relationship with several lenders for processing home loan applications, each lender having its own implementation. Since the service definition requirement for DummyMortgages is the same for all partners, it could publish the service definition tModel as a standard for all of its partners. The several lenders can reference the DummyMortgages' service definition and publish their own service implementation details. The concept of tModel allows various entities like DummyMortgages or standard bodies to publish abstract service specifications that can then be used by other partners that implement services. By referencing to the tModel, the partners agree to be compliant with the service specification dictated by the tModel.

Figure 8 lists the elements in the <tModel> structure.

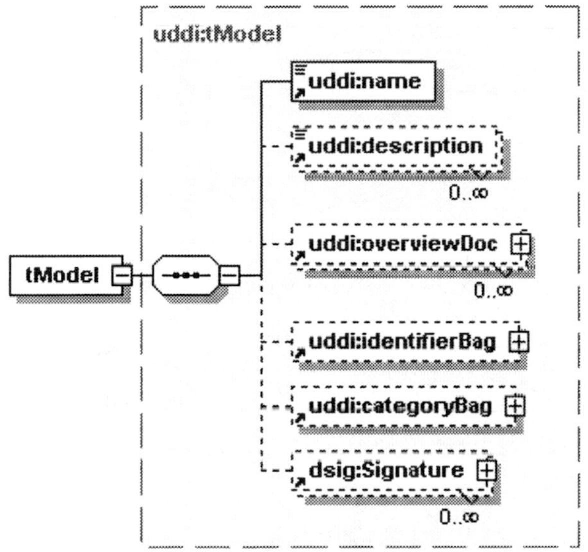

Figure 8. TModel

2.2.5. Relationships: The PublisherAssertion Element

Many businesses and organizations are not effectively represented by a single <businessEntity>. Examples include corporations with a variety of subsidiaries, private exchanges with sets of suppliers and their customers and industry consortiums with their members. An obvious solution is to publish several <businessEntity> structures. However, these entities are still under the same umbrella company and might want to be coupled with each other and make some of their relationships visible in their UDDI registrations. This is accomplished by using the

<publisherAssertion> structure. To eliminate the possibility that one publisher claims a relationship to another that is not reciprocated, both publishers must publish identical assertions for the relationship to become visible. Thus a company can claim a business relationship only if its partner asserts the same relationship. One company's assertion about a business relationship is not visible to the public until its partner creates a similar, but separate, <publisherAssertion> document for its own <businessEntity> structure. Thus, if Company A asserts a relationship with Company B (fromKey=A,toKey=B), then the relationship will become public when Company B asserts a relationship with Company A (fromKey=B,toKey=A).

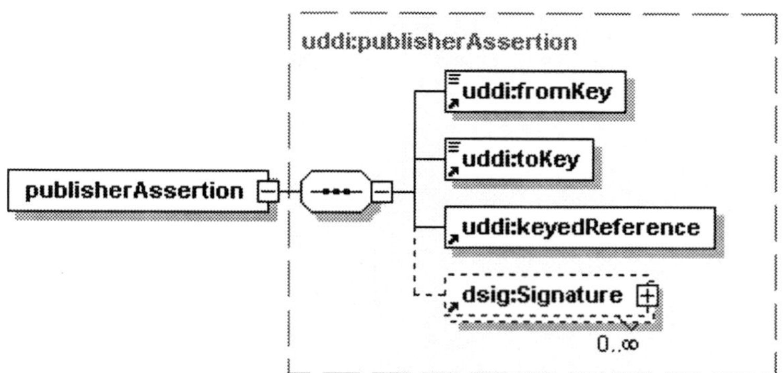

Figure 9. **PublisherAssertion**

2.2.6. Operations Information: The OperationalInfo Element

Information about a publishing operation is captured whenever a UDDI core data structure is published. This data includes the date and time that the data structure was created and modified, the identifier of the UDDI node at which the publish operation took place, and the identity of the publisher. The <operationalInfo> structure is used to convey the operational information for the UDDI core data structures, that is, the <businessEntity>, <businessService>, <bindingTemplate> and <tModel> structures. Figure 10 lists the elements of an <operationalInfo> structure.

2.3. UDDI Keys

When the above components are published in the registry, they are assigned a globally unique identifier or key. It is via that key that you refer to a registry entry. With the

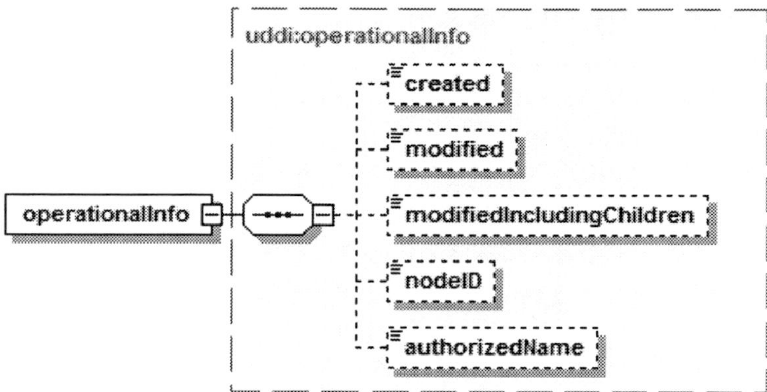

Figure 10. **OperationalInfo**

earlier versions of UDDI, the registry generated the keys. Version 3 of specifications allows businesses to suggest a key at the time of publishing the entry. With Version 3, the key can be generated either by the registry (`UUID/uddiKey`), or specified by the client (`domainKey`) or a combination of the above two (`derivedKey`). Let us examine the various key types.

2.3.1. UUID

Universally unique identifier, known as UUID is assigned when the data structure is first inserted into a UDDI registry and the user does not specify a key. They are 16 digit hexadecimal strings and the registry guarantees the generation of a unique identifier by concatenating the current time, hardware address, IP address, and random number in a specific fashion. An example of a uuid-based registry key is:

uddi: 4CD7E4BC-648B-426D-9936-443EAAC8AE23

2.3.2. DomainKey

`domainKey` allows the publisher to the register its domain name as part of the key and in a format that is more palatable for humans to read. Because domain keys are based on an organization's internet domain name, they also facilitate the aim of global uniqueness, and allow a business to define its own policy for generating their service keys. The following is an example of a valid domain key.

uddi: springer.com

2.3.3. DerivedKey

The derived key can be generated by appending a key appending string (KSS) to a `UUID` or a `domainKey`. A KSS may consist of any non-null alphanumeric ASCII character, as well as a few other special characters. The following listing illustrates a valid derived key based on `UUID`.

uddi: 4CD7E4BC-648B-426D-9936-443EAAC8AE23:Enterprise SOA Book

In a similar manner, a derived key can be generated using a `domainKey`

uddi: springer.com:Enterprise SOA Book

The introduction of domain keys and derived keys makes managing service keys much more organized. But even with user-specified keys, a UDDI registry still has to enforce global key uniqueness. When publishing a new registry entry, the UDDI registry checks with its internal key verification policy if the suggested registry key is acceptable. If it is, the entry will accept the provided registry key; otherwise, the UDDI registry will generate a UUID.

Data is only considered information if it can be discovered and used. It is worthless if it is lost within a mass of other data. If a client application cannot effectively find information within a registry, then the purpose of the registry service is considerably compromised.

2.4. Classification – Where Is My Data?

Depending on the number of entries in the registry and the search criteria, the result could be a large and unmanageable set. Providing the structure and modeling tools to address this problem is at the heart of UDDI's design. As illustrated in the previous section, the core components of UDDI, `businessEntity`, `businessService`, `bindingTemplate` and `tModels` have `categoryBag` and `identifierBag` elements to help discover these entities in the registry. In this section, we will look at categorization and identification.

Taxonomy – The term is derived from the Greek taxis ("arrangement") and nomos ("law"). It is defined as the science, laws, or principles of classification.

2.4.1. Categorization

Categorization allows data in a UDDI registry to be associated with an industry, product or geographic code set. UDDI facilitates a classification system to be used on every entity contained in the registry. It is generally recommended that all services be classified before being made publicly available. You can either use any of categorization schemes supported by the base specifications or create your own.

As part of the base specifications, UDDI supports three canonical taxonomies that be used for categorization of businesses and the services they offer. Each taxonomy categorization is registered as a `<tModel>` structure within UDDI. This registration means that each categorization has a `<tModel>` name and UUID that can be used to reference it. Table 1 summarizes the list.

***Table 1.* Taxonomies**

Taxonomy Name	TModel name	Description
NAICS	`ntis:gov:naics:1997`	The North American Industry Classification system jointly developed by US, Canada and Mexico. Provides classification for services and manufacturing including categories for "Dog and Cat Food", "Knit Outerwear" and "Computer Storage Devices". More information can be found at http://www.census.gov/epcd/www/naics.html
UNSPSC	`unspsc-org:unspsc:3-1`	The Universal Standard Products and Services Classification provides classification for products and services for worldwide use. More information can be found at http://www.unspsc.org
ISO 3166	`iso-ch:3166:1999`	International standard geographical regions. This taxonomy includes codes for countries and their administrative support staffs. More information can be found at http://www.din.de/gremien/nas/nabd/iso3166ma

UDDI registries also allow using your own classification schemes. Sometimes it is necessary to defined additional classification schemes particularly when you are defining businesses for internal registries. You could create a new taxonomy based on price, service or other factors. However, identifying categories for easy searching is not an easy proposition. Anyone who has ever searched the web for an item should be familiar with the problem. If the category is too broad, like manufacturing, it can return countless businesses and services thus overwhelming the client. If the category is too specific, like manufacturing yellow trucks in San Diego, it might be too restrictive to return any results. UDDI allows multiple classification schemes to be applied to a single entity. The categories are assigned with the use of `<categoryBag>` element that is part of the core UDDI entities.

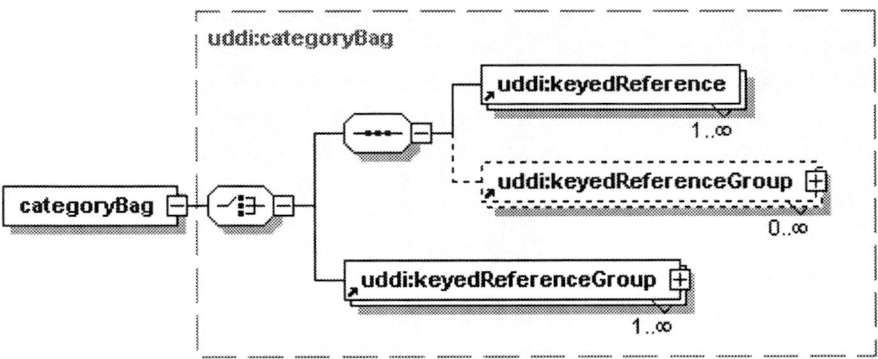

Figure 11. **CategoryBag**

A `<categoryBag>` structure contains zero or more `<keyedReference>` structures and may also contain a list of `keyedReferenceGroup` structures. Each `<keyedReference>` structure contains the name and value of a category to which the data element belongs. A `keyedReference` contains the three attributes `tModelKey`, `keyName` and `keyValue`.

For example, you would use the following code snippet in order to categorize a `businessEntity` as offering goods and services in California, USA, using the corresponding ISO 3166 `tModelKey` within the UDDI Business Registry.

```
<keyedReference
    tModelKey="uddi:uddi.org:ubr:categorization:iso3166"
    keyName="California, USA"
    keyValue="US-CA"/>
```

The `tModelKey` refers to the `tModel` that represents the categorization system, and the `keyValue` contains the actual categorization within this system. The `keyName` is optional and is used to provide a descriptive name of the categorization.

A `keyedReferenceGroup` is simply a list of `keyedReference` structures that logically belong together. It also contains a `tModelKey` attribute that specifies the structure and meaning of the `keyedReferences` contained in the group. For instance, the following listing illustrates a `keyedReferenceGroup` to categorize a `businessEntity` as being located at the geodetic point that is specified by the latitude/longitude pair 49.6827/8.2952 using the corresponding World Geodetic System 1984 (WGS 84) tModelKey within the UDDI Business Registry.

```
<keyedReferenceGroup tModelKey="uddi:uddi.org:ubr:
    categorizationGroup:wgs84">
    <keyedReference
        tModelKey="uddi:uddi.org:ubr:
        categorization:wgs84:latitude"
        keyName="WGS 84 Latitude"
        keyValue="+49.682700"/>
    <keyedReference
         tModelKey="uddi:uddi.org:ubr:categorization:
         wgs84:longitude"
         keyName="WGS 84 Longitude"
         keyValue="+008.295200"/>
</keyedReferenceGroup>
```

2.4.2. Identifiers

Another way to search an entity in the registry is by using a unique key or identifier. UDDI registry has the ability to mark entities with identifier. An identifier is a type of property or keyword that can be used to uniquely identify a business or specification. The purpose is to allow others to find the published information using more formal identifier systems. For instance, businesses may want to use their D-U-N-S® number, Global Location Number (GLN), or tax identifier in their UDDI registration data, since these identifiers are shared in a public or private community in order to unambiguously identify businesses. In UDDI registries that are only used in private communities, businesses may also want to use privately known identifiers. For example, in a UDDI registry that is used as a service registry in a private exchange, supplier identifiers that are only known in this community might be used to identify the businesses. Identifiers can be applied to `<businessEntity>` and `<tModel>` structures.

Identifiers and categorizations are implemented similarly. Identifiers are attached to `<businessEntity>` and `<tModel>` documents through an `<identifierBag>` structure. As illustrated in Figure 12, the `<identifierBag>` structure can have one or more `<keyedReference>` structures that provide the name, value and `<tModel>` UUID reference for locating more information.

For example, the following listing can be used to identify Springer publications using their Dun & Bradstreet D-U-N-S® Number and the corresponding tModelKey within the UDDI Business Registry:

Figure 12. **IdentifierBag**

```
<identifierBag>
    <keyedReference
       tModelKey="uddi:uddi.org:ubr:identifier:dnb.com:d-u-n-s"
       keyName="SAP AG"
       keyValue="31-626-8655"/>
</identifierBag>
```

However, as Figure 13 illustrates, more than one identifier can be attached to the entity.

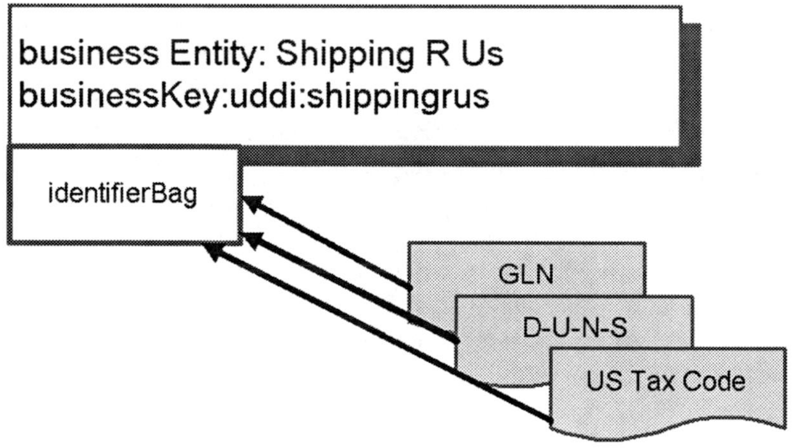

Figure 13. **IdentifierBag-businessEntity**

The `businessEntity` with the name "Shipping R Us" specified three identifiers in its `identifierBag`, D-U-N-S® number, a Global Location Number, and a US Tax Code identifier. Any of the identifiers can be used in a `find_business` call in order to locate the `businessEntity` in the UDDI registry. The description for `find_business` call is provided in the next section.

3. Programming UDDI

Three of the main API sets supported by UDDI specifications are for inquiry, publishing and subcription. The inquiry API locates information about a business, the services a business offers, the specifications of those services, and information about what to do in a failuare situation. Any read operation from a UDDI registry uses of one of the inquiry API's message. The inquiry API does not require authenticated access and is subsequently accessed using HTTP.

The publishing API is used to create, store or update information located in a UDDI registry. All functions in this API require authenticated access to a UDDI registry; the UDDI registry must have a logon identity, and the security credientials for this identity must be passed as a parameter of the XML document for each UDDI invocation. Because publishing requires authenticated access, it is accessed over HTTPS, with a different URL than the one used with the inquiry access point.

The subscription API, which has been introduced with UDDI v3 as an optional API allows consumers to register interest in the UDDI registry as a subscription. Whenever there is change in the registry that matches the subscription criteria, the register sends a notification to the client.

3.1. Searching with UDDI

UDDI defines an inquiry API to support the programmatic discovery of registry data. The API primarily consists of finder and retriever methods. The finder methods return result sets based upon general criteria, while the retriever methods return detailed information about a specific registry entry. Table 2 lists the available finder methods.

The finder methods (`find_xx`) are designed to return basic information about the structures. Given the key to one of the major data structures, you can drill down into the registry to get a full listing of the details in that structure.

The inquiry API provides a series of methods (`get_xx`) for retrieving information from the registry. Table 3 provides a listing.

The inquiry API provides three patterns that can be used to query the registry: the browse, drill-down and the invocation pattern.

Table 2. **Finder Methods**

Method Name	Return type	Description
`find_binding`	`<bindingDetail>`	Locates bindings within or across one ore more registered business services. The API call returns a `<bindingDetail>` that contains zero or more `<bindingTemplate>` structures.
`find_business`	`<businessList>`	Locates information about one or more businesses. The API call returns a `<businessList>` that contains zero or more `<businessInfo>` structures.
`find_relatedBusiness`	`<relatedBusinessesList>`	Locates information about `businessEntity` registrations that are related to a specific business entity whose key is passed in the inquiry.
`find_service`	`<serviceList>`	Locates one or more business services within registered business entities. The API call returns a `<serviceList>` that contains zero or more `<serviceInfo>` structures.
`find_tModel`	`<tModelList>`	Locates one or more `tModel` information structures. The API call returns a `<tModelList>` that contains zero or more `<tModelInfo>` structures.

3.1.1. Browse Pattern

The browse pattern characteristically involves starting with some broad information, performing a search, finding general result sets and then selecting more specific information for drill-down. The `find_xx` API methods listed in the above table are used to support the browse pattern. For instance, you might want to find out if a particular business has any information registered (`find_business`). Once you know the business name, you might want to know about the services offered by the business (`find_services`). The `find_xx` API let callers start with a broad notion of the kind of information they wish to retrieve from a registry, retrieve summary information, and then drill down to get details.

***Table 3.* Retriever Methods**

Method Name	Retrun type	Description
get_bindingDetail	<bindingDetail>	Returns the run-time binding-template information.
get_businessDetail	<businessDetail>	Returns one or more complete business-entity objects. The API call returns a <businessDetail> that contains a list of <businessEntity> structure corresponding to each of the businessKey values specified.
get_operationInfo	<operationalInfos>	Returns operational information pertaining to one or more entities. The API call returns an operationalInfo structure that contains an operationalInfo element for each entity requested by the inquirer.
get_serviceDetail	<serviceDetail>	Returns a complete service object. The API call returns a <serviceDetail> that contains a list of <businessService> structures corresponding to each of the serviceKey values specified.
get_tModelDetail	<tModelDetail>	Returns a complete tModel object. The API call returns a <tModelDetail> that contains a list of <tModel> structure corresponding to each of the tModelKey values specified.

3.1.2. Drill-Down Pattern

Drill-down patterns involves getting details information using the results returned by the find_xx operations. This is done using the retriever methods (get_xx) that are listed in Table 3. Each instance of the core data structures – businessEntity, businessService, bindingTemplate and tModel – has a key which is one of the items in the summary information retrieved by find_xx APIs. Given such a key, it is easy to retrieve the full registered details for the corresponding instance by passing the key to the relevant get_xx API. For instance, if you are looking to find information about a business, you could call the find_business method which will return a <businessList> structure. You can then use the businessKey (embedded in businessList) to retrieve more information about the business using the get_businessDetail method. Upon success, this API returns a businessDetail containing the full registered information, including the businessEntity structure for the entity whose key value was passed.

Most likely, you would use a tool with a graphical interface to achieve the above two patterns. It should allow you to find information on the basis of business, service or `tModel` and then let you drill down. It should further let you drill deeper, locating entities in the current context as your navigate through the registry.

3.1.3. Invocation Pattern

One of objectives with SOA applications is to have loose coupling between the participating businesses. Prior to SOA, a typical development approach for developing cross-application access was to define the interfaces in two locations. CORBA, J2EE among other distributed technologies also required the stub code to be available at the client location. In the SOA paradigm, services can be discovered dynamically and do not require stub code to be copied on the client location. Traditionally, discovering and identifying details about the inter-business call has been a task that is undertaken at the development time. The existence of UDDI registry entries makes it significantly easier to do dynamic binding using the invocation pattern. Here are the steps that you could execute to invoke a remote service.

- Using the above browse-and-drill-down patterns, you can browse the registry and retrieve bindingTemplate about the service that is of interest. The bindingTemplate contains the specific details about an instance of a given interface type, including the location at which a program starts interacting with the service.

- The calling application can then cache this information and uses it to contact the service at the registered address whenever it needs to communicate.

- If a call fails using cached, the client application could take the `bindingKey`, call the `get_bindingDetails` API and get a new `bindingTemplate`.

- If the new `bindingTemplate` returned is different from the cached information, the application should retry the invocation using the fresh information.

- If the result of this retry is successful, the new information can then update the cached information.

By using the invocation pattern, the client application can locate new service information about the partners without undue communication and coordination costs. Caching also helps in reducing the unnecessary round trips to the UDDI registry to locate services and binding information thus optimizing the service environment.

3.2. Publishing with UDDI

UDDI defines a publishing API to support the programmatic publication of registry data to a UDDI registry. All the publishing APIs are implemented as synchronous and "atomic" from the point of view of the caller. As discussed previously in Section 2.3 (UDDI Keys), the publisher can specify keys at the time of publishing. If no keys are specified, the registry generates a key at the time of registration. Unlike inquiry, publishing a message requires authenticated access to the registry. Publishing message requests use a different access points (HTTPS) than do the inquiry messages (HTTP). When information is inserted into an operator node, that site becomes the owner of that data's master copy. Any subsequent updates or changes to the data must be performed at the same operator node.

This API consists of four sets of methods that are used for the following purposes:

1. Adding or updating registry entries;
2. Removing registry entries;
3. Managing `publisherAssertions`; and
4. Retrieving the status of published entries.

Table 4 lists the methods used to add or update registry entries, whereas Table 5 lists the methods used to remove registry entries. Upon completion, all these methods return a `dispositionReport` structure with a single success indicator.

Table 6 lists the methods used to modify publisher assertions and Table 7 lists the methods used to retrieve status information about registry data.

The publication API supports a comprehensive set of methods to create, update and delete entries from the UDDI registry. There are also a good number of tools (e.g. Systinet) in the market that provides a web interface to achieve most of these functions.

3.3. Subscribing with UDDI

Subscription provides clients, known as subscribers, with the ability to register their interest in receiving information concerning changes made in a UDDI registry. The subscription API allows the monitoring of `businessEntity`, `businessService`, `bindingTemplate`, `tModel`, related `businessEntity` and

***Table 4.* Adding or Updating Registry Entries**

Method Name	Return type	Description
save_binding	<bindingDetail>	Inserts or updates a UDDI registry with the <bindingTemplate> documents passed as input. The method returns a <bindingDetail> structure containing the results of the call.
save_business	<businessDetail>	Inserts or updates a UDDI registry with the <businessEntity> documents passed as input. This API has the broadest scope of all of the save_xx API calls and can be used to control the full set of information about the entire business, including its businessService and bindingTemplate structures. It returns a <businessDetail> structure containing the final results of the call.
save_service	<serviceDetail>	Inserts of updates a UDDI registry with the <businessService> documents passed as input. This API can modify <businessService> and any references to <bindingTemplate> structures. It returns a <serviceDetail> structure containing the final results of the call.
save_tModel	<tModelDetail>	Inserts or updates a UDDI registry with the <tModel> documents passed as input. It returns a <tModelDetail> structure containing the final results of the call.

***Table 5.* Removing Registry Entries**

Method Name	Return Type	Description
delete_binding	<dispositionReport>	Removes existing bindingTemplate entry from the UDDI registry.
delete_business	<dispositionReport>	Removes existing businessEntity entry from the UDDI registry. Deleting these documents also causes the deletion of any contained <businessService> or <bindingTemplate> data.
delete_service	<dispositionReport>	Removes existing businessService entry from the UDDI registry.
delete_tModel	<dispositionReport>	Logically removes existing tModel entry from the UDDI registry by marking them as hidden. The documents are not actually destroyed. Hidden <tModel> documents are still accessible, via the get_registeredInfo and get_tModelDetail APIs, but are omitted from any results returned by calls to find_tModel.

***Table 6.* Modifying Publisher Assertions**

Method Name	Return Type	Description
add_publisherAssertions	<dispositionReport>	Adds a new relationship assertion to the current set of assertions. A publisher assertion creates an association between two businesses. The relationship becomes publicly visible only when both the businesses have added matching <publisherAssertion> documents to their collection.
delete_publisherAssertions	<dispositionReport>	Removes a specific publisherAssertion. Deleting an assertion causes any relationships based on that assertion to become incomplete.
set_publisherAssertions	<publisherAssertions>	Saves a new complete set of assertions for a publisher, completely replacing any previous assertions. The call returns a <publisherAssertions> document that contains the current collection as they are stored in the registry.

***Table 7.* Retrieving Status Data**

Method Name	Return Type	Description
get_assertionStatusReport	<assertionStatusReport>	Retrieves a report identifying all registered assertions and their current status for the requesting publisher.
get_publisherAssertions	<publisherAssertions>	Retrieves a list of all assertions for a particular publisher.
get_registeredInfo	<registeredInfo>	Retrieves an abbreviated list of <businessEntity> and <tModel> documents currently managed by a given publisher.

publisherAssertion. The subscribers register their interest and are notified if there is a new, updated or deleted entry for any of the above entities.

Let us illustrate the use of the above API by imagining a company, DummyMortgages, which provides a brokerage solution for home mortgages. Consumers or Mortgage buyers provide basic information about the type of loan required, and DummyMortgages supplies the best interest rate as available from its partners. DummyMortgages deals with many banks and financial institutions on a routine basis as increasing its partners network and providing the best interest rate for its customers is critical to its business growth. In order to integrate with its system, DummyMortgages asks its partners to implement a mortgage query service. The service would take the amount, and type of loan as the arguments and return the available interest rate. DummyMortgages publishes the interface definition of the expected service at its partners website so that a potential partner can implement the service and register it with the company's UDDI service. On a periodic basis, DummyMortgages business team queries the UDDI registry for a list of services that have implemented the mortgage query interface. If the list returns a new partner, the business team adds the name to its existing directory of partners. And from this point on, any consumer request for a loan will also be forwarded to this newly founded partner. The subscription API allows DummyMortgages to register its interest with the UDDI registry. Figure 14 illustrates the scenario.

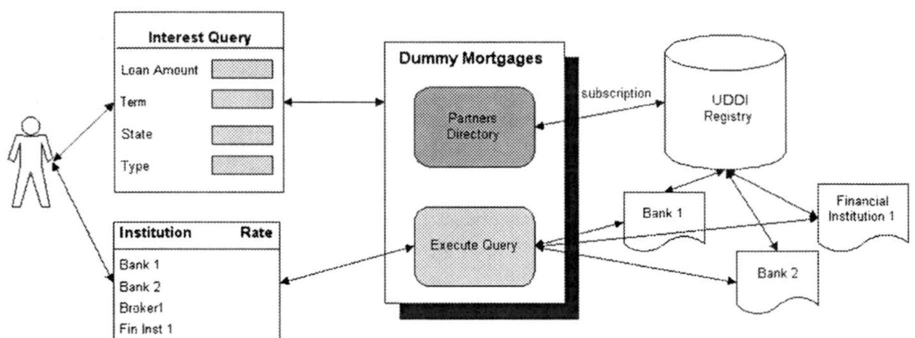

Figure 14. **Subscribing with UDDI**

Whenever a new partner publishes its service with the UDDI registry or an existing partner make changes to its registration, the registry will send notifications to DummyMortgages. This not only eliminates the need for DummyMortgages business team to keep polling the UDDI registry for new partners but it also speeds up the process of integrating new partner's services with the Dummy Mortgages' interest query service.

The business team would normally invoke the `find_service` method to retrieve the services that are compliant with the interest query tModel. The subscription API allows the query to be saved in the UDDI registry along with other parameters on how and when to notify the DummyMortgages' business team. It also allows specifying the length of time that the company is interested in monitoring the registry changes. The query and preferences are stored in the `subscription` structure that is shown in Figure 15. The subscription API supports two monitoring patterns.

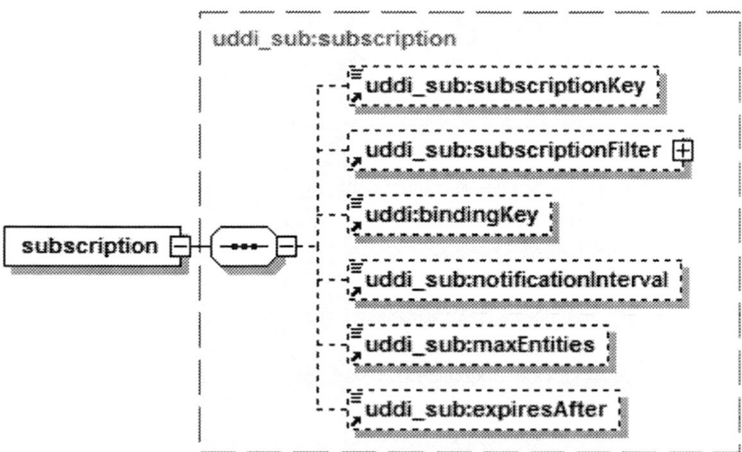

Figure 15. **Subscription Schema**

3.3.1. Asynchronous Notification

This pattern is also referred to as subscriber listener since it enables subscribers to inform the UDDI node that they wish to be directly notified when subscribed registry data changes. The subscription data structure allows registering a service or an email in the binding key element. Any time this is a change, the register either invokes the service or send an email notification about the change. Thus to be automatically notified of the new partners that have implemented the company's interest query service, the DummyMortgages' business team will save a subscription that uses the `find_service` call with the interest query service's `tModel` key as a parameter.

3.3.2. Synchronous Notification

This pattern is also referred as change tracking. It enables subscribing clients to issue a synchronous request to retrieve registry changes that match their subscription preferences. To support that *synchronous* subscription mode, you leave the subscription's binding key empty and invoke `get_subscriptionResults` method in a synchronous manner and it returns the same information what the registry would send in a notification.

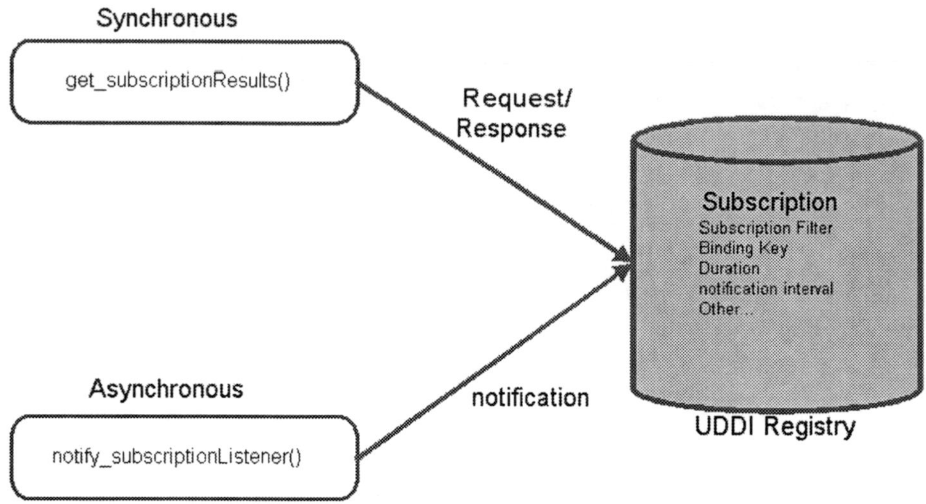

Figure 16. **Synchronous vs Asynchronous**

Note that the subscription API is optional and the UDDI registry is not required to support it. Table 8 lists the methods defined by the specification.

Table 8. **Subscription API**

Method Name	Return Type	Description
`delete_subscription`	`<DispositionReport>`	Deletes one or more subscriptions.
`get_subscriptionResults`	`<subscriptionResultsList>`	Synchronously returns registry data related to a particular subscription.
`get_subscriptions`	`<subscriptions>`	Returns current list of subscriptions associated with the subscriber.
`notify_subscriptionListener`	`<dispostionReport>`	Receives asynchronous notifications of changes to data that the subscriber is monitoring. The method is optional for client.
`save_subscription`	`<subscriptions>`	Registers a new subscription, or modifies or renews an existing one.

4. Internationalization

The U in UDDI stands for Universal and the one of the goals is to provide a registry solution for Universal description, discovery and integration of business entities and their services. The UDDI registry design includes support for internationalization features.ÿ Most of these internationalization features are directly exposed to end users through the API sets.ÿ Others are built into the design in order to enable the use of the UDDI registry as an international services discovery and description mechanism with multilingual descriptions of business entities worldwide. Version 3 of the UDDI specifications supports the ability to classify entities using multiple languages and multiple scripts of the same language. It also allows for additional language-specific sort orders and provides for consistent search results in a language-independent manner.

This section discusses the internationalization features supported by the UDDI specifications:

- multilingual descriptions, names and addresses;
- multiple names in the same language;
- internationalized address format; and
- language-dependent collation.

4.1. Multilingual Descriptions, Names and Addresses

UDDI registry allows names, descriptions and address elements to be specified in other languages that may have characters from language scripts other than the Latic script found in ASCII. For instance, if you have a shipping company that also provides services in China, you would want to register your business in that language too. The `xml:lang` attribute provides the solution.

```
<businessEntity ...>
  ........
<name xml:lang="en">ShippingRUs</name>
  <name xml:lang="zh">?????</name>
  .....
</businessEntity>
```

Similarly, variants of names, due to transliteration, e.g. romanization, to different languages can also be indicated through the use of the `xml:lang` attribute. The following shows an example of romanization where the primary name of the business (a Chinese flower shop) is in Chinese, and its alternative name is a romanization

```
<businessEntity ...>
  ........
  <name xml:lang="zh">?????</name>
  <name xml:lang="en">Rus Yun Shu Gong Si</name>
    .....
</businessEntity>
```

The following sample XML fragment shows an address written in two languages, English and Chinese, as indicated by the `xml:lang` attribute:

```
<address useType="Sales office" xml:lang="en"
tModelKey="uddi:...">
   <addressLine>7 F</addressLine>
   <addressLine>No. 245</addressLine>
   <addressLine>Sec. 1</addressLine>
   <addressLine>Tunhua South Road</addressLine>
   <addressLine>Taipei</addressLine>
</address>
</address><address useType="Sales office" xml:lang="zh"
tModelKey="uddi:...">
   <addressLine>???</addressLine>
   <addressLine>????</addressLine>
   <addressLine>??</addressLine>
   <addressLine>245</addressLine>
   <addressLine>7</addressLine>
   ...
</address>
```

4.2. Multiple Names in the Same Language

The registry also supports to publish muliple names in the same language. This is useful for multi-script languages. An example is Kanji and Katakana for Japanese where the registry allows publishing the name in both scripts for the same entity. It is also useful if you want to publish an acronym for your business. The following shows an example of use of multiple name elements to support a multi-script language and also the use of acronym. In the example, the first <name> element is the primary name of the business (a Japanese flower shop) in Japanese Kanji. The second <name> element is the business' name transliterated into Japanese Katakana. The third <name> element gives the business' full English name, and the fourth <name> element gives its English acronym:

```
<businessEntity ...>
  ........
  <name xml:lang="ja">???):</name>
  <name xml:lang="ja">......</name>
  <name xml:lang="en">ShippingRUs</name>
  <name xml:lang="en">SRU</name>
  .....
</businessEntity>
```

Where multiple name elements are published, the first name element is treated as the primary name, which is the name by which a business would be searched and sorted in case the business has multiple names.

4.3. Internationalized Address Format

Different parts of the world have their own ways of specifying their postal addresses using different elements such as lot numbers, floor numbers, city, street and so forth. In UDDI, the address is supported by the <address> element that is part of the businessEntity data structure. The address element contains a list of <addressLine> elements. UDDI Business Registry has a canonical tModel, ubr-uddi-org:postalAddress, that identifies a canonical postal address structure with common address sub-elements (e.g. states, cities). This canonical address structure describes address data via name/code pairs, enabling each common address sub-element to be identified by name or code. The following XML fragment illustrates a way to specify an address

```
<address useType="Sales office"
tModelKey="uddi:uddi.org:ubr:postaladdress">
   <addressLine keyName="Street"
   keyValue="40">SpringWell Road</addressLine>
   <addressLine keyName="House number"
   keyValue="70">181</addressLine>
   ...
   <addressLine keyName="Country"
   keyValue="30">United Kingdom</addressLine>
</address>
```

With the use of the `keyName/KeyValue` pair together with the codes assigned in the `ubr-uddi-org:postalAddress tModel`, you can programmatically determine the address semantics and evaluate them even if the sub-elements are specified in different sequence or language.

Since there is large variation in address sub-elements of different countries, the address structure also supports free form address lines.

4.4. Language-Dependent Collation

Each supported language within the registry is based on the Unicode 3.0 specification and ISO 10646, which support the majority of languages. Each language has its own unique behavior when it comes to sort-order collation. For instance, the languages that share the same alphabetic script, such as English, Spanish and French, the letters have different collation weights depending on the other languages with which they are used. For languages that have both upper and lowercase letters, sorting depends on whether sorting is specified as case-sensitive. The UDDI specifications allow the collation sequence of results returned by the Inquiry APIs to be specified via find qualifiers. For instance, the following snippet can be used to sort the entities by name in ascending order using the JIS X 4061 Japanese collation sequence.

```
<find\_business xmlns="urn:uddi-org:api\_v3">
...
  <findQualifiers>
   <findQualifier>
       uddi:uddi.org:sortorder:jis-4061
   </findQualifier>
   <findQualifier>
       uddi:uddi.org:findqualifier:sortbynameasc
   </findQualifier>
  </findQualifiers>
...
</find\_business>
```

4.5. Federation of Registries

The UDDI Version 3.0 specification addresses the complexity of registry topology, and defines how registries may form a *federation*. A key aspect of such federations is the mechanism by which a registry entity may be promoted from one registry to another and how global registry key uniqueness is maintained. In the earlier versions of UDDI specifications, only the UDDI node could generate keys and a publisher was not allowed to pre-assign the keys. In order to maintain the uniqueness of keys, a publisher could not import or export a UDDI registry entity in its entirety from one registry to another.

As we discussed earlier in this chapter, Version 3 of UDDI approaches the issue of key generation in a significantly different fashion and it allows the publisher to use its own keys while registering an entity. It therefore allows copying an entity from one registry to another while preserving the key. This behavior is called entity promotion and it permits data sharing between UDDI registries and it establishes UDDI as a more distributed registry solution. The publisher could potentially publish the entirety of a registry's contents into another registry, effectively mirroring the data. Or, the publisher might be interested in only a subset of data from another registry and only copy a portion of that data. However, while copying the entities across the registries, it is still critical to avoid key collisions. The recommended way to prevent such collisions is to establish a *root registry*, a registry that acts as the authority for key spaces. A root registry serves to delegate key partitions such that other registries can rely upon the root registry for verification and validation of a given key partition. All other registries that interact with the root registry are called *affiliate* registries. By relying on a common root registry as an arbitrator of key spaces, affiliate registries can share data with both the root registry and among one another with the knowledge that a given partition is unique.

An important example of a root registry is the UDDI Business Registry, which has a set of policies in place to generate unique `uuidKeys` as well as to validate `domainKeys` through signatures that correlate with DNS records. By acknowledging the UDDI Business Registry as a root, an affiliate registry can establish inter-registry communication policies and procedures with both the UDDI Business Registry and any other registry, which is an affiliate of the UDDI Business Registry. Following this approach, registries could form hierarchical relationships where they can share data with their parents and affiliate registries and form a federation.

The two scenarios below illustrate the use of inter-registry communication in real business situations.

4.6. Private Test Registry

Applications based on SOA follows the same laws of software development life cycle. You develop the application in a development environment, unit test it and promotes it to a test or staging environment. Once the system test and UAT is done, the

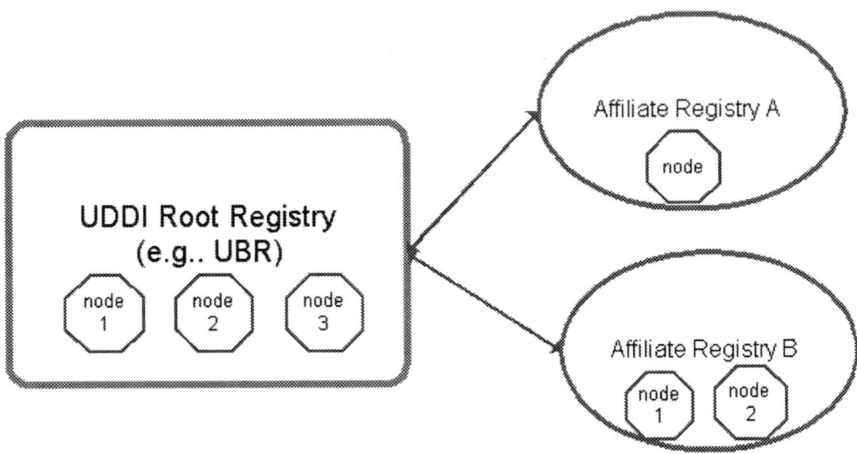

Figure 17. **Federation**

application is promoted to a production environment. Your registry should follow the same route as your service while progressing its way from a test registry to a production registry. In order to be close to the real-world production environment, it is desirable that the modifications required while switching from test to production mode are kept minimal. It is also critical that the development/test versions of software must not interfere with actual production systems. Because services can be highly distributed and are loosely coupled maintaining this distinction is paramount to ensure that dependencies are managed systematically. You would not want two hundred thousands copies of the same book delivered to your door step while load testing your book ordering application in test environment which by mistake was pointing to the production service.

The entity promotion facilitates the setup of a private test registry and the upgrade from test to production environment. When development versions of software have been fully tested and certified in the test environment, the registry entry in its entirety can be copied to the production sphere.

A number of companies are following the practice of setting up a private test registry for internal development and testing and then using standard operations procedures to migrate it to the production environment. Figure 18 illustrates the scenario.

4.7. Shared Registry

The enhanced security and federation of the UDDI registries also allows setting up shared registries that support collaboration among partners. The shared registries

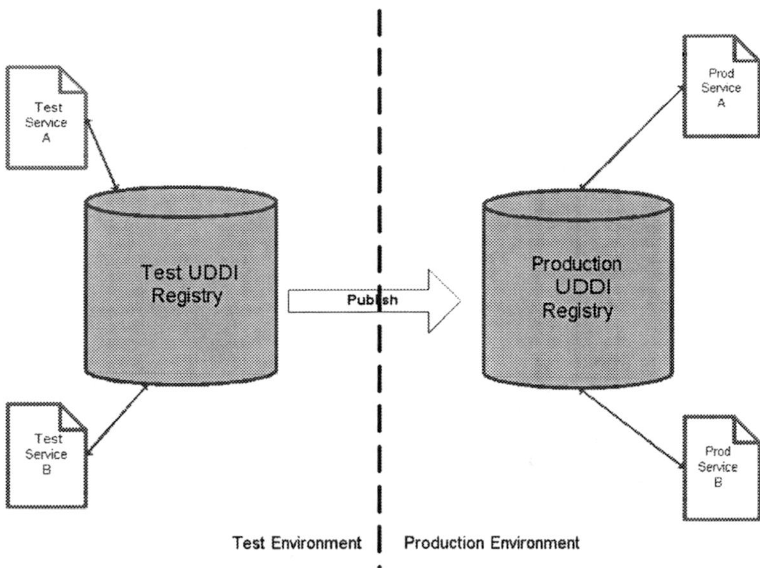

Figure 18. **Private Registry**

might reside outside a corporate firewall but with restricted access only to clients of trusted business partners. For instance, DummyMortgages from our earlier example can set up a shared UDDI registry and invite its partners to register relevant Web service implementations in it. Let us consider another scenario where a manufacturing business purchases raw material from its partners, fabricate it and sell it to its consumers. Being in the middle of the supply chain, it profits relies on its integration with its suppliers and consumers and the efficient management of its inventory system. Due to the disparate systems of its partners, SOA appears as the natural choice. In order to avoid separate integration and coordination efforts with each of its partners, it sets up shared partner registries where its partners can implement their services. In addition, by establishing subscription-based relationships with partner's registries, the company can ensure that the information is up-to-date and is processed in the most efficient manner. The registries can be deployed inside the DMZ trusted environment to limit the exposure of the registry. Figure 19 illustrates the scenario.

Such shared UDDI registries can either be hosted by companies or by industry-specific organizations or consortia. These shared registries will restrict access to its members and facilitate an electronic market place. For instance, all the automakers can setup a registry to unify their purchasing power on commodity parts. There are already some efforts underway to this effect. For instance, the Star Standard (http://www.starstandard.org/) is an auto-industry-wide initiative to define a standard way for automotive dealerships to communicate with car manufacturers; RosettaNet (http://www.rosettanet.org) is a consortium of major Information technology and

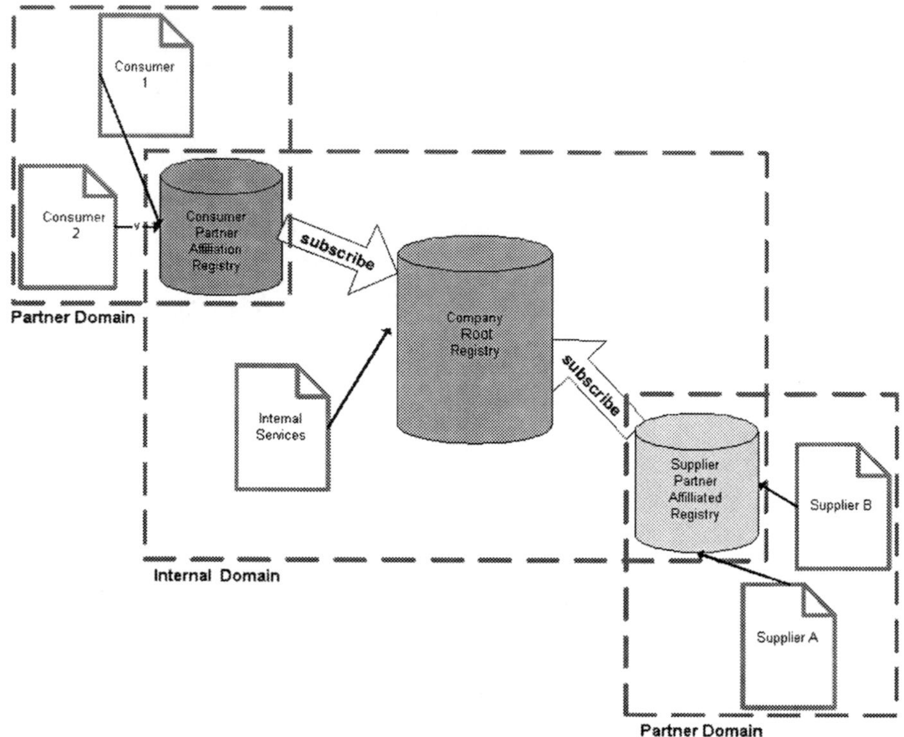

Figure 19. **Shared Registry**

manufacturing companies to define open e-business process standards for supply chain partners on a global basis. OpenTravel (http://www.opentravel.org) is a similar effort by major airlines, hoteliers, car rental companies, and travel agencies.

4.8. Security

The security model for a UDDI registry can be characterized by the collection of registry and node policies and the implementation of these policies by a UDDI node. The principal areas of security policies and mechanisms in the UDDI specification are related to data management, user identification, user authentication, user authorization, confidentiality of messages and integrity of data.

UDDI v3 also supports XML Digital Signatures on UDDI data. XML digital signature is discussed in depth in the next chapter on Security. In the context of UDDI, it enables consumers to verify the integrity of the data with respect to the publisher. Publishers of entities can now ensure that some malicious party who claims to own the entity does not misrepresent them. Furthermore, once a publisher signs the data, altering it in any way breaks the signature, providing confidence in the data's integrity. By verifying the signature, consumers using the registry can also be assured that a signed entity is valid and that the publisher represented by the signature created it. Consumers can also issue queries that only return results pertaining to signed data. The reliability of data is even more critical in the multi-registry environment. When signed data is copied between registries, you can guarantee its integrity by simply validating the signature. The use of digital signatures improves both the quality of data in UDDI and provides users with the trust and protection needed for service-oriented applications.

5. Summary

A registry solution is all about sharing business information, making it easier to publish your preferred means of doing business, finding trading partners and have them find you, and interoperate with these trading partners over the internet. It removes the barriers to rapid participation in the global economy and allows businesses to fully participate in the new digital economy. The automated application-to-application discovery and integration over the Internet helps eliminate many of the configuration and compatibility problems that are preventing businesses from more widely adopting B2B, despite B2B's potential for cost savings and improved efficiency. However, just like the early days of web, the registries have a Catch 22 situation. Users and businesses will not search the registries if there are not many services listed in the registry. With the scarcity of potential consumers, the providers will be reluctant to put the extra effort required to publish a service in the registry. The initial idea of the architects was to have a global registry where everybody can publish their services, but this has changed and the industry is now seeing many private and shared registries being used within the partner networks.

However, there are still a lot of places, where in spite of the service enablement of the business functions, the requestor and the provider binds directly to each other. True ESOA is only achieved when your organization accomplishes the dynamic interoperability between services. When the provider can announce a service and does not have to communicate individually with all the users. And a business analyst can select a service based on the functionality without worrying about the underlying infrastructure. There are a few key points that strongly support the value of a registry solution in an ESOA environment:

- Visibility: Without a registry solution, the business user or client cannot find what is available. You cannot use what you cannot find. The architects and the development teams can build a comprehensive set of services but without a standard mechanism to communicate these to the potential consumers, it is worthless. A registry works as the central point of reference for the distributed SOA assets built and deployed by an enterprise.

- Re-usability: It is one of the keys to the success of ESOA. The extra investment in enabling your business functions as services pays off, when it helps in avoiding the duplicate effort within the enterprise. However, without a registry solution, participants involved in creating, managing and consuming services will not know what others are planning and building and this will result in redundant, conflicting and overlapping services within the enterprise.
- Configurability and Adaptability: Registry provides a layer of abstraction between the consumer and the service provider. It allows for the modifications in the business requirements, policies or needs of the consumer as well as the implementation changes of the provider without affecting each other. It allows enterprises to assert new policies that define specific security, process, semantic, and governance constraints by which consumers can bind to specific business services, and for clients to adapt without having to redeploy applications.

The APIs provided by the registry solutions allows random searching for businesses. It is conceivable that software will eventually discover a service dynamically and use it without requiring human interaction. In the near future, the business analysts with specific knowledge of the problem at hand will use UDDI portals to discover potentially interesting services and partners, and technologists will write programs to use the services from companies that have already been discovered. UDDI portals and SOA management solutions are coming up fast in the market that provides user friendly interfaces and not only allows customized searches for business but also provides support to update information in a registry.

5
UNDERSTANDING ENTERPRISE SECURITY

The difficulties you meet will resolve themselves as you advance. Proceed, and light will dawn and shine with increasing clearness on your path.
Jim Rohn, Author of *The Art of Exceptional Living*

A key benefit of the service-oriented architectures is the ability to deliver integrated, interoperable solutions. Ensuring the integrity, confidentiality and security of these services through the application of a comprehensive security model is critical, both for organizations and their customers. Security is considered one of the most critical aspect of an enterprise system. According to Zapthink, "Security is the immediate roadblock facing widespread implementation of service oriented integrations across the enterprise." The advent of N-tier systems, enterprise application integrations and service-oriented applications has resulted in a more complex and fragmented application layer. Due to the distributed nature of the current enterprise systems, we have difficulty in administering security policies and bridging diverse security models. This leads to increased opportunities to make mistakes and leave security holes, hence the chance of accidental disclosure and the vulnerability to attack goes up.

The security infrastructure in the traditional distributed computing world resembles islands of security. Each component or network acts as an island, with its own perimeter security, and only users within the network are considered to be trusted. The arrival of Enterprise SOA breaks this "trusted vs untrusted" dichotomy. The promise of ESOA is to be able to locate and request a service on a different network or enterprise in a similar manner as if it is co-located.

The easy and historical approach to handle the security issue has been to put the responsibility on application developers. They have to discover the security policies of upstream providers and downstream requesters. Then they have to determine appropriate policies for the application layer and implement security infrastructure along side business code. This tactic of course results in intermingled code with business logic and security tightly coupled and a maintenance nightmare on hand. The other approach is to put the responsibility on security administrators. They have to understand the detailed security logistics of the different components, intermediaries and middleware infrastructure. However, without the proper knowledge and control of the security needs of other systems and to avoid the conflicts and interoperability concerns, this results in conservatively configured components.

The fundamental sources of these problems are twofold. First, middleware paradigms assume that the application is the center of the world. They often do not fully acknowledge the rest of the enterprise security ecology, which includes firewalls, directory servers, web servers, authentication providers, and databases. Second, the built-in security models of most middleware paradigms do not fully support the dynamic policies necessary to meet the realities of modern business processes. Evaluating who owns an account or the strength of encryption used on a connection is cumbersome if not impossible. The advent of SOA systems has extrapolated these security issues.

The solution lies in a change of perspective – middleware paradigms own the business logic but co-operate on security. Therefore, they should gather as much information from the rest of the security ecology as possible and enable the security administrators to evaluate this information before it ever reaches the business logic. However, in order to be interoperable and for administrators to understand this information, there is a need of mutually agreeable standards. For systems based on service-oriented architectures to be successful, there is a need of a security solution that is standards-based but powerful, flexible and extensible. It should be part of the application infrastructure and still separate from the application.

We will start this chapter explaining some of the prevalent security concepts. These concepts are valid whether it is a J2EE world or a .NET application, an online sale or a trip to your local mall. In the sections that follow, we will examine each of these concepts and how could be handled in an enterprise system. We will also look at the common specifications that are prevalent in the ESOA space. But before that, let us first discuss the need for a security solution where the security is built within the message.

1. Need for a Message Level Security Solution

Enterprise systems already have transport layer security mechanisms such as SSL/TLS and IPSec. Most of the applications, whether they are built on J2EE or .NET, also implement their own security framewok to block against outside attacks. Why this is not enough? The reason lies in the distributed and heterogeneous nature of the SOA systems. SOA enables application topologies that include a broad combination of mobile devices, gateways, proxies, middlewares, outsourced data centers, and globally distributed, dynamically configured systems. Many of the bigger problems involve sending the message along a path more complicated than request/response or over a transport that does not involve HTTP. In an SOA eco system, there are more than one endpoints that span the physical and application boundaries. Your application is only as secure as the weakest link (endpoint or intermediary) in the message flow. In the next few sections, we will discuss the issues that surfaces due to the distributed, heterogeneous nature of the SOA-based applications.

1.1. Point-to-Point vs End-to-End Security

Secure Socket Layer (SSL) along with the de facto Transport Layer Security (TLS) provides sufficient security for point-to-point systems. SSL/TLS offers several security features including authentication, data integrity and data confidentiality.

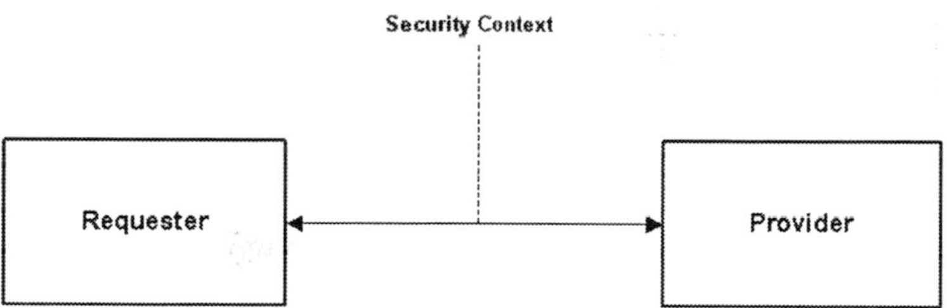

Figure 1. **Point-to-Point Security**

However, in service-oriented architecture a message travels from the originator to the ultimate destination, potentially by passing through a set of intermediaries along the message path. Intermediary is an application that is capable of both receiving and forwarding messages. When an intermediary receives a message, it processes header entries intended for it and must remove them before forwarding the message. It may also insert a similar header entry intended for another intermediary. The "actor" attribute of a header entry is used to indicate the URI of an intermediary who will process the header entry.

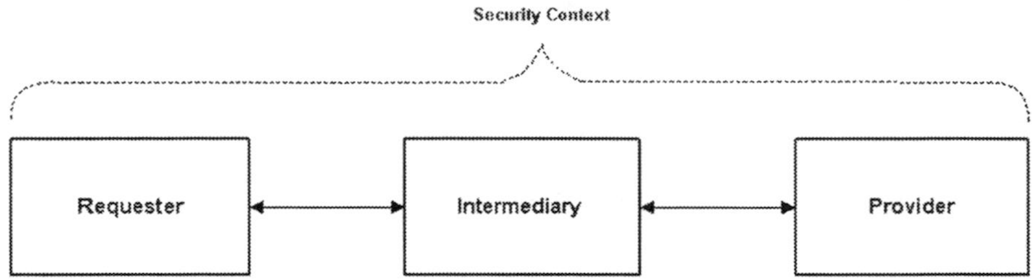

Figure 2. **End-to-End Security**

Transport level security ensures the integrity of data between the two end points. But it does not ensure data security within the intermediary's system. It forces any upstream message processors to rely on the security evaluations made by previous intermediaries and to completely trust their handling of the content of messages. Secure transport protocols can assure the security of messages during transmission. However, since messages are received and processed by intermediaries, secure end-to-end communication is not possible if these intermediaries are not completely trusted even though the communication links between them are trusted. End-to-end security is also compromised if any one of the communication links is not secured. A comprehensive end-to-end security architecture requires the security context to be propagated along with the data to all the listed actors.

The identity, integrity, and security of the message and the caller need to be preserved over multiple hops. More than one encryption key may be used along the route. Trust domains will be crossed. HTTP and its security mechanisms only address point-to-point security. More complex solutions need end-to-end security baked in. The solution needs to maintain a secure context over a multi-point message path.

1.2. Application Independence

End-to-end security ultimately needs to be achieved at the application level. This is because if there is any point between the communicating parties where messages are in plain text, it can be a potential point of attack. However, it is not an easy task to integrate cryptographic functionality into an application without introducing additional security vulnerabilities. Most of the available commercial cryptographic libraries are extremely flexible to meet many different levels of security requirements, and using them properly may require good understanding of cryptographic technologies. A standardized, application-independent security layer will provide good protection without worrying about cryptographic details. You should be able to change the security policies without really modifying the application. Consider the analogy to a secure physical filing system. When the security policy changes, you do not rewrite the document. You put it in a different filing cabinet. Or you change the key of the cabinet and a security officer controls the distribution of keys. Similarly, application developers should not have to change business logic when security policy changes. A security administrator should simply alter the protection given to related components. The other reason to have a separate security layer is to be able to handle security breaches more efficiently. It is a lot harder to test the security of every application component individually than a security system as a whole. For instance, to validate the adherence to the defined security policy for the filing system, you do not read all the documents in all the cabinets. You check the integrity of the locks. It is thus desirable, in most cases, to have security functionality as close to the application level as possible but not built into the application itself.

1.3. Technology Independence

Beyond doubt, every company in the ESOA space has a dream of standardizing each and every application, endpoint, middlewares to their platform. It will definitely make things simple but it is not going to happen. As the scope of your application increases, so does the count of technological variations. There is too much to administer, too many applications, too many variations, and too rapid a pace of technology change to design a single infrastructure to meet all requirements effectively. Extensible standards are required that can adapt to changing requirements, that can incorporate new technologies while continuing to work with legacy technologies, and that can be deployed modularly as needed without requiring use of unnecessary portions. The security solution should be able deal with different languages, cryptographic mechanisms, hashing algorithms among other things. In a computers world "abstraction has an answer for everything". The security solution should be flexible enough to abstract the security techniques used by a given system and have a mechanism to exchange it with other partners that are using a different standard.

2. Security Concepts

Technologies designed to meet the security requirements have evolved and have come a long way. However, the requirements have remained relatively constant. The risks of a system without a security infrastructure have not changed:

- Tampering – An unauthorized person changing the information in the transit. For instance, someone could change the shipping address of an order placed online.
- Eavesdropping – The data remains intact, but privacy of the data is compromised. For instance, someone could learn the credit card number used during an online order placement.
- Impersonation – Also referred to as identity theft where a person can pretend be someone else. Privacy laws of corporations both help and hurt this cause. For instance, with the number of free email providers available, it does not take much effort to get an email id with the words bill gates in it and start posting messages on the newsgroups.

In order to handle the risks above, there are five basic elements that are required for a secure application.

2.1. Authentication – Who Is It?

Determine the identity or role of a party attempting to perform some action such as accessing a resource or participating in a transaction. The recipient of the message must be able to confirm the identity of the sender of the message. Just like any online shopping site asks the user to login before allowing him to place an order, most service providers requires that consumers are authenticated before processing the service request. Security tokens either in the form of username/password or binary tokes (e.g. X.509 certificates) can be used to establish the user's identity. WS-Security allows the security tokens to be included in the SOAP header.

2.2. Authorization – What Can They Do?

Determine whether some party is allowed to perform a requested action, such as accessing a resource, making a transaction, viewing a web page or changing a password. Authorization is a means of ensuring that only authorized users are allowed to access the resources within a system. All authorization inquiries have the same general form: Can {Principal X} perform {Action Y} on {Resource Z}. The authorization queries can be answered by defining the authorization policies or rules. There are several ways to capture the above rules, for instance access control list (ACL) or role-based access. Later in this chapter, we will look at Extensible Access Control Markup Language (XACML) which is getting the maximum traction. XACML provides the XML Schema to capture the rules that specify the who, what, when, and how of information access.

2.3. Integrity – Ensure That Information Is Intact

Ensure that information is not changed, either due to malicious intent or by accident. The recipient of a message must be able to guarantee that a message has not been tampered with in transit. Remember, in a SOA system there may be multiple endpoints and intermediaries before the intended recipient gets the message. Digitally signing the message ensures the data integrity of the message as any data modifications during the message transit are detected in signature verification at the receiving end. XML Signature specifications, discussed later in the chapter, cover the syntax and processing of digitally signing the message.

2.4. Confidentiality – You Can't Read

Ensure that content may only be viewed by legitimate parties and the intruder of transmitted message can not read the data. For instance, consider if the message contains the credit card number of a customer. You not only need to verify that the data is not altered, but also ensure that the credit card information can only be read by the intended party. This basically involves encryption of the message using a mechanism such as SSL to ensure confidentiality. The sender authenticates the receiver and negotiates on the scheme of encryption with the receiver. The receiver has the option to authenticate the sender. The sender and receiver establish a connection exchanging the encrypted messages. XML Encryption specifications define the syntax and processing rules for encrypting and decrypting selected elements in an XML document. Since encryption/decryption algorithms are computationally expensive, it is required to be able to encrypt only the selected portions of the message.

2.5. Non-Repudiation – You Sent It, I Got Proof

The sender and the recipient of the message must be able to guarantee that the sender sent and the recipient received the message. It provides protection against false denial of involvement in a communication. For instance, in an online stock trading system, the broker must be able to verify that the given transaction was requested. XML Signature requires the sender to sign the document using its key and thus verify the sender's identity. Logging and auditing is another way to address non-repudiation claims.

Not exactly an absolute requirement but other useful features in the security infrastructure are given below.

2.6. Single Signon – How Many Times Do I Have to Tell You?

SSO allows users to gain access to resources in multiple domains without having to re-authenticate after initially logging in the first domain.

2.7. Key Management – Give Me a Key Chain

With the increased amount of data and the increasing number of parties involved, each signing and encrypting different elements using different keys, there is a need of key management solution so that the creation and location of the keys is outside the main application realm.

3. *Security Technologies*

With the growing acceptance of XML as de facto language for documents and protocols, it is only logical that security should be integrated with XML solutions. There are a number of XML Security standards to handle the security needs of service-oriented applications. These standards use legacy cryptographic and security technologies, as well as emerging XML technologies, to provide a flexible, extensible and practical solution toward meeting security requirements.

Figure 3 displays the building blocks required for the security framework.

The following items will be discussed in this chapter.

- Security Tokens.
- XML Digital Signature for integrity, Nonrepudiation and signing solutions.
- XML Encryption for confidentiality.
- XML Key Management (XKMS) for public key registration, location and validation.

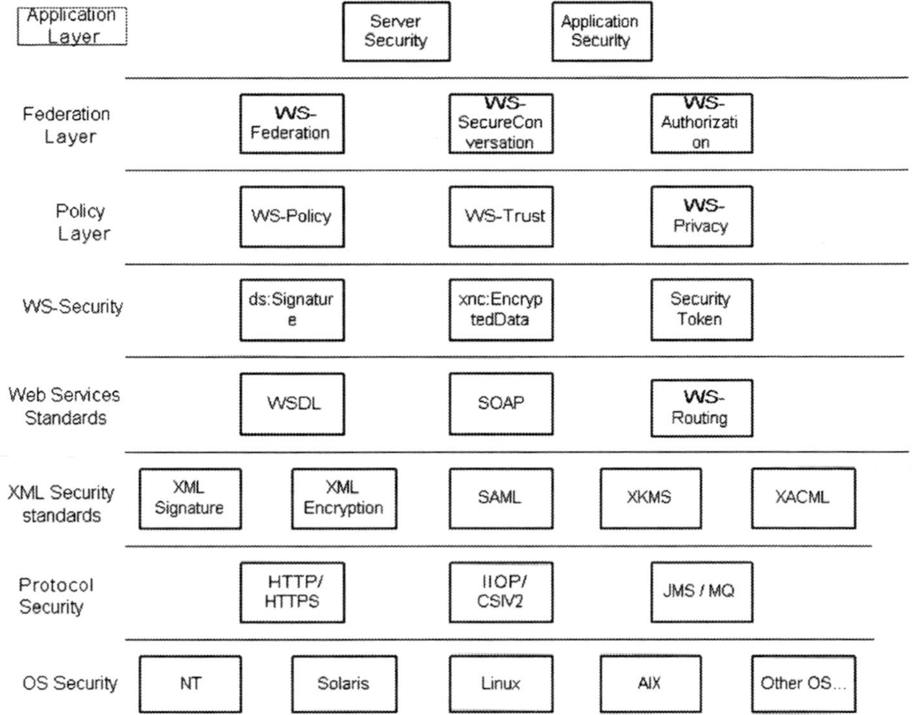

Figure 3. **Blocks for Security Framework**

- Security Assertion Markup Language (SAML) for conveying authentication, authorization and attribute assertions
- XML Access Control Markup Language (XACML) for defining access control rules.
- WS-Security and others – Relies on the above specifications to provide a comprehensive solution.
- Policy and Federation Layer.

3.1. Authenticaton and Security Tokens

Before a service provider allows the requestor any access to its resource, it needs to verify the credentials of the requesting party and verify its identity. For instance, if you go to a bank you need to show your driver's license or other proof of identity before you can withdraw money from your account. Or if you are in a different country, you need a passport to prove your identity. Both the driver's license and passport are credentials to vouch for your identity. However these documents do not perform authentication. Authentication is performed by a person based on these credentials. The bank teller or the immigration officer will verify the picture, signature or other attributes of these documents and validate that you are the rightful owner. In the software world, security tokens serves the purpose of driver's license or passport. Like the license bureau or passport authority, there are security token service providers that can issue security tokens that can be used by applications. The service provider will accept these tokens as part of the request and perform authentication before serving the request.

The requestor can send a security token along with the data as a proof if its identity. Security token is defined as a representation of security-related information (e.g. X.509 certificate, Kerberos tickets and authenticators, username, etc.). A security token is considered signed that contains a set of related claims cryptographically endorsed by an issuer. Examples of signed security tokens include X.509 certificates and Kerberos tickets. Username/password is considered unsigned security tokens. The requestor and provider can either have their own implementations to support the security token or they can rely on an external security token service. Figure 4 illustrates a common message flow.

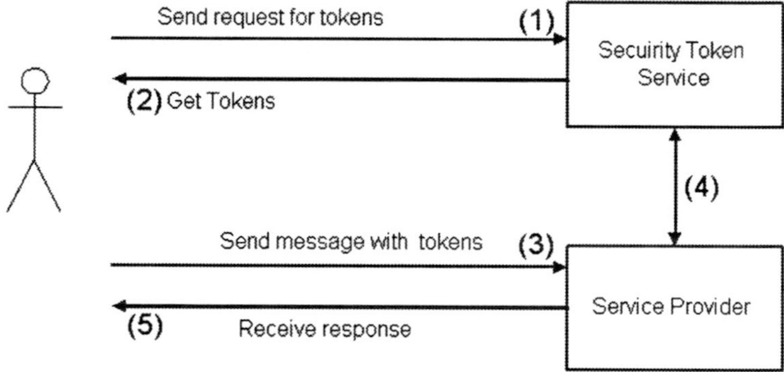

Figure 4. **Security Token Service**

3.1.1. Username/Password

The most common ways to pass around credentials is to use a username and password. The password can be sent along with the message in plain text or as a digest hash. The other option is to communicate the password in advance to avoid sending it with the message.

3.1.2. PKI through X.509 Certificates

Another option to use when authenticating uses is to simply send around an X.509 certificate. Using PKI, you can map the certificate to an existing user in your application. When a message sends along an X.509 certifcate, it will pass the public version of the certificate along the message. Anyone with the public version of the certificate can validate the identity of the sender.

3.1.3. Kerberos

To use Kerberos, a user presents a set of credentials such as username/password or an X.509 certficate. The security system them grants the user a ticket granting ticket (TGT). The TGT is an opaque piece of data that the user cannot read but must present in order to access other resources. The user will typically present the TGT in order to get a service ticket (ST). The way the system works is as follows:

1. A client authenticates to a Key Distribution Center (KDC) and is granted a TGT.

2. The client takes the TGT and uses it to access a Ticket Granting Service (TGS)

3. The client requests an ST for a particular network resource. The TGS then issues the ST to the client.

4. The client presents the ST to the network resource and begins accessing the resource with the permissions the ST indicated.

3.2. Integrity and Signing

Integrity means that the message has not been altered in the transit. If the message is signed, the receiver of the message knows that the signed elements have not changed en route. A signature is based on a digest created according to the content of the document that needs to be digitally signed. It verifies to the receiver:

- The user identified by the X.509 certificate, UsernameToken, or Kerberos ticket signed the message.

- The message has not been tempered with since it was signed.

Before we go in the details of signing in the SOA perspective and XML Signature, let us quickly review the basics of digital signature. The first step in the process is to use a one-way hash mechanism to generate a message digest for the actual content. Once created, it is not possible to change a message digest back into the original data from which it was created. The second step is to encrypt the message digest and create a signature. While sending the data, the sender appends the signature with the message data.

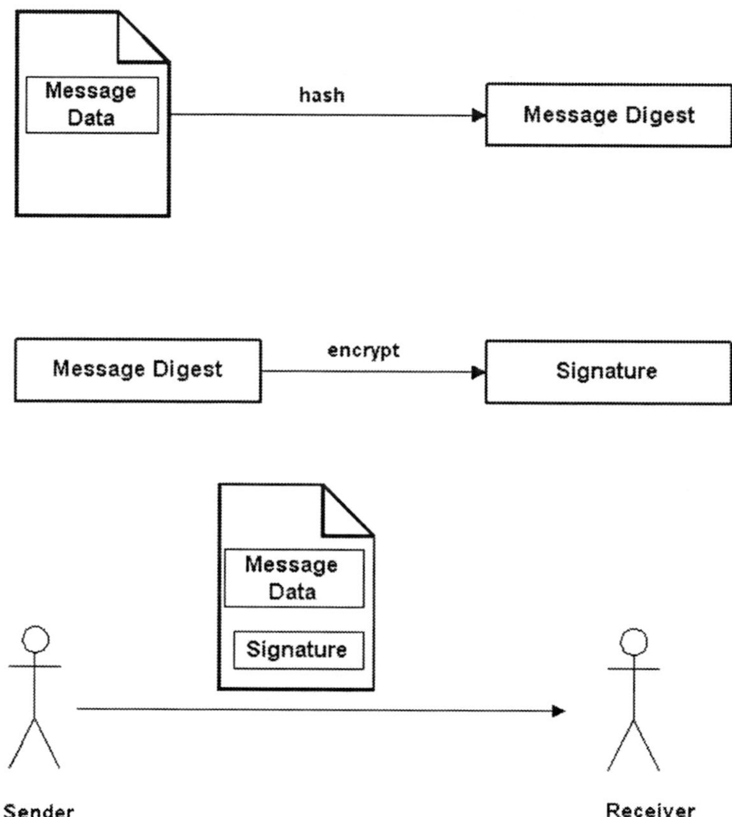

Figure 5. **Digital Signature**

The receiver decrypts the signature changing it back to a message digest. The next step is to hash the message data to generate a message digest in a similar fashion as the sender. If the message digest created by the above two steps are same, it ascertains that the data has not been altered in the transit.

All three of the authentication mechanisms mentioned in the previous section on security tokens provides a way to sign the message. X.509 allows the sender to sign the message using the private key. Kerberos provides a session key that the sender creates and transmits in the ticket. Only the intended receiver of that message can

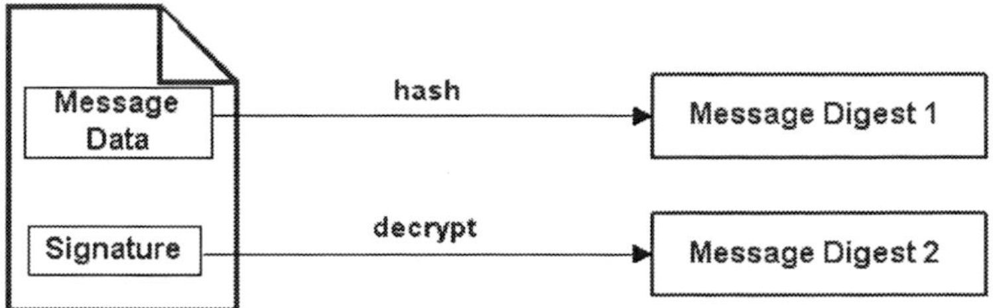

IF (Message Digest 1 == Message Digest 2)
THEN Message Data has not been altered.

***Figure 6.* Verification of Digital Signature**

read the ticket, discover the session key, and verify the authenticity of the signature. XML Signature, a W3C standard allows a mechanism for digitally signing XML documents using any of the above methods. Rather than reinvent what already exists, SOA implementations simply points to this existing specification and fills in a few details on how to use it with SOAP messages.

3.3. XML Signature

The project aims to develop XML syntax for representing digital signatures over any data type. The specification also defines procedures for computing and verifying such signatures. Like most of the other specifications in this space, XML Signature takes a very flexible approach. It allows you to sign any type of data and not just XML data and provides means to support diverse set of internet transaction models. For example, you can sign individual items or multiple items of an XML document. The document you sign can be local or even a remote object, as long as those objects can be referenced through a URI (Uniform Resource Identifier). Consider for instance, an order entry system where a user orders an item for the company's website. Behind the scene, the order flows through the inventory system, a credit card company, provisioning and billing systems, followed by shipping. XML Signature allows each system to sign and verify the sections related to them. Billing system for instance does not care for the shipping address or the item ordered and only wishes to verify the integrity of billing data.

XML digital signature also allows multiple signing levels for the same content, thus allowing flexible signing semantics. For example, the same content can be semantically signed, cosigned, witnessed, and notarized by different people.

You can associate a digital signature of an XML Document in different ways:

- Enveloped – The signature is a child of the data being signed.
- Enveloping – The signature encloses the data being signed.
- Detached – The signature is a sibling of the element being signed and is referenced by a local link, or it can be located elsewhere on the network.

Let us examine the structure of XML Signature. The main thing defined by the XML Signature specification is a <Signature> element whose contents include both the digital signature itself and the information about how this signature was produced. Later in the section, we will illustrate the process of signing a file (order.xml) to create a signed document (signature.xml) and to how to validate its integrity. Figure 7 is the schema generated from the signed document. Before we dive into the sample, let us examine the various elements of <Signature>.

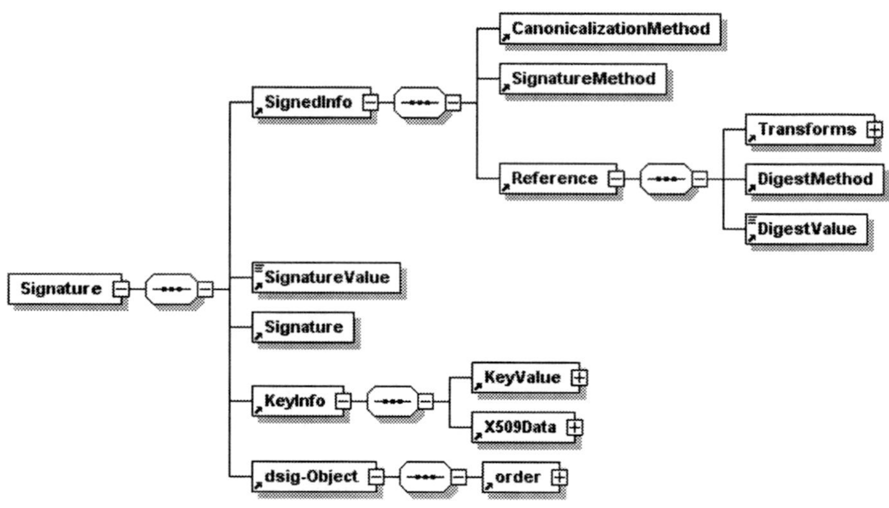

Figure 7. **Schema for Signature Element**

A typical instance of <Signature> as used with SOAP contains the <SignedInfo> and <KeyInfo> elements.

- <SignedInfo> element describes the information that is being signed. This element itself contains several subelements, each of which specifies something about the signed information. The most important of these include the following elements.
- <CanonicalizationMethod> identifies the algorithm that was used to convert this XML document into a standard form before the signature was generated.

This process is necessary because for digital signatures to work, each party's view of the signed document must be identical bit-for-bit. Canonicalization transforms an XML document into a standard form, ensuring that both parties view a document in the exact same way before signing it. We will look more into `Canonicalization` in a little bit.

- `<SignatureMethod>` identifies the algorithm used to create the digital signature. Both the XML Signature standard and WS-Security require support for the Digital Signature Standard, which uses Secure Hash Algorithm (SHA)-1 to create a message digest together with the DSA algorithm, and also recommend support for using SHA-1 together with the RSA algorithm.

- `<Reference>` identifies the information being signed, along with any transformations that were applied to it. When used with SOAP, this part of the signature typically references the signed parts of this SOAP message, such as the body and parts of the header. The `Reference` element also contains the two subelements: `<DigestMethod>` and `<DigestValue>`. The first of these identifies the algorithm used to create the message digest for this digital signature, while the second contains the message digest value itself.

- `<SignatureValue>`: This element contains the actual signature. As signatures are always binary data, XML DSIG specifies that the signature value is always a simple element with Base64-encoded content

- `<KeyInfo>` indicates what key should be used to validate this signature. The key can be identified in a variety of ways, such as referencing a certificate that contains the appropriate public key. This element can even be omitted entirely, since the recipient may know what key to use by some other means.

- `<dsig:Object>` element contains the actual data that is being sent and used in creating the digest.

The following example illustrates how XML Signatures work. We are using IBM's XML Security Suite to generate and verify the signature. The following listing displays the document `order.xml` that we will using in the next few examples:

```
<OrderData id="123">
   <CustomerData>
      <FirstName>John</FirstName>
      <LastName>Doe</LastName>
   <BillingData>
      <Street>123 MainStreet</Street>
      <City>Denver</City>
      <State>Colorado</State>
```

```
      <Country>US</Country>
      <ZipCode>80021</ZipCode>
   </BillingData>
   <ShippingData>
      <Street>123 MainStreet</Street>
      <City>Denver</City>
      <State>Colorado</State>
      <Country>US</Country>
      <ZipCode>80021</ZipCode>
   </ShippingData>
   <Payment Data>
   <CreditCardData>
      <Name>John Doe</Name>
      <Number>12232421l234343</Number>
      <Issuer>AmericanExpress</Issuer>
      <Expiry>20040405</Expiry>
   </CreditCardData>
   </PaymentData>
   </CustomerData>
   <ItemData>
      <Name>Enterprise SOA</Name>
      <Type>Book</Type>
      <Reference>83761761</Reference>
      <Quantity>1</Quantity>
      <Price>44.95</Price>
   </ItemData>
</Order>
```

3.3.1. Generate Certificate

In real world, to be able to create a digital signature you need a certificate, which is issued by certificate authorities such as Verisign. However, for our example here we will use the Java keytool command.

```
keytool -genkey -dname "CN=John Doe, OU=Enterprise SOA Book,
O=Manning, L=Denver, S=Colorado, C=US" -alias john
-storepass password -keypass security
// dname = distinguished name
// CN = Common Name
// OU = Organizational Unit
// O = Organization
```

```
// L = Location
// S = State
// C = Country
// alias = Alias for this certificate
// storepass = Password for the key store
// keypass = Pasword for the private key
```

3.3.2. Signing

To create digital signatures, we use the SampleSign2 application that is shipped with the IBM's XML Security Suite. The sample application can be used to create both detached and enveloping signatures. The application can be used as

```
java dsig.SampleSign2  <your-alias>  <your-storepassword>
<your-keypassword>   <resource><resource> ... > signature.xml
```

where resource is

- `-ext` URL for an external resource;
- `-embxml` URL for an embedded XML resource (content of specified URL is embedded in the signature).

Here is how `order.xml` is signed to generate `signature.xml`:

```
java dsig.SampleSign2 john password security -embxml
file:///d:/tools/xss4j/samples/order.xml > signature.xml
```

The alias, store password and key password are the ones that were generated in the previous step. The output is directed to a `signature.xml`, which will have the signature and the embedded data.

The following listing shows the content of the file `signature.xml`.

```
<Signature xmlns="http://www.w3.org/2000/09/xmldsig#">
<SignedInfo>
      <CanonicalizationMethod
            Algorithm="http://www.w3.org/TR/2001/
    REC-xml-c14n-20010315">
      </CanonicalizationMethod>
      <SignatureMethod
            Algorithm="http://www.w3.org/2000/09/
    xmldsig#dsa-sha1">
```

```
      </SignatureMethod>
      <Reference URI="#Res0">
            <Transforms>
                  <Transform
                  Algorithm="http://www.w3.org/TR/2001/
          REC-xml-c14n-20010315">
                  </Transform>
            </Transforms>
            <DigestMethod
                 Algorithm="http://www.w3.org/2000/09/
   xmldsig#sha1">
            </DigestMethod>
            <DigestValue>aJH0LRYgJaAtuqC/PJ/wfFiEI2A=
            </DigestValue>
      </Reference>
</SignedInfo>
<SignatureValue>
      XJjZ7OwwGn9Zhyga/t4ipuFKOnhREqX9UIDUaA2sPJVmhw+y3BksMA==
</SignatureValue>
<KeyInfo>
     <KeyValue>
           <DSAKeyValue>
                  <P>/X9TgR11EilS30qcLuzk5?</P>
                  <Q>l2BQjxUjC8yykrmCouuEC/BYHPU=</Q>
                  <G>9+GghdabPd7LvKtcNrhXuXmUr7?</G>
                  <Y>NTijOltictv5/SCbDZhUwKNlGlIOH?</Y>
           </DSAKeyValue>
     </KeyValue>
     <X509Data>
           <X509IssuerSerial>
                 <X509IssuerName>
                       CN=John Doe,OU=Enterprise SOA Book,
                       O=Manning,L=Denver,ST=Colorado,C=US
                 </X509IssuerName>
                 <X509SerialNumber>1079744797</X509SerialNumber>
           </X509IssuerSerial>
           <X509SubjectName>
                 CN=John Doe,OU=Enterprise SOA Book,
                 O=Manning,L=Denver,ST=Colorado,C=US
           </X509SubjectName>
           <X509Certificate>
                 MIIDHDCCAtoCBEBbmR0wCwYHKoZIzjg?
```

```
            </X509Certificate>
      </X509Data>
</KeyInfo>
<dsig:Object xmlns=""
      xmlns:dsig="http://www.w3.org/2000/09/xmldsig#" Id="Res0">
      <OrderData id="123">
            <CustomerData>
            ...
            </CustomerData>
      </OrderData>
</dsig:Object>
</Signature>
```

The actual signed data is underneath the `dsig:Object`. As we will see in the next section, any alteration with the data will result in a verification failure.

3.3.3. Verification

The XML Security Suite provides a utility, `VerifyGUI` that reports validity of each resource and validity of the signature. You can check a given signature to ensure that the signed resource has not changed, and you can check that the signature matches the information in the sender's certificate.

```
java dsig.VerifyGUI < signature.xml
```

If the signature and all of signed resources were not modified, VerifyGUI reports the result of verification as "Core Validity: OK".

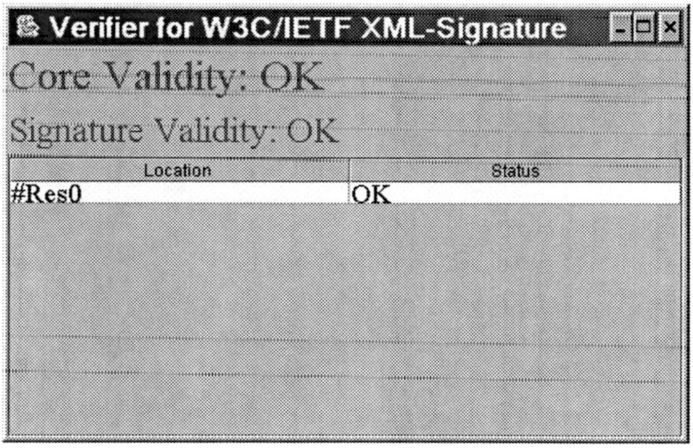

Figure 8. **VerifyGUI – Success**

If the signed file is changed, the signature will no longer be valid. To illustrate this, change the order id in the `signature.xml` to "234" and again run the utility. This time, VerifyGUI reports as "Core Validity: NG – Digest Value mismatch".

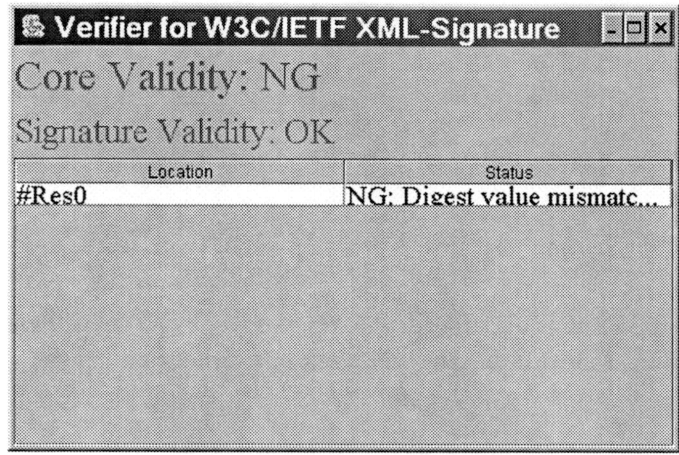

Figure 9. **VerifyGUI – Failure**

3.4. Canonicalization

XML documents can have the same logical meaning but different physical implementations based on several characteristics such as character encoding, attribute ordering or white spaces. Digital signature checks whether a message has changed along the way, but an XML document's physical representation can change during processing, even though its information content remains the same.

Let us examine the snippets below:

```
<OrderData id="123" type="web">
  <BillingData/>
</OrderData>
```

and

```
<order type="web" id="123">
   <BillingData>     </BillingData>
</order>
```

Though both snippets have identical information content, because of their permissible differences, their digests will definitely differ. XML Canonicalization solves this problem. The Canonical XML specification establishes the concept of equivalence between XML documents and provides the ability to test at the syntactic level. It enables the generation of the identical message digest and thus identical digital signatures for XML documents that are syntactically equivalent but different in appearance. By calculating the digest over a document's canonical form, we can ensure that, as long as the document's information content stays the same, its signature will still verify, even if the physical representation has somehow changed during processing.

XML Signature and message signing proves the sender's identity and ensures that the message has not been tempered. However, message signing does not prevent external parties to view the contents of the message. There are cases when data integrity is not enough and the receiver expects the data confidentiality, i.e. that the data has not been read in transit. For instance, if you are sending a credit card number as part of the message, validating the data is not sufficient enough. You would like the data encrypted in such a way that only the intended message recipient can read the message. Anyone watching the wire exchange should remain oblivious to the contents of the message. This is where encryption comes in.

3.5. Confidentiality and Encryption

Encryption involves the securing of messages exchanged between a sender and receiver. Figure 10 depicts the process involving encryption and decryption of messages.

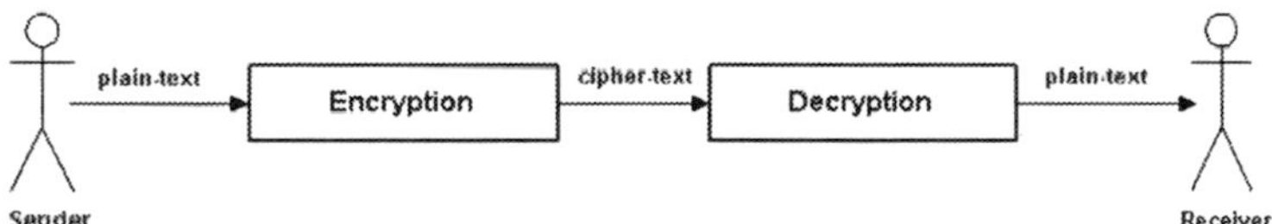

Figure 10. **Encryption**

In Figure 10, a sender wants to send a message over the internet to a receiver. The message is usually referred to as cleartext or plaintext. To preserve confidentiality, the message first undergoes a process called encryption. The encrypted message (also called as ciphertext) renders the actual message text invisible. When the message reaches the receiver, a process called decryption takes place, in which the encrypted message is converted to plaintext. Encryptions are done using complex mathematical techniques called as Cryptographic algorithms or ciphers. Most cryptographic algorithms can be divided into two main categories: one-way encryption and two-way encryption. In a one-way encryption scenario (e.g., RSA, MD4, MD5 and SHA), encryption and decryption involve a different key where in a two-way encryption, the same key is used for both operations.

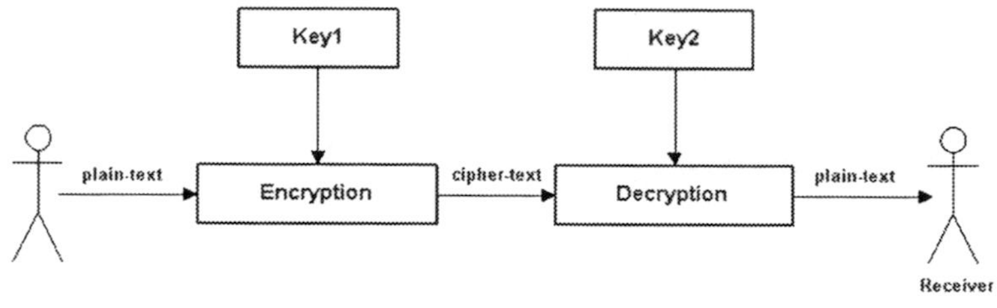

Figure 11. **One Way/Two Way Encryption**

When you encrypt data, you can choose either symmetric or asymmetric encryption.

3.5.1. Symmetric Encryption

Symmetric Encryption also known as secret-key cryptography requires a shared secret. This is a two-way encryption model because the same key is used for both encryption and decryption. Symmetric encryption is good if you control both endpoints and can trust the people and applications on both ends. The inherent problem with this encryption scheme is the distribution of the key. Prior to the invocation of the service, the key needs to be sent to the receiver using some other trusted mechanism. If a third party knows the key in can hack into message exchanges between the two parties.

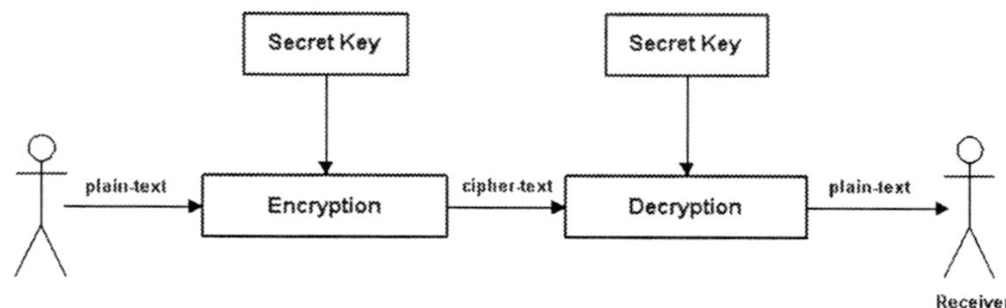

Figure 12. **Symmetric Encyrption**

1. A secret key is shared between sender and receiver.

2. Sender encrypts the plaintext using the secret key.

3. The ciphertext is sent to the receiver.

4. Receiver decrypts the ciphertext using the secret key.
5. Receiver retrieves the plaintext message.

3.5.2. Asymmetric Encryption

Asymmetric encryption, also known as Public-key cryptography is a one-way encryption model where two keys (public key and private key) are used for encrypting and decrypting data, respectively. In the asymmetric encryption, the endpoint receiving the data can publicly post its certificate and allow anyone and everyone to encrypt information using the public key. Only the receiver knows the private key and thus only the receiver can decrypt the data into something meaningful. This solves the key dispersal problem of the symmetric encryption model. Figure 13 explains the procedure.

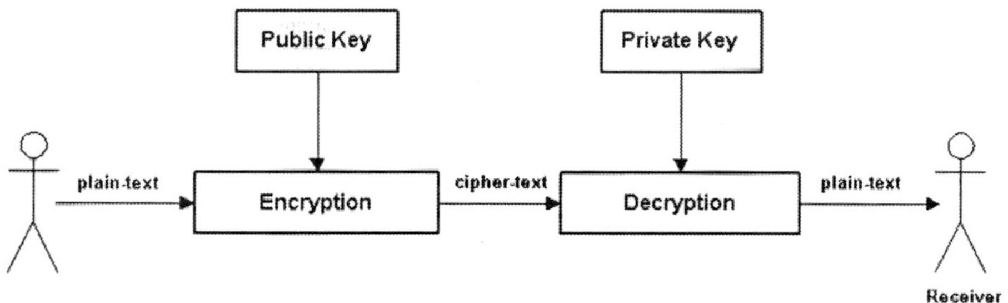

Figure 13. **Asymmetric Encryption**

1. Receiver holds the private key.
2. Sender encrypts the plaintext using the public key.
3. The message is sent to receiver in encrypted form.
4. Receiver decrypts the message using the private key.
5. Receiver retrieves the plaintext message.

Let us again look at the example that we mentioned in the earlier section where a user orders an item from a company website. The message (`order.xml`) travels back and forth between several parties. The message has information about the customer (e.g. credit card data) as well as the item that he ordered. The credit card company does not need to know about the item ordered and the shipping vendor does not need to know about the credit information. We can resolve this issue by selectively encrypting the data contents of the message, and the various parties will only be able to read the data that is meant for them.

Like everything else in the ESOA space, there is an XML solution to address the issue of encryption. The W3C and IETF have published a specification for encryption: XML Encryption.

3.6. XML Encryption

XML encryption extends the power of the XML digital signature system by enabling the encryption of the message that has been digitally signed. The specification outlines a standard way to encrypt any form of digital content and permits encryption of an entire XML message, a partial XML message, or an XML message that contains sections that were previously encrypted.

The following is the section from `order.xml` that pertains to credit card information.

```
<PaymentData>
<Name>John Smith</Name>
<CreditCardData>
   <CreditCard Limit='5,000' Currency='USD'>
      <Number>4019 2445 0277 5567</Number>
      <Issuer>American Express</Issuer>
      <Expiration>04/02</Expiration>
  </CreditCardData>
</PaymentData>
```

The application can encrypt just the credit card element.

```
<PaymentData>
<Name>John Smith</Name>
    <EncryptedData
    Type='http://www.w3.org/2001/04/xmlenc#Element'
     xmlns='http://www.w3.org/2001/04/xmlenc#'>
      <CipherData>
        <CipherValue>A23B45C56</CipherValue>
      </CipherData>
    </EncryptedData>
</PaymentData>
```

By encrypting the entire `<CreditCardData>` element from its start to end tags, the identity of the element itself is hidden. An eavesdropper does not know whether the transaction used a credit card, money transfer or a check. The CipherData element contains the encrypted serialization of the CreditCardData element. Figure 14 explains the structure of the encrypted data.

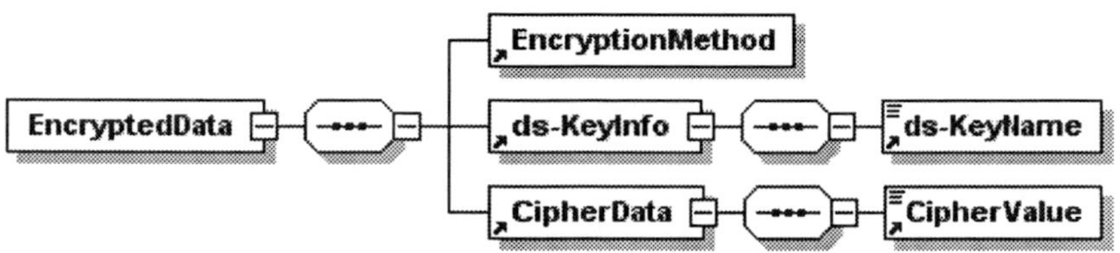

***Figure 14.* XML Encryption**

- <EncryptedData>: This is the core element of XML encryption and replaces the data being encrypted. It contains (via one of its children content) or identifies (via a URI reference) the cipher data.

- <CipherData> element is created to contain the encrypted serialization of the data. It either envelopes or references the raw encrypted data. If enveloping, the raw encryptied data is the <CipherValue> element's content; if referencing, the <CipherReference> element's URI attribute points to the location of the raw encrypted data.

- <CipherValue> element holds the encrypted result of the data.

- <EncryptionMethod> describes the method that used used for encryption such as RSA.

- <KeyInfo> borrowed from XML Signature. Here, it is assumed that both sides already know all of the keys available for use in encryption and decryption, so the only thing required is to inform the receiver of which one was chosen.

It is also possible to convey an encrypted key in the same message that carries data that was encrypted using that key. For instance when the data is encrypted using a symmetric key, then that symmetric key is encrypted using the public key of the message's recipient and sent along with the data. When the message arrives, the recipient can use its private key to decrypt the embedded symmetric key, then use this symmetric key to decrypt the actual data. The encrypted key can be sent using the element <EncryptedKey>. The format of <EncryptedKey> is much like <EncryptedData> has three main subelements: <EncryptionMethod>, <KeyInfo>, and <CipherData>. Rather than having the message data, these elements contain information about the key, how it has been encrypted and the encrypted value.

The following example demonstrates the use of XML Encryption. As in the previous section, we use IBM's XML Security Suite for the task. We will also reuse the certificate keys generated in the earlier section on XML Signature.

3.6.1. Encryption

We use the DomCipher application that is shipped with the IBM's XML Security Suite. The sample application can be used to create both detached and enveloping signatures. The application can be used as

```
java enc.DomCipher -e <provider> <keyinfo> <target>
[xpath template...]
//Encryption
```

and

```
java enc.DomCipher  -d <provider> <keyinfo> <target>
[xpath template...]
//Decryption
```

Here is how to encrypt `order.xml`

```
java enc.DOMCipher -e "*" john security password
file:///d:/tools/xss4j/samples/order.xml > encrypted.xml
```

The alias, store password and key password are the ones that were generated in the previous step. The output is directed to an `encrypted.xml`.

The application also allows us to encrypt parts of data. For instance, the following command will only encrypts the credit info in the `order.xml`

```
java enc.DOMCipher -e "*" john security password
file:///d:/tools/xss4j/samples/order.xml
"//*[name()='CreditCardData]"  >
encrypted.xml
```

3.6.2. Decryption

The XML Security Suite provides a utility, `VerifyGUI` that reports validity of each resource and validity of the signature. You can check a given signature to ensure that the signed resource has not changed, and you can check that the signature matches the information in the sender's certificate.

Here is how to decrypt `encrypted.xml`:

```
java enc.DOMCipher -d "*" john security password
file:///d:/tools/xss4j/samples/encrypted.xml > order.xml
```

3.7. Authorization

Security tokens provide a way of authentication and establish your identity. However, authentication does not allow you to perform a specific action or to access a resource. For instance, you can login into a database system using your login id and password. It will let you navigate around the tables and read the data but you will not be allowed to delete a table unless you are a DBA. Similarly, your credit card will prove your identity and who you are but you may not be allowed to make a million dollar transaction through it due to the policy of your credit card company. In a software language, a policy refers to the set of conditions and constraints that must be met in order for an entity to perform some type of operation. The requester can be a person or another application but it has to abide by the policies of the provider to be able to access its services. Extensible Access Control Markup Language (XACML) provides XML documents with support for defining access control and policies.

3.8. Extensible Access Control Markup Language (XACML)

XACML is an OASIS standard that describes both a policy language and an access control decision request/response language (both written in XML). The policy language is used to describe general access control requirements, and has standard extension points for defining new functions, data types, combining logic, etc. The request/response language lets you form a query to ask whether or not a given action should be allowed, and interpret the result.

3.8.1. Key Concepts

XACML includes the concepts of Policy Enforcement Point (PEP) and Policy Decision Point (PDP). PEP is the entity that is charged for access control. When a client makes a resource request, the PEP will form a request based on the requester's attributes, the resource in question, the action, and other information pertaining to the request. The PEP will then delegate the authorization decision to the PDP. Policy Decision Point will look at the request and the policy that applies to the request, and come up with an answer about whether access should be granted.

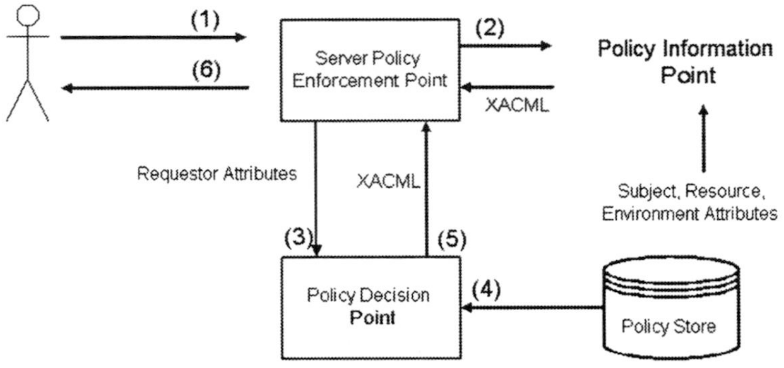

Figure 15. **XACML**

3.9. Top-Level Constructs: Policy and PolicySet

At the root of all XACML policies is a `Policy` or a `PolicySet`. A `PolicySet` is a container that can hold other `Policies` or `PolicySets`. The `Policy` element is composed principally of `Target`, `Rule` and `Obligation` elements and is evaluated at the `Policy Decision Point` to grant or deny access to the resource.

Since multiple policies may be found applicable to an access decision (and since a single policy can contain multiple Rules), XACML provides support for Combining Algorithms that are used to reconcile multiple outcomes into a single decision.

3.10. Key Management

Most of the concepts like authentication, digital signature, encryption discussed earlier, rely on public and private keys, digital certificates among others. There is a need to simplify the management of these security components and to keep them organized and secure. There are many PKI solutions available like X.509, Pretty Good Privacy (PGP) and Simple Public Key Infrastructure (SPKI). In an ESOA, to be able to talk to the other systems, each application needs to be aware of the PKI solutions used by other systems. For instance, if service A uses an X.509 PKI solution and sends encrypted documents to service B, which uses an SPKI solution, then service B will not be able to decrypt and use the document sent by A. For A and B to work together, one of them has to understand the other's PKI solution. If you extrapolate this scenario to a situation where multiple partners are involved, it becomes clear that all of the partners will have to be aware of each other's PKI solution, thus increasing each application's complexity many times.

The XML Key Management Specification (XKMS), another W3C standard aims to provide a standard XML-based solution for the management of keys for authentication, encryption and digital signature services.

3.11. XML Key Management Specification (XKMS)

XKMS allows application developers to outsource the processing of key management (registration, verification etc.) to trust services accessed over the internet. This trusted third paty will act as an intermediary that frees the SOA programmer from having to track the availability of keys or certificates and ensures their validity. XKMS specifications are made up of two other specifications.

3.11.1. XML Key Information Service Specification (XKISS)

XKISS allows the client applications to authenticate encrypted/signed data. The XKISS service specification defines the following two operations:

1. Locate: Locate resolves a `<ds:KeyInfo>` element that may be associated with XML encryption or XML signature, but it does not prove the validity of data binding in the `<ds:KeyInfo>` element.

2. Validate: This operation not only searches the public key corresponding to the `<ds:KeyInfo>` element, but also assures that the key binding information that it returns is trustworthy.

3.11.2. XML Key Registration Service Specification (XKRSS)

XRSS allows for registration and subsequent management of public key information. A client of a conforming service may request that the registration service bind information to a public key. The information bound may include a name, an identifier or extended attributes defined by the implementation.

An XKRSS service specification defines four operations:

1. Register: Information is bound to a key pair through key binding. During registration, either the client provides the public key, along with some proof of possession of the corresponding private key, or the service provider generates the key pair for the client. The service provider may request more information from the client before it registers the public key (and optionally the private key as well).

2. Re-issue: A previously registered key binding is re-issued. New credentials in the underlying PKI are generated using this operation. While there is no lifespan for the key binding information used by XKMS, the credentials issued by the underlying PKI occasionally do have a time span that must be renewed periodically.

3. Revoke: This operation allows clients to destroy the data objects to which a key is bound. For example, an X.509 certificate that is bound to an XKMS key is destroyed when this operation is called.

4. Recover: This operation allows clients to recover the private key. For this operation to be meaningful, the private key must have been registered with the service provider. One of the ways in which the service provider may have the private key is when the key pair is generated at the server rather than the client.

3.12. Single Sign-On

Single sign-on authentication is the ability for an end user or application to access other applications within a secure environment without needing to be validated by each application. For instance, you should be able to log into your corporate application infrastructure with a single username and password. Even if there are different subsystems underneath for providing payroll information, vacation details or 401K data, it should be oblivious to the user and he should be able to navigate across the subsystems seamlessly without entering the username/password for each sub-system.

The best approach to allow access to all applications without additional intervention after the initial sign-on is by using a profile that defines what the user is allowed to do. Many companies such as Ping Identity, RSA, Netegrity, support products for web-based, single sign-on authentication and authorization. In general, these products use an intermediary process that controls and manages the passing of user credentials from one application to another. The responsibility of authentication and authorization is shifted to a third party, leaving the application free to focus on implementation of business logic.

The implementation of SSO varies a bit according to the business scenario. In an ETrade like banking environment, the user can log into one module (say mortgage), and the system uses SSO to enable the user in other modules as banking, securities and options. If the user signs off from any of the module, the system signs off the user from all the other modules. The situation is a bit different in a scenario where there are more disparate applications participating in the SSO solution. Corporate intranet, that provides links to other internal sites such as HR and Payroll is a good example. When the user log in the intranet, he might not realize that he is also login into other secure sites like Payroll that are SSO enabled. This can pose a security risk if the user leaves his machine unlocked for an extended period of time. One solution is to implement a short SSO timeout that mitigates the risk of unauthorized access to sensitive applications.. The decision to enable an application for SSO lies with the business. But there are considerations like mentioned above that should be taken into account before enabling an application. One approach to handle the above issue is by implementing security levels. The enterprise security group can divide applications into security levels based on the application's sensitivity. The SSO is enabled within the security level. Therefore, if the user login into the intranet (with Security level 0), he has to login again to access the Payroll information which is set at a higher security level.

In ESOA, single sign-on is a subset of a bigger issue referred as identity management. Single sign-on only deals with username/password. However, each user has an identity and username/password can be considered as two of the many attributes that are associated with the identity. One of the approaches seen in SSO implementation is the use of attributes to dynamically determine the user's access or authorization. Thus when the user logs in, the SSO application (e.g. Netegrity) authenticates the user against the company directory server and populates the user's principal with selected attributes. The various business applications can then implement a message handler that can intercept the request and assign dynamic roles based on the attributes in the request. For instance, if the "manager" attribute is set to "true", the user is allowed to view the payroll information of other employees. With this implementation, the SSO application is only used for authentication, and the authorization decisions are made within the application's domain.

3.13. Identity Management

Identity represents the core of any business relationship. It encompasses attributes and characteristics critical to developing and deploying valuable services. Identity Management is a set of processes for the creation, maintenance, and use of identities and their attributes, as well as credentials and entitlements, plus a supporting infrastructure.

Users today have multiple login ids and passwords for several applications. One user-id and password for Amazon; another one for the mortgage lender; and one each for every bank account and credit card company. This leads to what is known as the "sticky note problem". Since each individual has many usernames and password, they end up writing them on sticky notes all over their desk posing a major security risk. Similarly in business-to-business interactions, each service requires has its own way of authenticating the request. The problem becomes even bigger in enterprise SOA where the service spawns the boundaries of many applications and operating systems, endpoints and intermediaries. Each component has its own mechanism for managing identity, credentials and policies, leading to a fragmented identity infrastructure. Such infrastructure contains overlapping identity repositories, inconsistent policy frameworks, and process discontinuities. Needless to say that the result is cumbersome and such infrastructures are expensive to manage, error prone, and can have weaknesses that can lead to security breaches. One of the challenges for a successful adoption of Enterprise SOA is to provide a simple and secure identity management solution.

There are several industry initiatives to address this issue. One of them is Liberty Alliance project, which we will explore in the next section. Single sign-on and federated network identity (a system for binding multiple accounts for a given user) are key to solving this. The basic philosophy is to have a separate identity management system that contains a centralized repository of identity and policy information that every component can access. When the user logs in, the system authenticates the user via the identity management system, and creates a token that identifies that user and the privileges that the user has. That token then remains with the user request as it traverses the service composition layer, the atomic Web Services, and finally to the back-end systems.

3.14. Liberty Alliance Project

Liberty Alliance project is a business alliance that was formed in 2001, with the goal of establishing an open standard for federated identity management. The goal is to make it easier for businesses and consumers to conduct commerce while providing protection mechanisms for privacy and identity information. The project has established a specification for an open standard of federated network identity that integrates with a variety of products and services.

The goal of the project is to enable the concept of network identity. Network identity is the fusion of network security and authentication, user provisioning and customer management, single sign-on technologies, and web services delivery. Internet users today have multiple login Ids, passwords and other aspects that make up an identity. The information is spread throughout the internet, buried in multiple sites. This is where Identity Providers can fit it. An identity provider can create, maintain and manage the identity information for "users" (or `subject` in security language). The "users" here represent an individual person, a group of individuals, a corporation or any entity that is requesting the service. The identity provider develops a relationship with the service providers(s) and provides the authentication services. With federation, the Identity Provider and Service Provider together establish an opaque identifier(s) to be used to refer to a particular user. (Subsequent communications use this agreed-upon pseudonym for the user). The Service Provider bases its trust in the Identity Provider's assertion through signatures, certificate chains, validity intervals and any other technical mechanism. When the users and service providers rely on identity providers as trusted sources for authenticated user information, it leads to a "circle of trust".

A circle of trust is a federation of service providers and identity providers that have business relationships based on Liberty architecture and operational agreements and with whom users can transact business in a secure and apparently seamless environment. For instance, as illustrated in the following diagram, the user's local bank can act as an identity provider and collaborate with a bill payment company to provide its services. The bill payment company in turn can then interact with external federated partners as Utilities Company, Phone Company, Credit card company and so on.

A federated identity architecture delivers the benefit of simplified sign-on to users by granting rapid access to resources to which they have permission, but it does not require the user's personal information to be stored centrally. Microsoft's Passport and WS-Federation are other technologies attempting to solve the similar problem. WS-Federation specifications are still in early stages but it will be interesting to follow their progress and how it converges with the Liberty Alliance Project. Since both are based on open standards and have industry support behind them but have overlapping goals.

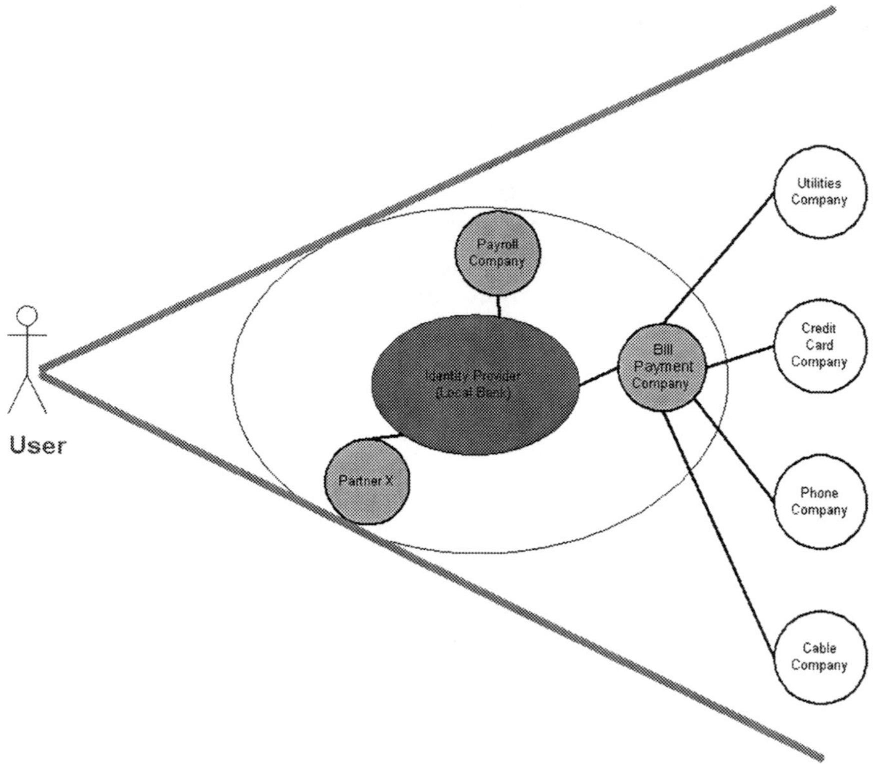

***Figure 16.* Circle of Trust**

Multiple systems (e.g. Credit Card company, Phone Company), coordinating user authentication decisions presents another challenge. The information about the authenticated user needs to be exchanged between trusting service providers. First, a user or a subject is likely to maintain different local identities with different service providers. For instance John Doe may be referred as jdoe with the phone company and johnd with the cable company. Similarly each system has its own way of expressing security assertions. The successful adoption of Single sign-on and identity management solutions required a common way to express assertion so that they can be shared between trusting parties. That need led to the development of an XML language to express security assertions, the Security Assertions Markup Language, or SAML. SAML itself is a merger of two previously competing XML-based languages aimed to specify security-related information, S2ML and AuthML. Currently, SAML is careering through the OASIS (Organization for the Advancement of Structured Information) open standards consortium and is poised to become the dominant security-specific XML language. The next section explains the language in more detail.

3.15. Security Assertion Markup Language (SAML)

Most security solutions that exist today are based on the assumption that the consumers and providers are located on the same physical (e.g. local LAN) and/or logical (e.g. VPN) network and therefore are under the realm of a single trust domain. A trust domain can be considered as a logical construct with a single set of access control policies. It is easy to establish and manage security within a single domain. For instance, obtaining access to an application within the single domain requires creation of a new user account in the domain and granting the appropriate access.

However, the collaboration of services in the ESOA world requires a standard way to communicate security attributes across the domains. If an individual identity has been established and verified in one trust domain, he should be allowed to assert his identity in another trust domain. Each domain could still control the local security policies to evaluate whether to grant access to its services. When the service request spans more than one domain, the security attributes and assertions must travel with the message. This form of portable security could be achieved using SAML.

The Security Assertion Markup Language (SAML) standard defines a framework for exchanging security information between online business partners.

SAML architecture is based on two key concepts: Asserting Party and Relying Party. Asserting parties that are also known as SAML authorities asserts information about a subject. For instance, the asserting party asserts that the user has been authenticated and has given associated attributes. The relying party relies on the information supplied by the asserting party. It still uses its local access policies to decide whether the subject may access the resources. The information passed around between asserting parties (SAML authorities) and relying parties is mostly in the form of XML and the format of these XML messages and assertions is defined in a pair of SAML XML schemas. SAML addresses the issue of SSO that allows the users to gain access to resources in multiple domains without having to re-authenticate after initially logging in to the first domain. To achieve SSO, the domains need to form a trust relationship before they can share an understanding of the user's identity that allows the necessary access.

The following listing illustrates how SAML can be used for authentication assertion.

```
<saml:Request MajorVersion="1" MinorVersion="0"
RequestID="123">
      <saml:AuthenticationQuery>
```

```
        <saml:Subject>
  <saml:NameIdentifier
                SecurityDomain="Enterprise SOA"
                        Name="JohnDoe"/>
</saml:Subject>
      </saml:AuthenticatationQuery>
</saml:Request>
```

In the above listing, the requesting party creates a assertion query for the subject "JohnDoe" in the "Enterprise SOA" Domain. The next listing shows the SAML response.

```
<saml:Response MajorVersion="1" MinorVersion="0"
InResponseTo="123" StatusCode="Success">
<saml:Assertion  MajorVersion="1" MinorVersion="0"
AssertionID="123"
        Issuer="Enterprise SOA"
IssueInstant="2004-03-22T05:45:00Z">
      <saml:Conditions
               <NotBefore="2004-03-22T05:45:00Z"
        <NotAfter="2004-03-22T09:45:00Z">
      </saml:Conditions>
      <saml:AuthenticationStatement
    AuthenticationMethod="Password"
    AuthenticationInstant="2004-03-22T05:45:00Z">
    <saml:Subject>
  <saml:NameIdentifier
SecurityDomain="Enterprise SOA"
Name="JohnDoe"/>
<saml:Subject>
      </saml:AuthenticationStatement>
       </saml:Assertion>
</saml:Response>
```

`<Conditions>` element specifies the conditions that must be considered when evaluating the assertion. For instance, in the above listing assertion is only valid for a specified time period. The statement types can be AuthenticationStatment, `AuthorizationDecisionStatement` or `AttributeStatement`. In the above listing, it is `AuthenticationStatement` and it states that the subject "JohnDoe" was authenticated at a certain time and it was authenticated using password authentication.

Many of the known industry players in the world of SOA Security (IBM, Microsoft, BEA, RSA) collectively proposed a number of new web services specifications related to security. We have reasons to believe that the intention is not just to cure the insomniacs. The goal for these specifications is to make it easier to apply business polices and to implement security for a wider range of applications. None of these specifications are an attempt to invent new security solutions but rather use the existing ones to work along with web services. In the next section, we will look at the some of most commons one.

4. Web Services Security (WSS)

Web Service Security specification was specifically created for using the security technologies that we discussed earlier in the chapter in the context of a SOAP message. Web Services Security (WSS) describes enhancements to SOAP messaging in order to provide quality of protection through message integrity, and single message authentication. The specifications provide three main mechanisms: ability to send security tokens as part of a message, message integrity, and message confidentiality. These mechanisms can be used to accommodate a wide variety of security models and encryption technologies.

WS-Security addresses security by leveraging existing standards and specifications. This avoids the necessity to define a complete security solution within WS-Security. The industry has solved many of these problems. Kerberos and X.509 address authentication. XML Encryption and XML Signature describe ways of encrypting and signing the contents of XML messages. XML Canonicalization describes ways of making the XML ready to be signed and encrypted. What WS-Security adds to existing specifications is a framework to embed these mechanisms into a SOAP message. This is done in a transport-neutral fashion. WS-Security defines a SOAP header element to carry security-related data.

The WS-Security specification defines a new SOAP header:

```
<xs:element name="Security">
   <xs:complexType>
      <xs:sequence>
   <xs:any processContents="lax"
      minOccurs="0" maxOccurs="unbounded">
   </xs:any>
   </xs:sequence>
   <xs:anyAttribute processContents="lax"/>
   </xs:complexType>
</xs:element>
```

The security header element allows any XML element or attribute to live within it. This allows the header to adapt to whatever security mechanisms your application needs.

WS-Security needs this type of structure because of what the header must do. It must be able to carry multiple security tokens to identify the caller's rights and identity. If the message is signed, the header must contain information about how it was signed and where the information regarding the key is stored. The key may be in the message or stored elsewhere and merely referenced. Finally, information about encryption must also be able to be carried in this header. In an ESOA application, the same message flows through a number of intermediaries and endpoints. For each of these components, the SOAP message can have multiple security headers identified by a unique actor. The actor attribute in any SOAP header is meant to say "this header is meant for any endpoint acting in the capacity indicated by the actor URI". This means that the intermediary may act in varying capacities and may consume zero, one or more headers. Let us look at some examples of how WS-Security can be used to exchange security information.

4.1. Security Tokens

The security tokens can be passed either as a username/password or X.509 Certificates or Kerberos. To pass user credentials as username/password manner, WS-Security has defined the `UsernameToken` element. When passing a `UsernameToken` in a SOAP message, the XML may come across as following:

```
<wsse:UsernameToken>
   <wsse:Username>scott</wsse:Username>
   <wsse:Password Type="wsse:PasswordText">tiger</wsse:Password>
</wsse:UsernameToken>
```

The above example shows the password being sent as plain text. To be a little more secure, the password can be sent in as a digest hash.

```
<wsse:UsernameToken>
   <wsse:Username>scott</wsse:Username>
   <wsse:Password Type="wsse:PasswordDigest">
      X456DXTQALOY!ADT&ADYT
   </wsse:Password>
</wsse:UsernameToken>
```

Credential using .509 Certificate or Kerberos can be passed using the `BinaryTokenElement`. The following listing shows an example:

```
<wsse:BinarySecurityToken
   ValueType="wsse:X509v3"
   EncodingType="wsse:Base64Binary"
   Id="SecurityToken-f32456fasdfft62......"
</wsse:BinarySecurityToken >
```

The valueType may be any of the following values, defined by the ValueTypeEnum in the WS-Security schema document:

- wsse:X509v3: An X.509, version 3 certificate.
- wsse:Kerberossv5TGT: A ticket granting ticket as defined by Section 5.3.1 of the Kerberos specification.
- wsse:kerberossv5ST: A service ticket as defined by Section 5.3.1 of the Kerberos specification.

The EncodingType attribute indicates the encoding method and can be set to either wsse:Base64Binary or wsse:HexBinary.

4.2. Signature

Message integrity is provided by leveraging XML Signature in conjunction with security tokens (which may contain or imply key data) to ensure that messages are transmitted without modifications. The integrity mechanisms are designed to support multiple signatures, potentially by multiple actors, and to be extensible to support additional signature formats. The following listing displays a sample signed SOAP message.

```
<?xml version="1.0" encoding="utf-8"?>
<s:Envelope
 xmlns:s="http://schemas.xmlsoap.org/soap/envelope/"
 xmlns:wsse="http://schemas.xmlsoap.org/ws/2002/12/secext"
 xmlns:wsu="http://schemas.xmlsoap.org/ws/2002/07/utility">
 <s:Header>
  <wsse:Security>
   <ds:Signature xmlns:ds="http://www.w3.org/2000/09/xmldsig#">
    <ds:SignedInfo>
     <ds:CanonicalizationMethod
       Algorithm="http://www.w3.org/2001/10/xml-exc-c14N"/>
     <ds:SignatureMethod
       Algorithm="http://www.w3.org/2000/09/xmldsig#rsa-sha1"/>
     <ds:Reference URI="#MessageBody">
```

```
      <ds:DigestMethod
        Algorithm="http://www.w3.org/2000/09/xmldsig#sha1"/>
      <ds:DigestValue>
        a0bd8914kjfdsi...
      </ds:DigestValue>
     </ds:Reference>
    </ds:SignedInfo>
    <ds:SignatureValue>
      jlkfds90dfl...
    </ds:SignatureValue>
    <ds:KeyInfo>
     <wsse:SecurityTokenReference>
      <wsse:Reference URI="#X509Cert"/>
     </wsse:SecurityTokenReference>
    </ds:KeyInfo>
   </ds:Signature>
  </wsse:Security>
 </s:Header>
 <s:Body wsu:Id="MessageBody">
  ...
 </s:Body>
</s:Envelope>
```

4.3. Encryption

In the same way they addressed the question of integrity, the authors of WS-Security chose to build on existing standards (XML Encryption) for confidentiality rather than create something new. The following listing shows an example of encrypted message:

```
<s:Envelope
 xmlns:s="http://schemas.xmlsoap.org/soap/envelope/"
 xmlns:ds="http://www.w3.org/2000/09/xmldsig#"
 xmlns:xenc="http://www.w3.org/2001/04/xmlenc#">
 <s:Body>
  <xenc:EncryptedData>
   <EncryptionMethod
     Algorithm='http://www.w3.org/2001/04/xmlenc#tripledes-cbc'/>
   <ds:KeyInfo>
    <ds:KeyName>
      CN=ESOA, C=US
```

```
    </ds:KeyName>
   </ds:KeyInfo>
   <xenc:CipherData>
    <xenc:CipherValue>
      r5Kipsslkr490dDV ...
    </xenc:CipherValue>
   </xenc:CipherData>
  </xenc:EncryptedData>
 </s:Body>
</s:Envelope>
```

As we mentioned earlier in this section, the purpose of WS-Security standard is not to invent new standards for security but to use the existing ones. It achieves that be defining a SOAP security header and thus providing a standard place to list security artifacts. The following listing represents a consolidated basic WS-Security SOAP Header:

```
<s:Envelope>
<s:Header>
        </wsse:Security>

        <!-- Security Token -->
<wsse:UsernameToken>
...
</wsse:UsernameToken>

<!-- XML Signature -->
<ds:Signature>
...
</ds:Signature>

<!-- XML Encryption -->
<xenc:ReferenceList>
<xenc:DataReference URI="#body"/>
<xenc:ReferenceList>
</wsse:Security>

</s:Header>
 <s:Body>
  <xenc:EncryptedData>
   <EncryptionMethod
     Algorithm='http://www.w3.org/2001/04/xmlenc#tripledes-cbc'/>
        ...
```

```
  </xenc:EncryptedData>
 </s:Body>
</s:Envelope>
```

WS-Security standard form a foundation upon which several other security specifications rely on. The vision is to have several security components, each addressing a unique security puzzle to work in unison with each other. The dream is still far from reality but WS-Security provides a framework to support this unifying approach. Figure 17 depicts the other security standards that are being built on the WS-Security foundation.

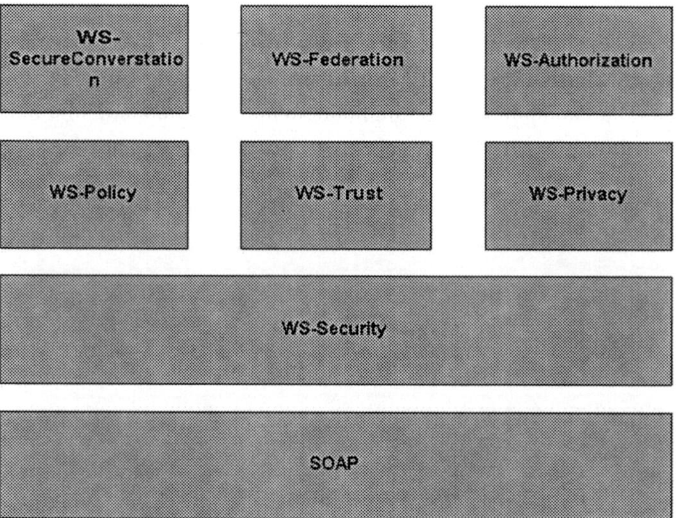

Figure 17. **WS-Security Foundation**

5. WS-Policy

The Web Services Policy Framework (WS-Policy) is a specification jointly developed by IBM, Microsoft, BEA and SAP. It specifies how senders and receivers can state their requirements and capabilities regarding policies they require to conduct business in an electronic format. The specification is highly flexible and supports an extensible grammar for expressing the capabilities, requirements and general characteristics of entities in an XML Web Services-based system. It defines a framework and a model for the expression of these properties as policies. A policy is expressed as policy assertions. A policy assertion represents a capability or a requirement. Policy assertions are defined in a companion specification (Web Services Policy Assertions

Language or WS-PolicyAssertions). WS-Policy expressions are associated with various Web services components using the Web Services Policy Attachment specification (WS-PolicyAttachment).

The following example illustrates a policy:

```
1 <wsp:Policy xmlns:wsse="..." xnlns:wsp="...">
2    <wsp:ExactlyOne>
3       <wsse:SecurityToken wsp:Usage="wsp:Required"
        wsp:Preference="100">
4          <wsse:TokenType>wsse:Kerberosv5TGT</wsse:TokenType>
5       </wsse:SecurityToken>
6       <wsse:SecurityToken wsp:Usage="wsp:Required"
        wsp:Preference="1">
7          <wsse:TokenType>wsse:X509v3</wsse:TokenType>
8       </wsse:SecurityToken>
9    </wsp:ExactlyOne>
10 <wsp:Policy>
```

Illustrate the expression of a security policy using assertions defined in WS-SecurityPolicy. Lines to 10 represent a set of policy assertions for authentication.

Lines 2 to 9 represent the `<wsp:ExactlyOne>` policy operator that is used to group policy assertions into policy sets. That is, a valid policy can contain any one of the contained assertions (lines 3 to 8).

Lines 3 to 5 and 6 to 8 represent two specific security policy assertions that indicate that two types of authentication are supported and that of the two types, Kerberos authentication is preferred over X509 authentication.

6. WS-Trust

The Web Services Trust Language (WS-Trust) is a specification jointly developed by IBM, Microsoft, Verisign, and RSA. In order for a secure communication between two parties, they must exchange security credentials (either directly or indirectly). However, each party needs to determine if they can "trust" the asserted credentials of the other party. WS-Trust specifications describe the model for establishing both direct and brokered trust relationships (including third parties and intermediaries). It provides a framework to support:

- methods for issuing and exchanging security tokens, and

- ways to establish and access the presence of trust relationships.

Typically, WS-Trust allows a client to send a request (using a X.509 certificate or any other security token supported by WS-Security) to a Security Token Service (STS) via a gateway. The STS maps the X.509 certificate to the security token expected by the receiving party, for example a SAML assertion, and then returns the trusted (i.e. signed) SAML assertion to the client. The client can now use the security token expected by the receiving party.

7. WS-Privacy

Personal information becomes public in many ways. For instance, sharing of customer data among partner companies, unsecured personal information stored on the internet. WS-Privacy allows organizations to state their privacy policies and require that incoming requests make claims about the initiator's adherence to these policies. The specification describes a model for how a privacy language may be embedded into WS-Policy descriptions and how WS-Security may be used to associate privacy claims with a message. WS-Privacy also describes how WS-Trust mechanisms can be used to evaluate privacy claims for organizational practice as well as user preferences. As many governments pass laws to protect sharing of personal information, this specification will grow in importance.

8. WS-SecureConversation

WS-SecureConversation jointly proposed by IBM, Microsoft, RSA and Verisign, describe how to manage and authenticate message exchanges between parties including security context exchange and establishing and deriving session keys. WS-SecureConveration is the SOAP layer equivalent of SSL at the transport layer. The mechanisms defined in WS-Security provide the basic mechanisms on top of which secure messaging can be defined. WS-Security is well suited for a single message authentication model in which the message contains all the security attributes necessary to authenticate itself. However, for multi-message conversation, this model becomes inefficient since each message has to go through the same authentication / verification process. Parties that wish to exchange multiple messages typically establish a secure security context in which to exchange multiple messages. A security context is shared among the communicating parties for the lifetime of a communications association. WS-SecureConversation specification defines extensions to allow security context establishment and sharing, session key derivation. The primary goals of this specification are:

- Define how security contexts are established, and
- Specify how derived keys are computed and passed.

9. WS-Federation

Web Services Federation Language (WS-Federation) is a specification jointly being developed by IBM, Microsoft, BEA, Verisign and RSA. It will provide support for secure propagation of identity, attribute, authentication, and authorization information. The specifications describe how to manage and broker the trust relationships in a heterogeneous federated environment including support for federated identities. WS-Federation addresses the issue where the requestor in one trust domain interacts with a service in another trust domain using different security models. For instance, how does a consumer service using Kerberos invoke a producer service based on X.509 in a trusted fashion. Liberty Alliance project and Microsoft Passport are an attempt to solve the same issue and WS-Federation is working towards providing a standard, generic approach to handle identity federation.

10. WS-Authorization

WS-Authorization specifications describe how to manage authorization data and authorization policies. It covers the description of how assertions can be made within security tokens as well as how they will be interpreted by each endpoint. This specification is designed to be flexible and extensible with respect to both authorization format and authorization language. This is important because each security provider may have a different authorization format and language.

11. Summary

The loosely coupled nature of ESOA systems makes it easy for applications to interoperate but it also opens the door for unauthorized access. The fragmented nature of ESOA systems only adds to the problem. With a lot of industry momentum behind ESOA, practical implementations have started to emerge in the market place and companies have begun to realize the need and complexity of security around these systems. The security standards mentioned in this chapter are essential for the successful adoption of ESOA. Many of the specifications are still in early stages and it will take time for the vendors to catch up and provide robust implementations around these specifications. On the plus side, the proposed architecture is flexible enough and does not require a change to the existing security implementations.

6 SOA MANAGEMENT

Management means, in the last analysis, the substitution of thought for brawn and muscle, of knowledge for folkways and superstition, and of cooperation for force. It means the substitution of responsibility for obedience to rank, and of authority of performance for the authority of rank
Peter Drucker

Service-Oriented Architectures can be deployed across corporate firewalls where services can be accessed both internal and external to the enterprise. What makes SOA beneficial is the very thing that also makes them challenging. Once services are accessed outside of the administrative control of the creators of the service, IT development teams and infrastructure groups are now placed on the critical path for all business processes that leverage that service.

Enterprise systems complexity increases over time and becomes increasingly important that these systems and the services they offer support manageability. It is highly desirable to dynamically view and control the state associated with all services used within an application. Since services can be developed using a multitude of languages, strategies surrounding management need to be provided using a platform-independent methodology.

In this chapter, we will cover:

- Systems Management,
- Lifecycle Management,
- Business Processes,
- Architecture Management.

1. Problem Space

In previous chapters, you learned that a fundamental element of an SOA is the contract which is a first class citizen and which serves to define the syntax of a service. The contract also describes semantics of the service using comments contained within an embedded description element or grouping of methods and/or operations. Many discussions of SOA specify the sole contract as defining the business interface. In reality, there are two contracts of which management is less defined within the industry.

In web services, the contract is described within a WSDL document and describes an interface in two ways. First, it provides an abstract description of messages and types. Second, it provides one or more concrete descriptions that bind the abstract definition of the service to the selected messaging transport. WSDL can be extended to support other transport bindings, marshalling mechanisms and even proprietary binding protocols but how this is accomplished is not well documented.

> *WSDL documents should be segmented to separate the business contract from the services technical binding.*

We have also learned that while the vast majority of current SOA implementations are point-to-point, we may need for our services to interoperate in a loosely coupled manner where producer and consumer of services have no prior knowledge of each other. WSDL is typically created using wizard type tools that tie the producer and consumer together since the binding information and endpoint information may be actually contained within the WSDL document. WSDL can be used to describe service and operation names, message parts, data types and a return value but can also be inappropriately used for more than it was originally intended to support.

In order to further understand the problem, let us pretend you have developed a service that provides quoting for business partners and is secured using SSL. A simple modification of the WSDL will allow you to change the transport from HTTP to HTTPS in the address element of the location attribute. Over time, this service may become used by a multitude of parties and becomes successful. After the service reaches critical mass, the head of the corporate security department creates a new policy where all electronic communications with third parties must be encrypted using either 168-bit Triple DES or RC4 algorithms. The problem now becomes harder than simply changing a single element in WSDL.

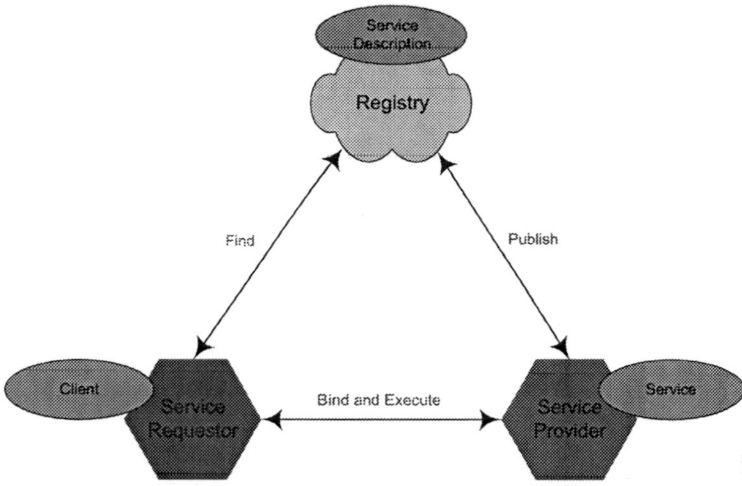

Figure 1. **Find Bind and Execute**

Solving this problem may require opening your favorite SOAP development kit and creating and/or substituting a new encryption layer. This task becomes difficult to realize for all but the most talented developers in our industry. Even if you have figured out a clever way to modify your SOAP stack to support the new enterprise security requirements, what about all the other service consumers who use this service but will have their own release schedules of when they can support messages using the newly chosen algorithm. In many enterprises, the business customer will demand that security be downgraded to support protocols that are easier to implement for external parties and suggest using username and password using HTTP digest mechanisms. Now you have to support two different approaches to security and the endless loop has begun.

Administrators within many enterprises are responsible for keeping the systems running and ensuring the overall health of the system at run-time. This may include determining the optimal number of instances of a service that should be running at any one time, whether the service has stopped accepting requests and so on. IT operations are usually the first to respond with violations of service level agreements and/or complaints from customers related to response times. Traditional tools provided by network management vendors currently are limited to understanding network and operating system metrics alone.

Conventional applications periodically encounter run-time errors that will show up either in a log file and/or operator's console that will allow operations to diagnose how to solve the problem. Services however, generally do not have the same benefit as they may be silently implemented within the bowels of its hosting application. Visibility into the internals of an application is sometimes warranted. The ideal situation is the ability for the enterprise to have a console that can allow for management of all service-oriented applications.

SOA also encourages reuse of services for internal consumption. Laws tied to legislative acts such as Sarbanes Oxley, Graham Leach, and Bliley may force authentication of access to consumers internal to the enterprise. The enterprise may require internal service consumers to authenticate to the service using client-side certificates using PKI technologies. A pattern emerges; an SOA starts out loosely coupled but mysteriously and quickly becomes tightly coupled.

The example previously described hints towards issues that can arise for service providers but can be extended to service consumers as well. Hopefully, you are now asking yourself in the above scenarios how would you implement these options into a service as well as support future management requirements without jeopardizing existing service dependencies.

The problem space is not limited to just security concerns but can become pervasive problems for other aspects of the infrastructure. Pressure surrounding business reporting and controls surrounding legislative concerns and compliance to trade agreements within a service-oriented architecture are equally challenging. Sarbanes Oxley requires that both the Chief Executive Officer (CEO) and Chief Financial Officer (CFO) must certify "the appropriateness of the financial statements and disclosures contained in the (annual) report, and that those financial statements and disclosures fairly present, in all material respects, the operations and financial condition of the issuer" and will be held personally liable for willful violations of the section. This clearly places the responsibility of accurate controls of services on the CEO. Developers simply adding in code to each service may no longer be acceptable.

If one were to analyze Sarbanes Oxley and its impact on a service-oriented architecture, one would include that services cannot be simply left to grow organically and must be supported by a management strategy. In Table 1 we look at elements of Sarbanes Oxley and the requirements it brings to managing an SOA.

So far, we have outlined problems with rolling out service-oriented architectures Now that the problem space of services is starting to emerge, lets start exploring scenarios in which one can start managing enterprise SOAs.

***Table 1.* Sarbanes Oxley Effect on Service-Oriented Architectures**

<table>
<tr><td>Compliance Requirements</td><td>Management Problem</td></tr>
<tr><td colspan="2">Section 302 – Corporate Responsibility for Financial Audits</td></tr>
<tr><td>• The CEO and CFO need to attest that the financial statement and disclosures are accurate.
• Signing officers are responsible for establishing appropriate internal controls.</td><td>• Ability to define enterprise-wide audit trails and comprehensive logging of all service transactions.
• Ability to create processes to ensure that all requirements related to compliance and performance are automatically handled.
• Ability to enforce segregation of service interactions (where appropriate) and establish that all corporate information policies are fully adhered to.</td></tr>
<tr><td colspan="2">Section 401 – Disclosures in Periodic Reports</td></tr>
<tr><td>• Adequate and comprehensive disclosures are required where relationships with customers and/or suppliers are disclosed where there may be some conflict, etc.</td><td>• The ability to provide a quick view of potential deals that need to be reported on financial reports.
• The ability to provide variant alerts based on certain transaction types and/or deals with specific customers/partners.
• Tracking of all types of service requests for a stakeholder that is deemed important.
• Ability to track all forms of electronic communications in a non-reputable manner.</td></tr>
<tr><td colspan="2">Section 404 – Management Assessment of Internal Controls</td></tr>
<tr><td>• Each annual report must include an "internal control report", which has to:
State that management is responsible for creating and maintaining an adequate internal control structure and procedures for financial reporting.
Contain an assessment of the effectiveness of the internal control structure and the procedures of the issuer for financial reporting.
• The company's auditor is required to attest to and report on the company's internal control report as part of the annual report.</td><td>• The ability to determine service routing rules based on defined monetary values where specific approvals are required.
• The ability to define a managed approval chain.
• The ability to define specialized audit trails that captures the approval and/or rejection of service transactions and providing centralized transaction history.
• Comprehensive ad-hoc reporting.</td></tr>
</table>

***Table 1.* Continued**

Compliance Requirements	Management Problem
Section 409 – Real Time Issuer Disclosures	
• Issuers must disclose information on material changes in the financial condition or operations of the issuer on a rapid or current basis.	• Information used for reporting purposes must be accessible in a near real-time manner.
Section 802 – Records Management and Retention	
• Provisions related to the destruction, alternation or falsification of records in federal investigations and bankruptcy. • Fine and/or imprisonment of not more than 20 years for "whoever knowingly alters, destroys, mutilates, conceals, covers up, falsifies, or makes a false entry in any record, document or tangible object with the intent to impede, obstruct or influence".	• Strategy surrounding non-repudiation of all service invocations and logging and auditing related services. • Comprehensive workflow that defines both happy path use cases as well as exception handling in a centralized manner. • Audit records must be centralized and have archival and retention strategies.
Section 906 – Corporate Responsibility for Financial Reports	
• The CEO and CFO must each certify the material representation of the company's financial condition in all financial reporting.	• Clearly defined system of records for all financial transactions.

1.1. Management Scenarios

The ability to management services can be accomplished in a variety of manners. A basic model principle may be for applications and services to write log information to a file or event logging service, which is useful in diagnostics but requires manual intervention in most situations in order to determine whether errors have occurred that require attention. In the vast majority of enterprises, log files are typically not looked at until the service is down; although it may contain useful clues that could have prevented an outage in the first place.

Another approach that can be used is to ensure that all services within the enterprise implement one or more common management interfaces that will allow external management consoles to query the service for its status. A good strategy that can be incorporated into the enterprise architecture will be for services to implement an interface for application level pings, returning the service version and the ability to shutdown a service remotely. Let us look at representative WSDL snippets that outline this concept:

```
<?xml version="1.0" encoding="UTF-8"?>
<definitions
    name="Quote"
    targetNamespace="http://www.canaxia.com/Quote.wsdl"
    xmlns="http://schemas.xmlsoap.org/wsdl/"
    xmlns:soap="http://schemas.xmlsoap.org/wsdl/soap/"
    xmlns:tns="http://www.canaxia.com/Quote.wsdl"
    xmlns:xsd="http://www.w3.org/2001/XMLSchema"
    xmlns:xsd1="http://www.canaxia.com/Quote.xsd1">
    <types>
        <xsd:schema
            targetNamespace="http://www.canaxia.com/Quote.xsd1"
            xmlns="http://schemas.xmlsoap.org/wsdl/"
            xmlns:SOAP-ENC="http://schemas.xmlsoap.org/soap/
            encoding/"
            xmlns:xsd="http://www.w3.org/2001/XMLSchema"
            xmlns:xsd1="http://www.canaxia.com/Quote.xsd1">
        </xsd:schema>
    </types>
    <message name="ShutdownResponse">   </message>
    <message name="ShutdownRequest">
        <part name="username" type="xsd:string"/>
        <part name="password" type="xsd:string"/>
    </message>
    <message name="VersionResponse">   </message>
    <message name="PingResponse">   </message>
    <portType name="ManagementPortType">
        <operation name="Ping">
            <documentation>Verify that the service is listening
            and ready to accept messages</documentation>
            <output message="tns:PingResponse"/>
        </operation>
        <operation name="Shutdown">
            <documentation>Shuts down the service</documentation>
            <input message="tns:ShutdownRequest"/>
            <output message="tns:ShutdownResponse"/>
        </operation>
        <operation name="Version">
            <documentation>Displays the version of
            the service</documentation>
```

```
        <output message="tns:VersionResponse"/>
    </operation>
</portType>
<binding name="ManagementPortTypeBinding"
type="tns:ManagementPortType">
    <soap:binding style="rpc"
    transport="http://schemas.xmlsoap.org/soap/http"/>
    <operation name="Ping">
        <soap:operation soapAction="capeconnect:Quote:
        ManagementPortType#Ping"/>
        <input>
            <soap:body use="literal"/>
        </input>
        <output>
            <soap:body use="literal"/>
        </output>
    </operation>
    <operation name="Shutdown">
        <soap:operation soapAction="capeconnect:Quote:
        ManagementPortType#Shutdown"/>
        <input>
            <soap:body use="literal"/>
        </input>
        <output>
            <soap:body use="literal"/>
        </output>
    </operation>
    <operation name="Version">
        <soap:operation soapAction="capeconnect:Quote:
ManagementPortType#Version"/>
        <input>
            <soap:body use="literal"/>
        </input>
        <output>
            <soap:body use="literal"/>
        </output>
    </operation>
</binding>
<service name="Quote">
    <port binding="tns:QuoteBinding" name="QuotePort">
        <soap:address
        location="http://localhost:8000/ccx/Quote"/>
```

```
        </port>
    </service>
</definitions>
```

Code 1. WSDL to define management interfaces

Within the WSDL document, we defined the shutdown operation as taking a username and password to prevent arbitrary shutdown by unauthorized personnel as well as a version service that can return meta-information about the service itself. This approach allows application developers to include entry-level management capabilities into their services by implementing the enterprise defined service interfaces. Common interfaces used consistently throughout the enterprise makes the task of adding management capabilities easily scoped and, more importantly, repeatable. An enterprise can begin to create their own framework that can proactively check the status of a service via simple polling constructs.

The proposed service interfaces are useful in creating a strategy whereby internal management applications can be custom developed to understand the state of the services network and while an improvement over simple logging, it will still introduce problems of their own including who can call the services, in what context and how often.

The real question that should be asked is whether application developers should be implementing management functionality into services at construction time or whether this concern should be externally managed. Enterprises are under constant pressure to externalize systems, deliver quicker. This requires IT to leverage agile methods for developing software and deferring many tasks to later phases that never actually happen. Development teams would love visibility into the run-time behavior of their service offerings but usually their requirements come second to business demand.

Teams may be able to develop and deploy services quickly without management capabilities. However, this often leads to disruptions of new development and missed deadlines because the teams must triage and diagnose run-time service problems with very little real-time information. The enterprise should consider approaches where management is externalized from the services themselves.

The ideal abstraction would suggest having an enterprise framework that has responsibility for management of services. A robust framework should provide support for answering the following questions regarding management of services:

- What services have to be managed?
- What are the properties of the service?

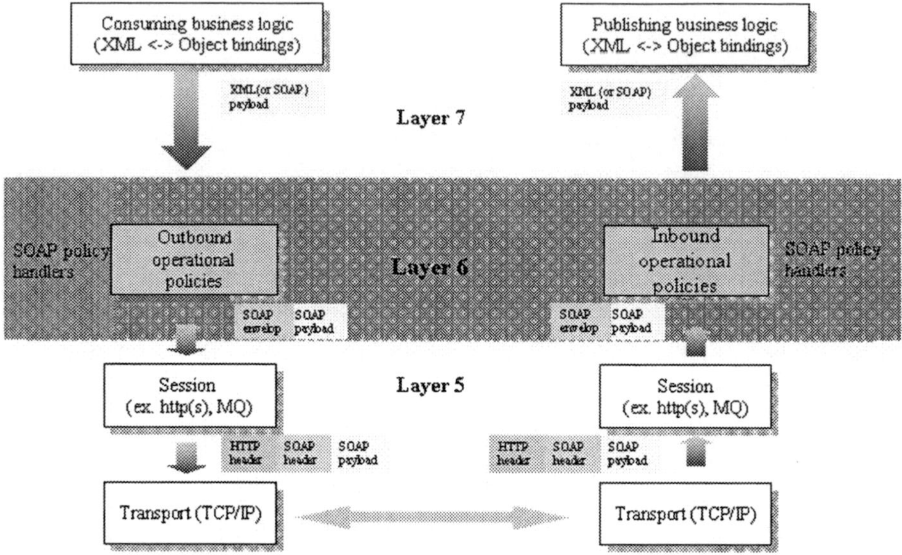

Figure 2. **Management Separation of Concerns (OSI Model)**

- What if some service(s) fail?
- How to properly secure and manage security of services?
- Protocols used for exchanging management information including operations, notifications and protocols?
- Relationships between managed services?

The ability to provide management of services is best realized by using a framework-based approach that can encapsulate the interactions with sets of managed services. The framework itself may be reminiscent of a typical object-oriented system in that services under management are analogous to an object hierarchy.

2. *Systems Management*

Managing service-oriented architectures can be thought of as a new layer of functionality on top of traditional management frameworks (i.e. Tivoli, BMC, CA/Unicenter) that can understand and interact with the underlying infrastructure and provide a mapping layer to how services behave on it. Traditional management infrastructures provide visible and control of the underlying infrastructure but do not provide management at the service request level which maps directly to a business process.

A framework that understands services can provide additional value over traditional management infrastructures in that it can not only alert but can make informed decisions and provide alternatives to increase service reliability. Service-oriented management frameworks can permit or deny service requests based on the identity of the requestor, its content and/or its context. Frameworks in this space can reroute requests to alternative service providers, provide load balancing across servers or even data centers, transform messages and provide analytics surrounding run-time performance and utilization.

Systems Management is comprised of the following components:

- Logging,
- Auditing,
- Monitoring,
- Alerting,
- Provisioning.

Management of XML-based services is enabled via the principle of introspection. While it is possible to have services that do not use XML, without the ability to inject into the architecture third party components become difficult to manage and usually require serialization, rebuilding and recompiling to change. Introspection of XML can occur at run-time with default implementations and can be used to rapidly instrument services without the service implementation changing.

2.1. Logging

Access to services from consuming applications should be logged at a minimum. These logs can be used for various operational processes including services provisioning, monitoring, performance evaluations, and business trend analysis.

Listed in Table 2 are some of the elements that we believe should be centrally logged upon every service invocation.

Corporate security policies and software development standards should dictate which elements of a log message are required vs. optional. From a software development perspective, the framework component that handles capturing of logging records

Table 2. **Logging Properties**

Property	Data type	Description
Service Name	String	Name of the service
Service Protocol	String	Transport protocol used to invoke the service.
Credential	String	Credential of the calling service consumer. Could be username, thumbprint or other credential type.
Credential Token	String	If service request required authentication and/or authorization, the log should store the unique identifier provided by the security service.
Request Start Timestamp	Timestamp	Time the service request was started. Should be logged to the 100 millisecond.
Request Finish Timestamp	Timestamp	Time the service request was completed.
Log Timestamp	Timestamp	In order to achieve scalability, it may be necessary to defer logging to background processes while retaining full traceability.
Request Message	Blob	Request message may exceed the limits of typical datatypes especially if store used is a relational database.
Response Message	Blob	Same as above. Ideally store could "shred" request/response XML into normalized fields for reporting purposes.
Severity	String	If service invocation resulted in an error, may want to indicate problem. Severity may be indicated as follows: • Error • Warning • Critical • Informational • Diagnostic
Signature	Binary String	Field used to store digital signature of log entry and can be used for non-repudiation purposes. Ideally it will be signed using an algorithm that supports one-way encryption such as MD5 or SHA1.

needs to be built with more system qualities than anything else within the enterprise as it must reliably keep records of security-related and business transaction events. Minimally, the logs will serve as a useful audit trail and can be used to confirm compliance with government regulations and internal enterprise security policies, detect breaches in security and helping diagnose production problems.

2.2. Auditing

In accounting, an audit trail provides a recorded log of sequences that help in either validating or invalidating accounting entries. For services, the audit log may track all changes to policies, starting and stopping security related services or other administrative actions. Auditing can be considered an extension to logging but is also used for different purposes. Logging often contains diagnostic information and information regarding service requests while audit logs contain information about the management framework itself in order to maintain higher order conceptual integrity.

Auditing also requires dependencies on external services in order to maintain integrity. Some of the services required are given in Table 3.

***Table 3.* Auditing Requirements**

Service	Description
Public Key Infrastructure	Audit logs may require non-repudiation. Use of digital signatures may be used as a mechanism to accomplish this.
Secure Time Service	If the audit logs use timestamps, a trusted time service is required. Usually this time service will be indexed to the Naval Observatory or other Stratum 1 time service.
Secure Storage	The audit information will ultimately need to be persisted in a form of secured database.

In reality, auditing is a hybrid requirement that is someone between logging and security and shares characteristics with both depending upon its context. Let us look at the differences:

- Auditing assists in the detection and avoidance of violations in security related policies, while security is applied in order to prevent future denials of service consumer, producer or administration actions.
- Logging is passive and ideally accomplished out-of-band from the service request, where auditing should always be handled in-band and fail the entire service transaction if the auditing record cannot be created.
- Auditing is active in that it can react immediately to violations such as locking a user account, where actions may be invoked on logging entries but will be handled at a later time. Actions on log entries is often manual, so no automated action can be taken on it.
- Auditing records are usually centralized and may have daemon processes that perform checks on them periodically, while logging can be accomplished decentralized and replicated centrally in the future for analysis.

For more information on network time protocols and stratum, see Internet RFC 1769.

2.3. Monitoring

The ability to determine the health of the services network is vital to run-time reliability. Operational snapshots that show the health of all services by averaging values from the services connected through a single component (gateway or agent) is mandatory. Usually, this information is best rendered in the form of a console that displays the health of the selected component. Components can be optionally compared to their specified service level agreement (SLA). An ideal approach is to color key the display as shown in Table 4.

***Table 4.* Monitoring Color Key**

Color	Run-time Description	SLA Description
Green	Service(s) is experiencing no errors.	Service(s) performing within SLA.
Yellow	Service(s) is experiencing errors, user experience not impacted. Service may have failover or been re-routed.	Service(s) performing close to limit of SLA.
Red	User experience is impacted. Services are returning errors.	Service(s) performing outside limit of SLA.

The ability to view run-time information on various components and services within specified time periods allows one to quickly determine the overall health of the services network and take action accordingly. Ideally, the management framework should provide other metrics and views, see Table 5.

***Table 5.* Service Metrics**

Metric	Description
Downtime	Information when the service is considered no longer able to process service requests.
Execution Failure	Metrics expressed as a percentage/count of the number of successful service executions vs number of service failures.
Latency	The amount of processing time overhead the policies have added to the to service requests.
Access Violations	Number of service invocations that are failing due to security considerations.

If the service is accessed via a gateway, downtime can show the start and end times of when the specified service started to fail and then started again to successfully process service requests. For agents, this can indicate the amount of time where a centralized facility that performs service-level pings has not completed. Execution failures should be specified as a percentage for high-volume services and as a count for low-volume services. For example, if the Yahoo® Stock Quote service has a billion requests per day, having a threshold count will create either too many false positives or not show that anything is wrong. A better way in this situation may be to indicate that monitoring should show yellow if the number of failed invocations goes over 1% within core business-hours and red if over 2%.

Latency is an expression of how much time it takes for a request to travel from one designated point to another. A service will have zero latency if all data in the request can be transmitted instantly between one point and another. Adding gateways and agents will introduce application-level latency but this will also occur based on the underlying network topology.

Latency of service invocations occurs due to several factors including:

- Propagation,
- Transmission,
- Routing, and
- Miscellaneous processing.

Propagation is the time it takes for a service request and response to travel between producer and consumer respectively. Transmission of service requests occurs over a multitude of physical network components (i.e. routers, fiber, T1s, ATM, and so on) that introduce their own delays. Service components such as gateways and agents may need to examine the payload to determine next hop or provide additional processing such as transformation and/or validating the service request came from an authorized user.

High latency in routing and propagation tend to indicate performance bottlenecks in the infrastructure while latency in routing and miscellaneous processing usually occur due to sub-optimal service run-time resources, bad services design or service components that require optimization. Latency can be improved by implementing pre-fetching (anticipating the need for supplemental information) and introducing multi-threading constructs that will allow processing to occur in parallel across multiple threads of execution.

Access violations are useful in determining whether the services network is receiving an increased amount of failed service invocations due to security considerations and will help determine service-level denial-of-service, malformed requests or other forms of attacks.

3. Alerting

Business alerts allow you to specify an action in response to a specific type of business event. Alerts provide notification when a service is not meeting its service-level agreement or not seeing the level of service requests expected. An alert can watch for specific types of business events and initiate an action in response. Alerts can be created on both message traffic patterns and other forms of system and aggregated data.

Alerts can be created to notify individuals and distribution lists in a variety of manners as well as invoke predetermined services. Some of the possible alerting facilities that should be supported in a framework include:

- Email notification (user and/or distribution list),
- SNMP Traps, and
- Service invocation.

Alerting can also be used for technical considerations. It may make sense for the operations staff to classify all alerts into the following alert categories:

- Response time,
- Transaction size,
- System fault, and
- Trending.

3.1. Round Trip

Response time for services measure the total elapsed time from the detection of the service request to the completion of the response to the service request. This is known as measuring the round trip execution time for service requests. This is useful in detecting situations where high-volume services such as a real-time stock quoting service exceeds its desired response time.

3.2. Transaction Size

The amount of data transmitted as part of a service request may give hints to identifying operations that sent or receive large amounts of information. The size of the payload could have the effect of slowing down overall service response times especially in situations where XML is used. It may be useful to operations personnel to be notified in situations where an individual service request sent a 10 MB XML document where the typical document is 1 MB. Transaction size may also be used in aggregation situations for operations personnel. For example, you may desire to be notified if the average request size during any one-hour period has exceeded 50 MB.

3.3. System Fault

Alerts can be useful for tracking the availability and operational status of individual services. Alerts may be sent if a service request could not be processed correctly either due to the service not responding or the service returning a fault. Management frameworks may optionally implement a heartbeat monitor that periodically directs a predefined service request to the service and alerts upon failure.

3.4. Trending

Over time service request transaction times may deviate from expected values. Using threshold scenarios in alerting situations can sometimes result in not getting alerted when it is important to or on the other side receiving too many false positives. One solution to this problem is the introduction of non-threshold-based analysis. One of the more popular approaches is the use of Bayesian Belief Networks.

Bayes theorem is named after the Reverend Thomas Bayes who worked on the problem of computing a distribution for the parameter of a binomial distribution. In simple terms, he defined a mathematical formula based on probability inference, which is a means of calculating, from the number of times an event has not occurred, the probability that it will occur in the future.

Bayesian belief networks are used to develop knowledge-based management frameworks where usage patterns are characterized by inherent uncertainty. The ability to apply reasoning with uncertainty sometimes overlaps with conventional knowledge-based capture techniques. For example, a stock quoting service may receive an average of 1,000 requests per minute on days where the stock market is open, say Monday thru Friday from 9am to 4pm eastern time excluding holidays. During this period, if the number of requests goes over 5,000 an alert can be set using traditional approaches, but what happens on Saturdays if the request volume is 750 requests per minute when weekend traffic is lower? Now imagine the alert threshold being correlated to news such as peace in the Middle East. You could not define the alerting criteria in advance but the system could learn trading volumes and take into considerations trends such as increased trading volume near year end or even inverse patterns such as the number of buy orders is dropping but the number of sell orders is increasing.

For more information on Thomas Bayes and Bayesian Beliefs, see: http://www.bayesian.org/bayesian/bayes.html.

4. Provisioning

A management framework should be responsible for defining services behavior based on its exposed business and technical functionality. Service consumers in enterprises that implement per-usage chargeback mechanisms or for external service consumers who are charged for usage should use a management framework that supports a metering construct. Service usage can be billed based on usage/subscription patterns.

The logic for provisioning services should be built into a subscription engine that exposes itself as a service. Service consumers can search for services against registries where they have been given access and then apply for a subscription to the desired services. Likewise, subscription policies can be defined as metadata in the registry in which the management framework is responsible for enforcing.

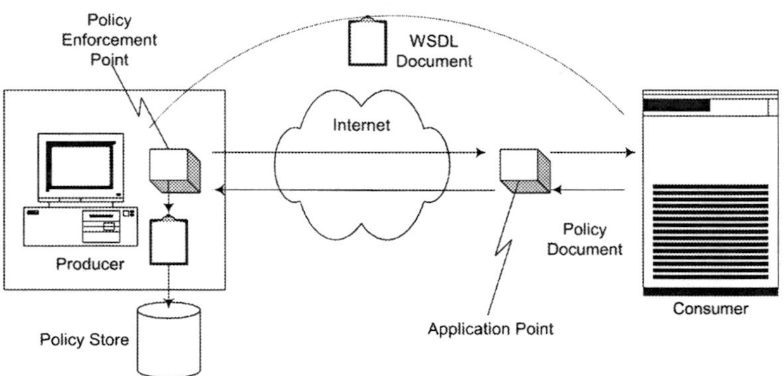

Figure 3. **Service Invocation – Producer Policies**

Ultimately service consumers will access services based upon the contract based upon their subscription. In order to effectively bill for usage, the framework will need to be aware of the statistics of the contract, committed service levels and implied qualities of services. When services are consumed, a separate function of the framework that handles metering may allow/disallow access to the service, throttle the number of requests within a specific time period and ultimately will create input to be used by a billing service.

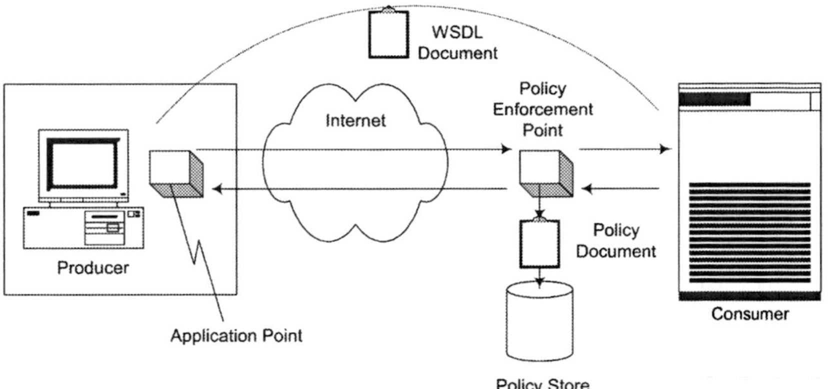

Figure 4. **Service Invocation – External**

5. Leasing

A lease is a grant of guaranteed access over a time period. When the lease runs out, the consumer must request a new one. Leases are negotiated between consumers and the provider of the service as part of the service contract. Leasing helps prevent stale caching information from queries to UDDI registries and other locator-based services. The concept of a lease is necessary for SOA when services need to maintain the state of information about the binding between consumers and producers. The lease defines the amount of time for which the state may be maintained. Leasing reduces coupling between service consumers and service producers by limiting the amount of time consumers and providers may be bound. Without a leasing construct, consumers could bind to a service forever and never rebind to its contract again.

When service producers need to change the implementation of a service, it can do so when the leases held by consumers expire. This allows service implementations to change without affecting the execution of the service consumers, because those consumers must request a new contract and lease. When the new contract and lease are obtained, they are not guaranteed to be identical to the previous ones.

Leases can be implemented so that they are either exclusive or non-exclusive. Exclusive leases insure that no one else may access the resource during the period of the lease; non-exclusive leases allow multiple service consumers to invoke the same service.

Leases can also be implemented using finite or infinite constructs. A finite lease can be used immediately or based on a future lease. Finite leases require service providers to define the exact period for which the service should be made available for discovery in the registry. The lease period is restricted by the maximum allowable lease period defined by the administrator.

Future leases allow a service provider to make the service discoverable once the lease has been activated. Infinite leases allow for the maximum allowable time for the lease to change. This is useful in circumstances where a service provider wants to ask for service consumers to periodically check back for changes in service contracts. Usually infinite leases should be constrained based on either a time period or ratio.

Leasing can be integrated into the provisioning system in which the elements are static upon each request. This would require knowledge of how to handle leasing terms at the service proxy and gateway. Alternatively, leasing can be implemented at the gateway itself as a type of policy. This would allow consumers that do not understand leasing constructs to function while maintaining loose coupling. Leasing can also be tied into components that provide authentication, encryption and non-repudiation.

6. *Billing*

The billing service is responsible for creating and storing billing records. It has the responsibility of creating billing entries into a separate billing provider system. For internal usage, the billing service can create billing entries for chargeback purposes into general ledger applications such as Peoplesoft, SAP or Oracle Financials. Table 6 shows the elements of a typical billing record.

Ideally, the billing service should expose an interface that can provide up to date billing information for service consumers. The billing provider should physically separate this interface from the billing services interface that is used to store billing records as well as the interfaces actually used. It may be a good idea to consider separating consumer access (query) from billing creation in order to deter fraudulent access.

***Table 6.* Recommended Elements of a Billing Record**

Element	Description
User	The user ID of the service requestor.
Record Date	Date and time of service usage.
Duration	Duration of service usage. Can be a count if aggregated, CPU time or similar metric.
Reference	A pointer to the contract (provisioning record if applicable) which governed service access.
Service Name	Name of the service(s) consumed.
Host	Host unique identifier that the service executed on.

7. Pricing/Chargeback Models

Service level agreements establish the foundation for pricing and chargeback models. Within most business models there will be services offered with no quality of service guarantee and therefore may be freely available. Likewise, services that are used in business transactions where quality of service is important, then pricing and chargeback models become applicable.

In order to support effective pricing models, identifying the service consumer in a non-repudiated manner may be required and may optionally support the usage of digitally signed XML messages. The ability to collect revenue on services helps fund future service enhancements and fund operations.

Several models for pricing & charge backs for services include:

- Per User,
- Per Transaction,
- Percentage of Revenue,
- Fixed Fee/Subscription,
- Lease/License,
- Business Partnership, and
- Registration.

While decisions based on pricing models can be made at service construction time, embedding this type of information within each service minimally will require breaking of the provided service interfaces. If multiple models are employed, solving for this at design-time becomes a fragile value proposition. Let us look at each of the models in detail.

7.1. Per Transaction

Fee per use models are the most primitive of all commerce and are based upon a pre-established relationship between two trading partners. In this model, the notion of a charge per transaction can be implemented using payment instruments such as debit and credit cards. Service consumers may be given discounts for various transaction volume levels.

7.2. Fixed Fee/Subscription

Subscription models depend upon the establishment of user accounts and supporting the appropriate validation mechanisms as part of the service request. This support can be incorporated into an overall provisioning strategy where users specify their anticipated service usage. A service provider may desire to create tiers of membership levels to allow for classification of service consumers. Architecturally, it becomes important to consider whether this model happens within the service itself, externalized to a management framework and/or handled through out-of-band provisioning and reconciliation.

Service providers may charge additional fees, such as a management fee that covers the costs associated with operations personnel, bandwidth, hardware and other data center charges. Fees for support services are also common.

7.3. Lease/License

Leasing and licensing are common for large volume usage scenarios and are usually based upon customized agreements. Service providers may charge based on the number of service requests or the volume of requesting components (i.e. seats) within the service requestor's infrastructure. Leasing and licensing always occur via out-of-band provisioning mechanisms.

7.4. Business Partnership/Percentage of Revenue

A visit to many software vendors web sites will uncover the notion of partnering whereby a vendor will establish mutual usage agreements with other vendors in order to increase the number of customers for reference purposes and as a money saving mechanism. Bartering of services can be done based on equality or a percentage of gross revenue (i.e. link referral model) of the requestor in third-party service branding scenarios.

Percentage of revenue (i.e. slice of the pie) is similar to the per-transaction model in that the amount charged to service consumers may fluctuate based each billing cycle. The difference between the per-transaction model and percentage of revenue is the model's price calculations correlate to the amount of revenue the service consumer generates each billing cycle.

7.5. Registration

Many web search engines now charge for registering Internet web sites in order to for the site to be generally accessible. The same thinking can be applied to services that will be externally accessed. One model may be to use a management framework that intercepts publish requests to a UDDI registry and charges based on a pay to be viewed concept as shown in Figure 5. This model assumes that if a service provider wants to offer services, they will be willing to pay a registration fee.

The pricing/chargeback models discussed in this chapter are generally applicable to any market segment and/or industry vertical.

8. *Lifecycle Management*

Traditional lifecycle processes focus on methodologies used to support developers during the development process but fall short in considering what happens at deployment time. A complete strategy should include all aspects of a service's lifecycle and follow the path of a service from its conception to its retirement. Lifecycles for services really have two viewpoints, the development aspect which is developer driven and the operational aspect which is driven by operations personnel.

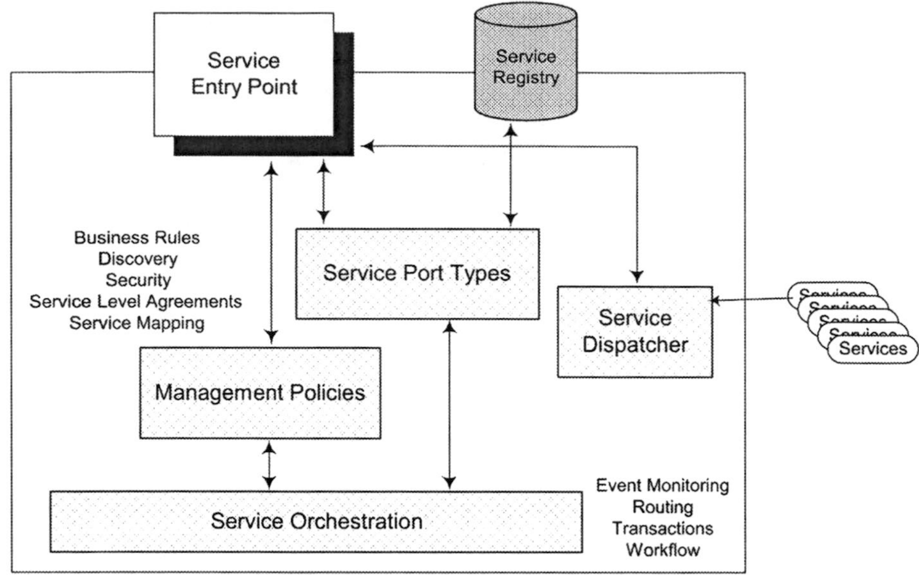

Figure 5. **UDDI Registry Management**

Operations staff typically manages deployment and run-time aspects of services and develop plans for reacting quickly to deployment related problems. This strategy may include rolling back services or in situations of disaster routing request to alternate providers. Ongoing support for services may include infrastructure tuning and stability improvements to help services meet service-level agreements. Over time services will need to be retired or wholesale replaced. Usually this is the most difficult discipline to accomplish since enterprises tend to be reluctant to change especially when services still meet their needs. For example, there is a large portion of end-users who still run Windows NT and Windows 2000 although its replacement has been available for several years. The management strategy must include identification and planning to support service obsolescence.

Lifecycle management for services can be realized in a multitude of ways and are comprised of the following aspects:

- Routing,
- Transformation,
- Versioning,
- Deprecation,

- Provisioning, and
- Quality Assurance.

8.1. Routing

One of the tenets to Service-Oriented infrastructure (SOI) will be to eliminate single points of failure within the enterprise. Usually this is accomplished by making sure that a particular service has more than one instance either on a single machine and/or on different machines. The services can also be spread across different geographic locations. Ideally, location transparency should be incorporated into the architecture so that clients are unaware to the physical location of each service and maintains a single stable endpoint address.

A management framework may use load-balancing approach to make sure that requests are evenly distributed across instances of a particular service. Different service reception points may share a common queue provided by the framework in which downstream service endpoints may be invoked in a round-robin fashion. Invocation may also contain pluggable strategies to talk into account algorithms such as affinity, weighted averaging, availability and quiescence.

To quiesce is to put a service or other computer resource into a temporarily inactive state whereby in-progress requests are serviced but new requests are denied.

Support for affinity is important in two different situations. The first usage of affinity is to support service requests that are stateful by nature. Stateful services are highly discouraged but the management framework should support it anyway. The second usage for affinity is to increase performance of services where it may internally cache access to downstream data sources such as relational databases, file systems or other resources. An advanced form of affinity is known as Class affinity where groups of services say from a particular user population (i.e. VIP customers, partners) may be routed to a different set of services. Ideally, affinity will be defined on a per service basis in a weak manner (for stateless services) where the vast majority of requests for affinity are desired but not guaranteed or strongly where it is. Strong affinity will return an error condition back to the consumer in case the target server cannot handle the request.

Affinity is an approach to load balancing that directs multiple incoming requests from the same consumer are always to the same producer. Service affinity disables workload management after initial service invocation by forcing requests to always return to the initial connection endpoint.

Management frameworks may support advanced load balancing where consumers are balanced across multiple physical services. If one or services (grouping) have zero consumers, then those services alone are considered for load balancing. One all the services within the group have at least one active consumer, then standard load balancing approaches are used.

8.2. Versioning and Deprecation

Change management is one of the most difficult disciplines to master. Service-oriented architectures compound the problem in that traditional disciplines usually assume that producers and consumers are under the same administrative control. Once a service has been deployed to production and has gained widespread usage, opportunities for improvement will emerge. The difficulty is how to support change to production services without forcing all consumers to upgrade at the same time.

Forced upgrades simply do not work in service-oriented architectures as the principle of decoupling producer from consumer has the effect of separation of concerns from a design perspective but does not address run-time considerations. In production environments, it is a requirement that different versions of a service be simultaneously supported. A management framework should provide a public interface to each service and optionally upgrade/downgrade service requests to backend services as appropriate. This strategy will allow for decommissioning older versions of a service without consumer disruption.

Several strategies emerge to support this problem space. At development time, if interfaces are made immutable then you can upgrade components and other services that leverage components without breaking code that relies on old version. Microsoft's COM takes an interesting approach in that it assigns each interface a globally unique identifier (GUID). A developer cannot modify an interface and therefore must create a new one if they wish to modify the behavior. This means that once a client is compiled using the specified interface, the developer can be assured that the interface will never change.

> *A GUID is a 128-bit integer that is unique across both space and time.*

If the interface uses a document-style approach where an arbitrary number of parameters can be passed using either an XML tagged approach as a string and/or strongly typed object such as a property bag, then versioning can be implemented inside of the service itself. Let us look at a code snippet in Java that demonstrates this concept:

```
public class OrderDTO extends VectorDTO {
private static final long serialVersionUID = 1;
protected Vector bag;
}
```

Code 2. Data transfer object
Let us now extend to OrderDTO to contain the currency type used when placing an order:

```
public class OrderDTO extends VectorDTO {
private static final long serialVersionUID = 2;
protected Vector bag;
public Currency typeOfMoney;
}
```

Code 3. Extending a DTO

The DTO can be passed to a method that may have the following signature:

```
public Boolean Process(OrderDTO order)
```

Within the process method, you can determine if the DTO is the version you expect by using a method that exposes the value of serialVersionUID and can optionally upgrade the interface as appropriate without forcing all clients to recompile. Development time changes can be accomplished with you have administrative control over both the client and the server but otherwise is limiting. Versioning as a problem space is not limited to strictly producer side concerns but can also occur if you are a consumer that needs to talk to an upgraded service but cannot modify your own code.

Versioning of services has similarities with traditional object-based approaches but also varies in subtle ways. A management framework attempts to externalize versioning concerns out of code and keeping this information centralized. By having versioning handled by a framework, it affords several opportunities including:

- Ability to perform version upgrades of services without reducing service availability.
- Hot deployment and maintenance of new parallel version of services.
- Creation and support of multiple mirrors support each version of the service.
- The ability to commission and decommission servers in both provider and consumer modes.

Versioning will also afford the enterprise the ability to combine versioning constructs with provisioning constructs. For example, a free version of the service could be offered that supports an older version of a service while paid customers can access newer versions of the service. The ability to establish version-based access control is especially important for high-volume consumer driven architectures. In this same situations, the ability to externalize versioning information within the application will allow for centralized notification to consumers when newer versions of the service are available and/or when currently supported services will be deprecated.

Service-oriented architectures that leverage XML as the transport make versioning easier since a framework can provide introspection capabilities on the payload and upgrade/downgrade as appropriate through transformation constructs. If your SOA uses binary protocols such as classes, an intermediary may be capable (although not usually the case) of converting objects from one type to another. It may be useful to provide routing to the service that has the highest numerical version unless the client specifies otherwise.

Upgrading of interfaces can be accomplished by software that supports either/both the Proxy Pattern or Intercepting Filter Pattern. These patterns can also for the creation of framework components that can intercept the message upon service invocation by changing the message in-flight while passing the request to and from the service.

For more information on patterns, please see Gamma et al. (1994). The Intercepting Filter pattern is covered in detail in Alur et al. (2003).

Use of document-style services is order of magnitudes easier to implement versioning constructs over document style approaches. Document style allows for the usage of XML and allows for situations in which versioning is not so direct. Since XML processing allows for addition of elements, older clients will simply ignore them. Document-style enables versioning of interfaces that use queuing approaches, since elements may need to be accessed externally to the document itself such as priority.

8.3. Transformation

Transformations of XML payloads by management frameworks allow services to bridge the information models and business processes within composable services architecture. If you ask yourself, how do I get the message into the right format for its next destination, the requirement for transformation becomes clearer.

The management framework should provide the ability to handle complex transformation of messages and the ability to map between message formats. In services that are purchased off the shelf, the vocabulary used could be wide-ranging. For example, fields named given name and surname may need to be converted to fields named first name and last name in order to be processed by downstream services.

Messages may also be required to be broken into a number of new messages each with their own routing. Let us look at one example:

```
<?xml version="1.0"?>
<!DOCTYPE ORDER SYSTEM "order.dtd">
<?xml-stylesheet type="text/css" href="xmlorderpart.css"?>
<Orders>
<Customer>
   <CustNumber>BICHE1</CustNumber>
   <CompanyName>Budhoorams Auto Body</CompanyName>
   <ContactName>Khaimraj Kelon</ContactName>
   <ContactTitle>CEO</ContactTitle>
   <CountryCode>TT</CountryCode>
   <Phone>868-666-0123</Phone>
</Customer>
...
<Customer>
   <CustNumber>SHOOP1</CustNumber>
   <CompanyName>Little Red Zuper Car</CompanyName>
   <ContactName>James Franklin</ContactName>
   <ContactTitle>CEO</ContactTitle>
   <CountryCode>US</CountryCode>
   <Phone>860-242-8050</Phone>
</Customer>
</Orders>
```

Code 4. Composite order message

In the above code, we have a composite order that contains two different customers in different countries (Trinidad and the United States). In this situation, we may need to route the request to two different services, which will require breaking up the document into two distinct messages as follows:

```
<?xml version="1.0"?>
<!DOCTYPE ORDER SYSTEM "order.dtd">
<?xml-stylesheet type="text/css" href="xmlorderpart.css"?>
<Orders>
<Customer>
   <CustNumber>BICHE1</CustNumber>
```

```
   <CompanyName>Budhoorams Auto Body</CompanyName>
   <ContactName>Khaimraj Kelon</ContactName>
   <ContactTitle>CEO</ContactTitle>
   <CountryCode>TT</CountryCode>
   <Phone>868-666-0123</Phone>
</Customer>
</Orders>
```

Code 5. Order message – Trinidad

```
<?xml version="1.0"?>
<!DOCTYPE ORDER SYSTEM "order.dtd">
<?xml-stylesheet type="text/css" href="xmlorderpart.css"?>
<Orders>
<Customer>
   <CustNumber>SHOOP1</CustNumber>
   <CompanyName>Little Red Zuper Car</CompanyName>
   <ContactName>James Franklin</ContactName>
   <ContactTitle>CEO</ContactTitle>
   <CountryCode>US</CountryCode>
   <Phone>860-242-8050</Phone>
</Customer>
</Orders>
```

Code 6. Order message – United States

The ability to convert from one message format to another is a fundamental principle in enterprise integration. A framework can accept incoming XML data and perform specialized XML transformations using XSLT and XPATH. Usually the least non-performing aspect of any XML-based SOA is related to transformation. The ability to first externalize this from services to a framework will allow the enterprise to take advantage of newer parsers without disturbing existing service code bases.

XML transformations can also be offloaded to specialized XML appliances that implement XML transformation within hardware. Hardware-based solutions have a performance gain of factors of 20 to 1 or even greater. XML encryption and digital signatures can also be offloaded to specialized cards in order to provide additional performance benefits. Ideally, the framework will allow for transformation engines to be configured using approaches such as Java's API for XML Processing (JAXP).

Datapower, Sarvega, Reactivity and Tarari are the leading vendors in this space.

8.4. Provisioning

Services are expressed in business terms and so should service levels. Traditional service level agreements were based on technical constructs and had no tie to business benefit. A framework should provide a comprehensive way of translating a service level agreement into the allocation of resourced required by consumers of the service and may be comprised of required security profiles, policies surrounding prioritization of traffic and the number of requested that be executed during a given time period.

Service level agreements are abstract concepts that provide a mechanism for partner's to understand each other's capabilities, to negotiate service parameters and assist with providing a management goal. Service level agreements ideally provide a level of separation between partners in managing concerns between them. A well-defined service level agreement is given in Table 7.

***Table 7.* Components of a Service Level Agreement**

Constraint Type	Elements	Description
Date	Start Date End Date Next Evaluation Date (optional)	Specifies the date the service level agreement starts and ends (i.e. 16 February 1977 to 10 September 2001) and the date in which the agreement can be re-evaluated.
Function	Name	Could describe systems, services or other technical constructs.
Day Time	Days of week Hours	Should be expressed in terms of days of week (i.e. Monday thru Friday, working days, holidays, etc.) and hours (8am to 4pm) and include time zone (GMT) and observation of daylight savings time.
Process	Name (optional)	Processes can describe sub-aspects of functional systems and/or services.
Construct	Description	A construct describes how the process operates and/or message exchange patterns.
Measured Item	Name Location	One or more items to be measured for system qualities and determines where measurements will occur (producer, consumer).

A service-level agreement attempts to completely define mutual terms in a measurable manner. For example, an agreement may contain a phrase like "Starting March 1st, 2004 to March 1st, 2005, from 8am to 4pm eastern standard time, Monday thru Friday except holidays, the average response time for the ten longest running quote transactions as measured from the gateway should be less than five seconds". In this example, we have specified constraints on date, day/time, a group of processes and where the agreement will be measured.

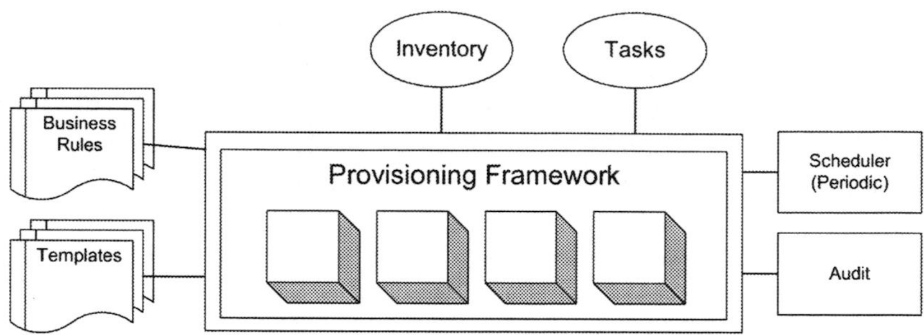

Figure 6. **Provisioning Framework**

A key to gaining control over service-level agreements is to not simply limit measurement to compliance points contained within agreements but to fundamentally build a comprehensive understanding of run-time information. The ability to measure between producer and consumers, and even intermediaries becomes vital. For example, the orders service from company ABC promises to deliver order items to company 123 within three business days but uses the shipping service of company XYZ to deliver orders. In this scenario several measurement challenges emerge. First, company ABC can only measure its service-level by consulting either 123 or XYZ. Second, 123 and XYZ will measure service-levels locally but will distribute measurement information to external frameworks.

A service level agreement may be specified to a service consumer in general terms or may be guaranteed at the time access to services is provisioned. Minimally, provisioning engines need to support the following interface types:

- Creation,
- Activation,
- Modification,
- Suspension,
- Deactivation,
- Deletion, and
- Interrogation.

Provisioning engines attempt to unify and centralize business rules around provisioning requirements. This may be implemented using a gateway approach in a distributed manner that may synchronously or asynchronously update the provisioning system of record. The gateway can be considered a provisioning service point or can optionally manage a separate provisioning service.

8.5. Quality Assurance

Quality assurance is the discipline used in a systematic process of checking to see whether a service being developed or deployed meets specified requirements. Within most enterprises, there will exist a separate departments dedicated to quality assurance practices. A quality assurance system is said to increase customer confidence and organizational credibility. Quality assurance systems emphasize catching defects before they get into production.

A sound quality assurance practice will minimally test prior to production the following elements of a service:

- The service must work functionally for a single user (i.e. functionality).
- The service must provide a response within a reasonable amount of time, scaling or performing well in relation to the required number of simultaneous users. This aspect assurance conformance to service level agreements (i.e. performance, scalability).
- The service must not crash in response to the anticipated number of simultaneous users (i.e. reliability).
- The service must never return invalid responses for any number of simultaneous users even when under duress.

Testing services under load increases in importance especially in situations where services will be accessed from service consumers not under the same administrative control. Stress testing services traditionally is the method least tested but the most important attribute especially if the service is accessed outside of the enterprise and contains transactional, medical, financial, or legal data. The business and legal repercussions of providing inaccurate information to customers and partners can be severe.

Services are usually implemented as part of a larger enterprise application. Traditional quality assurance practices change when a service model is introduced. In the past, practices such as regression testing entire applications were encouraged. This was practical in that regression really tested systems under the same administrative control.

Since services can reside within the enterprise or external, it becomes important that testing instead concentrate on services within administrative control due to issues of causing unnecessary load from the external party's perspective.

SOA starts with the notion of a contract that is published by the service provider in which consumers will leverage. Quality assurance in an SOA needs to concentrate on making sure that the contract does not change between releases, that interfaces over the lifetime of a service remain immutable and that developers have employed appropriate defensive coding techniques within the application to handle invalid data being passed to the service. Of even greater importance is figuring if services adhere to applicable industry standard schemas (where appropriate) and following enterprise and industry vertical semantic constructs.

Management frameworks assist in quality assurance initiatives in several important ways. First, they provide the ability to capture logging and diagnostic information that will assist in quality assurance. The ability to quantify the amount of successful requests vs. failed requests is a simplistic feature of a framework. Second, the ability to have a strategy that can intercept specified requests to services external to the enterprise or in situations where the service has usage costs and/or updates transactional production systems becomes important. For example, if you are testing your internal general ledger and it leverages a funds transfer service to your local bank, it becomes viable to perform regression tests on all internal services with the ability to simply return a predefined message on behalf of the funds transfer service without actually invoking it.

8.6. Business Processes

The discipline of business process management seeks to coordinate the end-to-end activities (manual and automated) that provides value to end customers. Enterprises have always sought to optimize their unique business processes that provide competitive advantage and product differentiation. In order to realize this goal, a strategy that covers the complete process lifecycle including deployment, discovery, optimization and analysis is required.

Business people quickly understand business processes when expressed in business terms, however the level of understanding is not realized within the enterprise due to IT practices of "digitizing" business processes using their own specialized notations such as reference architectures. Ideally, service operations that are related to business processes should be separated from management-oriented operations and ideally contained in their own interface definitions in order to break the coupling between business process and technical implementation.

Business processes minimally include constructs that support the following notions:

- Message Prioritization.
- Business Activity Monitoring.

Let us discuss what these areas mean and how we can incorporate them into a services management strategy.

8.7. Message Prioritization

The need to ensure that your most important customers receive better service than other customers is vital to a services model. The ability to provide service request prioritization based on requirements such as who is requesting the service and the context of the request as it relates to business processes, contracts terms or other business driven criteria may be necessary.

Prioritization may use implemented using queuing strategies for asynchronous service requests, buffering or advanced forms of routing for synchronous requests. The ability to prioritize can be based upon a supplied user credential contained within the message where priority is this determined based on a lookup against the provisioning service, an indicator within a header that either describes its context or indicates its priority or based upon constructs supported at the transport level when using message queues.

8.8. Business Activity Monitoring

Business activity monitoring is a crosscutting concern and leverages the technical aspects of monitoring and alerting. From a business perspective, the ability to create alerts based on business processes becomes crucial in order to comply with governmental regulations, internal audit procedures and enterprise security concerns. Minimally, you should ask yourself do you have a mechanism to determine if your most important customers are using your services, how are they using your services and how often?

The idea behind business activity monitoring is simple. In the business world there is a continuous production of information related to sales, production, logistics, financial operations and other business concerns that many times goes unnoticed until it is too late. Traditional IT systems usually do not have capability to analyze information in real time, creating alerts when problematic or anomalous situations arise. Business activity monitoring can provide both real-time and historical services activity monitoring and visualization and traffic information.

There are three high-level goals of business activity monitoring:

1. Ability to create a dashboard for executives who need aggregated information on business activity at anytime, anywhere.

2. Monitor of business processes and activities in real-time to anticipate and manage problems before they impact the bottom line.

3. Streamline operations with real-time access to the information line managers need when they need it.

Business activity monitoring leverages the management framework's ability to introspect service request traffic and uses not only for technical considerations but business focused events. It also incorporates disciplines found elsewhere within the enterprise such as business intelligence built into data warehouses.

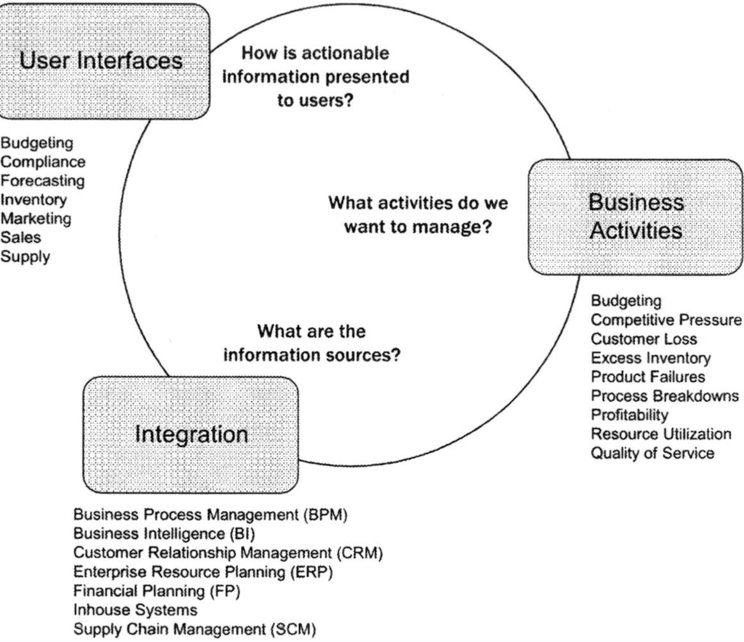

Figure 7. **Business Activity Monitoring**

If you wanted to analyze historical trends to determine peak usage levels for services, then the data warehouse may fit the enterprise requirement. But if say the enterprise wanted to be notified when say order inquiry requests exceed a certain volume, the ability to drill-down and see if it has a common root cause, the requirement to see information in real-time becomes crucial. Using a service management approach not only provides you with information but also context.

9. Management Architecture

A well-defined management strategy for services will lead to the conclusion that execution can be distributed but management should be centralized. Management can be accomplished using two basic methods, gateways and agents. Gateways are a specialized proxy that intercept requests, enforce policies and forward requests to downstream services. Agents are deployed as intercepting filters into services containers such as Axis, Systinet's WASP or in-house frameworks and enforce policies in the address space of the service.

Let us look at the architecture of the following components:

- Gateways,
- Agents, and
- Centralized Policies.

9.1. Gateways

In many enterprises, the infrastructure includes use of a proxy server that acts as an intermediary between an internal computer resource and the Internet so that the enterprise can ensure security, administrative control and caching to reduce bandwidth usage. Proxy servers serve to separate the enterprise network from the outside network.

Traditional proxy servers operate on the packet level. A network router functions by examining TCP/IP packet headers and performing network routing decisions based on rules that specify observed patterns in the packet flow. Firewalls block packet flow by disallowing traffic that does not comply with specified policies and allowable parameters.

There is also what is known as a reverse proxy server where users external to the enterprise may make a request for an Internet service such as web page that resides on an internal web server. If the request passes filtering requirements, the proxy server will return the page to the user. If the proxy server implements caching, it will serve the request out of is local store. If the request cannot be served out of its local store will uses one of its own IP addresses to request the page from the server and forward the response to the user on the Internet. To the Internet user, the proxy server is invisible; all requests and responses appear to be answered directly by the proxy.

Use of TCP/IP ports and HTTP header information is insufficient for making routing decisions based on XML-based content. Proxies that understand XML are capable of examining traffic at the content level can serve as a mediator for both client and server operations and perform operations itself or simply allow XML traffic to flow through. When an intermediary can handle both situations it is referred to as a gateway.

In services architecture, a gateway can be thought of as a specialized proxy that understands request for services. A gateway is also analogous to a router in that it knows where to direct a given packet of data that arrives at the gateway and a switch that furnishes the actual path in and out of the gateway for a given packet.

Gateways when used with services will act as an intermediary for service request and responses and enforce policies for each connected service. Gateways will require that each service that will pass through it be registered and will create a new URL for intercepting the request that can be published to other parties. The URL of the service on the gateway will be the one published in a UDDI registry (Figure 8).

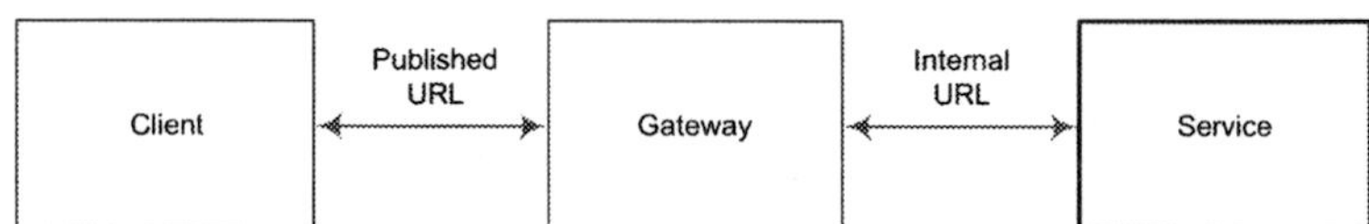

Figure 8. **Gateway Service Registration**

9.2. Agents

Agents run in context of the service's address space and usually are implemented as an intercepting filter. As agents are configured to run in the services container, they can intercept all incoming requests and do not require generation of a proxy URL in the same manner that gateways require. This approach also allows for services to be globally managed vs having per-service registration requirements.

***Figure 9.* Agent Service Registration**

Both gateways and agents internally can implement the pipes and filter architectural pattern so that the same component filters can be deployed using both models.

For more about the intercepting filter pattern, see: http://java.sun.com/blueprints/corej2eepatterns/Patterns/InterceptingFilter.html

9.3. Centralized Policies

Many IT budgets are consumed by maintenance of currently deployed services to support new application-level policies that do not modify core business logic. The need to externalize policies goes way beyond development time considerations and has an effect on quality assurance efforts even for simple upgrades. IT security departments need to govern security related standards used throughout the enterprise and periodically need to verify compliance to the policy. Having policies embedded within enterprise applications makes these tasks difficult.

The elements of a policy are comprised of:

- Operational Rules,
- Components, and
- Persistent Storage.

Policies are a central concept to managing an SOA. Let us review the elements of a policy.

9.4. Operational Rules

Policies may be defined that trigger actions from sending alerts to operations staff or storing diagnostic information in a database for future analysis. In these situations, policies are defined as conditional and will be invoked based upon specific conditions occurring. Operational rules are composed of a conditional expression that is Boolean and an action. For example, a rule can be defined to log all quotes from users who reside in the state of Connecticut. Rules can be classified broadly in two categories (see Table 8).

***Table 8.* Operational Rules**

Rule Type	Description
General	Inspect all service invocations and take action each time rule conditions are satisfied.
Aggregation	Rules that are applied based on consolidated metrics and takes action based on aggregated view of conditions.

General rules when tied to processing instructions such as alerting allows contextual information about specific events to be preserved but also can cause a flood in scenarios where service failures occur in high throughput systems. General rules should be applied in controlled situations as processing of the rules themselves could have an adverse impact on the entire service network.

Aggregated rules provide a benefit in that they are applied to summarized information and therefore will generate less actions. This can be useful in scenarios where high-throughput services experience a failure but also have its own limitations in that specific information about particular events may not be captured (for rule criteria, see Table 9).

***Table 9.* Rule Criteria**

Element	Description
Name	Name of the rule.
Type	Specify whether this rule is general or an aggregate.
Description	Description of the rule.
Action	The action(s) that should be performed if this rule is fired. This can range from creating an alert to logging.
Condition	Conditions in which this rule is fired. Ideally this is best captured using an Xpath expression.

Conditional rules may contain one or more fields within an XML message and correspond to a specified value. Rule conditions are usually best expressed when composed of two operands and a comparator. Optional support for XQuery expressions should be supported in management frameworks.

For more information on XQuery, see McGovern et al. (2003).

9.5. Components

Policies are ultimately executed on either/both gateways and agents. Many of the management concerns such as logging, metering and monitoring can be implemented as both gateways and agents. However some management concerns may be limited to one or the other. Let us look at concerns that have limited implementation in Table 10.

Table 10. **Management Attributes Matrix**

Attribute	Category	Limitation
Routing	Systems Management	Gateway
Non-Repudiation	Security	Agent
Message Prioritization	Business Process	Gateway

Routing determines which service endpoint a particular request gets routed to. Since agents run in context of the target service, the ability to change the target is already too late. If you implement your own SOA framework and do not rely on SOAP or other message formats, then it is possible to develop a custom message similar to the HTTP protocol and its support for redirect headers (http status 302).

Non-repudiation is the ability to ensure that a party to a conversation (request/response) cannot deny the authenticity of their signature on a document or the sending of a message that they originated. Since gateways serve as intermediaries to service requests and have the ability to modify requests, they cannot be used to provide end-to-end non-repudiation. The gateway can participate in non-repudiation but ultimately the end service requiring non-repudiation related policies are required to run as an agent in the address space of the service.

How to implement non-repudiation is covered in detail in Chapter 4.

Message prioritization can be implemented as either an advanced form of routing and/or a buffering strategy. Buffering of traffic within the service in order to gain prioritization would require adding cross-request scheduling internal to each service. Although it is technically possible to perform this task by making worker threads go to sleep for services that are multi-threaded, this would make service development more complex than required and therefore is discouraged.

9.6. Persistent Storage

Management frameworks that leverage policy-based approaches should ideally make sure that policies physically reside in multiple locations in order to ensure high-availability and disaster recovery. The framework themselves should treat policies as dynamic entities that change during run-time and therefore must rely on either synchronization/replication models.

Replication relies on background processes that copies policy data from one policy store to another. When the background process completes replicating data from the primary policy store to the secondary policy stores, it should synchronize its data with the other policy stores in order to maintain consistency of policy implementation across all gateways and agents.

Synchronization is the process of updating replicated data (policies) from one policy store to another and ensures that all policies are identical across the enterprise. When a new gateway or agent is added to the infrastructure, it is automatically synchronized with all other peers. Several models for implementing synchronization exist, including but not limited to the ones given in Table 11.

***Table 11.* Synchronization Models**

Model	Description
Change-Based	Receives notification when synchronized policy data changes. The changed content is updated automatically and immediately on all members in the synchronization loop.
Cluster	This serves to synchronize all member policy services under the same administrative federation.
Interval-Based	Synchronization occurs based on predefined interval or schedule.
Member	This serves to synchronize a single member policy service with a master policy service.
On-Demand	This form of synchronization only occurs when an administrator specifically requests it.

Synchronization can be accomplished in either a coarse-grained manner or more granular depending upon the actual run-time services infrastructure approach. Considerations for providing synchronization mechanisms to synchronize content across management boundaries in some situations may be warranted.

10. Policy Architecture

Policies can be defined with the appropriate constructs to support business goals and service level agreements within and across administrative domains and should map to resources being managed (i.e. services). The ability to map higher-level policies to low level resources requires a canonical representation to their meaning. Business policies need to be translated into canonical form so that lower level components can understand their intent.

In order for a framework to support policies, it must fulfill the following requirements:

- A canonical representation for expressing policies (this is best accomplished using XML).
- An interface that policy consumers (gateways and agents) can use to fetch policies for services under its control.
- Interfaces that support the creation, distribution, transformation, enforcement, security and conflict resolution of policies.
- Interfaces that allow for storage of policies in a secure store.

Depending on how policies are distributed throughout the environment (push vs. pull) service consumers may interact with policy managers in a publish/subscribe model whereby they are notified when centralized policies change. Policy enforcement points will interpret policies and perform run-time configuration changes on services under their control.

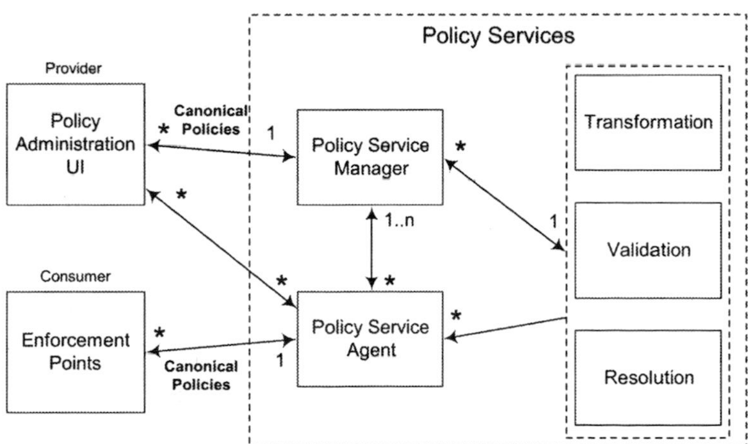

Figure 10. **Policy Architecture**

In order to ensure integrity of the policies themselves, the policy management architecture needs to incorporate minimally validation and conflict resolution interfaces. This will allow automated consistency checking. Interfaces are required to translate policies to and from the canonical form so that service consumers that use their own policy formats can plug into the service. Translation policies is applicable when you want to have consistent management of services yet have a separate security architecture provided by another vendor with its own set of policies (i.e. Netegrity, Oblix, etc.).

Run-time resolution of policy conflicts which may require specific knowledge about services in order to determine costs for violating a service-level agreement or legal consideration that can measure impact and decide accordingly may also be required.

10.1. Policy Execution

Events can trigger a sequence of processing steps from logging to sending email. One architectural pattern that can assist in dividing the overall processing tasks tied to a particular event into a sequence of smaller independent processing steps (filters) is the Pipes and Filters pattern.

A common usage may be when Agile Healthcare receives a patient's medical history from a hospital and wants to ensure that the message is encrypted as well as ensure that the message was not tampered with while in transit. It also wants to log receipt of the message and update the medical history database with the latest information. In Figure 11 an example pipeline is given to understand how this would work.

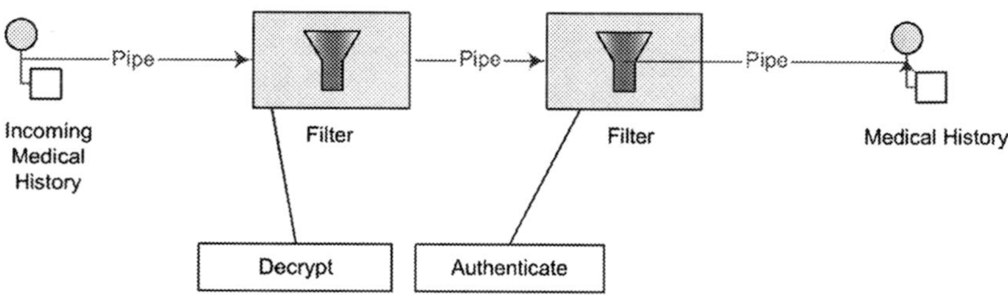

Figure 11. **Policy Pipeline Using Pipes and Filter as Architectural Style**

Filters are implemented with a generic interface that allows for reuse. The pipeline will have several filters registered to it that will when receiving messages on the inbound pipe, the filter will process the message and return the results back to the outbound pipeline in a manner that allows them to be chained. Using this pattern for components will allow you to add new filters, remove ones that are no longer needed or even rearrange them into new sequences without having to touch the filter code itself.

For more information on pipes and filters, see Buschmann et al. (1996).

Generic components can be developed and reused on both agents and gateways when using the pipes and filters pattern. Listed in Table 12 are several recommended components.

***Table 12.* Policy Pipeline Components**

Name	Category	Description
Authentication	Security	Validate that the service request is coming from an authorized user.
Authorization	Security	Check to see has been granted rights to the specified service.
Certificate	Security	If the service requires client-side SSL then validate the certificate and check against the certificate revocation list (CRL).
SAML	Security	Generate and/or validate creation of a security assertion.
Log	Logging	Write a record to the event log based upon specified criteria.
Transform	Transformation	Transform request/response using specified stylesheets.
Validate	Transformation	Compare incoming XML message to specified XML schema.

11. Framework Vendors

There are several vendors that provide frameworks for managing service-oriented architectures. Table 13 shows some of the ones the author team recommend for enterprise consideration.

***Table 13.* SOA Management Frameworks**

Vendor	Product	Web Site
Oblix	CoreSV	http://www.oblix.com/confluent/index.html
Blue Titan	Network Director	http://www.bluetitan.com
Actional	Looking Glass	http://www.actional.com
Digital Evolution	Management Server	http://www.digev.com
Infravio	Ensemble	http://www.infravio.com

12. Summary

Software as a service is important to enterprises not only to build internal systems but also to extend the enterprise to partners, suppliers and consumers. As services allow applications to become modular, and access to domains outside of administrative control, traditional issues that require operational attention become even more challenging. Services in this model must have a comprehensive management strategy required for profitable operation of the business. Management of services includes the entire service value chain and collecting information about the health and availability of services. All of these requirements can be accomplished in a vendor-neutral manner.

7 TRANSACTIONS

Life is an error-making and error-correcting process.
Jonas Salk, developer of the polio vaccine

As the concept of SOA has evolved as a means to integrate processes and applications at an inter-enterprise level, traditional transaction semantics and protocols have proven to be inappropriate. SOA-based transactions differ from traditional transactions in that they execute over long periods, they require commitments to the transaction to be "negotiated" at run-time, and isolation levels have to be relaxed. These kinds of business-to-business transactions often require an extended transaction model that builds on existing SOA standards and defines an interoperable transaction protocol and message flows that help negotiate transactions guarantees at the inter-enterprise level.

In this chapter we will look at the area of transactions as they apply to SOA and Web Services in particular. We will show how although this is still an active area of work, it is an extremely important one for the overall SOA environment; without transaction capabilities, it is impossible to build complex composite applications that people can trust to ensure consistent state changes, even in the presence of failures. However, before examining the kinds of SOA transaction protocols that have been developed, we need to first examine what are often referred to as *traditional ACID transaction systems*.

1. What Are ACID Transactions?

The concept of *atomic transactions* has played a cornerstone role in creating today's enterprise application environments by providing guaranteed consistent outcome in complex multiparty business operations and a separation of concerns in applications yielding well-designed business process implementations (Gray and Reuter, 1993; Bernstein and Newcomer, 1997).

So just what is an atomic transaction (often abbreviated to just *transaction*)? Put simply, a transaction provides an "all-or-nothing" (atomic) property to work that is conducted within its scope, whilst at the same time ensuring that shared resources are isolated from concurrent users. Importantly application programmers typically only have to start and end a transaction; all of the complex work necessary to provide the transaction's properties is hidden by the transaction system, leaving the programmer free to concentrate on the more functional aspects of the application at hand.

Let us take a look at just how a transaction system could help in a real-world application environment. Consider the case of an on-line cinema reservation system (shown in Figure 1). In this figure, the cinema has many seats that can be reserved individually, and the state of a seat is either RESERVED or UNRESERVED. The cinema service exports two operations, `reserveSeat` and `unreserveSeat` (we will ignore the other operations that are obviously required to make this service truly usable). Finally we will assume that there is a transaction manager service that will be used to manage any transactions that the cinema may require in order to process the user's requests.

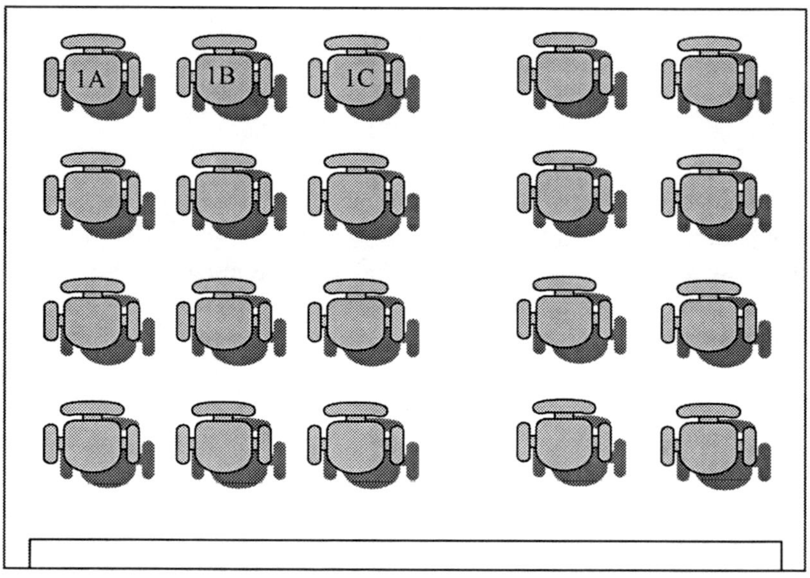

***Figure 1.* The On-Line Cinema Booking System**

Let us consider a very simple example: imagine that Mr. Doe wants to reserve a block of seats for his family (1A, 1B and 1C as shown in the figure). Now, the service only allows a single seat to be reserved through the `reserveSeat` operation, so this will require Mr. Doe to call it three times, once for each seat.

Unfortunately the reservation process may be affected by failures of software or hardware that could affect the overall consistency of the system in a number of ways. For example, if a failure occurs after reserving 1A, then obviously none of the other seats will have been reserved. Mr. Doe can try to complete the reservation when (assuming) the cinema service eventually recovers, but by this time someone else may have reserved the seats.

What Mr. Doe really wants is the ability to reserve multiple seats as an atomic (indivisible) block. This means that despite failures and concurrent access, either all of the seats Mr. Doe requires will be reserved for him, or none will. At first glance this may seem like a fairly straightforward thing to achieve, but it actually requires a lot of effort to ensure that these requirements can be guaranteed. Fortunately atomic transactions possess the following (*ACID*) properties that make them suitable for this kind of scenario:

- *Atomicity*: The transaction completes successfully (commits) or if it fails (aborts) all of its effects are undone (rolled back).
- *Consistency*: Transactions produce consistent results and preserve application specific invariants.
- *Isolation*: Intermediate states produced while a transaction is executing are not visible to others. Furthermore, transactions appear to execute *serially*, even if they are actually executed concurrently. Typically this is accomplished through the use of concurrency control techniques (e.g., locks) associated with shared resources.
- *Durability*: The effects of a committed transaction are never lost (except by a catastrophic failure).

A transaction can be terminated in two ways: *committed* or *aborted* (rolled back). When a transaction is committed, all changes made within it are made durable (forced on to stable storage, e.g., disk). When a transaction is aborted, all of the changes are undone. Atomic transactions can also be nested, and in which case the effects of a nested action are provisional upon the commit/abort of the outermost (*top-level*) atomic transaction.

Associated with every transaction is a *coordinator*, which is responsible for governing the outcome of the transaction. The coordinator may be implemented as a separate service or may be co-located with the user for improved performance. It communicates with enlisted participants to inform them of the desired termination requirements, i.e., whether they should accept (*commit*) or reject (*roll back*) the work done within the scope of the given transaction. For example, whether to purchase the (provisionally reserved) flight tickets for the user or to release them. A *transaction manager factory* is typically responsible for managing coordinators for many transactions. The initiator of the transaction (e.g., the client) communicates with a transaction manager and asks it to start a new transaction and associate a coordinator with the transaction.

Traditional transaction systems use a two-phase protocol to achieve atomicity between participants, as illustrated in Figure 2: during the first (preparation) phase, an individual participant must make durable any state changes that occurred during the scope of the transaction, such that these changes can either be rolled back or committed later once the transaction outcome has been determined. Assuming no failures occurred during the first phase, in the second (commitment) phase participants may "overwrite" the original state with the state made durable during the first phase.

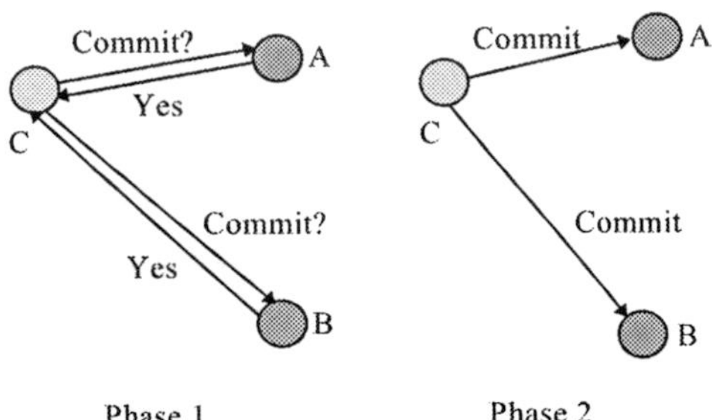

Figure 2. **Two-Phase Commit Protocol**

In order to guarantee consensus, two-phase commit is necessarily a blocking protocol: after returning the first phase response, each participant who returned a commit response must remain blocked until it has received the coordinator's phase 2 message. Until they receive this message, any resources used by the participant are unavailable for use by other transactions, since to do so may result in non-ACID behavior. If the coordinator fails before delivery of the second phase message these resources remain blocked until it recovers.

As we have already mentioned, transactions are required to provide fault tolerance. What this means is that information about running transactions (often referred to as *in-flight transactions*) and the participants involved must survive failures and be accessible during recovery. This information (the *transaction log*) is held in some durable state-store. Typically the transaction log is scanned to determine whether there are transactions mentioned in it that require recovery to be performed. If there are, then the information within the log is used to recreate the transaction and the recovery subsystem will then continue to complete the transaction.

Failures are not restricted to just the transaction coordinator. Therefore, participants must retain sufficient information in durable store so that they too can be recovered in the event of a failure. What information is recorded will obviously depend upon the participant implementation.

1.1. The Synchronization Protocol

As well as the two-phase commit protocol, traditional transaction processing systems employ an additional protocol, often referred to as the *synchronization protocol.* If you recall the original ACID properties, then you will remember that Durability is important in the case where state changes have to be available despite failures. What this means is that applications interact with a persistence store of some kind (e.g., a database) and this can impose a significant overhead – disk access is orders of magnitude slower than access to main computer memory.

One apparently obvious solution to this problem would be to cache the state in main memory and only operate on that for the duration of a transaction. Unfortunately, you would then need some way of being able to flush the state back to the persistent *store* before the transaction terminates, or risk losing the full ACID properties. This is what the synchronization protocol does, with Synchronization participants.

Synchronizations are informed that a transaction is *about* to commit, so they can, for example, flush cached state, which may be being used to improve performance of an application, to a durable representation prior to the transaction committing. They are then informed when the transaction has completed and in what state it completed.

Synchronizations essentially turn the two-phase commit protocol into a four-phase protocol:

- Before the transaction starts the two-phase commit, all registered Synchronizations are informed. Any failure at this point will cause the transaction to roll back.
- The coordinator then conducts the normal two-phase commit protocol.
- Once the transaction has terminated, all registered Synchronizations are informed. However, this is a courtesy invocation because any failures at this stage are ignored: the transaction has terminated so there is nothing to affect.

Unlike the two-phase commit protocol, the synchronization protocol does not have the same failure requirements. For example, Synchronization participants do not need to make sure they can recover in the event of failures; this is because any failure before the two-phase commit protocol completes means the transaction will roll back, and failures after it has completed cannot affect the data the Synchronization participants were managing.

1.2. Optimizations to the Protocol

There are several variants to the standard two-phase commit protocol that are worth knowing about because they can have an impact on performance and failure recovery. We shall briefly describe those that are the most common variants on the protocol and found in all of the Web services transactions specifications we will examine:

- *Presumed abort*: if a transaction is going to roll back then it may simply record this information locally and tell all enlisted participants. Failure to contact a participant has no affect on the transaction outcome; the transaction is effectively informing participants as a courtesy. Once all participants have been contacted the information about the transaction can be removed. If a subsequent request for the status of the transaction occurs there will be no information available and the requestor can assume that the transaction has aborted (rolled back). This optimization has the benefit that no information about participants need be made persistent until the transaction has decided to commit (i.e., progressed to the end of the prepare phase), since any failure prior to this point will be assumed to be an abort of the transaction.

- *One-phase*: if there is only a single participant involved in the transaction, the coordinator need not drive it through the prepare phase. Thus, the participant will simply be told to commit and the coordinator need not record information about the decision since the outcome of the transaction is solely down to the participant.

- *Read-only*: when a participant is asked to prepare, it can indicate to the coordinator that no information or data that it controls has been modified during the transaction. Such a participant does not need to be informed about the outcome of the transaction since the fate of the participant has no affect on the transaction. As such, a read-only participant can be omitted from the second phase of the commit protocol.

1.3. Non-Atomic Transactions and Heuristic Outcomes

We have already seen that in order to guarantee atomicity, the two-phase commit protocol is necessarily blocking. What this means is that as a result of failures, participants may remain blocked for an indefinite period of time even if failure recovery mechanisms exist. Some applications and participants simply cannot tolerate this blocking.

To break this blocking nature, participants that have got past the prepare phase are allowed to make autonomous decisions as to whether they commit or roll back: such a participant *must* record this decision in case it is eventually contacted to complete the original transaction. If the coordinator eventually informs the participant of the transaction outcome and it is the same as the choice the participant made, then there is no problem. However, if it is contrary, then a non-atomic outcome has obviously happened: a *heuristic outcome.*

How this heuristic outcome is reported to the application and resolved is usually the domain of complex, manually driven system administration tools, since in order to attempt an automatic resolution requires semantic information about the nature of participants involved in the transactions.

Precisely when a participant makes a heuristic decision is obviously implementation dependent. Likewise, the choice the participant makes (to commit or to roll back) will depend upon the implementation and possibly the application/environment in which it finds itself. The possible heuristic outcomes are:

- Heuristic rollback: the commit operation failed because some or all of the participants unilaterally rolled back the transaction.
- Heuristic commit: an attempted rollback operation failed because all of the participants unilaterally committed. This may happen if, for example, the coordinator was able to successfully prepare the transaction but then decided to roll it back (e.g., it could not update its log) but in the meanwhile the participants decided to commit.
- Heuristic mixed: some updates (participants) were committed while others were rolled back.
- Heuristic hazard: the disposition of some of the updates is unknown. For those which are known, they have either all been committed or all rolled back.

Heuristic decisions should be used with care and only in exceptional circumstances since there is the possibility that the decision will differ from that determined by the transaction service and will thus lead to a loss of integrity in the system. Having to perform resolution of heuristics is something you should try to avoid, either by working with services/participants that do not cause heuristics, or by using a transaction service that provides assistance in the resolution process.

Now that we have described the advantages that ACID transactions offer, you may be asking yourself why they are not sufficient for use in an SOA environment. An ACID transaction provides failure atomicity, isolation from concurrent users etc. so would appear to be an ideal tool for use when building complex distributed applications. Unfortunately as we will see in the next section, this is often not the case.

2. Why ACID Is Too Strong for Web Services

As we saw earlier, ACID transactions use a blocking two-phase commit protocol to ensure consensus. If the transaction coordinator fails, participants may remain blocked for extended periods of time while waiting for the coordinator to recover. Furthermore, to ensure isolation semantics, resources acquired during an ACID transaction may remain locked until the transaction completes; again in the event of a failure this could be a long time. For example, imagine an online bookstore that had to operate using ACID transactions; whenever you placed a book into your shopping cart, the store would essentially have to reserve that book exclusively for you until you decided whether to buy or not. That could take days or even weeks, making this an impractical solution.

Therefore, structuring certain activities from long-running transactions can reduce the amount of concurrency within an application or (in the event of failures) require work to be performed again. For example, there are certain types of application where it is known that resources acquired within a transaction can be released "early", rather than having to wait until the transaction terminates; in the event of the transaction rolling back, however, certain compensation activities may be necessary to restore the system to a consistent state.

Long-running activities can be structured as many independent, short-duration transactions, to form a "logical" long-running transaction. This structuring allows an activity to acquire and use resources for only the required duration of this long-running activity. This is illustrated in Figure 3, where an application activity (shown by the dotted ellipse) has been split into different, coordinated short-duration transactions. Assume that the application activity is concerned with booking a taxi (t1), reserving a table at a restaurant (t2), reserving a seat at the theatre (t3), and then booking a room at a hotel (t4), and so on. If all of these operations were performed as a single transaction then resources acquired during t1 would not be released until the transaction has terminated. If subsequent activities t2, t3 etc. do not require those resources, then they will be needlessly unavailable to other clients.

However, if failures and concurrent access occur during the lifetime of these individual transactional activities then the behavior of the entire "logical long-running transaction" may not possess ACID properties. Therefore, some form of compensation may be required to attempt to return the state of the system to consistency. For example, let us assume that t4 aborts. Further assume that the application can continue to make forward progress, but in order to do so must now undo some state changes made prior to the start of t4 (by t1, t2 or t3). Therefore, new activities are started; tc1 which is a compensation activity that will attempt to undo state changes performed, by say t2, and t3 which will continue the application once tc1 has completed. t5 and t6 are new activities that continue after compensation, e.g., since it was not possible to reserve the theatre, restaurant and hotel, it is decided to book tickets at the cinema.

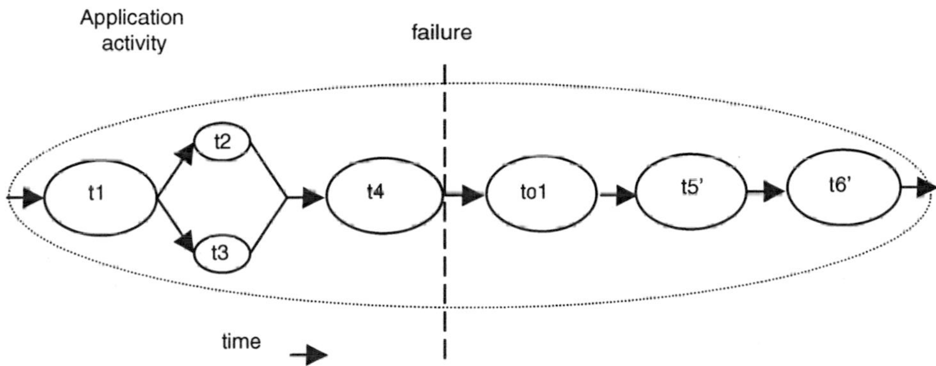

***Figure 3.* An Example of a Logical Long-Running "Transaction", with Failure**

Previous transaction processing systems shared a great deal of commonality in terms of the crux of the problem that they address and the abstractions they use to address it. Specifically, transaction processing systems were developed for particular platforms and each system assumes that it is in sole control of the transaction domain and hence does not generally have to interoperate with other transaction processing systems (though interoperability with lower-level components like databases is generally well supported via interfaces like X/Open XA, see The Open Group, 1991). Early attempts at transaction interoperability (e.g., the Object Transaction Service from the Object

Management Group, see OTS) did not manage to get past the "vendor lock-in" barrier, and attempts at using transactions across enterprise boundaries failed because in such systems transactions are assumed to exhibit ACID properties.

Web services present a different kind of problem: they are specifically about fostering systems interoperability. This presents some interesting problems from a transaction management point of view. What makes Web services so interesting is the fact that the architecture is deliberately not prescriptive about what happens behind service endpoints – Web services are ultimately only concerned with the transfer of structured data between parties, plus any meta-level information to safeguard such transfers (e.g., by encrypting or digitally signing messages) – yet it is behind service endpoints that we find traditional transaction processing architectures supporting business activities.

Thus we are presented with a paradox. The Web services platform provides a service-oriented, loosely coupled, and potentially asynchronous means of propagating information between parties, whilst in the background we have traditional transaction processing infrastructures whose behavior is neither or mutually interoperable. Furthermore, the fact that transactions in these systems are assumed to exhibit ACID properties potentially leads to problems when exposing resources to third parties, since it presents opportunities to those parties to tie up resources and prevent transactions from making progress. Thus if transactions were to be supported in the Web services architecture then it is clear that some re-addressing of the problem is required.

As you might imagine from what we have said earlier, since transactions are an important aspect of distributed systems in general and almost an imperative to ensure SOAs can scale to enterprise applications, there has been quite a lot of activity in the area of developing SOA transaction models. In the next section we will look at the current leading specifications for Web services transactions; it is important to realize that these specifications are applicable to other SOA environments.

3. A Brief History of Web Services Transactions

So far there have been three efforts to incorporate transactions into Web services and in the rest of this chapter we will examine the most important two. You may wonder why you need to know about them both and the answer to that question is straightforward: at this moment it is not possible to say which of these attempts (if any) will become the standard for Web services transactions.

The first attempt at defining a standard for Web Services transactions was the OASIS Business Transaction Protocol (BTP) in 2001; this was then followed by the Web Services Transactions specification (WS-Tx, now renamed WS-AtomicTransaction (see WSAA) and WS-BusinessActivity (see WSBA)) from IBM, Microsoft and BEA in August 2002, and more recently by the Web Services Transaction Management specification (WS-Transaction Management) from Arjuna Technologies, Fujitsu, IONA Technologies, Oracle and Sun in August 2003 (part of the OASIS Web Services Composite Application Framework, see WSCAF).

Although originally having the backing of BEA, Hewlett-Packard and Oracle, the OASIS BTP has been overtaken by the other two specifications. There are a number of technical reasons often cited for this, including the complexity of the protocol, the fact that it was not designed solely for Web Services (often coupled with its complexity) and lack of immediate interoperability with existing transaction processing infrastructures. However, it is likely to be the lack of support for this protocol from major vendors that will ultimately consign it to a niche area of history (as seems to be the case in Web services, the political factors almost always outweigh any technical benefits). As such, in the rest of this chapter we will concentrate solely on WS-AtomicTransaction and WS-BusinessActivity (we will refer to them collectively as WS-Tx) and WS-TransactionManagement (WS-TXM).

In the following sections we will examine these specifications. However, because of space constraints we cannot cover them all in detail. Rather, we will look at the commonality that exists between them and discuss the impact that the models they provide will have on developing SOA applications.

4. The Coordination Frameworks

The first area of commonality between WS-Tx and WS-TXM is in the area of *coordination*. In general terms, coordination is the act of one entity (known as the *coordinator*) disseminating information to a number of *participants* for some domain-specific reason. This reason could be in order to reach consensus on a decision like in a distributed transaction protocol, or simply to guarantee that all participants obtain a specific message, as occurs in a reliable multicast environment. When parties are being coordinated, information known as the *coordination context* is propagated to tie together operations which are logically part of the same coordinated work. The context is critical to coordination since it contains the information necessary for services to participate in the protocol. It provides the glue to bind all of the application's constituent Web services together into a single coordinated application whole.

Context information can flow implicitly (opaquely to the application) within normal messages sent to the participants, or it may be an explicit action on behalf of the client/service. This information is specific to the type of coordination being performed, e.g., to identify the coordinator(s), the other participants in an activity, recovery information in the event of a failure, etc. Furthermore, it may be required that additional application specific context information (e.g., extra SOAP header information) flow to these participants or the services which use them.

Coordination is an integral part of any distributed system, but there is no single type of coordination protocol that can suffice for all problem domains. For example a security coordination service will propagate differently formed contexts than a transaction coordinator.

Despite the fact that there are many different types of distributed application that require coordination, it should not come as a surprise to learn that each domain typically uses a different coordination protocol. In the case of transactions, for example, the OASIS BTP and the Object Management Group's OTS are solutions to specific problem domains and which are not applicable to others since they are based on different architectural styles. Given the domain-specific nature of these protocols (i.e., loosely coupled transactional Web services and tightly coupled transactional CORBA objects) there is no way of providing a universal solution without jeopardizing efficiency and scalability in each individual domain. However, both of these protocols have the underlying requirement for propagating contextual information to participants, and therefore it would make some sense if that mechanism could be made generic, and thus re-used. On closer examination it is possible to see that even solely within the Web services domain there are situations where coordination is a requirement of several different types of problem domain, such as workflow management and transaction processing, but where the overall models are very different.

Therefore, what is needed is a common *Coordination Framework* that allows users and services to tie into it and customize it. A suitably designed coordination service should provide enough flexibility and extensibility to its users that allow it to be tailored, statically or dynamically, to fit any requirement.

As a result, both the WS-Tx and WS-TXM specifications build upon their own coordination frameworks: Web Services Coordination (WS-C) in the case of IBM, Microsoft and BEA (see WSC), and Web Services Coordination Framework (WS-CoordinationFramework) in the case of Oracle, Sun et al. As you might imagine, there is a lot of commonality in the two coordination frameworks. In the following sections we will look at the general architecture that both frameworks share and indicate where differences arise.

Before we do so though, it is worth mentioning the interaction patterns that both sets of specifications assume. In order to support both synchronous request/response and message interactions, all interactions are described in terms of correlated messages, which an implementation may abstract at a higher level into request/response pairs. As such, all communicated messages are required to contain response endpoint addresses solely for the purposes of each interaction, and a correlation identifier such that incoming and outgoing invocations can be associated.

This has the immediate benefit of allowing loose coupling of application entities: the sender of a given message that requires a response need not be the same as the ultimate receiver of that response. This allows for great flexibility in choosing service deployments, particularly in environments that may be error prone or require dynamic changes to roles and responsibilities. However, one consequence of these interactions is that faults and errors which may occur when a service is invoked are communicated back to interested parties via messages which are themselves part of the standard protocol – and does not use the fault mechanisms of the underlying SOAP-based transport.

4.1. Coordination Architecture

Both specifications talks in terms of *activities*, which are distributed units of work, involving one or more parties. At this level, an activity is minimally specified and is simply *created*, made to *run*, and then *completed*. At the termination of an activity a coordination protocol is executed by an associated coordinator. This is where the first main difference exists between WS-C and WS-CoordinationFramework: WS-C only supports coordination at activity boundaries, whereas WS-CoordinationFramework allows coordination to occur at arbitrary points during the lifetime of an activity; obviously this may be restricted by whether or not the specific coordinator implementation supports it, but at least it is in the basic model.

In Figure 4, you can see that the framework could be used for propagating security, workflow, or replication contexts. Whatever coordination protocol is used, and in whatever domain it is deployed, the same generic requirements are present:

- Instantiation (or activation) of a new coordinator for the specific coordination protocol, for a particular application instance;
- Registration of participants with the coordinator, such that they will receive that coordinator's protocol messages during (some part of) the application's lifetime;

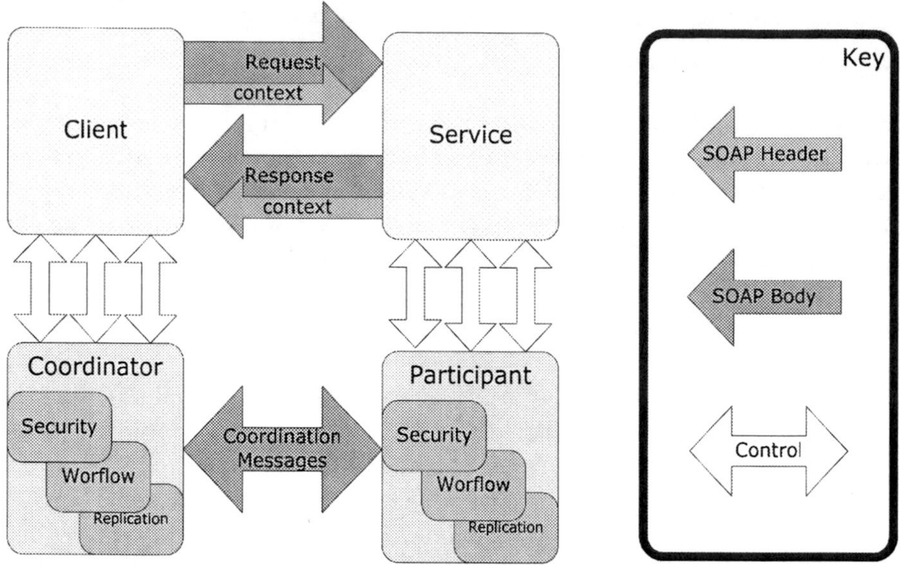

Figure 4. **The Architecture of a Coordination Framework**

- Propagation of contextual information between Web services that comprise the application;
- An entity to drive the coordination protocol through to completion.

The first three of these points are directly the concern of the coordination frameworks while the fourth is the responsibility of a third-party entity, usually the client application that controls the application as a whole.

4.2. Creating a Coordinator

Both WS-C and WS-CoordinationFramework have the notion of what WS-C terms an *Activation Service* and WS-CoordinationFramework calls an *Activity Lifecycle Service*: this is the service that supports the creation of coordinators for specific protocols and their associated contexts. In line with the interaction style mentioned earlier, the process of invoking this service is done asynchronously, and so the specifications define both the interface of the creation service itself and that of the invoking service, so that the creation service can call back to deliver the results of the coordinator creation (activation) – namely a context that identifies the protocol type and coordinator location.

For simplicity we will only show the WS-C interfaces for its Activation Service in Listing 1. The service has a one-way operation that expects to receive a CreateCoordinationContext message and the service that sent the CreateCoordinationContext message expects to be called back with a CreateCoordinationContextResponse message, or informed of a problem via an Error message.

```
<!-- Activation Service portType Declaration -->
<wsdl:portType name="ActivationCoordinatorPortType">
  <wsdl:operation name="CreateCoordinationContext">
    <wsdl:input
     message="wscoor:CreateCoordinationContext"/>
  </wsdl:operation>
</wsdl:portType>

<!-- Activation Requester portType Declaration -->
<wsdl:portType name="ActivationRequesterPortType">
  <wsdl:operation
    name="CreateCoordinationContextResponse">
    <wsdl:input
     message="wscoor:CreateCoordinationContextResponse"/>
  </wsdl:operation>
  <wsdl:operation name="Error">
    <wsdl:input message="wscoor:Error"/>
  </wsdl:operation>
```

Listing 1. The WS-Coordination Activation Service interface

4.3. The Context

The context is critical to coordination since it contains the information necessary for services to participate in the protocol. Since we are considering generic coordination frameworks, contexts have to be tailored to meet the needs of specific coordination protocols that are plugged into the framework. The format of contexts for WS-C and WS-CoordinationFramework is specifically designed to be third-party extensible and its contents are as follows:

- A coordination identifier with guaranteed global uniqueness for an individual coordinator in the form of a URI.
- An address of a registration service endpoint where parties receiving a context can register participants into the protocol.
- A time-to-live value which indicates for how long the context should be considered valid.

- Extensible protocol-specific information particular to the actual coordination protocol supported by the coordinator.

Since both frameworks are generic, the context is of very little use to some applications without the ability to augment it. This is shown in Listing 2 where the schema states that a context consists of a URI that uniquely identifies the type of coordination that is required (`tns:ProtocolReferenceType`), an endpoint where participants to be coordinated can be registered (`tns:CoordinatorReferenceType`), and an extensibility element designed to carry specific coordination protocol context payload (`xs:any`), which can carry arbitrary XML payload.

```
<xs:complexType name="ContextType">
   <xs:complexContent>
<xs:extension base="wsctx:ContextType">
        <xs:sequence>
<xs:element name="protocol-reference"
type="tns:ProtocolReferenceType"/>
<xs:element name="coordinator-reference"
  type="tns:CoordinatorReferenceType" maxOccurs="unbounded"/>
<xs:any namespace="##any" processContents="lax"
maxOccurs="unbounded"/>
    </xs:sequence>
</xs:extension>
   </xs:complexContent>
</xs:complexType>
```

Listing 2. The WS-CoordinationFramework context definition

Note that the reference to `wsctx:ContextType` above is because WS-CoordinationFramework builds on a separate context service specification, WS-Context; this specification defines a basic context type for use by a wide range of services and not just coordination. WS-CoordinationFramework simply extends this context definition.

4.4. Registering Participants

Both coordination frameworks make a distinction between an application Web service and a coordination participant Web service. This distinction is typically made from the perspective of the model, and implementations are free to blur the line. So, what is meant by an application Web service? This is the service that encapsulates some portion of the business logic of your application, e.g., an on-line airline reservation service.

However, what about the participant service? Normally it is the case that only some aspect if the work that the service does will require coordination, and in fact this may be an aspect that the original service provider did not know about at the time the service was designed and implemented.

For example, let us take the case of a transactional Web service. In this case, the transactional capabilities of the service are often not exposed to users of that service, as they are typically considered to be non-functional aspects of its work. It is frequently the case that many transactional services or components began life as non-transactional, and were "upgraded" as requirements for fault-tolerance and reliability changed. In the case of the on-line airline reservation service, for instance, the fact that individual seats are reserved and unreserved atomically is not noticed by its users, since that is an implementation detail (e.g., provided by the database technology that the service implementer has used to store information about individual aircraft).

Because of this, it has been the case over many decades that transaction systems usually separate out the work that is required to make a service transactional from the usual business logic. This separation has been taken and generalized by the coordination frameworks: the coordination participant is the service that controls this work and is driven by a specific coordinator. This has obvious benefits in that a non-transactional service can be made transactional without having to change its interface – the interface is managed separately by the participant. If the application Web service actually needs to participate in multiple different types of coordination (e.g., security and transactions), then it would typically possess a participant for each type.

Let us return to the coordination framework and see how this maps. Once a coordinator has been instantiated and a corresponding context created, there is going to be a need to be able to register participants with the coordinator. Rather than assume that the service that created the context is also the one that handles participant registration (that is an implementation choice, after all), both frameworks separate this out into what WS-C calls a *Registration Service* and WS-CoordinationFramework calls a *Coordinator Service*. Regardless of its name, this service allows participants to register to receive protocol messages associated with a particular coordinator.

Like the activation service, the registration service assumes asynchronous communication and so specifies WSDL for both the service that registers and the service that receives the result of registering. In Listing 3 we will only show the partial interfaces for the `ServiceCoordinator` and the `ServiceRespondant`.

```
<wsdl:binding name="ServiceCoordinatorPortTypeSOAPBinding"
type="tns:ServiceCoordinatorPortType">
   <soap:binding transport="http://schemas.xmlsoap.org/soap/http"
   style="document"/>
      <wsdl:operation name="addParticipant">
        <soap:operation
        soapAction="http://www.webservicestransactions.org
        /wsdl/wscf/2003/03/addParticipant" style="document"/>
<wsdl:input>
    <soap:body use="literal"/>
    <soap:header part="content" use="literal"
           message="tns:ContextMessage"/>
</wsdl:input>
      </wsdl:operation>
</wsdl:binding>

<wsdl:binding name="ServiceRespondantPortTypeSOAPBinding"
type="tns:ServiceRespondantPortType">
   <soap:binding transport="http://schemas.xmlsoap.org/soap/http"
   style="document"/>
      <wsdl:operation name="participantAdded">
           <soap:operation
           soapAction="http://www.webservicestransactions.org
           /wsdl/wscf/2003/03/participantAdded"
           style="document"/>
<wsdl:input>
<soap:body use="literal"/>
<soap:header part="content" use="literal"
message="tns:ContextMessage"/>
</wsdl:input>
      </wsdl:operation>
</wsdl:binding>
```

Listing 3. Partial WSDL for the WS-CoordinationFramework registration service

Once a participant has been registered with a coordinator, it receives messages that the coordinator sends (for example, "prepare to complete" and "complete" messages if a two-phase protocol is used).

At this point it is interesting to note another difference between WS-CoordinationFramework and WS-C: the WS-CoordinationFramework model allows participants to asynchronously call back to the coordinator and register results before the coordinator has even started the coordination protocol. This may seem strange (and is obviously only possible if the coordinator implementation supports it), but there are actually cases where this could help. Let us return to the case of a transactional service, where its participant knows that even though the transaction may last for many more hours, it is response to being told to prepare will never change; as a result, the participant can tell the coordinator what that response is immediately (and perhaps even be garbage collected). This can help to improve performance and in some cases tolerance to failures.

4.5. Terminating the Coordinator

The role of terminator is generally played by the client application, which at an appropriate point will ask the coordinator to perform its particular coordination function with any registered participants – to drive to protocol through to its completion. On completion, the client application may be informed of an outcome for the activity which may vary from simple succeeded/failed notification through to complex structured data detailing the activity's status.

At this stage we have described the two coordination frameworks. By themselves they are of extremely limited use. It is obviously when they are extended (or plugged into) that their real power becomes evident. In the next section we will look at how transaction models for Web services have been developed using these frameworks.

5. Web Services Transactions

Given that the traditional ACID transaction model is not appropriate for Web services, let us pose the question, "what type of model or protocol is appropriate"? According to the proponents of the two main Web services transactions specifications, the answer to that question is that that no one specific protocol is likely to be sufficient, given the wide range of situations that Web service transactions are likely to be deployed within. Fortunately, at present there seems to be a general consensus between the different specifications on the types of transaction model to support:

- ACID transactions: Web services are for interoperability in closely coupled environments such as corporate intranets as much as they are for the Web. Interoperability between heterogeneous transaction service implementations is a requirement and yet has been difficult to achieve in practice. This transaction model is designed to support interoperability of existing transaction processing systems via Web services, given such systems already form the backbone of enterprise class applications. Although ACID transactions may not be suitable for all Web services, they are most definitely suitable for some, and particularly high-value interactions such as those involved in the finance sector. For example, in a J2EE environment where the Java Transaction API is the standard way of interacting with the transaction service (JTA), JTA-to-JTA interoperability is supported through the JTS specification (JTS), but this is neither mandated nor universally implemented.

- Forward compensation-based transactions: this model is designed for those business interactions that are long in duration, where traditional ACID transactions are inappropriate. With this model, all work performed within the scope of an application should be able to be compensated such that an application's work is either performed successfully or undone. However, how individual Web services perform their work and ensure it can be undone if compensation is required, is an implementation choice. The model simply defines the triggers for compensation actions and the conditions under which those triggers are executed.

Both the specifications from IBM et al. and Oracle et al. provide models that fall into these categories. At the moment, the WS-TransactionManagement specification provides an additional model that you will not find elsewhere, so we will look at that separately later in this chapter.

To give you an idea of how the transaction specifications plug into and enhance their respective coordination frameworks, take a look at Figure 5. As you can see, the basic coordination framework components are activation and registration as we previously described. However, each transaction model has an associated protocol that is made available to an application by being plugged into the generic coordination framework.

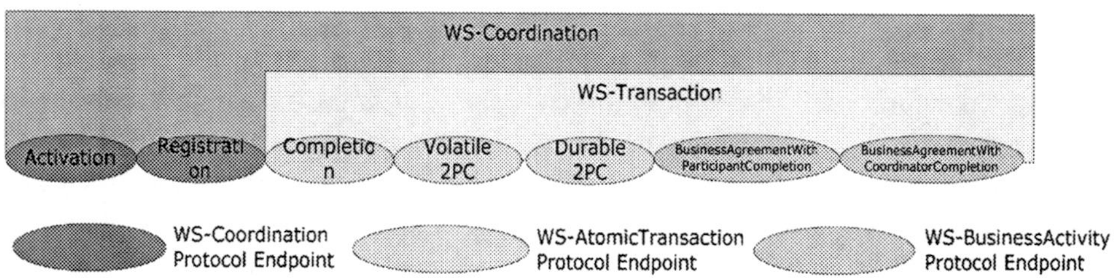

***Figure 5.* An Example of the Transaction Protocol Dependency on a Coordination Framework**

What this means in practice is that the basic coordination context is augmented with information that is specific to the transaction model. We will look at exactly what is in this additional information in the following sections.

5.1. Atomic Transaction

Within this model it is assumed that all services (and associated participants) provide ACID semantics and that any use of atomic transactions occurs in environments and situations where this is appropriate: in a trusted domain, over short durations. This model is supported by the WS-AtomicTransaction specification, and by the ACID Transaction model in the WS-TransactionManagement specification.

As you would expect, in order to begin an atomic transaction, the client application firstly locates a coordinator service that supports the right protocol. How that location occurs is conveniently ignored by the various specifications, so you are in the hands of your favorite implementation. However, once located, the client requests a new coordinator be created. As we saw earlier, in the WS-C specification this would require the client to send a `CreateCoordinationContext` message to the Activation Service. Importantly, the client must specify the type of transaction required; for example, for WS-AtomicTransaction this is done by using the http://schemas.xmlsoap.org/ws/2003/09/wsat URI in the creation message. The activation service uses this information to make sure that it can support the desired protocol (users often make mistakes!)

In both the WS-AtomicTransaction and WS-TransactionManagement specifications, the returned context has the type of transaction encoded within the context. As we mentioned earlier, in order to allow participants to be enlisted with the transaction, the context also contains a reference to the atomic transaction coordinator endpoint (what we called the registration service earlier). We have illustrated this for the WS-AtomicTransaction specification in Listing 4.

```
<!-- Create atomic transaction context message -->
<CreateCoordinationContext>
  <ActivationService>
    <wsu:Address>
      http://example.org/ws-transaction/activation
    </wsu:Address>
  </ActivationService>
  <RequesterReference>
    <wsu:Address>
      http://example.org/ws-transaction/client-app
    </wsu:Address>
  </RequesterReference>
  <CoordinationType>
    http://schemas.xmlsoap.org/ws/2003/09/wsat
  </CoordinationType>
```

```
</CreateCoordinationContext>

<!-- Atomic transaction context -->
<wscoor:CoordinationContext
  xmlns:wscoor="http://schemas.xmlsoap.org/ws/2002/08/wscoor"
  xmlns:wsu="http://schemas.xmlsoap.org/ws/2002/07/utility">
  <wsu:Identifier>
    http://example.org/tx-id/aabb-1122-ddee-3344-ff00
  </wsu:Identifier>
  <wsu:Expires>2003-06-30T00:00:00-08:00</wsu:Expires>
  <wscoor:CoordinationType>
    http://schemas.xmlsoap.org/ws/2003/09/wsat
  </wscoor:CoordinationType>
  <wscoor:RegistrationService>
    <wsu:Address>
      http://example.org/ws-transaction/registration
    </wsu:Address>
  </wscoor:RegistrationService>
</wscoor:CoordinationContext>
```

Listing 4. Atomic transaction context

After obtaining a transaction context from the coordinator, the client application then proceeds to interact with Web services to accomplish its business-level work. Neither specification defines how a client can determine whether or not a service is transactional and hence can deal with the associated context. Currently there is no equivalent of the J2EE deployment descriptor for services, or the OMG's Object Transaction Service for defining that a service is transactional and as such requires a valid context to be carried on all client-service interactions. No doubt this oversight will be removed when the likes of WS-Policy statements are extended to transactional semantics. Until that happens, however, each invocation on a business service requires the client to propagate the context, such that the each invocation is implicitly scoped by the transaction.

5.1.1. Supported Protocols

Both WS-AtomicTransaction and ACID Transaction support the two-phase commit protocol we described earlier. As you should expect by now, all interactions between the coordinator and participants are defined in terms of one-way messages. This is illustrates in Listing 9-5, where we show the WSDL for the two-phase commit participant (`twoPCParticipantPortType`) from the ACID Transaction protocol as well as the callback WSDL for the coordinator (`CoordinatorParticipantPortType`).

```
<wsdl:portType name="twoPCParticipantPortType">
  <wsdl:operation name="prepare">
    <wsdl:input message="tns:PrepareMessage"/>
  </wsdl:operation>
  <wsdl:operation name="onePhaseCommit">
    <wsdl:input message="tns:OnePhaseCommitMessage"/>
  </wsdl:operation>
  <wsdl:operation name="rollback">
    <wsdl:input message="tns:RollbackMessage"/>
  </wsdl:operation>
  <wsdl:operation name="commit">
    <wsdl:input message="tns:CommitMessage"/>
  </wsdl:operation>
  <wsdl:operation name="forgetHeuristic">
    <wsdl:input message="tns:ForgetHeuristicMessage"/>
  </wsdl:operation>
</wsdl:portType>

<wsdl:portType name="CoordinatorParticipantPortType">
  <wsdl:operation name="committed">
    <wsdl:input message="tns:CommittedMessage"/>
  </wsdl:operation>
  <wsdl:operation name="rolledBack">
    <wsdl:input message="tns:RolledBackMessage"/>
  </wsdl:operation>
  <wsdl:operation name="vote">
    <wsdl:input message="tns:VoteMessage"/>
  </wsdl:operation>
  <wsdl:operation name="heuristicForgotten">
    <wsdl:input message="tns:HeuristicForgottenMessage"/>
  </wsdl:operation>
  <wsdl:operation name="heuristicFault">
    <wsdl:input message="tns:HeuristicFaultMessage"/>
  </wsdl:operation>
</wsdl:portType>
```

Listing 5. The two-phase commit participant and coordinator WSDL

Transaction termination normally uses the two-phase commit protocol. If a transaction involves only a single participant, both models support a one-phase commit optimization similar to that in traditional transaction systems. Figure 6 shows the state transitions of an atomic transaction.

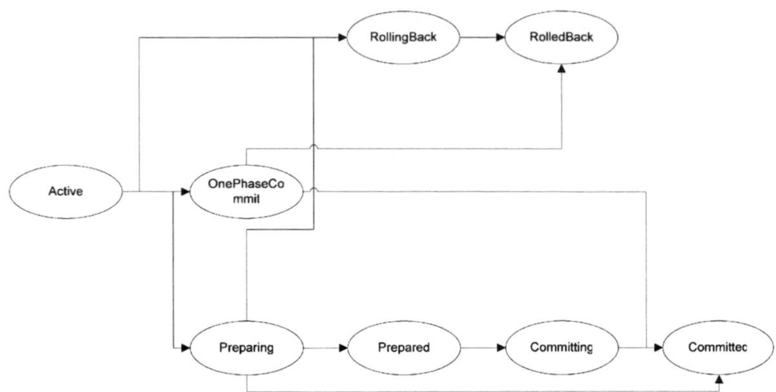

Figure 6. **Two-Phase Commit State Transitions**

As well as the two-phase commit protocol, both WS-AtomicTransaction and ACID Transaction support the synchronization protocol, though there are slight differences in the name. In WS-AtomicTransaction it is called the Volatile 2PC protocol, whereas in ACID Transaction it is given the more obvious name of the Synchronization protocol. Once again, using the WS-TXM WSDL as an example, Listing 6 shows the one-way interaction style common to both specifications.

```
<wsdl:portType name="SynchronizationPortType">
  <wsdl:operation name="beforeCompletion">
    <wsdl:input message="tns:BeforeCompletionMessage"/>
  </wsdl:operation>
  <wsdl:operation name="afterCompletion">
    <wsdl:input message="tns:AfterCompletionMessage"/>
  </wsdl:operation>
</wsdl:portType>

<wsdl:portType name="CoordinatorParticipantPortType">
  <wsdl:operation name="beforeCompletionParticipantRegistered">
    <wsdl:input message=
    "tns:BeforeCompletionParticipantRegisteredMessage"/>
  </wsdl:operation>
  <wsdl:operation name="afterCompletionParticipantRegistered">
    <wsdl:input message=
    "tns:AfterCompletionParticipantRegisteredMessage"/>
  </wsdl:operation>
</wsdl:portType>
```

Listing 6. The Synchronization protocol WSDL

A subtle, but important difference between the WS-AtomicTransaction and ACID Transaction models is that the former does not support heuristic outcomes. Although this may well change as the specification develops, at present not being able to propagate heuristic results from participants to the coordinator, or from the coordinator to the driving application, will have significant impact on the manageability of any application that uses WS-AtomicTransaction.

5.2. Business Activity

Most business-to-business applications require transactional support in order to guarantee consistent outcome and correct execution. These applications often involve long running computations, loosely coupled systems and components that do not share data, location, or administration and it is difficult to incorporate atomic transactions within such architectures. For example, an online bookshop may reserve books for an individual for a specific period of time, but if the individual does not purchase the books within that period they will be "put back onto the shelf" for others to buy.

Let us term this type of transaction a *business activity*, in line with the WS-BusinessActivity specification. The WS-TransactionManagement specification calls this a Long Running Action. A business activity is designed specifically for long-duration interactions, where exclusively locking resources is impossible or impractical. In this model services are assumed to encapsulate work that can be compensated later (possibly by executing another business activity).

As you would expect, each business activity is managed by a coordinator and when services do work, they enlist participants with the coordinator, such that if the activity later cancels the activity (needs to undo the work), these participants are informed and can then compensate for the work previously performed. What this means is that in essence, each service has a compensation element that can be used to undo the work later and this element is controlled by the participant (*compensator*).

While the full ACID semantics are not maintained by a business activity, consistency can still be maintained through compensation, though the task of writing correct compensating actions (and thus overall system consistency) is delegated to the developers of the services.

Central to business activities is the notion of *scopes* and defining activity-to-task relationships. A business activity may be partitioned into scopes, where a scope is a business task or unit of work using a collection of Web services. The Long Running Action model explicitly maps these scopes to nested activities, whereas the

WS-BusinessActivity model is less well defined. Such scopes can be nested to arbitrary levels, forming parent and child relationships. A parent scope has the ability to select which child tasks are to be included in the overall outcome protocol for a specific business activity, and so clearly non-atomic outcomes are possible. A business activity defines a consensus group that allows the relaxation of atomicity based on business level decisions. If a child task experiences an error, it can be caught by the parent who may be able to compensate and continue processing.

Nested scopes are important for a number of reasons, including:

- *Fault-isolation*: if sub-scope fails (e.g., because a service it was using fails) then this does not require the enclosing scope to fail, thus undoing all of the work performed so far.

- *Modularity*: if there is already a scope associated with a call when a new scope is begun, then the scope will be nested within it. Therefore, a programmer who knows that a service requires scopes can use them within the service: if the service's methods are invoked without a parent scope, then the service's scopes will simply be top-level; otherwise, they will be nested within the scope of the client.

When a child task completes it can either leave the business activity or signal to the parent that the work it has done can be compensated later. In the latter case, the compensation task may be called by the parent should it ultimately need to undo the work performed by the child.

Underpinning the business activity model are three fundamental assumptions:

1. All state transitions are reliably recorded, including application state and coordination metadata (the record of sent and received messages);

2. All request messages are acknowledged, so that problems are detected as early as possible. This avoids executing unnecessary tasks and can also detect a problem earlier when rectifying it is simpler and less expensive; and

3. As with atomic transactions, a response is defined as a separate operation and not as the output of the request. Message input-output implementations will typically have timeouts that are too short for some business activity responses. If the response is not received after a timeout, it is resent. This is repeated until a response is received. The request receiver discards all but one identical request received.

Most workflow systems do not distinguish compensate activities from forward progress activities: an activity is an activity and it just does some work. If that work happens to compensate for some previous work then so be it. In addition, most services you will find already have compensate operations written into their definitions, like "cancel seat reservation" or "cancel holiday" and they don't need to be driven by some other transaction/coordination engine that then sends "prepare" or "commit" or "roll back" to a participant which then has to determine how to talk to the service to accomplish the same goal.

Although similar in their goals, there are fundamental protocol differences between the WS-BusinessActivity and Long Running Action models. From an application programmer's perspective it is very unlikely that you will notice these differences. However, we will now briefly cover these differences.

5.2.1. WS-BusinessActivity

The WS-BusinessActivity model defines two sub-protocols, the `BusinessAgreementWithCoordinatorComplete` and `BusinessAgreement-WithParticipantComplete`. The only difference is that in the case of `BusinessAgreementWithCoordinatorComplete` the child scope cannot autonomously decide to end its participation in the business activity, even if it can be compensated. Rather the child task relies upon the parent to inform it when the child has received all requests for it to perform work which the parent does this by sending the *complete* message to the child.

A child activity is initially created in the active state; if it finishes the work it was created to do and no more participation is required within the scope of the business agreement (such as when the activity operates on immutable data), then the child can unilaterally send an *exited* message to the parent. However, if the child task finishes and wishes to continue in the business activity then it must be able to compensate for the work it has performed (e.g., un-reserve the seat on the flight). In this case it sends a *completed* message to the parent and waits to receive the final outcome of the parent. This outcome will either be a *close* message, meaning the business activity has completed successfully or a *compensate* message indicating that the parent activity requires that the child task reverse its work.

5.2.2. Long Running Action

In this (LRA) model, each application is bound to the scope of a compensation interaction. For example, when a user reserves a seat on a flight, the airline reservation centre may take an optimistic approach and actually book the seat and debit the users account, relying on the fact that most of their customers who reserve seats later book them; the compensation action for this activity would obviously be to un-book the seat and credit the user's account. Work performed within the scope of a nested

LRA must remain compensatable until an enclosing service informs the individual service(s) that it is no longer required.

Listing 7 shows the WSDL for the Compensator (`CompensatorPortType`) and the coordinator that drives it (`CoordinatorPortType`).

```
<wsdl:portType name="CompensatorPortType">
     <wsdl:operation name="compensate">
          <wsdl:input message="tns:CompensateMessage"/>
     </wsdl:operation>
     <wsdl:operation name="complete">
          <wsdl:input message="tns:CompleteMessage"/>
     </wsdl:operation>
     <wsdl:operation name="forget">
          <wsdl:input message="tns:ForgetMessage"/>
     </wsdl:operation>
</wsdl:portType>

<wsdl:portType name="CoordinatorPortType">
     <wsdl:operation name="compensated">
          <wsdl:input message="tns:CompensatedMessage"/>
     </wsdl:operation>
     <wsdl:operation name="completed">
          <wsdl:input message="tns:CompletedMessage"/>
     </wsdl:operation>
     <wsdl:operation name="forgot">
          <wsdl:input message="tns:ForgotMessage"/>
     </wsdl:operation>
     <wsdl:operation name="unknownCompensator">
          <wsdl:input
          message="tns:UnknownCompensatorFaultMessage"/>
     </wsdl:operation>
     <wsdl:operation name="cannotCompensate">
          <wsdl:input
          message="tns:CannotCompensateFaultMessage"/>
     </wsdl:operation>
     <wsdl:operation name="cannotComplete">
          <wsdl:input message="tns:CannotCompleteFaultMessage"/>
     </wsdl:operation>
</wsdl:portType>
```

Listing 7. The LRA Compensator WSDL

Let us consider the example of an online travel agent. The travel agent is concerned with booking a taxi, reserving a table at a restaurant, reserving a seat at the theatre, and then booking a room at a hotel. If all of these operations were performed as a single transaction then resources acquired during booking the taxi (for example) would not be released until the top-level transaction has terminated. If subsequent activities do not require those resources, then they will be needlessly unavailable to other clients.

Figure 7 shows how part of the night-out may be mapped into LRAs. All of the individual activities are compensatable. For example, this means that if LRA1 fails or the user decides to not accept the booked taxi, the work will be undone automatically. Because LRA1 is nested within another LRA, once LRA1 completes successfully any compensation mechanisms for its work may be passed to LRA5: this is an implementation choice for the Compensator. In the event that LRA5 completes successfully, no work is required to be compensated, otherwise all work performed within the scope of LRA5 (LRA1 to LRA4) will be compensated.

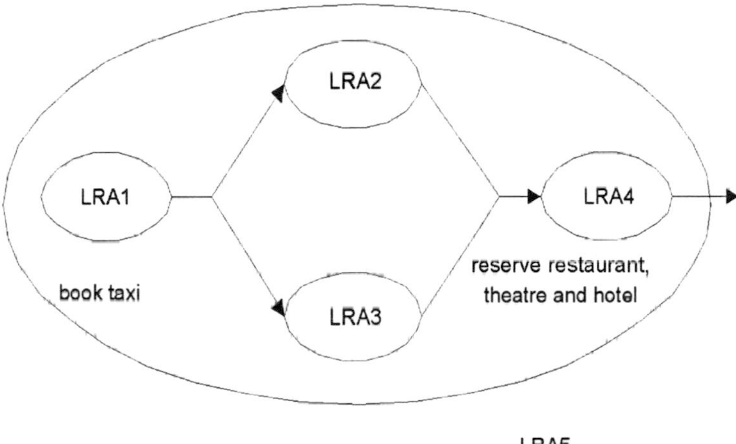

***Figure 7.* LRA Example**

A *Compensator* is the LRA participant that operates on behalf of a service to undo the work it performs within the scope of an LRA. How compensation is carried out will obviously be dependent upon the service; compensation work may be carried out by other LRAs which themselves have Compensators.

When a service performs work that may have to be later compensated within the scope of an LRA, it enlists a Compensator participant with the LRA coordinator. The coordinator will send the Compensator one of the following messages when the activity terminates:

- *Success*: the activity has completed successfully. If the activity is nested then Compensators may propagate themselves (or new Compensators) to the enclosing LRA. Otherwise the Compensators are informed that the activity has terminated and they can perform any necessary cleanups.

- *Fail*: the activity has completed unsuccessfully. All Compensators that are registered with the LRA will be invoked to perform compensation in the reverse order. The coordinator forgets about all Compensators that indicated they operated correctly. Otherwise, compensation may be attempted again (possibly after a period of time) or alternatively a compensation violation has occurred and must be logged.

Each service is required to log sufficient information in order to ensure (with best effort) that compensation is possible.

So far we have not really considered the relationship between LRAs in an application. Obviously LRAs may be used sequentially and concurrently, where the termination of an LRA signals the start of some other unit of work within an application. However, LRAs are units of compensatable work and an application may have as many such units of work operating simultaneously as it needs to accomplish its tasks. Furthermore, the outcome of work within LRAs may determine how other LRAs are terminated.

An application can be structured to so that LRAs are used to assemble units of compensatable work and then held in the active state while the application performs other work in the scope of different (concurrent or sequential) LRAs. Only when the right subset of work (LRAs) is arrived at by the application will that subset be confirmed; all other LRAs will be told to cancel (complete in a failure state).

At the start of this chapter we mentioned that although the WS-Transaction and WS-TransactionManagement specifications share many things in common, the latter specification possesses an additional protocol that the IBM, Microsoft and BEA specifications do not: the *business process model*. In the following section we will briefly talk about this model.

5.3. Business Process Model

The business process (BP) model is different from any of the other transaction models we have looked at so far. This model is specifically aimed at tying together heterogeneous transaction domains into a single business-to-business transaction. So, for example, with this model it is possible to have a long-running business transaction span messaging, workflow and traditional ACID transactions. The reason for this is to allow business to leverage their existing corporate IT investment.

In the business process transaction model all parties involved in a business process reside within *business domains*, which may themselves use business processes to perform work. Business process transactions are responsible for managing interactions *between* these domains. A business process (business-to-business interaction) is split into *business tasks* and each task executes within a specific business domain. A business domain may itself be subdivided into other business domains (business processes) in a recursive manner.

Each domain may represent a different transaction model if such a federation of models is more appropriate to the activity. Each business task (which may be modeled as a scope) may provide implementation specific counter-effects in the event that the enclosing scope must cancel. In addition, periodically the controlling application may request that all business domains checkpoint their state such that they can either be consistently rolled back to that checkpoint by the application or restarted from the checkpoint in the event of a failure.

An individual task may require multiple services to work. Each task is assumed to be a compensatable unit of work. However, as with the LRA model, how compensation is provided is an implementation choice for the task.

For example, let us return to our travel agent and see how it might be mapped into the BP model. If you look at Figure 8 you can see that the on-line travel agent interacts with its specific suppliers, each of which resides in its own business domain. The work necessary to obtain each component is modeled as a separate task, or Web service. In this example, the Flight reservation task is actually composed of two sub-tasks; one that gets the flight and the other that gets the necessary travel insurance.

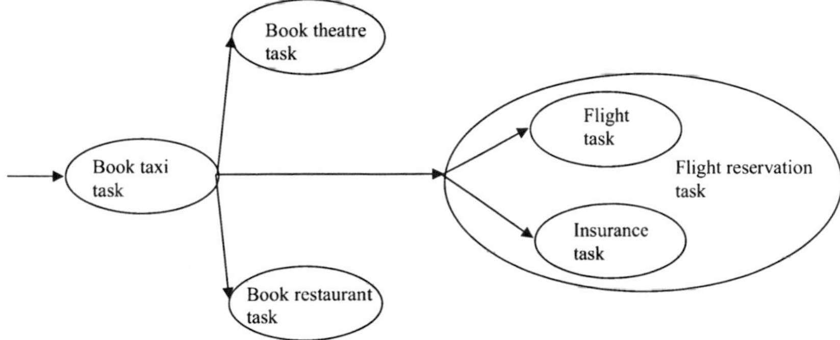

***Figure 8.* Business Processes and Tasks for a Travel Agent**

The user may interact synchronously with the travel agent to build up the details of the holiday required. Alternatively, the user may submit an order (possibly with a list of alternate requirements, such as destinations, dates, etc.) to the agent who will eventually call back when it has been filled; likewise, the travel agent then submits orders to each supplier, requiring them to call back when each component is available (or is known to be unavailable).

The business process transaction model supports this synchronous and asynchronous interaction pattern. Business domains are instructed to perform work within the scope of a global business process. The business process has an overall manager that may be informed by individual tasks when they have completed their work (either successfully or unsuccessfully), or it may periodically communicate with each task to determine its current status. In addition, each task may make period checkpoints of its progress such that if a failure occurs, it may be restarted from that point rather than having to start from the beginning. A business process can either terminate in a confirmed (successful) manner in which case *all* of the work requested will have been performed, or it will terminate in a cancelled (unsuccessful) manner, in which case all of the work will be undone.

If it cannot be undone, then this fact must be logged. One key difference between the business process transaction model and that of traditional 2PC is that it assumes success: the BP model is optimistic and assumes the failure case is the minority and can be handled or resolved offline if necessary, or through replay/void/compensation, but not always automatically, often requiring human interaction.

So far we have seen how useful transactions (ACID or not) can be when developing distributed applications. However, throughout the previous descriptions there has been an implicit assumption: a user can trust a transaction coordinator and a transaction coordinator can trust the participants. In the sorts of closely coupled environments where transactions originated these kinds of trust relationships are possible. As you can see in the chapter or Security, in the loosely coupled SOA environment, trust is something that cannot be taken as a given. In the next section we will give a brief overview of the kinds of issues that could arise when trust is not readily available.

6. Security Implications

There are several implicit security issues in the use of distributed transactions, regardless of the model that is employed. As we have seen, in any of the transaction models there are essentially three actors:

1. The participant that is driven through the termination protocol.
2. The coordinator, with whom participants register and who drives them through the termination protocol.
3. The application logic that tells the coordinator when and how to terminate.

Whatever the application logic might want (e.g., to commit) is never guaranteed by the coordinator, simply because failures can occur that force the transaction to roll back. However, within the basic protocols, the coordinator will always try to do what the application tells it and the coordinator cannot determine whether or not requests to terminate come from valid sources. What this means is that if some illegal user were to obtain a reference to the coordinator, it could force it to do work that is different from that which the legal user (application) would want.

Now let us consider the case where one of the participants is deliberately going to try to subvert the transaction protocol. By being involved in a transaction, a participant has knowledge of its outcome and can also affect that outcome. Having knowledge that a specific transaction has committed or rolled back, for example, could be important (e.g., insider share trading). Likewise, being able to affect the outcome of the transaction is obviously important too.

However, can the coordinator always be trusted? The coordinator always has the final say on the actual outcome of the transaction. Just because the application logic says to roll back, does not mean that the coordinator actually has to roll back the participants – it could lie. Likewise, if the application logic says to commit and all participants say they can commit, the coordinator could still roll them back. Even more threatening (especially to application consistency) is the fact that the coordinator could tell some participants to commit, and others to roll back!

What this brief overview of the security assumptions should show you is that just because there are transaction protocols for Web services does not mean that they alone can be used to solve all of your problems. Security and transactions have gone hand-in-hand for several years in traditional transaction processing systems, particularly in loosely coupled environments where no single trust domain exists. Unfortunately at this time there is no single standard for Web services security and neither of the Web services transactions specifications indicates how any kind of security infrastructure should be tied in. At best they simply say "security is required" and reference a specific security specification. For example, the WS-AtomicTransaction specification is quite clear in the fact that it should be used in conjunction with the WS-Security specification to ensure that transactions only ever span trusted domains. The chapter on Security provides a good insight into what it means to make your Web Services secure and you should read that chapter in conjunction with this section to understand the implications of making a Web Services transaction protocol secure.

7. Interoperability Considerations

As you might expect, there are some interesting interoperability issues presented by having multiple transactions specifications. However, there are also interoperability issues within the specifications. So let us first look at whether interoperability between heterogeneous implementations of the same Web services transactions specification is possible.

Unfortunately both WS-Tx and WS-TransactionManagement define message exchange patterns for their various models that allow for vendor-specific enhancements. For example, if we look again at the `CoordinationContext` structure defined by the WS-Coordination specification and shown in Listing 2, we can see that there is an any in the context. This is intended to allow for implementation specific enhancements to the basic context. Individual implementations can add whatever information they require in order to function, and this then extends to the WS-Transaction specifications that leverage the context.

Although it is possible to implement the various transaction protocols without recourse to the extensibility elements of the contexts or messages, it is likely that some vendors will use these to implement protocol optimizations. If these implementations used the optimizations with some foresight for interoperability then they should be able to continue to work in the absence of the extensibility elements (albeit in a less optimized manner). However, we have yet to find an implementation that does this, i.e., those that use the extensibility, require it to be present in all messages in order for the protocols to work. Obviously this significantly affects interoperability!

So although interoperability by implementations of the same specifications is possible, it is not necessarily a requirement of all vendors. You should be careful when choosing an implementation if interoperability is a requirement now or in then future.

If you thought interoperability within a specification was simple, then hopefully it should not come as a surprise to learn that interoperability between the two specifications is more complex. Despite the fact that the specifications share many requirements and have models in common, the on-the-wire message formats and WSDL are different. It is possible that as these specifications evolve (neither of them have yet to be ratified as a standard), they may move closer and perhaps even merge. In the meanwhile, direct interoperability (where, for example, an ACID Transaction two-phase participant can enroll with a WS-AtomicTransaction coordinator), is not possible. However, there are some vendors (e.g., Arjuna Technologies, ATL) who are working closely with both specifications (and their authors) to provide products that can opaquely to an application bridge between the different transaction protocols.

Although all of this might sound like we have a considerable way to go before interoperability is a fact of life, it is worth remembering that there is another type of interoperability that is at least as important, and which we can cater for now: interoperability with (and between) existing legacy transaction systems. Both WS-AtomicTransaction and ACID Transaction models are meant specifically for integration with back-end infrastructures easier.

Web Services are for interoperability as much as for the Internet. As such, interoperability of existing transaction processing systems will be an important part of Web Services transactions: such systems already form the backbone of enterprise level applications and will continue to do so for the Web services equivalent. Business-to-business activities will involve back-end transaction processing systems either directly or indirectly and being able to tie together these environments will be the key to the successful take-up of Web Services transactions. Leveraging existing infrastructural investments in terms of transaction systems and services that use them are extremely important, and both sets of specifications are ideal for this purpose.

8. Summary

We have looked at the two main candidates vying for the title of Web services transactions standard. All of the main Web services heavyweights are backing either WS-Transaction or WS-TransactionManagement. Whether there a single standard will ever evolve is unknown and is probably more in the realm of politics than technology.

As we have seen, although ACID transactions are not for all Web Services because of their blocking nature, they are still a requirement for some use cases, especially where interoperability is important. Interoperability of heterogeneous ACID transaction systems is now possible and has been an often unfulfilled requirement for many enterprises for a long time. Although Web Services represent a new arena of distributed system that is loosely coupled, potentially large scale and heterogeneous, they are for interoperability as much as for the Internet. As such, interoperability of existing transaction processing systems will be an important part of Web Services transactions: such systems already form the backbone of enterprise level applications and will continue to do so for the Web services equivalent.

Business-to-business activities will involve back-end transaction processing systems either directly or indirectly and being able to tie together these environments will be the key to the successful take-up of Web Services transactions. Web services will operate as the glue between different environments (e.g., corporate domains) and application components will be implemented using tried and tested technologies such as J2EE, CORBA and .NET. Compensation transactions such as the WS-TransactionManagement Long Running Action model or other extended transaction models will be important in areas where ACID transactions are inappropriate.

Finally we looked at the various security and interoperability issues that are still unresolved. Because this is still a relatively new area, it is perhaps unreasonable to assume that all of the "glitches" have been solved. However, when deploying implementations, you should be aware of the issues and be able to determine whether they are important now or in the future. Just because these problems have not been fully addressed by the specifications does not mean that a vendor implementation cannot (or should not) provide a good solution.

8
EVENT-DRIVEN ARCHITECTURE

Let me tell you the secret that has led me to my goal:
My strength lies solely in my tenacity.
Louis Pasteur

Early in many of our careers, we would have remembered the days of batch systems, transaction processing monitors such as CICS and other components of the mainframe that were used to run many mission-critical systems. As time passed and Moore's law provided us with the ability to double computing capacity every 18 months, we began to develop systems that provided information in real-time. With increasing computing capacity, we were able to ignore the architecture principles learned by our forefathers and instead preferred to create systems that did processing inline. This had the effect of making systems over time less scalable and more susceptible to outages especially when downstream services the application depended on were unavailable.

Event-driven architectures are one of the few instances in which the real-world benefits of an architectural approach were realized before the hype. The phrase "event-driven architecture" refers to applications and services that have the ability to react to changes in conditions, regardless of whether the change is a failure in a downstream system or a sudden change in the marketplace such as a meltdown on Wall Street.

An event is a change in the state of a resource or request for processing.

A time honored approach still holds true in service-oriented architecture of if it does not need to be done in real-time, do it asynchronously. Asynchronous behavior within applications is not just a technical construct but the way business itself operates. Remembering one of our core principles, that services should model the business, we can conclude that being event-driven is mandatory for the creation of an Enterprise SOA.

If you have meticulously read this book, you may have noticed a subtle but crucial difference between traditional service-oriented architectures and being event-driven. To this point, we have achieved the goal of articulating how to gain loose coupling amongst services but need to take it one step further. Event-driven architecture will help us become decoupled to a much greater degree. Coupling of services occurs at the level of the service contract (In Web Services, the WSDL document). With an event-driven approach, there is no need for any such contract. The only connection between event producers and consumers are the subscription and publication activities between them.

Let the reader be warned, this chapter may require multiple passes before one fully understands its content. In this chapter, we will cover:

- Service Design,
- Enterprise Service Bus,
- Business Rules,
- Pools,
- Patterns,
- Agents,
- Callbacks,
- Finite State Machines,
- Notifications,
- Brokered Notifications,
- Security concerns, and
- Practical Considerations.

1. Overview

Event-driven architecture as a paradigm focuses on the notion of an event as its primary abstraction. Events can be generally classified as any occurrence, activity or change in state. Events also have attributes such as location (where it occurred), interval (how often it occurred) and time (when it occurred). Events themselves are usually processed with some form of delay, which affords the opportunity to ignore particular events, delay response or immediately start processing. Abstracting business activities into a event-driven paradigm will help enterprises scale and align services with real world business process. Within the vast majority of enterprises, event handling within applications occurs via messaging paradigms.

Traditional applications may use queuing products and interact with other applications on a request-reply basis. Applications in this scenario send a message (event) to other applications via queues and wait for reply before continuing processing. Application level queues in this scenario may decouple the transport layer from a connectivity perspective but does not provide features to aid in scalability or availability since both applications become coupled to each other in a point-to-point interaction.

Usage of queues does not guarantee asynchronous application interaction. The event-driven approach to service development has similarities with traditional object-oriented development but departs in subtle ways. The first departure comes by the techniques used to capture and model the business domain. The traditional object-oriented approach may start with a UML class diagram that captures objects and their attributes. In this approach, the attributes determine their state and methods describe an object's behavior. In an event-driven approach, modeling may start by capturing the participants in an event, the roles they play in the specified scenario and modeling of state transitions.

Classes and their relationships traditionally captured are discarded in pure event-driven architectures. Within an event-driven approach, state is determined by event binding amongst participants and not within an object itself. Likewise, constraints on state transitions are modeled as conditional rejections. Events themselves have a transactional nature to them when put into a state context in that they can become classified as reversible or irreversible states.

Let us dive deeper into the details of being event-driven.

2. Events

Events can be loosely classified into the following categories:

- Descriptive,
- Prescriptive,
- Factual, and
- Assumptive.

Let us look into the details of each event classification.

2.1. Descriptive

Descriptive events are declarative in their approach and may be typically used to classify scenarios. Events can be further grouped into hierarchies and can also serve as aliases. For example, a participant (customer) in an event-driven scenario interacting with a consumer order entry service may also be classified as an individual (if single) or as a household (more than one person at the shipping address).

Descriptive events can also place participants into named groups (sets) as well as leverage a set of criteria. For example, an income tax service may classify wealthy Americans as those individuals who have an annual income greater than $40,000 per year and own a car. Events can belong to multiple groups at the same time. In the preceding example, the subject could be separately classified as both wealthy and American.

2.2. Prescriptive

Prescriptive events either serve to quantify or constrain. For example, a university course registration service may constrain students (participants) to how many courses they can take in a single semester. Constraints can either specify exact quantities or lower and upper boundaries in terms of ranges or intervals.

Constraints are usually applied to events that have a limited duration from a time perspective. For example, an insurance policy may constrain the reporting of physical property damage to the effective date of the policy to five business days after the policy expiration date. Constraints can also be applied to contingent scenarios whereby events are dependent upon a series of other events occurring. For example, a product warranty may trigger an obligation to repair an appliance at no charge if the product is damaged during normal product usage within one year from the date of purchase provided that the consumer purchased additional warranty coverage within ninety days of purchase.

2.3. Factual

Factual events are events that have occurred and can include both business and user-interface events. Business events include contractual events which specify the rights (descriptive) and responsibilities (prescriptive) of each participant. Contractual events are descriptive in that they incorporate definitions of the rights and responsibilities. Contractual events are also prescriptive in they specify authorizations and obligations on both parties. Factual events can also include workflow events which demonstrate the fulfillment of responsibility.

2.4. Assumptive

Assumptive events are events that may or may not have actually occurred. They may assumed to have occurred or anticipated to do so in the future. When the enterprise wants to develop systems that are predictive in nature, it may allow for assumptive events to be created. Sometimes it is useful for a semi-informed event to be created. For example, an event monitoring service may need to may certain assumptions if it receives multiple events that are part of a business transaction out of order. In this situation, any actions taken by a service need to allow for events that later prove or disprove the particular action taken.

2.5. Business Rules

Many enterprises have adopted the usage of business rules engines as a strategy of allowing flexibility in changing business rules without having to involve IT resources to write in a proprietary language. The process of capturing and modeling business rules is very similar to modeling of an event-driven architecture. In the event-driven paradigm, a business rule can be thought of as a business policy as it describes how specifications should be implemented in a prescriptive manner.

Policies have several components:

- Participants,

- Roles,
- Conditions,
- Events, and
- Classification/Scenario.

Examples of participants in business rules are customers, suppliers, supervisors, etc., whose activities occur in context of a role such as purchaser, approver, or authorizers. Business rules also have conditions such as under which circumstances can an authorization event will be triggered. Usually the entire rule will occur in some particular context/scenario and a classification scheme applied to it such as order entry, quoting, claims submission, etc.

Traditional business rules processing however is usually implemented in short-lived transactional scenarios. Event-driven architecture can be considered a superset in that it captures the lifecycle of all policies (business rules). When a rule fires, it only maintains context from its entry point but otherwise becomes isolated from other events within the enterprise. Sometimes it is necessary to understand the state of transactions outside of the currently executing context. Rules such as the trading service can only accept trades from six wealthy individuals concurrently that are submit limit orders for after hours on securities that trade on NASDAQ and the last trade was an up tick would be difficult at best to construct using a pure rules-driven approach and would require tons of awkward logic.

Traditional approaches to rules engines operate on the notion of forward chaining. Rather than specifying an expression for evaluation, the rule set is run against the current knowledge base allowing it to assert the facts for each rule has it is preconditions satisfied. Rules engines generally iterate until no rules have all of their preconditions satisfied. The problem with this approach is that the knowledge base is somewhat static in that another rule in another set may invalidate conditions that would have caused the rule to execute.

Some rules engine implementations will allow a user to leverage backward chaining. Backward chaining starts with just a set of preconditions and no assertions. The engine will search the knowledge base to find the facts that satisfy the constraints. Backward chaining is useful for constraint-based searching and can result sets can be returned iteratively instead of running to completion. Backward chaining is closer in spirit to event-driven architecture but forward chaining has won the popularity contest.

To learn more about Business Rules, we recommend Ross (2003).

3. Agents

Imagine a situation where a client from one enterprise wants to conduct dynamic business with another enterprise in an integrated supply chain manner. The ability to provide run-time integration and service provisioning at run-time is crucial. In this particular scenario, if no particular service existed that could satisfy the functionality required by the first enterprise, there should exist the possibility of combining existing services together in order to fulfill the request.

One challenge that has not yet emerged within the enterprise is the ability to understand the limitations of human capability to analyze the required services within a transaction and create compositions using approaches such as BPEL manually. At the heart of the matter is the notion of service composition as it is more complex than it appears at first and cannot be solved without good architectural discipline and several degrees of automation.

Enterprise SOAs that are event-driven will introduce the notion of an agent. An agent can launch several responses based on a business event, each of which can be executed independently often requiring no further action from the initiating agent. Agents can be configured statically or learn dynamically to watch for a range of events that may or may not happen, and may occur in an order that is difficult to design for upfront. Building applications and services that can be assembled in arbitrary ways usually requires heroic efforts when not using an event-driven approach. Until now, only a few services were constructed using event-driven approaches such as trading applications but have now became realizable for the enterprise to incorporate into all enterprise applications.

Before we jump into business events, agents and other advanced concepts, let us revisit some of the principles we discussed in previous chapters and put them into an event-driven context.

In Chapter 4, we learned techniques for describing and registering services. Many typical implementations of registries permit services to be referred to by function signatures that are somewhat opaque and provide virtually no indication of the nature of the services being managed. Services themselves in their description, require a level of expressiveness in order to work in an agent-based model. The description of a service needs to include its meaning and intent rather than simply ascribing a name to it.

> *The term Ontology is borrowed from philosophy and represents a systematic account of existence.*

For example, a semantically poor description of a service interface would be that it takes as input an integer and three strings are returned as output. A semantically rich description for this service interface would be that it takes the name of a company and returns (i) the stock exchange it trades, (ii) the email address of the CEO, and (iii) the CEO's shoe size.

> *Semantic is the study of meaning and the changes in meaning.*

One of the more important attributes of an enterprise SOA is that services should be composable. The dynamic composition of services requires the location of services based on their capabilities and the recognition of those services that can be matched to create a composite offering. Approaches that XML markups such as BPEL when taken to their logical conclusion simply will result in yet another legacy. BPEL relies on the nature of static binding of services in order to form composition and does not provide the ability to discover possible execution paths at run-time creating another form of coupling. Semantic understanding is the only thing that will assist in solving this problem.

For example, a web retailer wants to sell products similar to those on Amazon.com and wants to expose a web services interface. Likewise, a consumer is shopping for products related to ancient Chinese folklore and specifically interested in learning more about the legend of Fong Sai Yuk. The transaction requires choreography between two different services; an online language translation service and a dictionary service. The language translation service can handle translating text between several languages where as the dictionary service can return the meaning in English. The problem with describing this type of interaction in WSDL is that it would only contain a description of strings as input and output rather than the concept of how they can be combined.

Current practices around service descriptions will over time become exposed as being impoverished. The savage pursuit of describing the functional signature of a service and its interfaces instead of characterizing their meaning will simply result in yet another integration problem down the road. The ability for the enterprise to support service discovery services (above and beyond registries) is an essential component to achieving loose coupling.

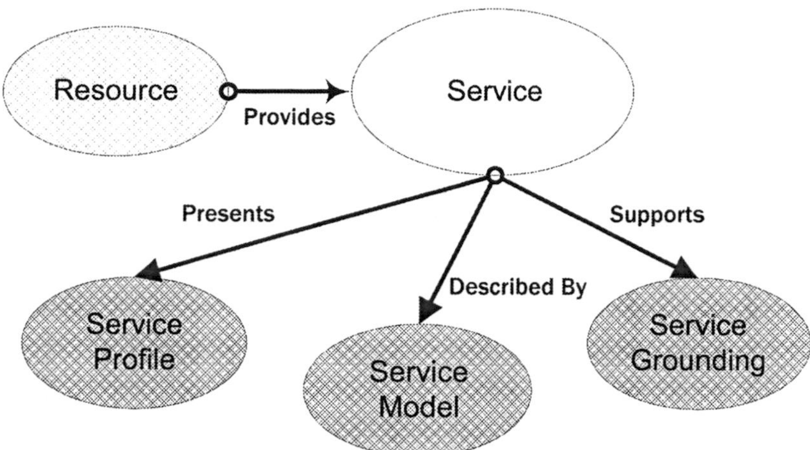

Figure 1. **Service Ontology**

The service profile describes what the service does, what it requires of consumers or other agents and what it provides for them. The service model describes how the service works and the service grounding describes to the service can be accessed.

The service as shown in Figure 1 provides an organizational point of reference for declaration of services. The properties presents, described by and supports are properties of the declared service. The classes Service Profile, Service Model and Service Grounding represent the declared ranges of those properties.

Service profiles state what the service does and give the types of information required by an agent seeking services (or its intermediaries) to determine whether the service meets its needs. The profile is also used to state the requirements of the agent seeking services so that an intermediary such as a matchmaking service which will pair parties together has a convenient dual-purpose representation on which its operations can be formed.

Service models state how the service works. For services that are composed of several steps which occur over an extended period of time, the model will provide a description that can be leveraged by agents. The description can be used by the agent to perform the following tasks:

- Direct the agent to perform an in-depth analysis of whether the service meets its needs.
- Create a composite service description from multiple services to perform a specific task.

- Under service invocation, allow the agent to coordinate the activities of different participants.
- Provide the ability for the agent to monitor the execution of the service.

Service groundings state the details of how agents can access the service and will contain information on which communication protocols to use, message formats and other service-specific details required to interact with the service. The service grounding also contains specifications for how to exchange data elements for abstract types contained within the service model. This could be a specification on how to serialize/deserialize the data type.

Current service interactions typically show a client querying a centralized registry (find) to discover the location of a service endpoint (bind and execute). What is not taken into consideration is the ability of a service provider to locate potential consumers of a service and provide pieces of the puzzle to the client in which the required interaction has not been predefined. Architectures that are agent-based can provide the opportunity for a service provider to become proactive in the service composition process.

To learn more about agent-based approaches to services, visit http://www.daml.org.

3.1. Service Design

The first stage of service design and development used within many enterprises starts with a highly synchronous interaction between producers and consumers. While we can use management approaches to load balance services to achieve scalability, it is important to talk about proper service construction techniques. The ability for the service itself to perform asynchronously will yield higher performance over other approaches and sustain response times with huge variations in load.

One commonly used approach to handling huge variations in load is to overprovision resources. Many web sites simply procure enough servers to handle the anticipated peak load and use various load balancing approaches to cause even utilization between them. Usually this strategy works well in situations when resources used are commodity in nature, low cost and readily available but otherwise will fail when the ratio of peak to average load is very high. It would be unrealistic to purchase hundreds of machines to support peak loads when the average load could be served by only a few machines. The traditional approach of building "farms" in this scenario will not meet the scalability requirements but will also result in wasted expense. The cost of managing a large number of servers over time can grow significantly higher than the multiplicative cost of the servers themselves.

The mindset within the enterprise needs to move away from the mindset of developing infrastructure to support peak loads to developing services that are mission-critical to be well-conditioned to handle load. A well-conditioned service has the characteristic that when the number of requests exceeds its intended capacity, it will minimally not over commit usage of operating system and downstream resources that ultimately degrade the responses of all clients.

Services that can detect overload conditions and attempt to adapt their resources to them can use strategies to shed load in a predictable fashion by returning a predefined response to the consumers when it is saturated or by degrading the quality of service based on either amount of data returned and/or actual response times. Ideally, this should be a configurable behavior within each service instance. The ability to inform service consumers that the service is overloaded is far better than dropping service requests.

The architecture used to develop services should also address:

- Handling large variations in service utilization.
- The ability to support massive concurrency of service requests.
- Decoupling event handling and load management from service logic.
- Allowing policies for load management to be configurable.
- The ability to provide classification in a generalized manner to service requests.

There are many approaches that can be used in creating highly adaptable services that realize the above goals. Some of the techniques that can be used are:

- Resource Pools,
- Multi-threaded Designs,
- Soft References.

In order to understand how they can be implemented within an enterprise, we will need to revisit several software engineering concepts and see how they can be applied to an enterprise SOA.

3.2. Pools

Pooling mechanisms are useful in situations where resources are limited and can cause performance bottlenecks where there are not enough resources to meet the demands of incoming service requests. Connections to relational databases are a good usage of a pooled approach since the performance costs of creating and destroying the connection is reduced.

Pools can provide functionality to allow clients to reserve resources in advance of their usage and return the resource to the pool when it is no longer needed. Pools can also solve for resource related slowdowns in situations when there are more connections to a resource, the longer it takes to create new connections.

Pools are used in situations where users of the pool assume that all resources contained within it are interchangeable. For example, if a user needs to query a relational database and the database connection is in a state that will accept queries, it does not matter to the client application which particular connection is used.

Sometimes pools are implemented as singletons where a generic pool will hold a variety of connection types. In other situations, there may be a different pool for each resource type (this is highly recommended). Most application servers provide a generic pooling mechanism for relational databases but do not provide pooling support for other connection types such as directory services, legacy applications and so on.

```
public interface PoolableObjectFactory {
Object create();
void activate(Object obj);
void passivate(Object obj);
void destroy(Object obj);
```

Code 1. Poolable Object Factory

A pool may sometimes implement other patterns such as Factory to ensure consistent lifecycle support. This will allow a pool to be written in a manner that will allow a client to select pooling behavior independent from the types of resources contained within them. An example is contained in Code 1.

Pools themselves can provide configurable constraints on entities contained within it such as maximum number of connections, who can use them and for how long and load balancing / failover in situations where connections to existing resources fail. Pools can also make service startup and recovery faster as they can delay creation of connections to other resources until they are required for timely client response times.

4. Threads

Many enterprise applications leverage frameworks and application servers that provide a simplistic approach to simultaneously support multiple concurrent requests. These frameworks hide the complexity of developing multithreaded applications from developers and meet their goal of making application development simpler. In most situations, the approach used by application servers and frameworks provide a sufficient level of concurrency with appropriate response times. However these same frameworks and application servers will most often fail in situations with unpredictable load.

Modern operating systems support the notion of a thread of execution in which the operating system determines what will execute. A thread executes in context of a process. Processes are used to group resources together and threads are the resource in which the operating system scheduler will schedule for execution on the CPU.

Usages of threads are a common approach to improving the parallelism of applications. The operating system will rapidly switch execution of threads to give the illusion of parallel execution. Threads like services can be in any of multiple states; running, blocked, ready, terminated. Threads can be useful in applications that are required to do more than one task at a time but can be detrimental in any application that has a sequential process that cannot be divided into parallel tasks as they would block until the previous one completes.

There are two pervasive approaches used in developing multithreaded applications:

1. Thread per Request, and

2. Thread Pools.

4.1. Thread per Request

Thread per request approaches are used by most architectures that are based on remote procedure call style of interaction. Microsoft's Distributed Component Object Model (DCOM) and Java's Remote Method Invocation (RMI) use this approach. In the thread per request, each accepted request is dispatched to a thread which processes the request. Locking techniques based on semaphores are utilized to protect the integrity of internal data structures and shared resources.

Semaphores are a technique for coordinating or synchronizing activities in which multiple processes compete for the same operating system resource.

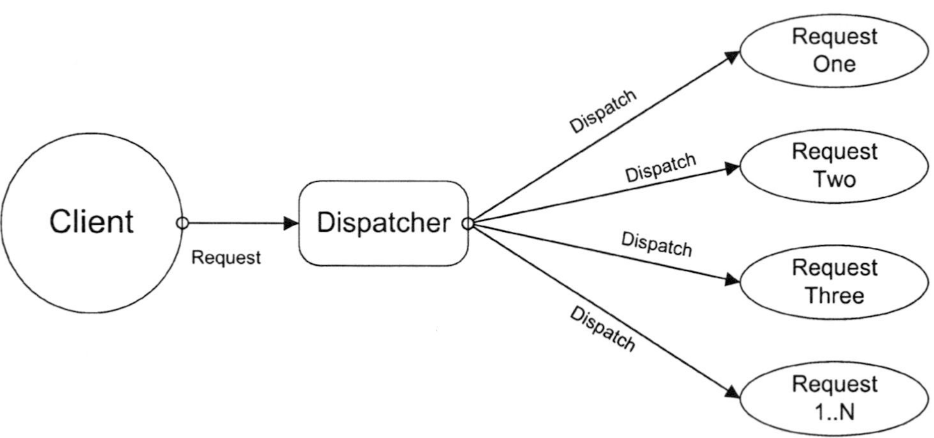

***Figure 2.* Thread per Request**

In the thread per request model (Figure 2), incoming service requests are dispatched to separate threads. In this model, each thread is responsible for performing all activities of the process and returning the result to the client. Each thread may use operating system resources such as accessing files which are also incorporated into each threads process.

Thread per request is commonly used because of its ease of programming as all tasks can be thought of as and are executed inline. This model also provides isolation from all other currently executing requests and only becomes noticeable when handling shared resources or state.

The original reason for usage of threads within operating systems was in support of timesharing. When the number of threads that need to execute concurrently grows significantly passed the number of processors contained within a server, the operating system will start to thrash. The operating system's scheduler will experience scheduling overhead and increased cache misses resulting in a rapidly increasing slowdown of all operations. The thread per request model has serious limitations in that it provides zero capability in terms of resource management.

4.2. Thread Pools

The second approach used in many application servers such as BEA Weblogic, IBM Websphere and Oracle 10g Application Server is the notion of thread pools which serve to bind the number of threads associated with a service. Thread pools dispatch to a bounded pool of threads. When all threads within a pool are busy processing requests, outstanding requests are queued until a thread within the pool becomes free.

Many application servers may dedicate a fixed number of threads (sometimes configurable) to handle incoming client connections. When the service has more connections than it can handle, additional clients that attempt to connect may be dropped even though additional worker threads may be free. In this situation, the perceived performance from the client may be dramatically different than the performance of the actual service.

Most communication between service consumer and the services themselves will use the TCP/IP protocol. When the service cannot handle additional connections, it may simply ignore the request and not provide any response back to the client. The client in this situation will usually know that the service is unavailable based solely on network level timeouts. In situations, where the connection was processed but the transmission of the request is overloaded due to unavailability of worker threads this may also result in a rapid decline of perceived service response time.

The TCP/IP protocol uses an exponentially increasing timeout value for retransmitting connection attempts (SYN) and will result in long connection delays on the part of clients. This will also have the added effect of providing good response times to those who are already connected while penalizing those clients who have not yet connected.

An enterprise SOA should always prioritize client access based on business policies.

Use of thread pools themselves requires choosing the right size for bounding. The vast majority of application servers allow for an administrator to statically define the maximum number of threads within the pool. Defining the thread pool with too few threads will result in underutilization of server resources and not providing maximum throughput. By defining thread pools too high, will result in severe degradation of response times and server resources under heavy utilization.

Usage of thread pools in many environments may also result in the consumption of all available threads with long-running requests which will prevent requests that consume fewer resources to be turned around quickly. It will also starve requests that are of a higher priority. Many application servers will solve the former problem by segmenting pools based on the type of request but do not necessarily provide a solution to the latter.

The usage of queuing via dispatching may help in some situations but since most implementations of queues use first-in, first-out (FIFO), there is no ability to support the prioritization of requests based on either business priority or resource requirements. The dispatcher approach is also limited in that it cannot preempt a busy thread for another thread that contains a request that uses less resources or of higher business priority.

A clever enterprise developer may be able to develop a framework that solves for the threading issues discussed to date, but this would be missing the entire point. The author team recommends leveraging existing frameworks and application servers where appropriate but to consider alternative approaches to commonly used techniques that were held over from client/server, J2EE Blueprints and other paradigms of the past.

5. Alternative Pattern-Based Approaches

One approach that can be used to develop intra-service communications is to consider leveraging several commonly used design patterns such as:

- Strategy,
- Chain of Responsibility,
- Interpreter,
- Flyweight, and
- Memento.

For additional information on design patterns, we recommend Shalloway and Trott (2004).

5.1. Strategy Pattern

The intent of the strategy pattern is to define a family of algorithms, encapsulate each one and make them interchangeable. The strategy pattern lets the algorithm vary independently from the services that use it. The implementation of a strategy usually uses internal variables to record the state of the algorithm and may also keep the results in this structure.

If services have potentially generic routines embedded within them such as determining business priority and/or resource utilization handling, at a minimum it becomes difficult to re-use these algorithms and dynamically exchange them. Use of the strategy pattern will allow new strategies to become pluggable and assist in decoupling different layers of functionality. Strategies will also allow you to vary your choice of policy at run-time.

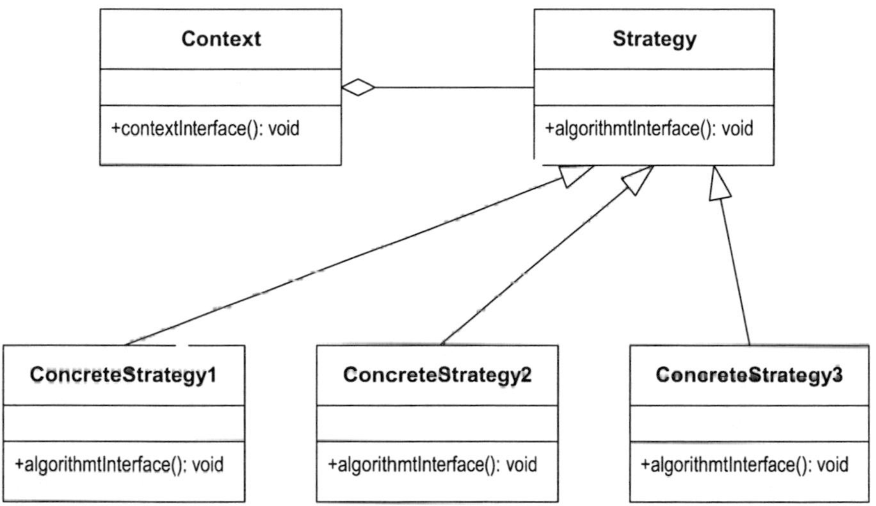

Figure 3. **Strategy Pattern**

Usage of the strategy pattern for queuing and resource access can allow the prioritization of requests based on resource consumption and business priority.

5.2. Chain of Responsibility Pattern

The intent of the chain of responsibility pattern is to help avoid coupling the sender of a request to its receiver by giving more than one object a chance to handle the request. Objects are placed in a chain and the request is passed to each object until one decides to handle it. The number and types of objects that can handle the request are not known at design time and thus can be configured dynamically. The approached used to chain objects typically use recursive composition to allow an unlimited number of objects (handlers) to be linked together.

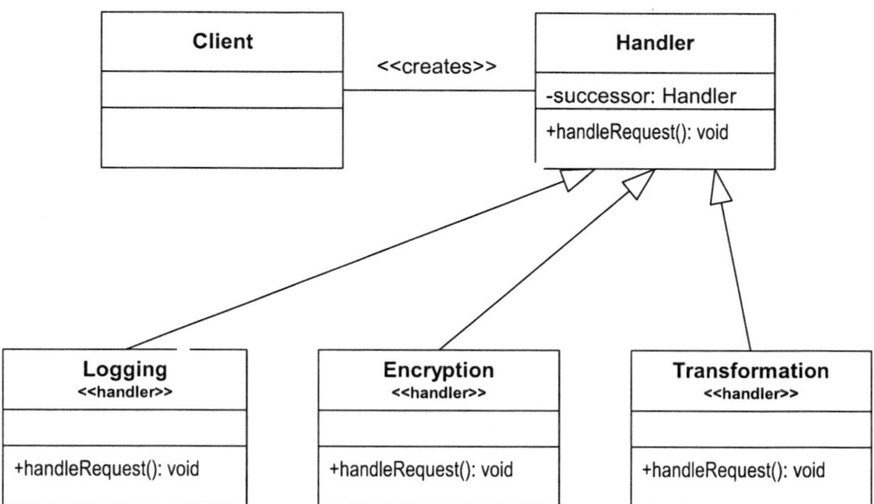

Figure 4. **Chain of Responsibility**

Chain of responsibility reduces communication and connections between objects. Each sender keeps a single reference to the head of the chain, while each receiver keeps a single reference to its immediate successor in the chain.

Generic handlers can be developed to commonly used functionality without requiring changes to underlying services. This approach is used by .NET remoting to implement the concept of channels. The client will make a method call that gets passed to a formatter sink that handles serialization of the request over the wire. In turn the receiver uses a transport sink to receive all incoming requests. The transport sink further passes along requests to the formatter sink which deserialize the request which passes it to a dispatcher sink which in turn makes the actual method call and returns the results to the client back through the chain.

Use of the chain of responsibility in a services paradigm can be used to add additional processing steps into a service call without requiring recompilation and can be done to handle business policies. Technical features such as logging, encryption, translations, load-balancing and replication are ideally implemented using this approach.

5.3. Interpreter Pattern

The intent of the interpreter pattern is given a language to define a representation for its grammar along with an interpreter that uses the representation to interpret sentences in the language.

Interpreter is best used in situations where your problem domain can be expressed as a mini-language. Typically, the interpreter will translate each instruction by assigning a grammar rule to a designated class. Rules about production can be defined as objects, instead of classes that result in lighter weight code processing.

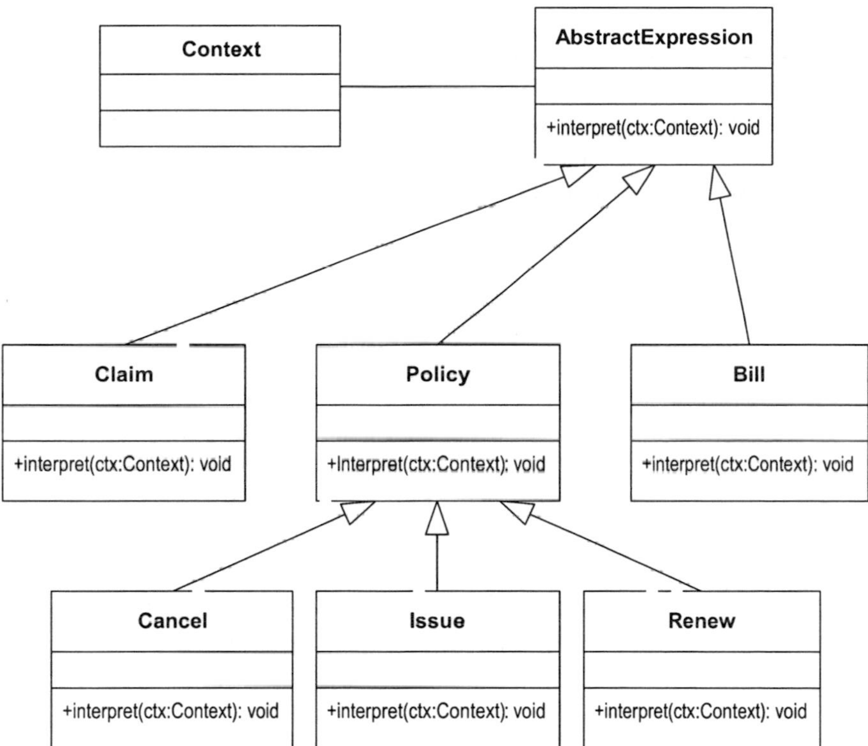

Figure 5. **Interpreter Pattern**

When services use the interpreter pattern, they can interpret the incoming request and effectively use switch-based processing instead of threading to handle requests. Interpreter pattern is used to take requests and determine which queue a request should be placed. Ideally it is used with a multiple queue approach or in situations where incoming messages contain hints of actual business priority within the message payload itself. Logic can be processed and tuned via configuration over time without requiring recompilation.

In Figure 3, the UML class diagram demonstrates a small portion of a policy administration system that could be used within the insurance industry. Using this approach, a developer could quickly add additional functionality such as supporting endorsements (additional coverages) that are not part of the standard policy process by implementing it in a separate class without requiring changes to other aspects of the system.

5.4. Flyweight Pattern

The intent of the flyweight pattern is to use sharing to support large numbers of fine-grained objects efficiently. Since many SOAs use XML, the flyweight pattern can be applied to the message in situations where the same information is included at many different points in a document. If the same data contained within the document is repeated at multiple locations and the data changes, every occurrence of the data must be located and updated.

The flyweight pattern has the potential to increase performance but is sometimes counter-intuitive to object-oriented design. Principles of object orientation usually suggest that it is best to encapsulate everything within an object so they can be uniformly accessed, extended and re-used. Within a large enterprise, there exist thousands of potential objects. The time to properly model all the potential objects combined with the run-time performance of them, will almost guarantee sub par performance. The approach of everything is an object was implemented in several languages including Smalltalk. From a purist's perspective, it allowed near perfect architectures but fell apart in performance. Modern languages such as Java and C# understand this simple truth and provide a mixed implementation of both objects and intrinsic types.

In Figure 6, we show the relationship between pools of objects for a stock quoting service. The quoting service needs to respond to quotes in a timely manner. There is data that experiences lots of changes (market pricing, highs and lows) as well as data that is relatively static (such as institutional investors, which indexes it is part of, or if the security is an index, which securities are contained within it and so on).

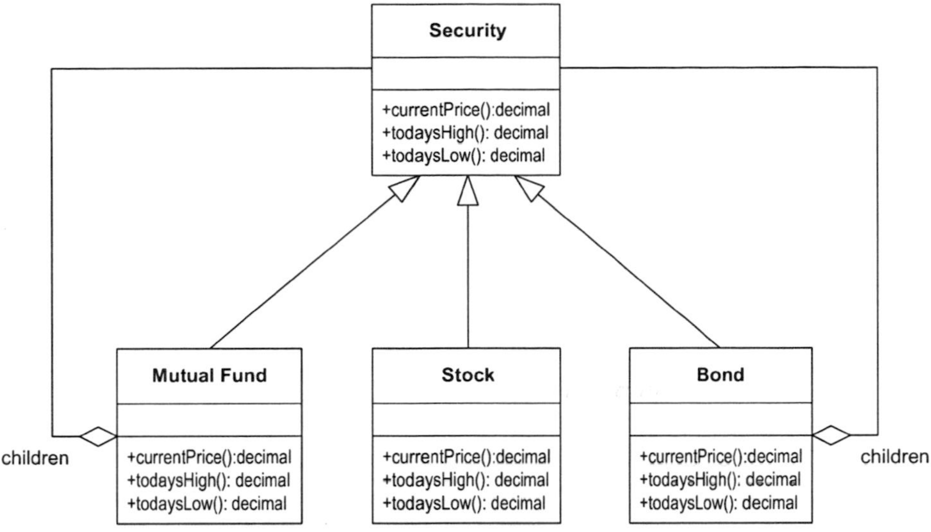

Figure 6. **Flyweight Pattern**

5.5. Memento Pattern

The memento pattern can be used to provide solutions to multiple problems with increasing concurrency.

The first usage of the memento pattern is in the development of a scheduler that figures out optimal utilization of resources as an alternative to FIFO-based queuing. The scheduler can implement an optimization routine that requires no knowledge of the internal implementation details of resource or how a particular schedule involving those resources is evaluated. The routine can simply be supplied with a sequence of requests to be executed and returns a weighting representing the quality of the proposed execution path. It can also reorder the sequence of requests and try again to see if it can get a better weighting. The optimizer may determine scheduling based on prior knowledge of how long previous tasks took to run. The problem becomes evaluating sequences from the beginning each time. The optimizer can choose to evaluate the state periodically and store a memento which then becomes the equivalent up to the corresponding point in the sequence and will allow optimization execute significantly faster.

The quote system referenced using flyweights can also leverage mementos. The quote system may maintain current information on thousands of securities. As we previously mentioned, some of this information changes frequently while other aspects are relatively static. When a quote is requested for a particular security, a

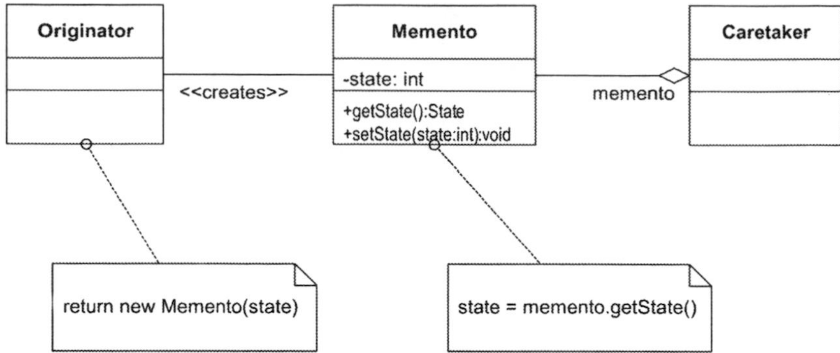

Figure 7. **Memento Pattern**

template is used to provide formatting of the output of the response. The memento pattern in this situation can take the data elements that have changed, encapsulate the translator state and store it requiring us to only retranslate a subset of the response.

Another usage of mementos may be in situations where the framework has the ability to preempt currently running tasks. The framework can swap out currently existing tasks and store them to persistent storage. If it is running in context of a chain of responsibility, it can also implement check pointing type functionality whereby the framework provides a cache of every n-th request of a particular type allowing checkpoint restart.

6. Language Specific Constructs

Many modern languages use a virtual machine paradigm and prevent developers from creating unstable applications via the usage of pointers. Instead, they dereference actual memory address access via objects and performance cleanup on memory using garbage collection approaches. Typical approaches to development when incorporating event-driven approaches may in many situations result in resource starvation. Let us look at three language specific constructs that are useful in an event-driven paradigm:

1. Soft References,
2. Forking, and
3. Non-blocking I/O.

6.1. Soft References

In the example of our stock quoting service, we had references to thousands of objects. In situations where memory is stressed, we do not want the service to not respond nor return an error to the end user. We also would like to avoid out of memory exceptions whenever possible. In the design of the stock quoting service, it can use reference objects to create a situation in which the garbage collector can reclaim individual security objects when heap memory runs low.

Our scheduler can implement a form of a reference queue to create a situation where it is notified when a certain object or set of objects are reachable only through reference objects. Upon notification, the scheduler can proceed with clean-up operations, checkpoint state, deserialize other dependent objects within the chain and make them eligible for garbage collection as well.

Java provides three different forms of references:

1. Soft,

2. Weak, and

3. Phantom.

Soft references are used in Java applications in situations where there are lots of fine grained cached type objects and not knowing in advance if the service will actually re-use cache entries. If the garbage collector reclaims objects that are softly referenced usually do to lack of access over an extended period, the service will need to recreate the object. Using soft references will allow a service to become aware of its own resources. Additionally, within most virtual machines, the garbage collector is required to clear all software references before throwing an Out of Memory Error.

Weak references are usually used in services that need to hold a reference to an immutable object and may contain supplemental information about it. Our stock quoting service may have an index constructed as a composite object that holds multiple weak references to underlying securities that make up the index. If the weak reference to an individual security gets destroyed, the index can be notified of this event and perform any required cleanup of the associated object which could range from displaying an older cached price to displaying a message that current pricing is unavailable.

Phantom references are not recommended for usage in services and therefore not discussed.

6.2. Forking

In certain situations, instead of taking on the difficult task of creating multithreaded services, especially if you are not using an application server that provides a framework, a simplistic approach may be to create new processes dynamically based on load. Web servers such as Apache use this approach to create highly scalable, fair processing HTTP services.

The ability to create new processes based on incoming requests provides the capability to use third-party non-thread safe libraries for services. Creation of new processes per request will also provide a level of isolation for each request so that if a problem arises with a single request, it will not with others.

Services that use forking techniques will have a single control process that is responsible for launching child processes which listen for connections and service client requests directly. The control process will also maintain several idle server processes so that clients do not need to wait for new child processes to be forked.

Fork is a feature of most operating systems that creates a new process. A forked process will inherit various properties from its parent process.

6.3. Non-Blocking I/O

Event-driven architectures place an important limitation on event-handling code by requiring it to be short and run to completion. When threads of execution process event handlers, they must avoid stalling processing and should ensure equality of execution across a large number of requests. This is best accomplished using asynchronous non-blocking I/O. I/O can be incorporated at multiple layers including when consumers connect to the service (sockets), to when the service writes files to disk (asynchronous file systems).

Java provides non-blocking I/O support via the java.nio package.

When comparing the various resources used in a computing environment such as CPU, Memory, Disk and I/O, I/O has been traditionally the hardest to optimize. I/O features of most general purpose operating systems were designed to provide maximum transparency to applications at the expense of being able to determine predictable behavior and a sometimes not so insignificant hit to scalability.

Even with the availability of commodity hardware such as Intel, free operating systems such as Linux and large hard drives generally available from Wal-Mart, enterprises still manage to not only keep their mainframes, but upgrade them on a frequent basis. Mainframes still exist as viable platforms to build services, not due to their blazing speed of execution (not!) nor the ability to support COBOL, but in their ability to handle I/O better than any other computing platform.

Mainframe architectures have had the ability to virtualize hardware resources, which is now only starting to become enterprise-class on other platforms. Most operating systems do not provide the ability for any applications to participate in enterprise-wide resource management decisions as services will typically execute across process and sometimes even server boundaries. The only implementation that the author team is aware of that affords this capability is IBM's Workload Manager.

6.4. Enterprise Service Bus

The concept of an Enterprise Service Bus (ESB) is a key component of an Enterprise SOA. Some will think it is a product that can be acquired from a vendor while others will think it is a set of standards (this is closer to the right answer) while those in the know, understand it is really about infrastructure capability that can be built in-house using tools and technologies that you may already own.

The Enterprise Service Bus support message and event-based interactions amongst services in heterogeneous environment while providing guaranteed delivery and queuing capabilities. The enterprise service bus provides multiple levels of infrastructure support to services including:

- Separation of transport (communication protocols) from service implementation to stress both location transparency and interoperability.
- Governance around the creation of implementation-independent service interfaces.
- Definition of services themselves that provide encapsulation of existing business functionality.

Enterprise SOA mandates that both applications and infrastructure support SOA principles. At the infrastructure level, SOA involves provisioning of the capabilities to route and deliver service requests to the correct service provider. The infrastructure must also support the ability to substitute one service implementation for another without clients being aware of the change from either an interface or response time perspective. In order for this goal to be achieved, clients must be able to invoke services in a way that invocation is independent of the service location and the transport used.

Many enterprise service buses can be implemented on top of existing messaging infrastructures but may require changes in how they are thought about and implemented. Traditional messaging infrastructures were described as hub-and-spoke architectures while services are usually described in a distributed fashion. In reality, the real problem space is the requirement of centralized control and distributed infrastructure.

The bus provides common interface to both consumers and providers as shown in Figure 8 as well as a centralized administration capability to control service addressing and naming. The consumer never directly binds to a provider and therefore both can involve independently of each other.

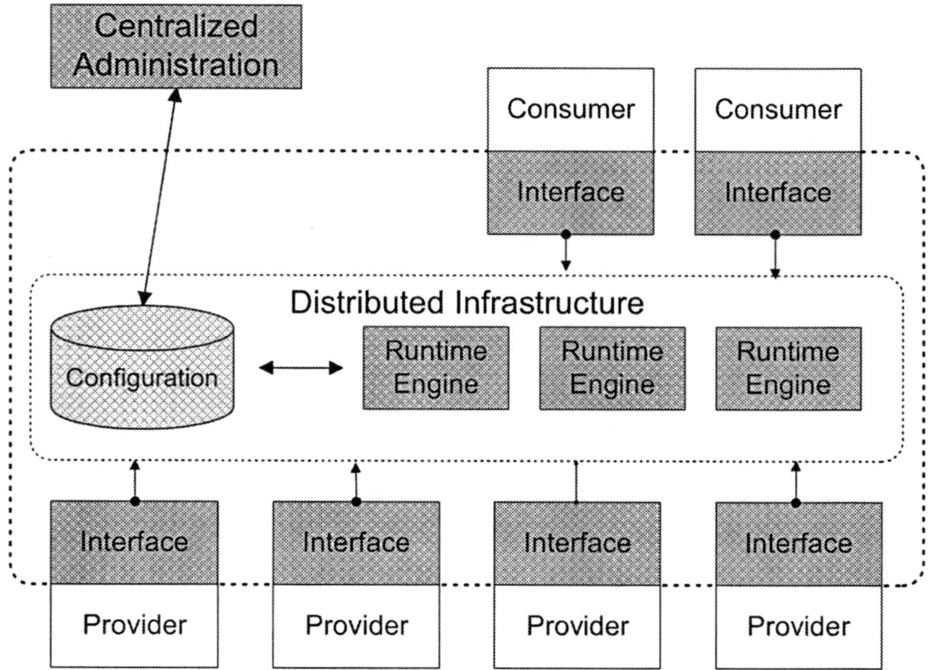

***Figure 8.* Logical View of Enterprise Service Bus**

The bus will usually support at least one form of message such as request/response, publish/subscribe, one-way and so on. It will also provide capabilities to support multiple transport protocols such as HTTP and JMS-based communications methods with the option of plugging in additional transports. Finally the bus may expose an interface to legacy applications without requiring them to create their own. Usually this is accomplished through various integration methods such as Java 2 Connectors, third-party adapters or proprietary protocols such as Siebel's EAN.

The ability to make many existing enterprise applications understand a common message format so they can participate in enterprise-level integrations is futile. The enterprise also has data stored within spreadsheets, flat files and other forms that would be ideal to incorporate but becomes challenging to wrap. The enterprise also must consider integration with current XML standards such as SWIFT, ACORD, Parlay and others where they are represented in XML but are not widely adopted and/or do not have standardized representations.

Loose coupling is formed by decoupling all interactions between consumer and provider and goes beyond typical point-to-point integration provided by basic web services. Basic web services provide zero centralized administration capability to control service addressing and/or naming. Service names are administered by each exposed service interface and routing is determined by the consumer's proxy interface.

Consumers typically know the address of specific service implementations and directly bind to them using specific protocols at specific addresses. Many enterprises have been smart by requiring all services to be published in a centralized registry (such as UDDI) but this is limited in that clients may still cache endpoints and there is no standard that forces clients to periodically query the registry for changes (such as leases) nor by avoiding the registry altogether and simply retrieving the WSDL directly. Substitution of one service for another becomes difficult and may even require changes to service consumer logic.

The bus can also implement functionality in a centralized manner to multicast events to multiple service endpoints. If a particular service is offline, it can optionally queue requests until the provider comes back online. Since the consumer and producer are not aware of each other, the bus can provide value added services such as implementing callbacks, notifications, publish and subscribe and the ability to have long-lived transactions. A consumer and provider interact with each other by simply placing events on the bus and continue processing without blocking.

Since both clients and services interact directly with the bus and not each other, the bus can provide admission control functionality and can even implement functionality to ensure that all services receive the same message at the same time or can prioritize service requests based on who the service consumer is and other business policies.

For additional information on ESB, check out Keen et al. (2004).

6.5. Callbacks

Many event-based applications under the hood implement implicit invocation of underlying services and limit asynchronous behavior at the service entry point. Usually this occurs because event-based services make correctness reasoning more difficult than simple procedural approaches. The ability to achieve further asynchronous behavior within the service can be accomplished by allowing a service to register a public interface for implementing callbacks.

Applications that subscribe to the principles of event-driven architectures when they cannot complete an operation immediately will register a callback and defer processing to a later time. Event-driven applications may poll for events and execute the appropriate callback when the event occurs. Callbacks can be done at the service interface or can even be implemented at each of the layers within an application.

> *A callback is a function that will be invoked whenever an event is received.*

When a consumer of the service contacts a service provider and the request cannot complete in real-time, the client may indicate a return address it wants the reply to the service request to be sent. If an application decides to implement callbacks at each layer in the software stack, it may decide to drive application logic by a loop that polls for events and executes the appropriate callback when the event occurs. Callback processing can execute indivisibly until a blocking operation occurs. Once a blocking operation happens, the layer processing the particular event will simply register a new callback and return control to the caller.

7. Finite State Machines

Finite State Machines (FSM) are used to model the behavior of a system that contains a limited number of defined conditions and transitions. The notion of state is actually encompassed into many applications. Each application may start with an initial state that change over time as it begins to service requests from end users. At any point in time, an application can be viewed a complex set of states. State machines have the following attributes:

- A description of the initial state.
- A set of input and output events.

- A set of states.
- Functions that map states and input to output.
- Functions that map states and inputs to states (This is known as state transition).
- Rules or conditions that must be met to allow a state transitions.

Finite state machines are limited in that they have a limited number (finite) of possible states. It is possible, but not practical to construct an infinite state machine due to the inability to define infinite transitions and the rules that must be met between them.

Finite state machines use an initial state as a starting point and keep track of the current state based on the last state transition. Input events serve as triggers which cause a rule or condition to fire that govern transition from the current state to future state. Finite state machines are traditionally used in artificial intelligence applications and services and whenever semantic networks are constructed.

Finite state machines are similar to rules-based approaches in many ways. For example, if all the antecedents of a rule is true then the rule is fired. Only one rule can fire at a time. If the potential for multiple rules to fire exists, then a conflict resolution strategy is required to determine which individual rule to select. This ultimately results in a state transition.

State may involve one or more actions.

Finite state machines may be implemented using the controller paradigm which serves as a switching mechanism for incoming events. Worker threads serve the controller by evaluating current state by execution of switch (case) statements and the resulting code for that state is executed. During the execution, one or more actions may be performed and all state transitions are noted. The controller may also implement pre-processing steps on the input for validation and security purposes and post-processing steps for auditing purposes.

The diagram in Figure 9 represents a simplistic view of placing an order via the stock market. A broker will list the stock order on a stock exchange where the order will be listed. The order may have preprocessing validation steps to validate elements of the order such as whether the stock trades in fractions or decimals, whether the ticker symbol is valid and if the exchange itself trades the specified security. Once the order has been accepted by the respective exchange, it stays valid for a period of 60 days (exchange rules) and if not executed within this time period may be automatically

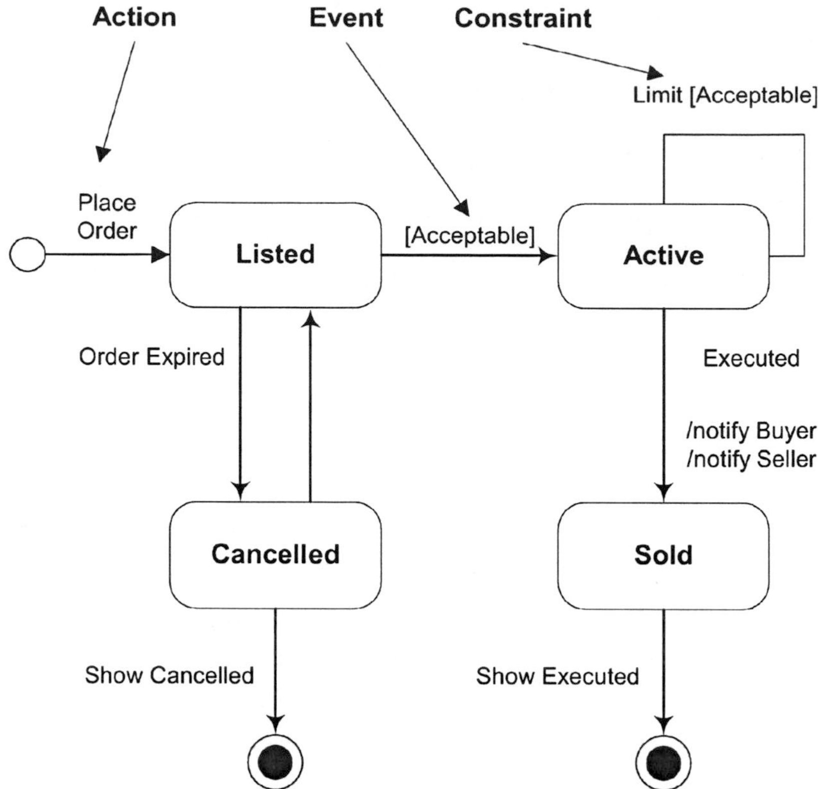

Figure 9. **State Transition Diagram**

cancelled. Likewise, if the order is executed, both buying and selling parties are notified and the clearing process begins.

Finite state machines are used in two different manners. First, the finite state machine specifies the type of operations which may be invoked on a service request. Any resulting transitions that are triggered will invoke the desired operation. This allows the service requester to invoke the operation at that point. In this scenario, the state machine does not specify the behavior of any service requests and resulting operations but merely records the change of state and determines which operations can be invoked.

Finite state machines can also specify the complete behavior of its context (such as a business process). In this scenario, Service consumers can send requests to the owner of the state machine (can be an orchestration engine, ESB or composite service) which the state machines receives the event and determines what the outcome will be by attaching actions to transitions complete specifications of operations are determined.

Finally, finite state machines can be deterministic or non-deterministic. Deterministic finite state machines work on the principle that the next state is uniquely determined by a single input event. Non-deterministic finite state machines not only depend on the current input event, but rely on an arbitrary number of future input events. Until these future events occur, it is impossible to determine the state the finite state machine is in.

Finite state machines can become complex over time and introduce difficult to code behaviors even with a few states. The optimal architecture for the enterprise assumes that there will be multiple distinct implementations of a finite state machine each with a specific task. One analogy to draw a parallel to is in the military. The decision-making processes that are used for launching airplanes off the flight deck of a carrier are distinct in nature from how the United States Marines may protect an embassy under siege.

For additional information on finite state machines, see Lawson (2003).

8. Event Notification

Event notification is similar to publish/subscribe in several ways but can also be considered its big brother. Publish/subscribe has been around for several decades and is based on the paradigm of message routing. Messages are delivered to receivers based on a set of criteria related to either metadata contained within the message or the message content. The message sender has no awareness of message receivers and the forwarding and delivery of messages is handled by middleware such as CORBA.

One or more notifications are emitted by an event producer and received or retrieved by one or more event consumers possibly through a broker.

Event notification unlike publish/subscribe adheres to a contract and uses the notion of an event-sink to request asynchronous delivery of specific events from an event source. Events can be considered an advanced form of callbacks in that they can leverage two different models: the push model and pull model.

The push model allows for suppliers of events to push an event into the event channel which is delivered to all consumers who registered interest in a specified event. The pull model occurs when the consumer of a service requests an event from the event channel which in turns requests the event from the supplier.

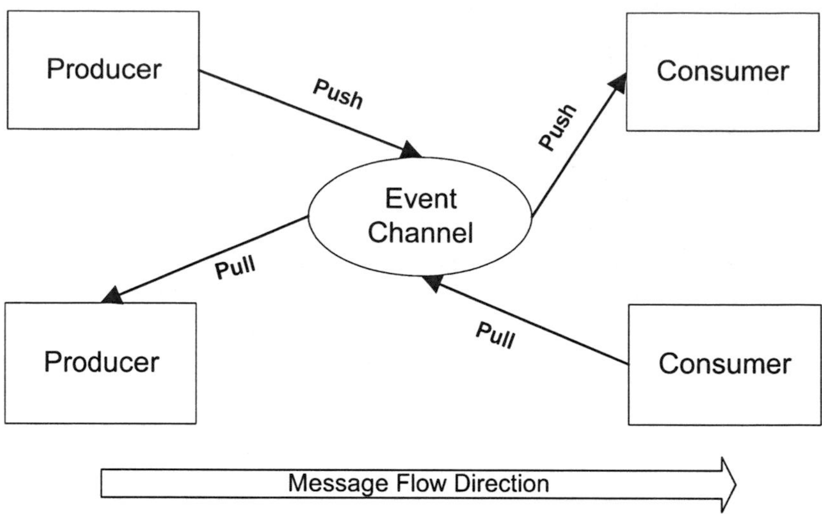

***Figure 10.* Push and Pull Models**

> *A channel is a proxy to the producer and consumer*

The notification model extends basic event handling by providing reliability, priority, expiry, earliest delivery time, maximum events per consumer, throttling and can even implement policies related to message delivery order or when messages such be discarded.

Notification services unlike events may implement policies that specify the order in which events are delivered including:

- Any order,
- First in First Out,
- Deadline,
- Business Priority, and
- Last in First Out.

Alternatively, may decide to implement a discard policy that tells it when to throw away messages. The stock order entry service may use this approach for consumers who request trades on various securities and choose to cancel the order if it cannot execute it within five seconds or other arbitrary number according to business policy.

Throttling allows a registered consumer or provider to not become overloaded in the event of unanticipated messages. Functionality of throttling may be implemented to specify the maximum amount of time events in a sequence will be collected before being delivered to an event consumer. This will allow service providers and consumers to make intelligent choices in optimizing usage of resources. For example, if a service uses a relational database that is low on memory and multiple queries for a particular customer are batched, the service will be able to respond faster as much of the data may already be in the database server's cache.

By using notification approaches, consumers are no longer tightly coupled to service providers. In fact, the only form of coupling that can exist in this model between consumer and service provider comes from actual subscription information in the form of a contract being shared amongst channels. Suppliers of events have the ability to query the channel for the desired event types desired by consumers. A supplier should not create events to place on the channel if no consumer has registered an interest in them. Consumers can also determine when new event types are being offered by suppliers so that can subscribe to new events as they become available.

The subscription mechanism will help reduce network traffic and the load on the infrastructure by ensuring that only traffic that is intended to be consumed will be produced. This helps in situations where providers may be sending out spurious events that no one actually desires.

Subscribers can alternatively use subscriptions to group one or more topics from publishers. The range of topics can be categorized in a tree like fashion where the subscriber can express an interest in a portion of the tree instead of each individual element. Publishers can provide notifications to subscribers to receive information on descendant topics without having prior knowledge of their existence.

8.1. Brokered Notification

Brokered notification allows publication of messages from entities that are not themselves service providers and includes standard message contracts and exchanges that allow both providers and consumers to participate in brokered interactions.

An event broker is an entity which routes notifications. Brokers typically aggregate and publish events from other producers. An event broker can also apply some transformation to the notifications it processes.

Brokers will be typically used in building of configurations where intermediaries are used to communicate with external parties in a federated fashion. Brokers within a federation can ideally implement sharing of administrative workload increasing scalability of all members within a federation.

8.2. Security Concerns

Event-driven architectures pose additional concerns above and beyond security mechanisms discussed so far. For example, notification messages themselves can contain empty bodies which should be signed so that content cannot be added by third-parties in transit.

The authors strongly recommend that all communications between services leverage strong message level authentication and encryption.

Depending upon the frequency of message exchange, different approaches to message security may be warranted. One off and low volume message exchanges can use public key infrastructure (PKI) for ensuring the integrity and confidentiality between publisher and consumer but will run into scalability and performance issues when volume increases. For high volume event-driven interactions, a better approach is to consider establishment of a secure context for events by incorporating the notion of trust.

The authors recommend implementation of WS-Trust and WS-SecureConversation for high performance event-driven architectures.

In addition to traditional attacks such as impersonation, message alteration or the ability for third-parties to intercept/read data not intended for them, event-driven also creates additional risk including but not limited to:

- Message Order alteration,
- Availability attacks,
- Replay, and
- Redirection Attacks.

8.3. Message Order Alteration

Imagine a situation where an event-driven approach is used in a stock trading scenario where a read-only message such as the price of a specified stock is allowed to reach selected parties before others. In this particular situation, the party that receives the message even ten seconds before another party has a potential advantage. On the receipt of bad news, the party may be able to sell their shares for less of a loss than parties receiving the message later. For a stock that is quickly rising in price, the first party may be able buy the stock cheaper than other parties and make more money.

The ability to protect against message order alteration is difficult and may require a mechanism for which no current specifications are provided. In this particular situation, one may have to resort to proprietary implementations of secured reliable delivery channels and other mechanisms.

8.4. Availability Attacks

Reliable delivery is also subject to a variety of attacks. Processing overhead for reliable delivery is higher than for general communication channels and therefore can be used to overload the services network with useless messages whose sole purpose is disruption. If the intent is to disrupt the network from processing messages in a timely manner, this can be accomplished by injecting certificates that have deep recursive relationships with other certificate authorities or by establishing authentication requests and immediately disconnecting since authentication is almost always synchronous in nature.

Availability attacks are difficult to secure but can be minimized by ensuring that the architecture takes into consideration the amount of state information maintained and that it is saved prior to any authentication related sequences.

8.5. Replay Attacks

In event-driven architectures, protection against messages being replayed is vital and is predicted to be the most popular of attacks. Replay attacks can easily be detected using mechanisms such as including a timestamp in the header along with a sequence identifier. Downstream services can decide to process only messages within a certain window of time and additionally keep track of not only whether a particular identifier was used but in what order it was received.

8.6. Redirection Attacks

Consider a situation in which a service is restricted to which consumers it can respond to. If an attacker can identify a naïve service, it can have it send the data contained within the response to the naïve service. The attacker could then potentially use the callback URL itself or even a message ID to encode the information it wishes to gain access to.

Redirection can also be used to launch attacks and have the attacker cover its tracks. Let us say that the quote service has a flaw in how it handles large messages (buffer overflow) but also register a callback URL of another machine resulting in the downstream service also potentially getting corrupted data and/or getting into an endless loop.

Redirection attacks cannot be prevented by simple access control lists that state who is authorized to access the service. In order to secure against this type of attack, the security policy will need to be extended to also support the ability to specify where responses can be authorized to be sent. Minimally, each service would need to be designed where the services themselves exchange authorization information before the entire message is sent (authorization should not be in the message itself).

Redirection attacks can also allow for hijacking of credentials. It becomes important that credentials are not transitive and can only be read by consumer and provider. This requires that both consumer and provider use the same security provider or that security providers are federated. Security in this situation should incorporate some form of hashing algorithm.

If you want your services to experience hijacking, the best way to accomplish this is by having developers be clever (being sarcastic here) in creating their own authentication schemes such as inspecting headers and comparing IP addresses to a list of known hosts.

To learn more about security, we recommend Ferguson and Schneier (2003).

9. Practical Considerations

Enterprises cannot realistically rewrite all of their applications, expose them all as services, incorporate all the events, and change them to exactly match all the business processes in a timely cost-effective manner so prioritization becomes crucial. The authors have constructed a simple straightforward approach to prioritization and have put them into four simple classifications:

1. Return on Investment (Bang for the buck),
2. Canonical Form,

3. Integration, and
4. Retirement.

9.1. Return on Investment

The first and foremost rule of an enterprise SOA is that it must provide business value. Value can be calculated in terms of making the cost of individual projects cheaper (internal rate of return) used to provide connectivity to external parties and to allow them access to internal applications or enabling a 360-degree view of the customer from a supply chain perspective. Regardless of the driving factor for SOA adoption, all decisions should be prioritized based on a stated objective of achieving a return on investment.

The ability to realize increased return on investment usually starts by modeling interactions from the customer perspective. For example, when an order for widgets is received via a Customer Relationship Management (CRM) application, this event can trigger other events such as payment systems, supply chain applications, inventory, resource scheduling and the general ledger in a loosely coupled manner allowing the enterprise to have an up-to-the-minute understanding from the customer perspective.

9.2. Canonical Form

The word canonical historically meant "according to religious law" but when applied to computing simply indicates a standard way of writing a formula. For example, the below HTML snippets are said to be equivalent because they mean the same thing, but could be interpreted differently depending upon who is consuming.

```
<color>white</color>
```

Code 2. HTML Example One

```
<color>rgb(255,255,255)</color>
```

Code 3. HMTL Example Two

The need to have message exchanges (especially XML-based) not only subscribe to syntactic standards but a specification also describing the physical representation, the canonical form is required. The requirement for canonical form aids not only in interoperability but is a fundamental component to many XML-based security schemes.

Enterprises that adopt a common and ideally industry-defined data model for business events which allows them to isolate their systems not only from each other but also ensures future interoperability. An enterprise having one common model allows change to occur in one system and the only change required is the particular interaction. Wherever appropriate, enterprises should not only use industry standard models, but should actively participate in their creation.

Enterprises wherever possible should not only use industry standard models where appropriate, but should actively participate in their creation.

If the canonical data model is defined in XML, the ability to convert between canonical form and internal implementations can be realized via simple XML transformations. The transformation can additionally be re-used in other parts of the enterprise allowing for additional interoperability.

To learn more about Canonical XML, visit http://www.w3.org/TR/xml-c14n.

9.3. Integration

Using an event-driven approach allows one to arbitrarily add additional applications into the supply chain without changing existing applications. New applications express an interest in specific enterprise-level messages and handle responses accordingly. This allows for the enterprise to add new applications at will and deal with previously unknown situations. Customizations to existing applications can also be accomplished in a loosely coupled manner.

9.4. Retirement

Taking event-driven approaches one step further will allow for the wholesale replacement of existing legacy applications with new ones. Minimally, when a consuming application doesn?t need to have understanding of the producing application will allow for its eventual replacement. Many enterprises desire to replace their CRM investments but are in a conundrum since upgrading costs are obscene. In this situation, the enterprise can replace the front-end of the CRM application using standards-based approaches such as portals and write a services wrapper on top of the CRM application to isolate changes in data.

The enterprise using this approach will first replace the front-end of the CRM application, working its way down the layers until it is able to wholesale replace the persistence tier. Event-driven architecture should be incorporated into any retirement strategy.

10. Summary

Event-driven architecture and service-oriented are distinct yet compatible concepts. The agile enterprise will require both. In constructing an enterprise service-oriented architecture, the enterprise will need to sense and respond to events as they occur rather than carry out predetermined processes developed using information based on historical occurrences.

In this chapter, we have learned how Service-Oriented Architectures provide the potential to improve the efficiency of IT systems and service offerings. While this book covered the technical know-how of how SOA can be realized, it is simply not enough to guarantee success. In order to be successful realizing an enterprise SOA one needs to be skilled in management and enterprise architecture. Enterprise SOA needs to be backed with the proper organizational structure, strong governance and agile software development approaches.

To learn more about governance, visit the IT Governance Institute at: http://www.itgi.org.

Enterprises that expect to use technology to gain and retain competitive advantage in the marketplace must adopt a business-driven event-based service-oriented architecture. Enterprises that have already started down the path have a distinct advantage over their peers. Enterprises that are just starting the journey to implementing an Enterprise SOA are well positioned to be fast followers. By learning from the experiences of others, their successes and failures, enterprises will be able to build the extended enterprise realizing the holy grail of lower total cost of ownership and business agility.

OUTTRO

How few there are who have courage enough to own their faults or resolution enough to mend them.
Benjamin Franklin

One of the most challenging aspects of writing a book on a vast topic like service-oriented architectures is knowing when the book should be published. Within the minds of most authors, books are never really complete. Authors are doubly challenged with the fact that they too may be consumers of books such as the one you hold in your hand. We too get upset when we spend our hard earned money and a book does not 100% answer all of our questions.

One of the challenges we faced while creating this book is whether it should cover topics of the moment that corporations are currently struggling with such as whether I should use SOAP internal to my enterprise. We took the stance, right or wrong that questions such as these are more appropriate for magazine articles and discussions with industry analyst firms. We felt that a book should not cover the issues of the minute but instead present information that is timeless in nature.

The authors also wanted to cover other aspects of service-oriented architectures but would have never finished the book if we kept adding to it. In order to be fair to both parties, we have decided to take a different approach. For purchasers of this book who register, we will be sending supplemental information in ebook format for no additional cost in hopes that we can not only meet your unstated desires in spending large sums of money to acquire knowledge, but to exceed it by leaps and bounds.

The ebook will discuss the following topics that are near and dear to your heart and criteria for success:

- Developing SOAs using the Enterprise Service Bus patterns,
- Integrating SOAs with Business Rules Engines,

- Extending Event-Driven Architecture to develop fault-tolerant SOA implementations,
- Case study on how SOA was used at a Fortune 100 enterprise in the insurance vertical to serve business partners and consumers, and
- A catalog of SOA architecture and design patterns.

In the meantime, if you have questions you would love answered, do not hesitate to ask. The author team has established a Yahoo Group at http://groups.yahoo.com/group/soabook for this purpose. Feel free to join and encourage others to participate ...

APPENDIX A: UNDERSTANDING DISTRIBUTED COMPUTING

Man has such a predilection for systems and abstract deductions that he is ready to distort the truth intentionally, he is ready to deny the evidence of his senses only to justify his logic
Fyodor Dostoevsky

The idea of service-oriented architectures have been around for over a decade and have been incorporated into many of the technologies that are pervasively used including the worldwide web, email and FTP. These concepts when applied to business, allow a new generation of enterprise applications to be created. SOA addresses many of the shortcomings in previous "old world" architectures based on monolithic independent applications.

Enterprises that leverage service-oriented architectures can bridge the traditional gap existing between business requirements and IT capabilities by providing the ability to find, bind and execute to providers of choice. SOA can help the enterprise with business goals that are based on technology in many ways including, but not limited to:

- Faster time to market,
- Less expensive application integration,
- Easier software construction,
- Ability to leverage existing IT investments, and
- And more ...

The rapid adoption of SOA is leading a shift in how enterprises leverage computing resources and deliver services to users. It is helping to provide tighter integration and alignment between business drivers and IT implementation. The ability unlock the assets contained with enterprise applications and provide the capability to mix and match services regardless of whether they reside within the enterprise or are provided by third-parties will allow IT to increase their own value to the enterprise.

Let us start with understanding the technical benefits of SOA and how it is based on the fundamentals of distributed computing.

1. Distributed Computing

Distributed computing is one key component in enabling the creation of the extended enterprise.The ability to have humans and systems interact with each other regardless if they reside within the same company or are located on the other side of the planet connected via the Internet has been a reality for many years now. The ability to interconnect systems via network using thousands of personal computers and various forms of networking technology has been commoditized.

Distributed computing is the ability to break down an application into discrete computing components that can be executed across a network of computers so they can work together to perform cooperative tasks. There are many approaches that can be used to accomplish this goal.

In this chapter, you will learn about the foundational principles used to distribute application execution across a network including:

- The anatomy of a distributed application.
- Remote Procedure Calls.
- Object Request Brokers.
- Transaction Monitors.
- Message-Oriented Middleware.

1.1. Anatomy of a Distributed Application

Distributed applications are constructed using layered approaches whereby each layer has a particular function. At the lowest level, the network layer provides connectivity to a group of computer so they can exchange information in a seamless manner. Use of pervasive industry standard protocols such as TCP/IP at the network layer provides packaging and addressing support for communicating to other applications that use the same network protocol. Higher-level services can be layered on top of the chosen network protocol, such as services that support security and directory services. By further extending this layer, a distributed application can be created that leverages lower layers to perform coordinated tasks across the network.

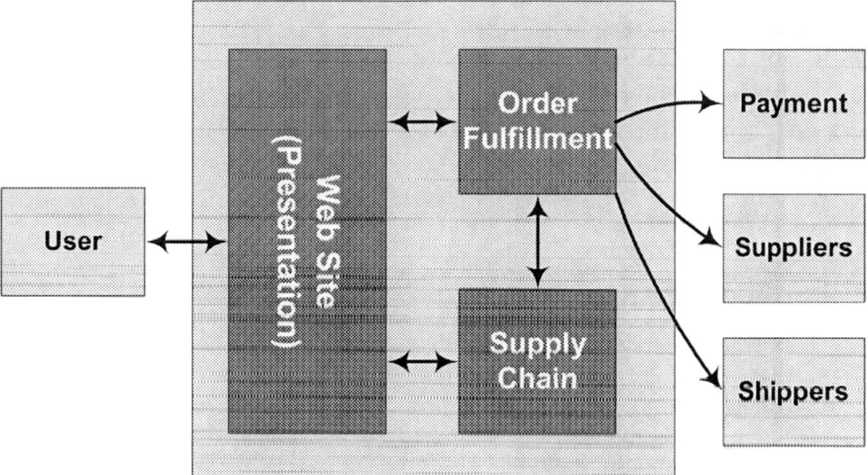

Figure 1. **Distributed Application**

Interoperability is increased when all of the layers use the same protocol. In a general sense, protocols define the sets of rules governing communication between nodes within a network. Protocols may specify timing, format, sequencing, error control, reliability, routing and security.

Each layer in a distributed application will specify its own set of rules for operation and data flow and therefore creates its own protocol.

Let us begin by taking a closer look at the foundation of a distributed application – the network layer.

1.1.1. Understanding the Network Layer

Fundamentals indicate that a computer network is simply a series of connections between computers and other network devices that allow them to communicate with each other. The size, speed, reliability and usage depend on the protocols and implementations used. Without protocol, networks would not successfully allow communication.

TCP/IP, one of the most widely used of protocols, actually is defined as a family of protocols in which TCP and IP are two. Protocols at the network layer were intentionally designed in a layered fashion and avoided monolithic approaches [typically seen at other layers. The original inventors of the TCP/IP protocol separated the suite of protocols into a discrete set of tasks with each layer that corresponds to a different facet of communication.

While implementations may blur the lines of actual layers to increase performance, the notion of layers at the TCP/IP are inherent within its architecture and is typically represented pictorially as a stack, as shown in Figure 2.

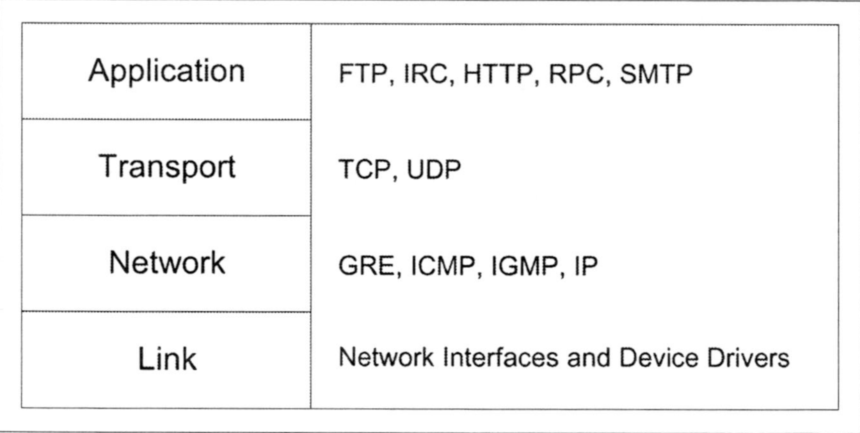

Application
FTP, IRC, HTTP, RPC, SMTP
Transport
TCP, UDP
Network
GRE, ICMP, IGMP, IP
Link
Network Interfaces and Device Drivers

Figure 2. **TCP/IP Protocol Layers**

The link layer is responsible for communicating with actual network hardware such as Ethernet cards. This layer transmits and receives data from the network and passes it along to the network layer. Likewise data received from the network layer is transmitted over the network by the link layer.

The network layer has responsibility for routing data to its destination. This layer is stateless and does not guarantee that data will reach its destination. Its sole responsibility is to decide where data should be sent. Because this layer is not concerned whether packets get to their final destination or the order in which packets arrive, its job is greatly simplified. If a packet arrives corrupted, the network layer simply discards it. The network layer requires that every network interface have a uniquely defined address. If the network layer is based on TCP/IP the uniquely defined address is known as the IP address.

The transport layer provides data flow (state) for the application layer where required. This layer performs guarantees of reliable delivery and ordering. Two of the more popular protocols in use at this layer are Transmission Control Protocol (TCP) and User Datagram Protocol (UDP). TCP provides end-to-end reliable communication. TCP creates virtual circuits between two processes and ensures that packets are received in the order they are sent (sequencing) and that lost packets are re-transmitted.

The application layer is where user applications interact with the network. Protocols such as Telnet, FTP, Email, IRC and others interoperate. Applications can use either/both TCP or UDP to communicate with other computers.

Let us look at a basic scenario on how TCP/IP is used within a Telnet application:

1. A user desires to connect to a machine via telnet named foxbat.soa.edu.
2. The machine name is converted via Domain Name Server (DNS) to an IP address (192.168.0.6).
3. Telnet informs the transport layer it wants to start a TCP connection with 192.168.0.6 on port 23.
4. TCP establishes a conversation with foxbat and uses IP to route packets.
5. Telnet retrieves a port number from the user's machine (say, 1742) and TCP places the source and destination ports in its packet header.
6. The packet is now handed to the network layer where IP routes the packet to the link layer.
7. The link layer takes the packet and places it on the network where it is transmitted via routers and switches to the Internet.
8. The process is repeated, one router at a time until it reaches the network segment in which foxbat is located on.
9. foxbat's TCP layer replies in a similar manner as outlined in step 8.
10. The telnet daemon on foxbat and the telnet client exchange terminal information and other parameters required for establishing an interactive session.

11. Control messages are sent in-band as an escape byte of 255 followed by a control byte. Control messages include: echo, status, terminal type, terminal speed, flow control, linemode and environment variables.

12. The user sees the login prompt from foxbat. After the login process is completed, data is sent back and forth until the session is terminated.

The benefit of layers, as originally envisioned by the inventors of TCP/IP, is that the network and transport layer would only have to be written once for each protocol. They would then provide a common interface to the network layer by writing different device drivers for each kind of network interface.

The principle of layering is pervasive in the vast majority of widely adopted architectures and adds simplicity. For TCP/IP, the transport layer provides a standard interface; network services that leverage the interface do not need to be rewritten or even recompiled if the transport layer code changes.

For more information on TCP/IP, see ftp://ftp.internic.net/rfc.

1.1.2. Building the Application Layer

In order to create a flexible component-based architecture that provides the ability to respond to increasingly complex business drivers and offer support to a diverse set of applications and service providers, use of a layered approach to constructing the application layer is warranted. Distributed applications as a core principle require logical partitioning of an application into at least three layers. A good approach to layering includes the separation of presentation, from business logic from data access and storage through controlled and managed interfaces.

In a simple distributed application, a client that provides the user interface communicates with a business logic layer. This layer may leverage an application server and custom-developed code that in turn communicates with either a database and/or file system that is responsible for storing application data.

Let us look at the function of each of these layers.

Presentation

The presentation layer includes the user interface to an application and can use either a rich or thin-client approach. Rich client interfaces provide full access to the underlying operating system user interface components. Thin clients leverage markup languages such as HTML and XML and provide benefits of portability and looser coupling at the expense of user interface expressiveness.

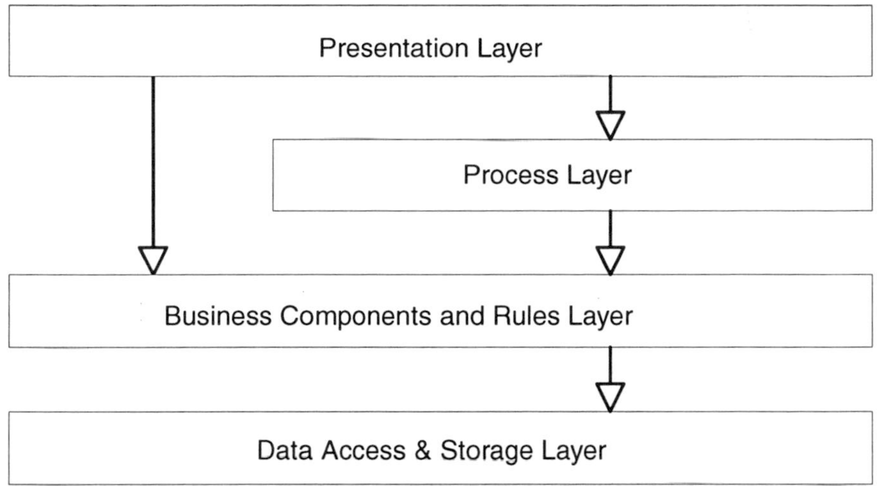

Figure 3. **Application Layer**

This layer may be implemented using the Model-view-controller architecture pattern to separate the business model (data and business logic), view (presentation code) and controller (response to user actions). If it uses a markup language, this layer can also provide additional inter-tier interaction. Examples of this may include embedding XML into HTML web pages.

One form of thin-client, web browsers not only understands loosely structured HTML but can also support XHTML, which is a well-formed version of HTML. Clients can receive XML and use XSLT to render XML into other markup formats including well-formed HTML. This approach provides separation of presentation from data. Alternative approaches include using of Cascading Style Sheets (CSS) that can be used by the thin-clients to present XML-based documents.

Business Logic/Services

The business logic layer incorporates your application's business logic and provides a well-defined interface to the presentation layer services. Business logic within many enterprises is typically hosted within an application server that allows the logic to support multiple simultaneous clients. The application servers themselves may also provide support for pooling of business logic in order to increase efficiency at run-time as well as protect selected portions of business logic from those who are not authorized to access specified processes.

In UML terms, the Actor can be a user interface (web browser, telephone, etc) or another system. The actor will issue a service request, which is defined as an event. This event is routed to the responsible business process component for execution

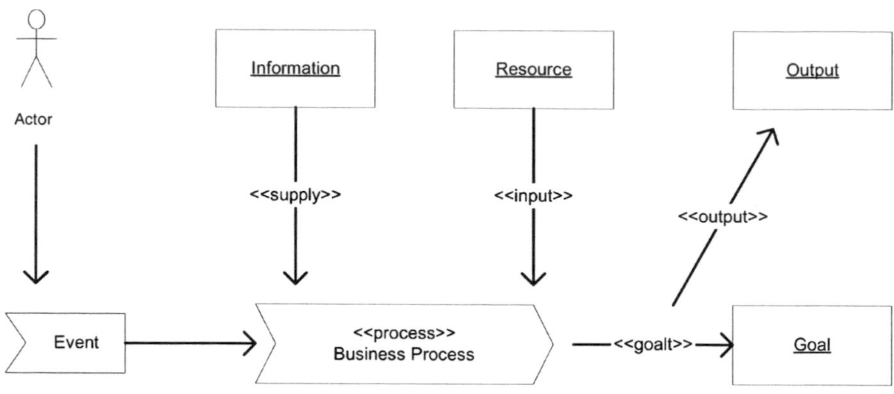

Figure 4. **Business Logic/Services**

and the results will be returned. The services tier is responsible for exposing business logic to client applications and hosts both business and technical services. Services are comprised of multiple components (hence component-based services) that expose common interfaces that are accessible via multiple clients.

Data Access and Storage

Data access and storage are usually part of the resource tier that mediates access to back-end systems of record that may include vendor packages such as Peoplesoft and Siebel, relational databases such as Oracle and legacy mainframe applications. Resources are exposed to various clients via the service tier.

Many relational databases provide the ability to take an XML document and persist it to normalized relational structures (shredding). This allows an application to work with self-describing well-formed XML documents while traditional tools that understand relational structure can also access the data directly increasing interoperability.

1.1.3. Operating System Components

An operating system provides its own set of services to applications and services that run on top of it. An operating system is responsible for providing scheduling and protection of multiple user processes ensuring equitable access to resources under its management.

Modern operating systems use a componentized approach in their own construction and operation. By understanding how operating systems work at a fundamental level, one can understand how applications and services that will execute on top of them can take advantage of the layered approach. Let us look at these three components.

Processes

A process is an instance of an application that is capable of running on one or more CPUs and contains a sequence of steps that the computer executes. A process also provides context that controls access to resources of the computer (CPU time, I/O, etc) via operating system calls. A process can initiate one or more sub-processes, which is called a child process. The child will refer to the process that initiated it as its parent. A child process is a replica of the parent process and shares many of its resources and is terminated when its parent is terminated. An application can be made up of one ore more processes. Likewise, a process can contain one or more applications.

Threads

A process is comprised of at least one thread of execution. All modern operating systems support the creation for multiple threads of execution within a single process. Each thread within a process can run independent of other threads but in practice usually require some form of synchronization amongst them.

Network-aware server applications are almost always developed as multi-threaded applications whereby a group of threads may be dedicated to monitoring input from a socket connection (users who are attempting to connect) while another group of threads may be dedicated to actual processing of logic. Synchronization is required when threads need to coordinate the transfer of data from the business logic portion of the application and send a response back to the requester.

When developing a multithreaded application, the number of simultaneously running threads can only be one for one with the actual number of CPUs. When there are more threads that desire to execute, the operating system will perform a context switch that allows other threads the opportunity to execute. Context switching is a core element of operating systems and occurs at both the process and thread levels. Context switching between two threads in a single process is lighter weight than a context switch between two processes.

Objects

Applications that were created using modern object-oriented languages are comprised of cooperating objects.A process is composed of one or more objects and one or more threads within a process access these objects. Objects themselves can be distributed across multiple systems within multiple processes using technologies such as CORBA, DCOM and RMI.

Common Object Request Broker Architecture (CORBA) is an architecture and specification for creating; distributing and managing distributed program objects within a network. CORBA allows applications at different locations to communicate through an interface broker. Distributed Component Object Model (DCOM) is a set of Microsoft concepts and program interfaces that provide underlying services of interface negotiation, lifecycle management, licensing and event services. Remote Method Invocation (RMI) is used in conjunction with applications written in Java and uses an object parameter-passing mechanism known as object serialization. RMI is designed to preserve the object model across a network.

For more information on CORBA, visit http://www.omg.org. For more information on RMI, visit http://java.sun.com/products/jdk/rmi/. For more information on COM, visit http://www.microsoft.com/com/dcom/dcom95/dcom1_3.asp.

1.2. Interprocess Communication

Operating systems execute processes within their own virtual address space and provide isolation from other processes. By default, processes cannot communicate with each other unless they use services provided by the operating system to do so. There are many times when interprocess communication is warranted.

Interprocess communication (IPC) is a set of interfaces that allow developers to create and manage individual application processes that can execute concurrently. IPC allows an application to handle many user requests simultaneously. Furthermore, a request from a single user may result in multiple processes executing within the operating system on the user's behalf, the processes need to communicate with each other.

Applications may use one or more IPC approaches including, but not limited to:

- Signals,
- Pipes and Named Pipes,
- Semaphores,
- Shared Memory, and
- Sockets.

Let us explore the details of each IPC mechanism.

Signals

Signals are used to signal asynchronous events between processes. A process may implement a signal handler to execute when an event occurs or may use the system default actions. Most signals received by an application can be ignored but some are required to be implemented. For example, within Java when a user wants to get a thread dump they can execute a kill –3 pid where pid is the operating system process ID. Likewise, to terminate an application, you would execute kill –9 pid that would terminate the process.

Pipes and Named Pipes

A pipe provides connectivity of the standard output (STDOUT) from one process to the standard input (STDIN) of another process. Pipes provide a method for one-way communication between processes in a parent-child relationship and may be sometimes referred to as half-duplex pipes.

For two-way communications between processes, two pipes can be established, one in each direction. When pipes are used for interprocess communication, they must have a common parent process. In both, one-way and two-way communications, the operating system buffers the data sent to the pipe until the receiving process reads it. Pipes themselves are created with a fixed size and cannot grow the amount of data they hold.

Named pipes work similarly to standard pipes but are implemented as a virtual device as part of the file system and use a First-in First Out (FIFO) approach. Unlike standard pipes, named pipes do not require processes to work in a parent-child relationship in order to communicate.

Semaphores

Semaphores are counters that are used to control access to shared resources accessed by multiple concurrent processes. Semaphores are frequently used as a locking mechanism to prevent processes from accessing a specified set of resources while another process is performing operations on them. Semaphores are a special function of the operating system kernel that each process can check and usually implemented as sets. Semaphores are common used to either share a common memory space and/or to share access to files.

Shared Memory

Shared memory provides the ability to map an area of memory into the address of more than one process. Shared memory is usually the best performing method for interprocess communication as processes do not need access to operating system kernel resources to share data. For example, a client process may send data to a server process in which would be modified and returned back to the client. Using other IPC mechanisms would require the client to write a file and the server to read it requiring kernel services. By using shared memory, the client would put data in shared memory after checking a semaphore value, writes the data to the shared memory area, and then resets the semaphore to signal the server that data has changed. The same process would occur with the server notifying the client of changes in data.

Sockets

Sockets provide two-way (full duplex) method for interprocess communication between client and server processes in a network. Sockets can also be used to communicate between processes on the same system. A socket is an endpoint of communication to which a name can be bound. Sockets can either be stream-based or datagram-based. Stream-based sockets provide guaranteed delivery and ensure sequenced unduplicated receipt of packets. Datagram sockets do not guarantee delivery or sequence and may allow for duplicated packets to exist but are usually faster at the network layer.

1.3. Communications Infrastructure

The infrastructure that enables processes to seamlessly communicate between each other over a network is typically referred to as middleware. Middleware is a layer of software that resides on the network and mediates information exchange between two different processes. Middleware helps applications work together across disparate operating systems and platforms and allow developers to write applications that interface with the middleware layer rather than recreating for each application the services provided by the middleware.

The ability to communicate across processes can be accomplished in a variety of manners including:

- Remote Procedure Calls,
- Object Request Brokers,
- Transaction Monitors, and
- Message-Oriented Middleware.

When used within the enterprise, middleware helps applications ranging from client/server to legacy mainframe applications to Web environments to participate in solving business goals in a distributed manner. Let us take a closer look at the various methods for communication in a distributed environment.

1.4. Remote Procedure Calls (RPC)

A procedure is a sequence of instructions that execute as part of an application. A procedure call is a request that is made by one procedure to another procedure for the specified service. Remote procedure calls reduce complexity in creation of applications that execute across multiple operating systems and network protocols (TCP/IP, IPX/SPX, etc.) by hiding the details of transport and marshalling from developers.

Remote Procedure Calls cannot be considered middleware in a strict sense in that it is embedded within actual applications. When client and server applications are compiled, a local stub is created and linked into the application. These stubs are invoked whenever the application requires access to a remote function.

RPC is typically implemented using synchronous request/reply exchange in which the client blocks execution until the server satisfies the result. RPC can be implemented to support asynchronous behavior through the use of a client-side proxy that either executes in another thread or implements polling/yielding behavior.

For more information on the Proxy pattern, see http://c2.com/cgi/wiki?ProxyPattern.

RPC can be used in client/server applications where the client can issue a service request and wait for the response from the server before continuing its own processing logic (blocking). Most implementations of RPC are not well suited to handle peer-to-peer, asynchronous or object-oriented programming and should be avoided in these situations.

1.5. Object Request Brokers (ORB)

Object request brokers are traditionally used in CORBA-based architectures and serve as a broker between a client's request for a service and the service itself. Object request brokers provide location transparency as the client can make service requests without having to know where the service is provided in a distributed network or what the actual interface needs to look like in order to carry out a successful invocation. The ability to understand interface definitions at run-time allows for run-time resolution.

The function provided by ORB technology can be loosely categorized into:

- Interface definition,
- Location and possible activation of remote objects, and

- Communication between clients and object.

Object request broker are analogous to a telephone network. ORB provides a directory of services and mediate communications between connected clients and services offered. For architectures that use an ORB-based approach, to the client all services appear as if they are local. The ORB in a sense is a framework that provides the cross-system communication between distributed objects.

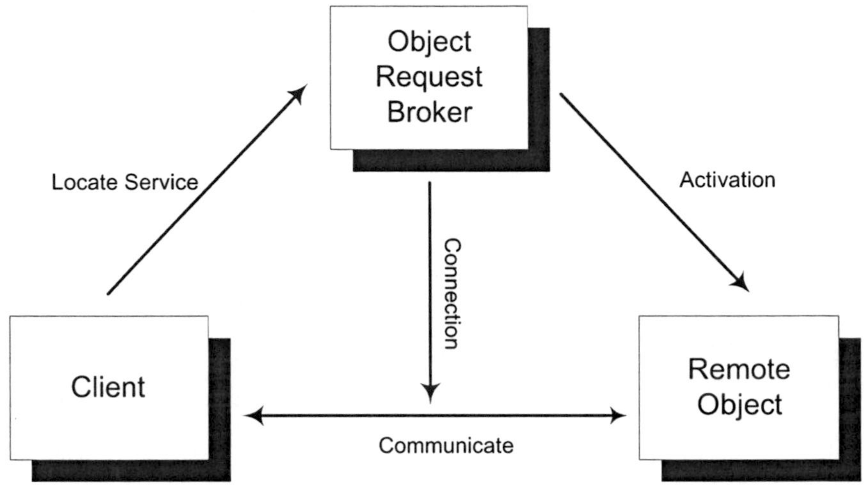

Figure 5. **Object Request Broker**

Depending upon the particular implementation of the ORB, it may be compiled into clients, executed as separate operating system processes or can even be embedded within an operating system kernel. Object request brokers may provide several services to both client and service provider including those shown in Table 1.

There are two major offerings of ORB-based approaches, one of which is championed by the Object Management Group (OMG) and their CORBA specification and one led by Microsoft known as the Component Object Model (COM).

Enterprises that adopt an ORB-based approach have to take into consideration vendor lock in, lack of pervasive interoperability and extensive software development and vendor acquisition costs. Usage of these approaches is good for integrating legacy technologies but is highly discouraged for modern software development.

Product offerings by vendors who produce object request brokers include:

- Iona Orbix – http://www.iona.com.
- Rogue Wave Noveau – http://www.roguewave.com/products/nouveau.

Table 1. **Services Provided by Object Request Brokers**

Services	Description
Lifecycle	Defines how objects and components are created and destroyed.
Persistence	Provides the ability to store data used by the service using a backing store such as a relational database and/or file system.
Naming	Allows a component to locate another component by name and can optionally be used to leverage existing naming services such as NIS or DCE.
Events	Components can register interest in receiving notification of selected events.
Concurrency control	Provides management of locks to data that transactions may compete for.
Transaction	Ensures that when a transaction is complemented, all changes are either committed or restored to their pre-transaction state.
Licensing	Supports measurement for purposes of compensation and may provide mechanisms to restrict usage based on session, instance creation or physical location.
Properties	Allows a component to provide a self-description that can be consumed by other components.
Security	Provides the ability for the service to authenticate and authorize all client related service requests.
Time	Provides the ability to keep two components to share the notion of time.

- ObjectSpace Voyager – http://www.objectspace.com/products/vgrOverview.htm.

1.6. Transaction Processing Monitors

Transaction processing monitors (TP Monitors) have been successfully used in order processing, airline reservation, customer service applications and scenarios where an online support environment has to concurrently operate in conjunction with batch processes. TP Monitors provide a strong ability to increase scalability of a distributed architecture and accomplishes this goal by multiplexing client transaction requests onto a predefined number of processing instances that support desired service requests.

Transaction Processing Monitors provides services that increase scalability, availability and management capability such as restarting failed processes, enforcement of consistent in distributed data stores and dynamic load balancing. TP monitors provide near linear scalability by adding more servers to service additional requests.

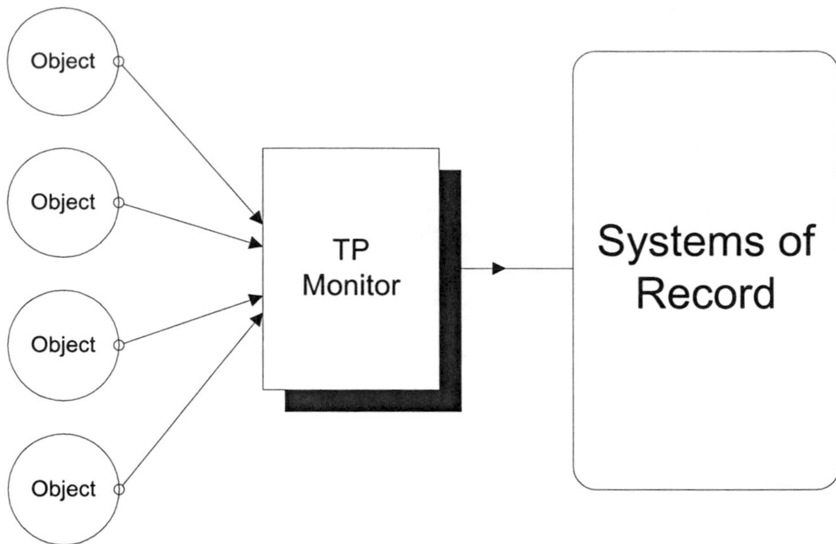

***Figure 6.* Transaction Processing Monitor**

Typical TP monitor implementations have built-in support for authentication and authorization of the clients attempting to use the services along with protecting the data they attempt to access. TP monitors typically support both synchronous and asynchronous communication models.

TP monitors break up complex applications into discrete small units of work (transactions) and provide a guaranteed commit/rollback mechanism. A typical unit of work may require performing multiple database actions (inserts, updates, deletes, etc.) across multiple databases yet ensuring a consistent state.

TP monitors offer the following functionality:

- Communication services – Support for synchronous, asynchronous, store-and-forward (similar to MOM) and conversational mechanisms (similar to RPC).

- Directory services – Physical data location independence to allow for cross-platform operations.

- High availability – Provide for routing user requests upon node failures as well as re-initialization and restart of failed services.

- Workload management – In environments where workloads are comprised of online and batch transactions, TP monitors provide scheduling capabilities that take into consideration, desired policies so that execution maintains a consistent throughput.

- Enhanced security – TP monitors provide security context for authorized users including their specific privileges and can optionally check against external security credential providers such as LDAP and relational databases.
- Online administration – TP monitor typically provide a console whereby an administrator can view all operations in progress, start, restart and shutdown services and gather statistical information on the platform.
- Vendor independence – TP monitors have been implemented pervasively and support multiple operating system platforms. Implementation of the X/Open consortium's XA (transaction) interface when communicating with resource managers is also standards-based.
- Legacy System Access – Use of TP monitors provide transactional connectivity to legacy technologies such as IMS, RDB and other legacy technologies.

The architectural framework provided by TP monitors allows enterprises to develop scalable applications in a heterogeneous environment with clients ranging from a few to thousands in a relatively simplistic manner.

Product offerings by vendors who produce transaction-processing monitors include:

- IBM CICS – http://www.ibm.com.
- NCR Top End – http://www.ncr.com.
- BEA Tuxedo – http://ww.bea.com.

1.7. Message-Oriented Middleware (MOM)

Message-oriented middleware is software that supports asynchronous calls between client and server applications and use message queues to provide temporary storage when the destination server is unavailable. Message-oriented middleware works in a services network in client/server, peer to peer and publish and subscribe. Message exchange mechanisms allow for logical decoupling in that sender does not have to know what platform the destination application uses.

Message-oriented middleware is best utilized for event-driven applications especially when developed using object-oriented paradigms. The asynchronous nature of message-oriented middleware unlike remote procedure calls (RPC) provides the ability for the client to not block when making service requests. This can in many circumstances provide for increased scalability (but reduced performance). Message-oriented middleware can have the ability to in stress situations overload the network when clients can send data faster than the server can process the incoming requests.

The vast majority of implementations of message-oriented middleware are implemented in a proprietary manner and do not interoperate with other implementations of MOM products without costly bridging products. Use of a single implementation of a MOM will likely result in a dependence on the MOM vendor future enhancements. Vendor lock in can be mitigated in some languages such as Java by coding to message product neutral APIs such as JMS.

MOM software usually requires installation on every platform within a network that will increase software-licensing costs. Administration of MOM software in a large distributed network can result in an increase in staff for maintenance especially in a heterogeneous environment. MOM may also consume additional CPU cycles and memory on each platform and must be taken into consideration at capacity planning time.

Product offerings by vendors who produce message-oriented middleware include:

- Oracle Advanced Queueing – http://www.oracle.com.
- Arjuna Messaging – http://www.arjuna.com.
- IBM MQSeries – http://www.ibm.com.
- Tibco Rendezvous – http://www.tibco.com.
- Open Source Message Queue – http://www.osmq.org.

1.8. Service Description

In order to achieve interoperability in a distributed computing environment, the architecture requires not only communication at the lower layers of the protocol stack but must have equivalent support at the application layer. Supporting interoperability at the application-layer requires the ability to have a common way of describing services. Web Services Description Language (WSDL) is an XML markup that provides an XML grammar for describing services as collections of communication endpoints capable of message exchange.

Description mechanisms will usually contain an abstract definition of endpoints and messages produced and consumed by the specified service. The service description should whenever appropriate separate the abstract definition of endpoints and messages from the concrete network deployment or data format bindings.

Mechanisms that support service description have existed in distributed computing environment for decades in the form of Interface Definition Language (IDL). IDL defines a system of interfaces, operations those interfaces support, data types used as parameters and return values for those operations.

1.9. Versioning

In the real world, an enterprise will create different versions of its software and services on a periodic basis. A service over time will increase the functionality provided to consumers. Supporting multiple versions of a service is different than the traditional methods used in support of multiple versions of a product due to loose coupling between layers and the separation of producer from consumer. It becomes important to support the formal evolution of services, which can be accomplished via a variety of mechanism including, but not limited to:

- Making interfaces immutable and defining a new interface for each change in service.
- Creating a document-style interface that allows a document to be passed to the service which contains versioning information.
- Allowing interfaces to be mutable and requiring clients to stay synchronized with changes.

Making interfaces immutable is a technique used by Microsoft's Component Object Model (COM) and helps prevent run-time binding errors by ensuring that clients always have access to a stable interface. Interface immutability will allow a client to bind to a specific version of an interface or if one is not specified, the client will be bound to the most current version.

Document passing is another technique where either a serialized string or value object is passed from the client to the service. The service itself takes on the responsibility for checking within the document, the actual version the client passed and making sure it is supported and syntactically valid. If it is not valid, the service itself will throw a fault. Defensive coding will usually require making a copy of the document before processing.

If you control both the producer and consumer of services then you can change interfaces at will and upgrade accordingly. This strategy however is fraught with issues if the service will be consumed outside of your administrative control.

Minimal support for versioning of XML-based services should adopt an approach that leverages unique XML namespace URIs.

Techniques for each of the three choices have been discussed in previous chapters.

1.10. Operations

Distributed computing platforms usually provide a mechanism for describing network services as collections of communication endpoints that support message exchange along with an abstract description of actions supported by the service.

Web services for example use the Web Services Description Language (WSDL) to describe operations across multiple services and capture this information using XML in a WSDL document. WSDL defined services as a collection of network endpoints and separates the abstract definition of endpoint and messages from their concrete deployment and data format.

Service operations can occur using both RPC-style and message-passing (document style) bindings. When operations use RPC-style, it becomes important to mirror the underlying interfaces signature since order of parameters becomes significant. For document style, list of parameters do not require the sender to adhere to a particular parameter order.

Typically, transmission of messages across a distributed computing environment can be classified in to one of four categories:

1. One-Way,
2. Request-response,
3. Solicit-response, or
4. Notification.

The above four primitives are better known as primitives and are represented in abstract terms. Understanding the basics of each of the four primitives is crucial to services. For example, some endpoints may only received messages if they are the result of a synchronous request/response operation while others can interoperate in an asynchronous manner. Let us look in detail as to how each of these operations can be defined using WSDL.

1.10.1. One-Way

A one-way operation sends data to an endpoint but does not expect any form of response. This form of operation is typically seen in message-queue-based architectures that allow clients to send and forget. Example grammar for a one-way operation is shown below.

```
<wsdl:definitions ... >
   <wsdl:portType ... > *
      <wsdl:operation name="nmtoken">
         <wsdl:input name="nmtoken"? message="qname"/>
      </wsdl:operation>
   </wsdl:portType >
</wsdl:definitions>
```

Code 1. One-way operation

In the above example, the portType element specifies a set of abstract operations. The input element specifies the abstract message format for the one-way operation. The name attribute of the input element defines a unique name for the operation. If it is not specified, the name defaults to the name of the operation with the operation type appended.

1.10.2. Request/Response

A request-response operation sends data to an endpoint and expects either a successful response or a fault to be returned. This form of operation is typically seen in scenarios where interaction between two services is synchronous in nature. Example grammar for a request-response operation is shown below.

```
<wsdl:definitions ... >
   <wsdl:portType ... > *
      <wsdl:operation name="nmtoken" parameterOrder="nmtokens">
         <wsdl:input name="nmtoken"? message="qname"/>
         <wsdl:output name="nmtoken"? message="qname"/>
         <wsdl:fault name="nmtoken" message="qname"/>*
      </wsdl:operation>
   </wsdl:portType >
</wsdl:definitions>
```

Code 2. Request/Response Operation

The input and output elements specify the abstract message format for the request and response, respectively. The fault element is optional and specified the abstract message format for any errors that may be returned by the service as a result of the operation. Each element within the fault must be named to allow a binding to specify the concrete format of the fault message. The name of the fault element is unique within the set of faults defined for an operation.

The request/response operation must specify a particular binding to determine how messages are actually sent within a single service conversation (such as HTTP request/response).

1.10.3. Solicit/Response

A solicit/response operation receives data from an endpoint and returns a successful response or a fault. This form of operation is similar to request/response in that it is synchronous in nature. Example grammar for a solicit/response operation is shown below.

```
<wsdl:definitions ... >
   <wsdl:portType ... > *
      <wsdl:operation name="nmtoken" parameterOrder="nmtokens">
         <wsdl:output name="nmtoken"? message="qname"/>
         <wsdl:input name="nmtoken"? message="qname"/>
         <wsdl:fault name="nmtoken" message="qname"/>*
      </wsdl:operation>
   </wsdl:portType >
</wsdl:definitions>
```

Code 3. Solicit/Response Operation

The output and input elements specify the abstract message format for the solicited request and response, respectively. The optional fault element specifies the abstract message format for any errors that may be returned from the service.

1.10.4. Notification

A notification operation receives data from an endpoint but does not send any form of acknowledgement. This form of operation is typically used to implement callback mechanisms for asynchronous processing. Example grammar for a notification operation is shown below.

```
<wsdl:definitions ... >
   <wsdl:portType ... > *
      <wsdl:operation name="nmtoken">
         <wsdl:output name="nmtoken"? message="qname"/>
      </wsdl:operation>
   </wsdl:portType >
</wsdl:definitions>
```

Code 4. Notification Operation

The notification operation is the inverse of one-way. The output element specifies the abstract message format for the notification operation.

1.11. Service Discovery

Services are not only required to be described in a consistent manner to ensure interoperability, but must support a mechanism that allows them to be discovered. The discovery of services within a distributed computing environment can occur using many approaches including passing configuration files to locating the service via a specialized directory service by name and/or specific attributes. In the past, directory services have supported browsing, drill-down and search engine type operations.

Applications and services can be built upon application infrastructure that operates in groups of interdependent servers usually known as clusters. Clusters coordinate their actions to provide increased scalability, availability and fault-tolerant services to applications.

Clustering architectures are classified based on how each member server within a cluster accesses memory, disk and whether servers share a copy of the operating and the I/O system. Clusters can be loosely defined into three categories.

1. Shared Memory,
2. Shared Disk, and
3. Shared Nothing.

Clusters that use the shared memory model have member servers within the cluster use the same primary memory, through which all traffic to the cluster is routed. The servers in the cluster also share a single copy of the operating system and I/O subsystems. Shared disk clusters provide each member server with its own memory but share common disks. In order to ensure data protection against simultaneous write operations, use of a distributed lock manager to control access to disk-based resources is required.

Shared nothing clusters provide each member server with its own memory and disks and use disk mirroring technologies to provide access to shared state. Hybrid models also exist where shared nothing architectures are ran on top of shared disk hardware. While only a single member server can access the disk at a time, it provides seamless failover in that another server can pickup the workload via checkpoint processes.

Cluster architectures have common attributes in how they operate and can be generally classified into four categories:

1. Active/Active,
2. Failover/Failback,
3. Switchover, and
4. Impersonation.

Active/active clusters require each server to run its own workload and can assume responsibility for another cluster member in the event of a failure. Failover/failback-based cluster will automatically transfer the workload of a failed server to another cluster member until the first server recovers, at which time its workload is automatically transferred back.

Clusters may also use switchover approaches that allow clients to find replacements for failed cluster member servers with a minimum of service disruption. Usually this approach requires a server to stand in for another server by taking over the IP address of a failed server. Impersonation allows clients to find a replacement server and reroutes network traffic intended for the failed server to the replacement server.

1.12. Application Services

Most distributed computing environments nowadays are built on top of application servers that provide security, load balancing, and transactional support and mediated access to allow for pooled operations in order to increase scalability and ensure reliability.

Services that are built on top of application servers can be classified into four basic models:

1. Stateless,
2. Conversational,
3. Cached, and
4. Singleton.

Let us look at each of the models:

1.12.1. Stateless Services

Stateless services do not maintain state in memory between service invocations. This allows a service to have the potential for increased scalability by allowing multiple instances of a service to be deployed across multiple servers in the services infrastructure. If the infrastructure provides load-balancing services that detect unresponsive services, using this model services can be made highly available.

1.12.2. Conversational Services

Conversational services maintain state between service invocations between clients and can be constructed by either having the client on each service request pass a session identifier or by having the infrastructure create an instance that is solely used by that client. Conversational services generally maintain transient state in memory and may optionally persist state between long-running transactions.

Service request from clients are usually grouped into sessions. A session is associated with the state that must be maintained by the service between service requests. A service may choose to save shared state between invocations in order to mimic stateless behavior.

If durability between invocations is not a requirement, there are multiple alternatives that can improve both scalability and performance. Session state can be serialized and passed to/from the client to the service as part of the request itself. The service can also leave session state in memory and periodically expire session data based on lack of activity.

When implementing conversational services, session affinity is required and may result in changes to the underlying network since network protocols will by default assume everything is stateless. Support for affinity is created when the session is built and all subsequent requests are routed to the chosen server. This can be implemented by using external IP-based mechanisms (i.e. F5 Big IP, Coyote Point, Cisco CSS and so on) that leverage DNS to return a single address for the service and/or support pass-through proxying in order to obtain stateful load balancing.

1.12.3. Cached Services

Cached services maintain state in memory and use its memory to process service requests from multiple clients. A cached service can increase scalability within a distributed computing environment in situations where request processing is CPU intensive and the results are not specific to the caller. Implementations of cached services vary in their implementation and can use alternative strategies for keeping copies of cached data consistent with each other. Cached services may also leverage a backing store when memory requirements are high.

One approach a cached service may implement is to have each cache flush itself at regular intervals according to a configurable time-to-live property. Using this approach removes any requirement for communication between the same instances of services but does require the client to tolerate a window of potential data inconsistency and/or staleness.

Another approach is to keep all copies of the data consistent with the backing store by using concurrency control in the caches. In order to ensure scalability, this is best accomplished by implementing optimistic concurrency where the service should flush the cache after updates to reduce the possibility of concurrency exceptions.

1.12.4. Singleton Services

Singleton services are active on exactly one server within a network at a time and handles service requests from multiple clients. Singletons are usually used in situations where unique values may need to be generated in a sequential manner. Depending upon the particular application server used, a singleton service may be migrated to a new server or simply restarted upon service failure.

Potential issues arise in failure/disaster scenarios where connectivity between services becomes disconnected. Singleton services upon migration can cause a "split-brain" whereby multiple instances of a service are running but not aware of each other. One technique that can increase availability while reducing the changes for the "split-brain" scenario to occur is by partitioning data and creating a singleton service for each partition.

We have covered many of the options you need to know about when implementing an SOA. In the next section, we look at some of the concepts you need to consider when putting them all together.

2. Practical Considerations

Distributed computing is difficult because it requires services to be constrained by the real world at each service/network boundary. Whenever a service interacts with other services and handles client requests, it also has to correctly handle a variety of conditions that may or may not be known at code time.

A distributed computing environment can reduce the potential number of errors a developer will face by providing layers of abstraction. For example, a service may return five different errors but a developer may want to abstract the details of the error away and simply think about success or failure.

Tim Berners-Lee when inventing the worldwide web realized that broken links are OK. The same thing can be said of developing web sites, cities or services. Successful service-oriented architecture is always on the border of chaos. Broken services are inherent to any complex adaptive system. The key to building an enterprise SOA are:

- Get the basics right.
- Prefer working software over intellectually pure pursuits of architecture.
- Merciless refactoring.

Put yourself in the shoes of the city planners for New York City. If they ever sought perfection, the city would never exist or have been a total failure. The truth of the matter is that New York City has only had a single electric blackout, water always flows (sometimes even overflows during Super Bowl half-time), and people get ran over by taxis, there is always construction and potholes that are in need of repair. The strategy for creation of services cannot be thought of in a big all encompassing plan upfront but needs to evolve over time to support the ever-changing needs of its users. An SOA is never complete and is always in the constant state of change.

Creation of an enterprise SOA does not require perfection but does require attention to detail, careful planning and informed opinion. The most successful services are the ones that exist.

3. Summary

In this chapter, we have learned about:

- Business rationale for service-oriented architectures.

- The foundational principles for distributed computing.
- Techniques for increasing interoperability amongst enterprise applications.

Distributed computing provides a cost effective model for enterprise level computing where multi-tier architectures and middleware will be key factors for success of electronic business. The rapid progress that has occurred in this area in order to assist with seamless integration of all system components is of increasing importance.

APPENDIX B: QUALITY ATTRIBUTES

The bitterness of poor quality lingers long after the sweetness of meeting schedules is forgotten.
Kathleen Byle, Sandia National Laboratories

1. System Qualities

System qualities are the attributes of architecture that define characteristics of how the system shall behave and/or its structural aspects should be implemented. The design of distributed computing architectures requires balance between competing system qualities. The five system qualities that are most important to incorporate early as design goal are:

1. Availability,
2. Manageability,
3. Performance,
4. Scalability, and
5. Security.

Let us look at each of the five system qualities.

1.1. Availability

Enterprise applications and services typically depend on multiple servers that may be accessed by thousands of users and use internal networks to connect to relational databases and legacy systems and even may leverage services outside the enterprise connected via the Internet. This may be composed of multiple infrastructure components that must operate in a predictable uniform manner. When any component within the enterprise application's nervous system fails, the interruption could result in loss of business revenue, tarnish the brand of the company, and deny customer access to data needed to perform customer self-service requests or other serious outcomes. Creation of a highly available distributed computing architecture becomes part of the business strategy.

Not all applications and services require 24 × 7 uptime with instantaneous response times. Some can support failure with zero consequences while other applications may be tolerant to unplanned downtime but require varying recovery approaches. Few mission-critical applications and services must provide high availability and use technology that supports replication to ensure instant, near real-time transparent recovery with no significant downtime.

Local application failures can usually be handled in an expedient manner. It becomes progressively more difficult to avoid failure, as software will always be used in scenarios above and beyond its original design supported. Typically, one or more of the following reasons can cause failures:

- Inadequate software testing.
- Lack of a real change management discipline.
- The inability to monitor the environment in real-time.
- No tools that allow for performing long-term trend analysis.
- Lack of quality software engineering processes.
- Operating environment failure (hardware failure, disaster, fire, flood, storms, cooling).
- Sudden changes in usage levels.

Based on our experience with several Fortune 100 enterprises, listed in Table 1 are breakdown percentages of failures.

Availability is typically a measure of how often an application and/or service is available for usage and is a percentage calculation based on how often the application is actually available to handle service requests when compared to the total planned run-time. The formal calculation for availability includes time for system maintenance because an application during this period is unavailable for use.

As higher levels of availability are achieved, hardware costs for service execution will increase due to server CPU utilization, network throughput and disk storage

Table 1. **Typical Availability Failure Scenarios in Order**

Reason	Percentage
Inadequate software testing	25
Lack of a real change management discipline	20
Lack of quality software engineering processes	20
The inability to monitor the environment in real-time	15
No tools that allow for performing long-term trend analysis	10
Operating environment failure	5
Sudden changes in usage levels	5

and redundancy. The discovery and identification of bottlenecks at higher levels will also require higher-skilled developers who have a skilled understanding in software engineering. Finally, higher levels of availability require automated comprehensive testing of every service that may affect your application at run-time.

1.2. Manageability

Distributed applications and services make customer access and data exchange with business partners easy but come at the expense with the difficulty in diagnosing and resolving capacity and resource access issues in a production environment. Quality assurance also becomes a run-time requirement that may introduce the need to perform audits and incorporate findings into maintenance upgrades. This can become difficult in infrastructures that are distributed across large geographic areas.

It becomes important to incorporate at design-time, interfaces that will allow not only for operational quality assurance but the continuous measurement of service health including such factors as resource consumption, faults, and statistics on consumer service requests and overall service performance.

1.3. Performance

In many enterprises, there is a widely held belief that performance and scalability are interchangeable terms when it reality they describe two different problem spaces and can be in many situations opposing. Performance is usually not apparent until a particular instance of a service is put under an increased load.

Conducting code reviews and/or using pair-programming style development can uncover performance bottlenecks. At run-time, performance testing of services should be conducted to identify bottlenecks checking for slow performing code routines or contention for resources.

1.4. Scalability

Scalability must be designed into a service early in its lifecycle, as this is the hardest attribute to support after the fact. Decisions made during design and early coding phases will dictate how well your services scale. Scaling of services also requires working knowledge of the deployment environment as it has dependencies on the underlying hardware.

Hardware-based scaling can be accomplished by scaling up which requires adding resources such as more memory, faster and/or more processors or even migrating to a newer class of machine. Typically, this approach permits some scalability increases without requiring changes to source and keeps administration simpler.

Scaling up can also have the effect of moving the bottleneck from one component to another. For example, a server that is at 99 percent CPU utilization could increase capacity by adding another CPU. However, this may shift the bottleneck from the CPU to the system memory. Adding CPUs does not increase performance in a linear fashion. In most servers, the performance gain curve tapers off as each additional processor is added. Minimally, in order to take advantage of adding multiple CPUs, your services should support multiple threads of execution.

Scaling out provides a different alternative to scaling up and hopes to leverage the economics of using commodity hardware to distributed processing across multiple smaller servers. Although scaling out is achieved by using many servers, the collection functions as a single resource. By dedicating multiple machines to a common task, service fault tolerance is increased at the expense of additional administration.

Scaling out provides a mechanism that results in near linear increases in scalability as more servers are added. The key attribute to achieving scaling in this manner is location transparency. Application code must not know what server is executing the service. In some rare situations, it is still possible to scale out when applications are aware of what servers are executing services. This situation is known as location affinity. Location affinity requires changes to code to scale from one server to many. It is easier to design services with location transparency at design time than refactoring later.

1.5. Security

The ability to provide security in a distributed computing environment is all about controlling access to a variety of resources (services, data, configuration, etc.). There are four main concepts on which security practices and providers are based:

1. Authentication,
2. Authorization,
3. Data Protection, and
4. Auditing.

Authentication is the process of confirming the identity of the caller and/or service. Before a service permits access, it may require confirming the identity of the service requestor. The requestor establishes an identity by providing a credential that is known only to the requestor and the authenticating service. In some situations, the requestor may also desire to validate the identity of the authentication service, which is known as mutual authentication.

Authorization is the process where verification of the authenticated party has the appropriate permissions to access a specified resource. You cannot assume that because someone has been authenticated that they are authorized for all actions.

Data protection is the process of ensuring the confidentiality, integrity and non-repudiation of data. Data, whether contained within a message in transit or on disk, requires protection. Encryption assists in protecting the confidentiality of data and renders it useless to parties who lack knowledge of which cryptographic algorithm was used and the key. Data integrity is realized through the use of hashing algorithms, digital signatures and message authentication codes. Auditing is the process of logging of security related events and can be used for forensic purposes.

2. *Design vs Run-Time*

Quality attributes are properties that govern how a system behaves over and above its functionality. There are two categories of quality attributes, those that can be determined at run-time and those that can only be estimated through inspection. It is the prime responsibility of architects to ensure that all systems within their portfolio have identified quality attributes and they are prioritized to those of which are most important.

Table 2. **Run-Time Quality Attributes**

Quality Attribute	Description
Availability	The amount of time that a system is up and running. This can be measured by the length of time between failures and how quickly the system is able to resume activity after a failure.
Performance	A measurement of system response time.
Reliability	The ability of a system to operate over time in a predictable manner. Reliability is measured by mean time between failure (MTBF).
Usability	A measure that determines how easy it is for a user of the system to understand and operate.

Table 3. **Inspection Time Quality Attributes**

Quality Attribute	Description
Buildability	The ability for a system to be constructed using the budget, time and staff available for the project in many cases is simply too ambitious to be completed given project constraints.
Conceptual integrity	The ability of the architecture to communicate a clear, complete vision for the system. Using agile methods, this is typically realized using metaphors. If it does not feel right, then conceptual integrity is lost.
Integrability	Systems over time will need to integrate with other systems. The Integrability of a system depends on the extent in which the system uses open standards, how well APIs are designed and the usage of approaches such as service-oriented architectures.
Modifiability	A measure of how easy it is to change the system to incorporate new functional requirements. There are two aspects to modifiability, time and cost. If a system uses an obscure or outdated technology that requires expensive consultants or other hard to find specialists, then even though it may be quick to change, its modifiability can still be low.
Portability	A system's platform may consist of hardware, operating systems, application server software and databases. The ability to measure the ease to move to different platforms.
Reusability	The reusability of a system is the ability to reuse portions of the system in other applications. Components that can be reused include: the run-time platform, source code, libraries and processes.
Security	The ability of a system to resist unauthorized attempts to access system resources while providing services to authorized users.
Subsetability	For incremental development approaches, a system that can execute to demonstrate small iterations demonstrates subsetability. This attribute becomes important if time and/or resources on the project are reduced. If the subsetability of the architecture is high, then a subset of features may still make it into production.
Testability	How easily can a system be tested using human effort, automated testing tools, code reviews and inspections and other forms of ensuring system quality.

In Table 2, the system qualities that can be evaluated at run-time are given, whereas Table 3 shows the system qualities that can only be reasonably evaluated through inspection.

The quality of an enterprise SOA is directly proportional to the quality incorporated into the enterprise architecture. A thorough understanding of system qualities not only for services but all components of an architecture will result in lower total cost of ownership and increased business agility.

APPENDIX C: REFERENCES

It is amazing what can be accomplished when nobody cares about who gets the credit
Robert Yates

Books

Alur, D., Malks, D. and Crupi, J. (2003) *Core J2EE Patterns: Best Practices and Design Strategies*. Prentice Hall.

Atkinson, C. et al. (2002) *Component-Based Product Line Engineering with UML*. Addison-Wesley.

Beer, S. (1979) *The Heart of Enterprise*. Wiley.

Bernstein, P.A. and Newcomer, E. (1997) *Principles of Transaction Processing*. Morgan Kaufmann.

Buschmann, F., Meunier, R., Rohnert, H., Sommerlad, P. and Stal, M. (1996) *Pattern Oriented Software Architecture*, Volume One. John Wiley and Sons.

Clements, P. and Northrop, L. (2002) *Software Product Lines*. Addison Wesley.

COD (1982) *The Concise Oxford Dictionary*. Oxford University Press.

Eeles, P. and Sims, O. (1998) *Building Business Objects*. Wiley.

Farley, J. (1998) *Java Distributed Computing*. New York: O'Reilly.

Ferguson, N. and Schneier, B. (2003) *Practical Cryptography*. John Wiley & Sons.

Gamma, E., Helm, R., Johnson, R. and Vlissides, J. (1994) *Design Patterns: Elements of Reusable Object-Oriented Software.* Addison Wesley.

Gamma, E. et al. (1995) *Design Patterns.* Addison Wesley.

Gray, J. and Reuter, A. (1993) *Transaction Processing: Concepts and Techniques.* Morgan Kaufmann.

Guttman, M. and Matthews, J. (1998/1999) *Migrating to Enterprise Component Computing.* Cutter Consortium.

Harmon, P., Rosen, M. and Guttman, M. (2001) *Developing E-Business Systems and Architectures.* Morgan Kaufmann.

Herzum, P. and Sims, O. (2000) *Business Component Factory.* Wiley.

Hubert, R. (2002) *Convergent Architecture.* Wiley.

Greenfield, J. and Short, K. (2004) *Software Factories.* Wiley.

Keen, M. et al. (2004) *Patterns: Implementing an SOA Using Enterprise Service Bus.* IBM Redbook.

Lawson, M. (2003) *Finite Automata.* CRC Press.

McGovern, J., Bothner, J., Cagle, K., Linn, J. and Nagarajan, V. (2003) *XQuery Kick Start.* Sams Publishing.

McGovern, J., Ambler, S., Stevens, M., Linn, J., Sharan, V. and Jo, E. (2003) *A Practical Guide to Enterprise Architecture.* Upper Saddle, NJ: Prentice Hall.

McGovern, J., Ambler, S., Caserio, C., Narayan, N., Tyagi, R. and Biggs, M. (2004) *Agile Enterprise Architecture.* Connecticut: Manning Publications.

Morgan, T. (2002) *Business Rules and Information Systems: Aligning IT with Business Goals.* Boston, MA: Addison Wesley.

Pawson, R. and Matthews, R. (2002) *Naked Objects.* Wiley.

Rector, B. (2003) *Introducing 'Longhorn' for Developers*, chapter 3. Microsoft.

Robinson, M., Tapscott, D. and Kalakota, R. (2000) *e-Business 2.0: Roadmap for Success*. New York: Pearson Educational.

Ross, R.G. (2003) *Principles of the Business Rule Approach*. Addison Wesley.

Shalloway, A. and Trott, J. (2004) *Design Patterns Explained: A New Perspective on Object-Oriented Design*, 2nd edition. Addison Wesley (first edition 2001).

Sims, O. (1994) *Business Objects*. McGraw-Hill.

Taylor, D.A. (1995) *Business Engineering with Object Technology*. Wiley.

Magazines

Mehta, T. (2003) Adaptive Web Services Management Solutions. *Enterprise Networks & Servers Magazine*, May.

Petzold, C. (2004) Create Real Apps Using New Code and Markup Model. *Microsoft MSDN Magazine*, January (http://msdn.microsoft.com/msdnmag/issues/04/01/Avalon/default.aspx).

Docs

Abrahams, A.S., Eyers, D.M. and Bacon, J.M., An Event-Based Paradigm for E-commerce Application Specification and Execution. Department of Operations and Information Management, The Wharton School, University of Pennsylvania.

Bray, T., Paoli, J., Sperberg-McQueen, C.M. and Male, E. (1998) Extensible Markup Language (XML) 1.0 (Second Edition), World Wide Web Consortium, 10 February.

Bray, T., Hollander, D. and Layman, A. (1999) Namespaces in XML, World Wide Web Consortium, 14 January.

Catania, N., Web Services Events, Web Services Management Framework, Hewlett Packard.

Combine (2003) Component-Based Interoperable Enterprise System Development – An EU Framework 5 Project, see http://www.opengroup.org/combine/overview.htm.

Cummins, F. (2002) White Paper on Web Services Integration Architecture. OMG Document bei/02-10-02.

Murry, B., WSMF Foundation, Web Services Management Framework, Hewlett Packard.

OMG1 (2003) MDA Guide version 1.0, OMG document omg/2003-05-01; also www.omg.org/mda.

OMG2 (2003) Unified Modeling Language Specification, OMG document formal/03-03-01 (http://www.omg.org/technology/documents/formal/uml.htm).

OMG2 (2004) UML Profile for Enterprise Distributed Object Computing (EDOC). OMG documents formal/04-02-01 through formal/04-02-08 (see http://www.omg.org/technology/documents/formal/edoc.htm).

OMG3 (2004) Unified Modeling Language Version 2.0 (see http://www.uml.org/#UML2.0).

OMG3 (2004) UML 2.0 Superstructure Specification. OMG Document ptc/04-10-02 (see also http://www.omg.org/technology/documents/formal/uml.htm).

The Open Group (1991) Distributed Transaction Processing: The XA Specification.

Rogers, S. (2003) An Integrated Web Services Management Approach, IDC, July.

Sims, O. (2001) Making Components Work. Cutter Consortium, Executive Report Vol. 4, No. 9.

Sims, O. (2002) A Component Architecture. Cutter Consortium, Executive Report Vol. 5, No. 5.

Understand Enterprise Service Bus Scenarios and Solutions in Service-Oriented Architecture, Part 1, IBM Developer Works.

Vambenepe, W., WSMF: Web Services Model, Web Services Management Framework, Hewlett Packard.

Weblogic Server 7.0, Distributed Computing with BEA Weblogic Server, BEA Systems.

Web Services RoadMap: Security in a Web Services World: A Proposed Architecture and Roadmap, A Joint White Paper from IBM Corporation and Microsoft Corporation April 7, 2002, Version 1.0, http://www-106.ibm.com/developerworks/security/library/ws-secmap/

XUL (2004) The Open XUL Alliance, http://xul.sourceforge.net/links.html (see also http://www.xulplanet.com/).

Web Sites

Agile Alliance, Agile Manifesto for Software Development, http://www.agilemanifesto.org

Arjuna Technologies Ltd., www.arjuna.com

IBM UDDI V3 Registry Site, https://uddi.ibm.com/beta/registry.html

IBM UDDI Test Registry Site, https://uddi.ibm.com/testregistry/registry.html

IBM's XML Security Suite, http://www.alphaworks.ibm.com/tech/xmlsecuritysuite

Java Transaction API 1.0.1B, http://java.sun.com/products/jta/index.html

Java Transaction Service 1.0, http://java.sun.com/products/jts/index.html

Kerberos: The Network Authentication Protocol, http://web.mit.edu/kerberos/www/

Microsoft Technet, various pages: http://www.microsoft.com/technet

Microsoft UDDI page, http://msdn.microsoft.com/library/default.asp?url=/library/en-us/dnuddispec/html/uddispecindex.asp

OASIS BTP Committee Specification, http://www.oasis-open.org/committees/business-transactions/

Object Request Broker, http://www.sei.cmu.edu/str/descriptions/orb.html

Object Transaction Service 1.3, http://www.omg.org/technology/documents/formal/transaction_service.htm

Portland Pattern Repository, various pages: http://www.c2.com/cgi/wiki?WelcomeVisitors

Public-Key Infrastructure (X.509) (pkix), http://www.ietf.org/html.charters/pkix-charter.html

Ryan, J., various articles, http://www.developer.com

Security Assertion Markup Language (SAML), http://www.oasis-open.org/committees/security/

Techtarget, various pages, http://whatis.techtarget.com

UDDI Specifications, http://uddi.org/pubs/uddi_v3.htm

WCAF, The Web Services Composite Application Framework Technical Committee, http://www.oasis-open.org/committees/documents.php?wg_abbrev=ws-caf

WSAA, The Web Services Atomic Transaction specification, http://msdn.microsoft.com/library/default.asp?url=/library/en-us/dnglobspec/html/wsat.asp

WSBA, The Web Services Business Activity specification, http://msdn.microsoft.com/library/default.asp?url=/library/en-us/dnglobspec/html/wsba.asp

WSBPEL, http://www-106.ibm.com/developerworks/webservices/library/ws-bpel/

WSC, The Web Services Coordination specification, http://msdn.microsoft.com/library/default.asp?url=/library/en-us/dnglobspec/html/wscoor.asp

WSDL Specifications, http://uddi.org/pubs/uddi_v3.htm

WS-Security, http://www.oasis-open.org/committees/tc_home.php?wg_abbrev=wss

XACML, http://www.oasis-open.org/committees/tc_home.php?wg_abbrev=xacml

XML Canonicalization, http://www.w3.org/TR/xml-exc-c14n/

XML Encryption, http://www.w3.org/TR/xmlenc-core/

XML Key Management Specification 2.0 (XKMS), http://www.w3.org/TR/xkms2/

XML Signature, http://www.w3.org/TR/xmldsig-core/

Presentations

XML on Wall Street, February 2004, James McGovern and Jeff Ryan, Enterprise SOA in Financial Services.

Tyndale-Biscoe, S., Sims, O., Sluman, C. and Wood, B. (2002) Business Modelling for Component Systems with UML. Paper given at the EDOC 2002 Conference.

APPENDIX D: ADDITIONAL READING

If someone is going down the wrong road, he doesn't need motivation to speed him up. What he needs is education to turn him around.
Jim Rohn

The author team has composed a list of its favorite books that will further guide you on the straight path of becoming a superior architect as we understand that creating a service-oriented architecture requires many distinct disciplines in order to be successful. The books listed below span multiple subject areas (in no particular order) and will put you on the road leading to mastery of service-oriented architectures.

Java Web Services Architecture, James McGovern, Sameer Tyagi, Michael E. Stevens, Sunil Mathew Morgan Kaufman, April 2003

False Prophets: The Gurus Who Created Modern Management and Why Their Ideas are Bad for Business Today, James Hoopes, Perseus Publishing, April 2003

The Pragmatic Programmer: From Journeyman to Master, Andrew Hunt, David Thomas, Ward Cunningham, Addison Wesley, October 1999

Agile Modeling: Effective Practices for Extreme Programming and the Unified Process, Scott Ambler, Ron Jeffries, John Wiley & Sons, March 2002

e-Enterprise: Business Models, Architecture and Components, Faisal Hoque, Cambridge University Press, April 2000

Software Architecture: Perspectives on an Emerging Discipline, Mary Shaw, David Garlan, Prentice Hall, April 1996

Software Product Lines: Practices and Patterns, Paul Clements, Linda M. Northrop, Addison Wesley, August 2001

Elements of UML Style, Scott Ambler, Cambridge University Press, December 2002

What's the Big Idea? Creating and Capitalizing on the Best New Management Thinking, Thomas Davenport, Laurence Prusak, H. Wilson, Harvard Business School Press, April 2003

How to Open Locks with Improvised Tools, Hans Conkel, Harper Collins, October 1997

Zen and the Art of Motorcycle Maintenance, Robert Pirsig, Bantam Books, April 1984

The Mythical Man-Month: Essays on Software Engineering, Frederick P. Brooks, Addison Wesley, August 1995

Data Access Patterns: Database Interactions in Object-Oriented Applications , Clifton Nock, Addison Wesley, September 2003

Domain-Driven Design: Tackling Complexity in the Heart of Software, Eric Evans, Addison Wesley, August 2003

Enterprise Integration Patterns: Designing, Building and Deploying Messaging Solutions, Gregor Hohpe, Bobby Woolf, Addison Wesley, October 2003

Survival Is Not Enough: Why Smart Companies Abandon Worry and Embrace Change, Seth Godin, Charles Darwin, Touchstone Books, December 2002

Smart Mobs: The Next Social Revolution, Howard Rheingold, Basic Books, October 2003

The Practical Guide to Enterprise Architecture, James McGovern, Scott W. Ambler, Michael E. Stevens, James Linn, Vikas Sharan, Elias Jo, Prentice Hall, November 2003

APPENDIX E: UPCOMING BOOKS

Leadership is not so much about technique and methods as it is about opening the heart. Leadership is about inspiration – of oneself and of others. Great leadership is about human experiences, not processes. Leadership is not a formula or a program, it is a human activity that comes from the heart and considers the hearts of others. It is an attitude, not a routine.
Lance Secretan

Listed below are books that members of this author team are currently working on and their anticipated release dates. We thank you for your continued support and hope to serve you well in the future.

Agile Enterprise Architecture – Fall 2006

Over the past decade, many enterprises have undertaken enterprise architecture efforts. While many of these programs have had varying success, the vast majority have failed – failed to gain management support, failed to deliver actionable results, or failed to result in meaningful change within the enterprise.

The lack of success in enterprise architecture is symptomatic of the lack of success in IT organizations in general. In most companies, IT is perceived to be dying a slow death. It is viewed as a necessary evil and not a critical part of the success of the broader enterprise. To achieve the status of strategic partner, IT must re-focus its architecture efforts from enabling the technology to enabling the business.

In order to achieve a chaordic balance in strategy, design and implementation, agile approaches to enterprise architecture must be employed. Methods for performing each of these activities will be explored along with practical considerations with a focus on the issues, strategies and practices of enabling business agility.

In this book, readers will learn about:

- IT Governance,
- Portfolio Management,
- Quality Assurance,
- Software Risk Management,
- Defect Management,
- Agile COTS Assessment,
- Architectural Assessment,
- Process Patterns,
- Agile Procurement Processes, and
- Thought Leadership.

Enterprise Portal Architecture – Fall 2006

Portals are a technology that allows for integrating various resources within the enterprise (applications, databases, and so on) available to end users through a unified user interface. Open source technology enables enterprises to construct highly dynamic enterprise portals with increased agility and minimal limitations. This book explains the fundamentals behind portal technologies and how to take full advantage of offerings in this space.

In this book, one will learn:

- The ability to develop a common approach to recurring problems within the portal space leveraging pattern-based approaches.
- Evaluating business requirements and planning for a successful implementation.
- Development of robust portal solutions using the premier open source portal: Liferay.
- Implement federated security and single sign on across multiple portals.

- Incorporate personalization and user profile concepts to tailor site content.
- Integrating portals with web services.
- Architectural and network diagrams that illustrate detailed portal implementations.
- Integration with leading ERP, CRM and supply chain vendors.
- Make better decisions empowering users to gain rapid access to crucial information.
- Practical considerations for implementing portals in large enterprises.
- Reduce the risk of project failures in large integration and portal implementation efforts.

Enterprise Open Source – Spring 2007

Use of open source software within the enterprise is gaining momentum. The vast majority of enterprises have some form of open source software used in production environments, which may include Linux, Apache, JBoss and so on. The enterprise architecture however needs to incorporate the best thinking of the industry that not only includes using open source but contributing to it.

The model in which open source software gets developed has practices, which could assist an organization in becoming agile in their software development practices, and allows them to develop software faster, with cheaper cost and of better quality.

In this book, one will learn:

- Two models of software development: The cathedral and the bazaar.
- Value proposition of using open source to executives.
- How much does free software really cost?
- Paying for software in forms less tangible than money.
- Making the build vs buy decision to include using open source.
- The effect of open source development on project management.
- Merging the open source development model into enterprise architecture.
- Reducing the total cost of ownership for software projects.

Enterprise BPM Patterns – Summer 2007

There is a lot of hype in industry trade journals about business process management (BPM). Some believe it is a revolutionary process that will create new categories of software used in developing enterprise applications. Others believe it is evolutionary in that it will help leverage existing business and technology assets create new value propositions. Along with any revolution comes confusion. Many will be confused with the terminology used. Some will ask is it workflow? While others will struggle with the notion of orchestration and choreographed business processes.

Business process management is really a paradigm shift. The nature of processes themselves presents severe, even insurmountable challenges for IT implementation. In many enterprises, the processes themselves have requirements far from classical automation. Change management and product lifecycle management as disciplines can also be thought of as processes in their own right. The ideal manner in which enterprises can learn about the concepts, practices and recommendations for business process management is using a pattern-based notation.

In this book, one will learn:

- The ability to have a common vocabulary and solution to recurring problems within the business process management space using a pattern-based approach.
- Practical considerations for implementing business process management in large enterprises.
- Reduce the risk of project failures in large integration and business process management efforts.

Printed in the United States
85381LV00001B/127-132/A

9 781402 037047